Coal Yard
Gar
Brownlow Str.
DRURY
LANE
Wild Street
L. Wild St.
Row
Fields
Portugal Row
Portugal Str.
Vere Str.
Princes S.
Stanhope St.
Clements Lane
Clare Market
New Inn
Broad Co.
Dukes Co.
THEATRE ROYAL DRURY LANE
Rufsell Str.
Bow
ROYAL GARDEN
Covent Garden Market
Bridges S.
Russell
York St.
Tavistock St.
W. Hart Pa.
Swan Yard
Wych Str
Holywell Str
78
83
THE STRAND
Exeter Street
Catherine St
Southampton St.
Surry Str.
Norfolk S.
Arundel S.
35
Adam S.
Salisbury Str
Cecil Str.
Savoy Sta.
Salisbury Sta.
Adelphia Buildings
York Buildings
York Stairs
Stamp, Victualing & other Offices.
Royal Academy, Cupers Bridge
Strand Bridge
Surry Sta.

The *Revels* History of Drama in English

GENERAL EDITORS

Clifford Leech
& T. W. Craik

The *Revels* History of Drama in English

VOLUME VI 1750-1880

*Michael R. Booth, Richard Southern,
Frederick & Lise-Lone Marker
& Robertson Davies*

Methuen & Co Ltd
London

First published 1975 by Methuen & Co Ltd
11 New Fetter Lane, London EC4P 4EE
© *1975 Michael R. Booth, Richard Southern,*
Frederick and Lise-Lone Marker and
Robertson Davies
Printed in Great Britain by
Richard Clay (The Chaucer Press), Ltd
Bungay, Suffolk

ISBN 0 416 13070 4 (*hardbound*)
ISBN 0 416 81380 1 (*paperback*)

Distributed in the USA by
HARPER AND ROW PUBLISHERS INC.
BARNES AND NOBLE IMPORT DIVISION

Contents

List of illustrations

Section three *between pages 226 and 227*

Acknowledgements

The authors and publishers would like to thank the following for permission to reproduce the illustrations appearing in this book:

The Theatre Collection, University of Bristol (Richard Southern Accession), for Nos. 3a, 3b, 4a, 4b, 5a, 5b, 6a, 6b, 7a, 7b, 7c, 8a, 8b, 9a, 9b, 10a, 10b, 11a, 11b, 12, 13a, 13b, 14a, 14b, 15a, 15b, 16a, 16b, 17, 18a, 18b, 23, 34, 39, 43b

The Garrick Club for No. 37

The National Portrait Gallery for Nos. 45 and 46

M. Newman, fine art dealers, for No. 1b

The Victoria and Albert Museum (Enthoven Collection) for Nos. 2a, 2b, 19, 20a, 20b, 21a, 21b, 22a, 22b, 24a, 24b, 25a, 25b, 26a, 26b, 28a, 28b, 30a, 31a, 31b, 32, 33a, 33b, 35, 36a, 36b, 36c, 38a, 40a, 40b, 41a, 41b, 42, 43a, 44, 47, 48

The Walker Art Gallery for No. 27a

Zürich Kunsthaus for No. 30b

Preface

This series of volumes on drama in English from medieval times to the twentieth century is published under the names of two editors, and it is proper here to inform the reader that the major responsibility for Volumes III and VI has been mine; in the volumes which will appear later Professor T. W. Craik of Dundee has taken my place, in every way to my delight, although I have been partially responsible for the selection of authors and have been able to read some of their contributions to the work.

I should like to take this opportunity of thanking all the contributors who have worked with me in the most friendly and cooperative way.

Clifford Leech

Chronological
table

The purpose of this table is to suggest relations between the plays and dramatists of the years 1750–1880 and historical events and the non-dramatic literature of the time. That non-dramatic writings and authors are more numerously presented than plays and playwrights will be no surprise to any student of the period: the dramatists were writing in a period when other kinds than theirs achieved the greater eminence. But it must be recognized that acting and production, if not often dramatic writing, were of major quality and significance in the English society of this time: new plays must therefore be seen in relation to the 'Theatrical events' listed in column 2.

References to continental and American writings are minimal: they include only such writings and authors as might be expected to have made an impact on dramatists in England (in some cases after the years covered by this volume). American drama will be dealt with separately in Volume VIII. As far as is possible, works have been assigned to the years in which they first appeared, rather than to those in which they were (in the case of plays) printed, or (in that of serialized writings) published in volume form; their titles have frequently been abbreviated. There is fairly substantial reference to events in the continental theatre.

Date	Historical events	Theatrical events	Non-dramatic literary events
1737		Licensing Act restricts acting of legitimate drama to two patent theatres, Drury Lane and Covent Garden	
1741		Drury Lane revival of *The Merchant of Venice* with Charles Macklin as Shylock; début of Garrick at Goodman's Fields	
1743			
1745			
1747		Garrick joint patentee at Drury Lane	Richardson, *Clarissa*
1748			Smollett, *Roderick Random*
1749			Fielding, *Tom Jones*; Johnson, *The Vanity of Human Wishes*
1750		Spranger Barry leaves Drury Lane for Covent Garden to engage in rivalry with Garrick	Gray, *Elegy in a Country Churchyard*; Johnson, *Rambler* (begins); Collins, *The Passions*
1751		James Quin retires	Fielding, *Amelia*; Smollett, *Peregrine Pickle*
1752		Local Licensing Act requires licensing by magistrates of all smaller productions; Lewis Hallam leaves with a troupe of players for America	
1753			Richardson, *Sir Charles Grandison*; Smollett, *Ferdinand Count Fathom*
1754			

...ths and deaths ...on-dramatic ...ers	First performances of notable UK plays	Births and deaths of notable UK playwrights	Continental theatrical events
		Hannah Cowley b.	
		Thomas Holcroft b.	
			Danish Royal Theatre, Scandinavia's first national theatre, opens; Voltaire's *Sémiramis*
			Lekain joins Comédie Française. Goldoni promises and completes, sixteen new comedies for following season in Venice
	Whitehead, *The Roman Father*		
		Sheridan b.	J.-F. Schönemann appointed court poet to Duke of Mecklenburg, first German nobleman to subsidize a company
...nny Burney b. ...atterton b.	Foote, *Taste*		
...rkeley b.	Glover, *Boadicea*; Foote, *The Englishman in Paris*; Moore, *The Gamester*	Elizabeth Inchbald b.	Konrad Ekhof's Schauspieler-Akademie begins
...abbe b. ...elding d.	Foote, *The Knights*		L. Holberg d.

Date	Historical events	Theatrical events	Non-dramatic literary events
1755	The Seven Years' War begins	Anti-French riots over Drury Lane production of Noverre's ballet *The Chinese Festival*	Johnson, *Dictionary*
1756			Gray, *The Bard*
1757	Pitt prime minister; Battle of Plassey		
1758			Johnson, *The Idler* (begins)
1759	Battle of Minden; Wolfe takes Quebec		Johnson, *Rasselas*; Voltaire, *Candide*
1760	George III accedes	Peg Woffington d.	Sterne, *Tristram Shandy* (begins)
1761	Bute prime minister	John Rich d.	Goldsmith, *The Citizen of t. World* (begins)
1762			
1763	Peace of Paris; Wedgwood establishes potteries	Garrick clears spectators from the stage, travels on the continent until 1765; Drury Lane and Covent Garden partially wrecked by rioters demanding half-price admittance after third act	Smart, *A Song to David*
1764	Hargreaves invents spinning jenny		Goldsmith, *The Traveller*

-ths and deaths non-dramatic -iters	First performances of notable UK plays	Births and deaths of notable UK playwrights	Continental theatrical events
			Lessing imitates English sentimental drama with *Miss Sarah Sampson*; Hippolyte Clairon and Lekain reform costuming in Voltaire's *L'Orphelin de la Chine* in Paris
)dwin b.		Frances Sheridan d.	
ake b.	Home, *Douglas*; Garrick, *The Male Coquette*	Colley Cibber d. Edward Moore d. J. P. Kemble b.	
	Home, *Agis*		Diderot's *Le Père de famille*, with appended essay 'On Dramatic Poetry', launches the *genre sérieux* in France
:ckford b. :rns b. -hiller b.)llins d.	Garrick, *The Guardian*; Murphy, *The Orphan of China*; Townley, *High Life below Stairs*		Spectators banished from stage of Comédie Française
	Foote, *The Minor*; Bickerstaff, *Thomas and Sally*; Colman, *Polly Honeycomb*		Noverre's revolutionary *Lettres sur la danse et les ballets*; Caroline Neuber d.
	Murphy, *The Way to Keep Him*		
	Bickerstaff, *Love in a Village*	G. Colman (the younger) b.	
obbett b.	Foote, *The Mayor of Garratt*; F. Sheridan, *The Discovery*		
. Radcliffe b.		Thomas Morton b. F. Reynolds b.	

Date	Historical events	Theatrical events	Non-dramatic literary events
1765	Stamp Act; first North American opposition to Stamp Act; Watt's steam engine		Walpole, *The Castle of Otranto*; Percy, *Reliques of Ancient English Poetry*
1766	Stamp Act repealed	Samuel Foote granted patent for Haymarket; Barry re-engaged by Garrick; Quin and Mrs Cibber d.	H. Brooke, *The Fool of Quality* (begins); Goldsmith *The Vicar of Wakefield*
1767			
1768	Arkwright invents spinning machine; Royal Academy founded	Mrs Pritchard d.	Sterne, *A Sentimental Journey*; *Encyclopaedia Britannica* begins; Walpole, *The Mysterious Mother*
1769		Rainy and tourist-minded jubilee at Stratford celebrating bicentennial of Shakespeare's birth	*Letters of Junius* (begin)
1770			Goldsmith, *The Deserted Village*
1771		Garrick engages pioneer scene-designer Philippe Jacques de Loutherbourg for Drury Lane	Smollett, *Humphry Clinker*
1772			
1773	Hastings governor-general of India; Boston tea riots		

Births and deaths of non-dramatic writers	First performances of notable UK plays	Births and deaths of notable UK playwrights	Continental theatrical events
›ung d.	Bickerstaff, *The Maid of the Mill*		
, Edgeworth b.	Colman and Garrick, *The Clandestine Marriage*	F. Sheridan d.	Second Drottningholm court theatre, designed by Adelcrantz, opens near Stockholm
›rne d.	Foote, *The Devil upon Two Sticks*; Kelly, *False Delicacy*; Goldsmith, *The Good Natur'd Man*		Beaumarchais' *Eugénie* at Comédie Française, published with 'Essay on Serious Drama'; founding of Hamburg National Theatre; Lessing's *Hamburgische Dramaturgie* (begins)
	Home, *The Fatal Discovery*		Molé is first French Hamlet
›ethoven b. ›ntham b. ›gel b. ›gg b. ›ordsworth b. ›atterton d.			
›ott b. ›ay d. ›nart d. ›nollett d.	Cumberland, *The West Indian*		
›leridge b. ›vedenborg d.	Murphy, *The Grecian Daughter*		Lessing's *Emilia Galotti*; the Belgian theatreman d'Hannetaire's reform programme, *Observations sur l'art du comédien*
›esterfield d.	Goldsmith, *She Stoops to Conquer*		Goethe's 'Sturm und Drang' play, *Goetz von Berlichingen*

Date	Historical events	Theatrical events	Non-dramatic literary events
1774		Henry Mossop d.	Chesterfield, *Letters to his Son*; Goethe, *Werther*
1775		Unsuccessful début of Sarah Siddons as Portia	Johnson, *Journey to the Western Islands*
1776	US Declaration of Independence	Garrick retires; Sheridan assumes control of Drury Lane; Thomas Weston d.	Gibbon, *The Decline and Fall of the Roman Empire* (begins); Smith, *The Wealth of Nations*
1777		Henderson's début at Haymarket; Spranger Barry and Henry Woodward d.	
1778			F. Burney, *Evelina*
1779		De Loutherbourg designs picturesque, topographically accurate scenery for *The Wonders of Derbyshire*; Garrick d.	Hume, *Dialogues concerning Natural Religion*; Johnson, *Lives of the Poets* (begins)
1780			
1781	End of US War of Independence (definitive peace 1783)		
1782		Successful return of Mrs Siddons to Drury Lane; Covent Garden altered and enlarged	
1783	The younger Pitt prime minister	J. P. Kemble's début as Hamlet	Crabbe, *The Village*; Day, *Sandford and Merton* (begins)

...hs and deaths ...on-dramatic ...ers	First performances of notable UK plays	Births and deaths of notable UK playwrights	Continental theatrical events
...they b.	Foote, *The Cozeners*	Goldsmith d.	
...usten b. ...b b. ...dor b. ...G. Lewis b.	Garrick, *Bon Ton, or High Life above Stairs* Sheridan, *The Rivals*	M. G. Lewis b.	Beaumarchais' *Le Barbier de Seville*
...ne d.		B. Thompson b.	Opening of Burgtheater in Vienna; E. T. A. Hoffmann, b.; F. L. Schröder produces *Hamlet*, first German production of Shakespeare, with Brockmann as Hamlet
	Sheridan, *The School for Scandal*	Foote d., Kelly d., W. H. Ireland b.	
...litt b. ...sseau d. ...taire d.	Sheridan, *The Critic*		Opening of Piermarini's Teatro al Scala in Milan; Diderot's *Paradoxe sur le comédien* completed (publ. 1830); Eckhof d.
...alt b. ...Moore b.		Garrick d.	Odéon in Paris built (completed 1782)
	H. Cowley, *The Belle's Stratagem*	J. Kenny b.	Schröder manager of Burgtheater
...sing d.	Holcroft, *Duplicity*; Macklin, *The Man of the World*		Leopoldstädter Theatre in Vienna opens; Schiller's *Die Räuber* produced at Mannheim with A. W. Iffland as Franz Moor
...Ferrier b.		J. Pocock b.	Pit is seated at the new Comédie Française; Royal Opera in Stockholm, designed by Adelcrantz, opens
...Irving b. ...ndhal b. ...Brooke d.	Cumberland, *The Mysterious Husband*		

Date	Historical events	Theatrical events	Non-dramatic literary event
1784			
1785		Dorothy Jordan joins Drury Lane company; Henderson d.	Boswell, *Journal of a Tour the Hebrides*; Cowper, *The Task*; Paley, *Principles of Moral and Political Philosof The Daily Universal Registe* (called *The Times* from 178 begins
1786	Trial of Warren Hastings		Beckford, *Vathek*
1787		Royalty Theatre opens in unsuccessful defiance of patentees	
1788		Kemble manager of Drury Lane	
1789	French States General meet; fall of Bastille	Macklin's last appearance as Shylock	Blake, *Songs of Innocence*; E. Darwin, *The Botanic Garden* (begins)
1790		Munden's début at Covent Garden	Blake, *Marriage of Heaven and Hell*; Burke, *Reflection on the French Revolution*; Malone, edition of Shakespeare; Tate Wilkin *Memoirs of his own Life*
1791	Louis XVI's flight and capture; many French emigrants		Boswell, *Life of Johnson*; Burns, *Tam o'Shanter*; Paine, *The Rights of Man*
1792	Hasting acquitted; imprisonment of French royal family; Robert Adam d.	Opening of enlarged Covent Garden	Cowper, translation of Homer
1793	Execution of Louis XVI and Marie Antoinette; Committee of Public Safety;		Godwin, *Political Justice*; Paine, *The Age of Reason* Wordsworth, *Descriptive Sketches*

Births and deaths of notable non-dramatic writers	First performances of notable UK plays	Births and deaths of notable UK playwrights	Continental theatrical events
...gh Hunt b. ...nson d.	Cumberland, *The Carmelite*	S. Knowles b.	Triumphant production of Beaumarchais' *Le Mariage de Figaro* at Comédie Française
...Quincey b. ...cock b.	Inchbald, *I'll Tell You What*	R. Glover d. W. Whitehead d.	Engel's *Ideen zu einer Mimik* published
	Burgoyne, *The Heiress* Colman the Younger, *Inkle and Yarico*; Holcroft, *Seduction*	J. Poole b.	Mozart, *The Marriage of Figaro* Début of François Joseph Talma at Comédie Française; Mozart, *Don Giovanni*
...openhauer b. ...on b.		Byron b.	Royal Dramatic Theatre (Dramaten) in Stockholm established
...Cooper b.	Reynolds, *The Dramatist*		Goethe's *Egmont*; Kotzebue's *Menschenhass und Reue* ('The Stranger')
...Franklin d. ...am Smith d.			Teatro La Fenice in Venice built by Selva (completed 1792); Mozart, *Così fan Tutte*
...zart d.			Mozart, *The Magic Flute*; Goethe begins his twenty-six-year management of the Weimar Court Theatre; theatre monopoly ended in Paris; Scribe, Grillparzer b.
...ble b. ...rryat b. ...elley b. ...ynolds d. ...re b.	Holcroft, *The Road to Ruin* Inchbald, *Every One has his Fault*	R. B. Peake b. E. Fitzball b. Burgoyne d.	Goldoni d.

Date	Historical events	Theatrical events	Non-dramatic literary events
	murder of Marat; France declares war on Britain		
1794	Danton executed; Robespierre executed; end of Terror	Kemble opens enlarged Drury Lane with *Macbeth*, with Sarah Siddons and (as Malcolm) Charles Kemble	Blake, *Songs of Experience*; Godwin, *Caleb Williams*; A. Radcliffe, *The Mysteries Udolpho*
1795	Bonaparte in Italy		
1796			Lewis, *The Monk*
1797	Mutinies at Spithead and the Nore; Bank of England suspends payment	Macklin d.	*The Anti-Jacobin*
1798	Battle of the Nile		Malthus, *Principle of Population*; Wordsworth and Coleridge, *Lyrical Ballads*
1799	Bonaparte First Consul		
1800	Highland clearances	G. F. Cooke is Richard III at Covent Garden	M. Edgeworth, *Castle Rackrent*; Wordsworth and Coleridge, *Lyrical Ballads*
1801	Pitt resigns on King's refusal to sign Catholic Emancipation Bill; Addington prime minister; Battle of Copenhagen		T. Moore, *Poems by Thomas Little*
1802	Peace of Amiens; Bonaparte First Consul for life	Kemble and Mrs Siddons move to Covent Garden	Paley, *Natural Theology*; Scott, *Minstrelsy of the Scottish Border* (begins); *Edinburgh Review* (begins); John Boydell's *Illustrated Shakespeare*: engravings by Reynolds, Stothard, Smirke

hs and deaths on-dramatic ers	First performances of notable UK plays	Births and deaths of notable UK playwrights	Continental theatrical events
bon d.	Kemble, *Lodoiska*	W. T. Moncrieff b.; Colman (the elder) d.	
yle b. ts b. vell d.		T. N. Talfourd b.	Début of Mlle Mars at Comédie Française
pherson d. 1s d.	Colman (the younger), *The Iron Chest*; Ireland, *Vortigern*	T. B. Planché b.	
1e b. ke d. pole d.	Colman (the younger), *The Heir at Law*; Lewis, *The Castle Spectre*		Shakespeare translations by Schlegel and Tieck (continuing to 1801)
pardi b.	Thompson, *The Stranger*		*Victor*, first melodrama by Pixérécourt, the 'Corneille of Melodrama'
ac b. d b. hkin b. imarchais d.	Sheridan, *Pizarro*		
aulay b. ey b. per d.	Morton, *Speed the Plough*		Schiller, *Maria Stuart*
Barnes b. yman b.			Schiller, *Jungfrau von Orleans*
o b.	Holcroft, *A Tale of Mystery*	J. B. Buckstone b. C. Selby b.	

Date	Historical events	Theatrical events	Non-dramatic literary even
			Romney, Fuseli, Opie, Ba West, A. Kauffman, West Hamilton *et al.*
1803	War renewed between Britain and France		
1804	Pitt prime minister; Napoleon Emperor; end of Holy Roman Empire		Blake, *Jerusalem*; *Milton*
1805	Battles of Trafalgar, Ulm and Austerlitz	Master Betty craze; Liston's début at Haymarket	Scott, *The Lay of the Last Minstrel*
1806	Pitt d.; Battle of Jena		Webster, *Dictionary*
1807	Treaty of Tilsit; French invasion of Spain and Portugal; abolition of slave trade		Byron, *Hours of Idleness*; Crabbe, *The Parish Regist* C. and M. Lamb, *Tales fi Shakespeare*; Wordsworth, *Poems in Two Volumes*
1808		Covent Garden burns	Lamb, *Specimens of the English Dramatic Poets*; Scott, *Marmion*; Hunts *Examiner* founded
1809		Drury Lane burns; Kemble's enlarged Covent Garden reopens; irate spectators resenting his price rises stage the fierce Old Price riots	Byron, *English Bards and Scotch Reviewers*; *Quarterl Review* founded
1810		Cooke leaves for America	Crabbe, *The Borough*; Sco *The Lady of the Lake*

Births and deaths [of] n-dramatic [write]rs	First performances of notable UK plays	Births and deaths of notable UK playwrights	Continental theatrical events
ow b. ...as père b. ...rson b.	Kenney, *Raising the Wind*	Jerrold b. Lytton b. M. A. Lovell b.	Schiller's preface to *Braut von Messina* rejects theatrical illusionism; Goethe's *Regeln für Schauspieler*
...aeli b. ...thorne b. ...te-Beuve b. ...t d. ...stley d.			Theatrical censorship re-established in Paris
...worth b. ...ees b. ...y d. ...C. Andersen b.	Lamb, *Mr H.*	Murphy d.	Schiller d. in Weimar; Beethoven, *Fidelio*
...Browning b. ...Mill b.			
...gfellow b.			Eight legitimate theatres given patents in Paris
			Goethe, *Faust* I (completed); Oehlenschläger, *Hakon Jarl*, produced at Danish Royal Theatre
...win b. ...gerald b. ...ol b. ...V. Holmes b. ...lake b. ...b. ...nyson b. ...e d.		H. Cowley d. Holcroft d.	Début of Ludwig Devrient in Breslau
...pin, b. ...mann b.	Rhodes, *Bombastes Furioso*		de Musset b.

Date	Historical events	Theatrical events	Non-dramatic literary even_
1811	Regency begins	Macready appears in Newcastle upon Tyne with Sarah Siddons in *The Gamester* and *Douglas* during 1811–12 season; Charles Kean d.	J. Austen, *Sense and Sensibility*
1812	War between Britain and US begins; Napoleon invades Russia	Rebuilt Drury Lane opens; Siddons's farewell to the stage; Cooke dies in New York	Byron, *Childe Harold* I an_ II; J. and H. Smith, *Rejec_ Addresses*
1813			J. Austen, *Pride and Prejudice*; Byron, *The Bri_ of Abydos*; Scott, *Rokeby*; Shelley, *Queen Mab*; Sout_ *Life of Nelson*
1814	Treaty of Ghent; Congress of Vienna begins	Edmund Kean's outstanding début as Shylock at Drury Lane; Elisa O'Neill's début; Dorothy Jordan retires	J. Austen, *Mansfield Park_* Byron, *The Corsair*; Scott, *Waverley*; Wordsworth, *T Excursion*; Wyss, *The Swi_ Family Robinson* (translate_
1815	Battle of Waterloo; Treaty of Vienna		Scott, *Guy Mannering*; *Th_ Lord of the Isles*
1816		Macready's début at Covent Garden	J. Austen, *Emma*; Byron, *Childe Harold* III; *The Prisoner of Chillon*; Coleri_ *Christabel*; *Kubla Khan*; Peacock, *Headlong Hall*; Scott, *The Antiquary*; *Old Mortality*; Shelley, *Alasto_ Memoirs of the Late Thom_ Holcroft* (ed. Hazlitt)
1817		Final appearance of J. P. Kemble; Drury Lane and Covent Garden stages lit by gas	Coleridge, *Biographia Literaria*; *Sibylline Leaves* Hazlitt, *Characters of Shakespeare's Plays* (begin_ T. Moore, *Lalla Rookh*; Peacock, *Melincourt*; Scot_ *Rob Roy*
1818		Opening of Royal Coburg Theatre	J. Austen, *Northanger Ab_ Persuasion*; Byron, *Childe Harold* IV; *Beppo*; S. Fer_ *Marriage*; Keats, *Endymio_ Hyperion* (begun); Peaco_

ths and deaths ion-dramatic ters	First performances of notable UK plays	Births and deaths of notable UK playwrights	Continental theatrical events
B. Stowe b. ackeray b.		Cumberland d.	Kleist, *Prinz von Homburg*; Kleist d.
wning b. kens b. Lear b. yhew b.		Bickerstaff d.	
rkegaard b.	Coleridge, *Remorse*; Pocock, *The Miller and his Men*		First production of *Hamlet* in Denmark; Büchner b.; Hebbel b.; Verdi b.; Wagner b.
Fanu b. montov b. s H. Wood b. Sade d.		C. Reade b.	Iffland d.
ollope b.			
Brontë b.	Planché, *Amoroso, King of Little Britain*	Sheridan d. B. Thompson d.	
vett b. oreau b. Austen d.		Tom Taylor b.	
rx b. ude b. rgenev b. Brontë b.	Moncrieff, *Rochester, or Charles the Second's Merry Days*	M. G. Lewis d.	

Date	Historical events	Theatrical events	Non-dramatic literary event
			Nightmare Abbey; Scott, *T. Heart of Midlothian*; M. Shelley, *Frankenstein*; Shelley, *The Revolt of Islan*
1819	Manchester massacre	Elisa O'Neill retires prematurely: Madame Vestris in *Giovanni in London* at Drury Lane; opening of Adelphi Theatre	Byron, *Don Juan* (begins); *Mazeppa*; Crabbe, *Tales of the Hall*; Scott, *The Bride Lammermoor*; *Ivanhoe*; Shelley, *The Masque of Anarchy*
1820	George IV accedes; Cato Street conspiracy		Keats, *The Eve of St Agnes Isabella*; *Odes*; Maturin, *Melmoth the Wanderer*; Shelley, *Prometheus Unboun The Sensitive Plant*
1821	Napoleon d.; Greek war of liberation begins	Opening of new Haymarket	Galt, *Annals of the Parish*; Scott, *Kenilworth*; Shelley, *Adonais*; *Epipsychidion*; *Hellas*
1822			Byron, *The Vision of Judgment*; De Quincey, *Confessions of an English Opium Eater*; Peacock, *Ma Marian*; Scott, *The Fortune of Nigel*; Scott, *Peveril of t Peak*
1823	Monroe Doctrine promulgated	Charles Kemble's authentic revival of *King John*; J. P. Kemble d.	Lamb, *Essays of Elia* I; *Quentin Durward*
1824		Munden retires	Landor, *Imaginary Conversations* (begins); Sco *Redgauntlet*
1825	John Quincy Adams president of US		Coleridge, *Aids to Reflectio* P. Egan, *The Life of an Act* Hazlitt, *The Spirit of the A* Scott, *The Talisman*
1826	University College, London, founded	Ira Aldridge's début at the Royalty	F. Cooper, *The Last of the Mohicans*; Scott, *Woodstoc*

Date	Historical events	Theatrical events	Non-dramatic literary event
1827	T. Arnold headmaster of Rugby	Début of Charles Kean; visit of English actors to Paris	E. W. Brayley, *Historical a Descriptive Account of the Theatres of London*
1828	Wellington prime minister		Lytton, *Pelham*
1829	Catholic emancipation		Peacock, *The Misfortunes o Elphin*; Balzac, *Comédie Humaine* (begins); Goethe. *Wilhelm Meister*
1830	William IV accedes; Greece independent; Liverpool and Manchester Railway opened	Madame Vestris begins her Olympic management	Cobbett, *Rural Rides*; Stendhal, *Le Rouge et le No*
1831	Faraday's electro-magnetic current	S. Siddons d.	Peacock, *Crotchet Castle*
1832	First Reform Bill becomes law; University of Durham founded		Genest, *Some Account of t English stage from the Restoration in 1660 to 1830* Lytton, *Eugene Aram*; *Fraser's Magazine* founded Tennyson, *Poems*, chiefly *Lyrical* (dated 1833)
1833	Oxford movement begins	Edmund Kean d.; Bunn manages both Drury Lane and Covent Garden; passage of Dramatic Copyright Act, made operative by formation of Dramatic Authors' Society, securing playwright's control over his work	Browning, *Pauline*; Carlyle *Sartor Resartus* (begins); Lamb, *Essays of Elia* II
1834	Peel prime minister		Ainsworth, *Rookwood*; Lytton, *The Last Days of Pompeii*

Date	Historical events	Theatrical events	Non-dramatic literary events
1835		Début of Charles Mathews Jr at the Olympic	
1836	University of London founded	Début of Helen Faucit at Covent Garden	Dickens, *Pickwick Papers* (begins); Landor, *Pericles a Aspatia*; Marryat, *Mr Midshipman Easy*
1837	Victoria accedes	Macready assumes management of Covent Garden; Webster begins his Haymarket management; Liston retires; first London appearance of Samuel Phelps	Dickens, *Oliver Twist* (begins); Carlyle, *The Fren Revolution*
1838	Formation of Anti-Corn-Law League	Madame Vestris relinquishes Olympic management	Dickens, *Nicholas Nickleby* (begins); Surtees, *Jorrocks' Jaunts and Jollities*
1839		Macready ends his Covent Garden management, assumed in turn by Madame Vestris and Mathews	Poe, *Tales of the Grotesque and Arabesque*; Stendhal, *L Chartreuse de Parme*
1840	Victoria's marriage to Prince Albert		Browning, *Sordello*
1841	Peel prime minister	Macready takes over Drury Lane; Rachel appears in London	Browning, *Bells and Pomegranates* I; Carlyle, *Heroes and Hero-Worship*; Dickens, *Barnaby Rudge*; *T Old Curiosity Shop*; *Punch* founded
1842			Macaulay, *Lays of Ancient Rome*; Tennyson, *Locksley Hall*; *Morte d'Arthur*; *Ulysses*; *Vision of Sin*

ths and deaths non-dramatic ters	First performances of notable UK plays	Births and deaths of notable UK playwrights	Continental theatrical events
Butler b. Twain b. bbett d. gg d.	Haines, *My Poll and My Partner Joe*	W. H. Ireland d.	
Besant b. t Harte b. nes Mill d.	Planché, *Riquet with the Tuft*	W. S. Gilbert b. G. Colman (the younger) d.	Gogol's *The Inspector-General* acted before Nicholas II at Imperial Theatre, Moscow, with Shchepkin in main role; Büchner's *Woyzeck* (published 1873); Raimund d.
inburne b. opardi d. shkin d.	Browning, *Strafford*; Knowles, *The Love Chase*; Rayner, *The Dumb Man of Manchester*		Lemaître stars in Hugo's *Ruy Blas* at the Odéon
Morley b.	Boucicault, *A Legend of the Devil's Dyke*; Lytton, *The Lady of Lyons*	J. Albery b. T. Morton d. H. Irving b.	Rachel appears as Camille in Corneille's *Horace* at the Comédie Française
de Morgan b. ida b. er b. t d.	Lytton, *Richelieu, or the Conspiracy*		
rdy b. A. Symonds b. a b. Burney d.	Lytton, *Money*		Immermann d.
montov d.	Boucicault, *London Assurance*	F. Reynolds d.	
larmé b. ndhal d.	W. Marston, *The Patrician's Daughter*; Pitt, *Sweeney Todd*; Selby, *Boots at the Swan*		

Date	Historical events	Theatrical events	Non-dramatic literary events
1843		Macready ends his Drury Lane management; theatre monopoly ended by Theatre Regulation Act	Borrow, *The Bible in Spain*; Dickens, *A Christmas Carol*, *Martin Chuzzlewit* (begins); Lytton, *The Last of the Barons*; Macaulay, *Essays*; Ruskin, *Modern Painters* (begins)
1844		Phelps begins his eighteen-year management of Sadler's Wells	Barnes, *Poems of Rural Life* I; Disraeli, *Coningsby*; Dumas, *The Count of Monte Cristo* (begins); Kinglake, *Eothen*; Thackeray, *Barry Lyndon*
1845		Charlotte Cushman's guest appearance at the Princess's	Disraeli, *Sybil*; Mérimée, *Carmen*
1846	Repeal of the Corn Laws		Melville, *Typee*
1847		Madame Vestris and Mathews begin their Lyceum management; Covent Garden becomes the Royal Italian Opera House	C. Brontë, *Jane Eyre*; E. Brontë, *Wuthering Heights*; Longfellow, *Evangeline*; Tennyson, *The Princess*; Thackeray, *Vanity Fair* (begins)
1848	Chartists suppressed	Royal theatricals begin at Windsor Castle	Dickens, *Dombey and Son*; E. Gaskell, *Mary Barton*; Kingsley, *Yeast*; Lytton, *Harold*; Thackeray, *Pendennis* (begins)
1849		Ellen Terry b.	Arnold, *The Strayed Reveller and other poems*; Dickens, *David Copperfield* (begins); Lytton, *The Caxtons*; Macaulay, *History of England* (begins); Ruskin, *The Seven Lamps of Architecture*; C. Brontë, *Shirley*
1850		Charles Kean begins his management of the Princess's	E. B. Browning, *Sonnets from the Portuguese*; Emerson, *Representative Men*;

...hs and deaths ...on-dramatic ...ers	First performances of notable UK plays	Births and deaths of notable UK playwrights	Continental theatrical events
...ghty b. ...ames b. ...homson II b. ...they d.			Rachel plays Phèdre, her most celebrated role
...ges b. ...tole France b. ...kins b. ...ang b. ...tzsche b. ...aine b. ...d d.			Hebbel, *Maria Magdalena*; Sarah Bernhardt b.
	Archer, *The Black Doctor*; Taylor, *Vanderdecken, or the Flying Dutchman*		Jean-Baptiste Gaspard Deburau (beloved Pierrot, Théâtre des Funambules) d.
...Meynell b. ...m Stoker b.	J. M. Morton, *Box and Cox*	R. B. Peake d.	de Musset's *Un Caprice* at the Comédie Française; Mlle Mars d.
...efferies b. ...rryat d. ...Brontë d.			
...se b. ...ley b. ...does d. ...d.		J. Kenny d.	Electricity introduced at Paris Opéra with Meyerbeer's *Prophète*; Ibsen finishes his first play, *Catiline*; Strindberg b.; Heinrich Laube begins seventeen-year tenure as director of Vienna Burgtheater
...Hearn b. ...i b. ...Maupassant b.	Taylor, *The Vicar of Wakefield*		Wagner's *Lohengrin* performed at Weimar under the baton of Franz Liszt

Date	Historical events	Theatrical events	Non-dramatic literary even
			Hawthorne, *The Scarlet Letter*; Tennyson, *In Memoriam*; Wordsworth, *Prelude*
1851	The Great Exhibition	Macready's farewell as Macbeth	Borrow, *Lavengro*; E. Gaskell, *Cranford* (begins) Hawthorne, *The House of Seven Gables*; Melville, *M Dick*; Ruskin, *The Stones Venice* (begins); H. B. Sto *Uncle Tom's Cabin*
1852		Barry Sullivan's début at Haymarket	Arnold, *Empedocles on Etn and Other Poems*; Dickens *Bleak House* (begins); Thackeray, *Henry Esmond*
1853		Buckstone takes over Haymarket management from Webster	Arnold, *Balder Dead*; *The Scholar Gipsy*; *Sohrab and Rustum*; C. Brontë, *Villett* E. Gaskell, *Ruth*; Lytton, *Novel*; Reade, *Peg Woffington*; Thackeray, *Th Newcomes* (begins); C. M. Yonge, *The Heir of Redcly*
1854	Crimean War begins	Madame Vestris retires; C. Kemble d.	Dickens, *Hard Times*; E. Gaskell, *North and Sou* (begins); Thoreau, *Walde*
1855			Browning, *Men and Wome* Dickens, *Little Dorrit* (begins); Kingsley, *Westn Ho!*; Longfellow, *Hiawat* Tennyson, *Maud*; Whitm *Leaves of Grass* (begins); *Saturday Review* begins
1856		Madame Vestris d.	E. B. Browning, *Aurora Leigh*; Froude, *History of England* (begins); Motley, *The Rise of the Dutch Republic*; Reade, *It is Nev Too Late to Mend*
1857	Indian Mutiny	Adelaide Ristori appears in London	Holmes, *The Autocrat at Breakfast Table* (begins); Melville, *The Confidence Man*; Trollope, *Barcheste Towers*; Thackeray, *The Virginians* (begins)

Births and deaths of non-dramatic writers	First performances of notable UK plays	Births and deaths of notable UK playwrights	Continental theatrical events
lzac d. ordsworth d.			
evenson b. Cooper d.	Lovell, *Ingomar*; Webster, *The Courier of Lyons*		Dingelstedt manages Munich Court Theatre; Wagner publishes *Oper und Drama*
dy Gregory b. Moore b. ogol d. Moore d.	Boucicault, *The Corsican Brothers*; Taylor and Reade, *Masks and Faces*	W. Poel b.	Ibsen becomes stage director and dramaturge at Bergens Norske Theater
all Caine b.		J. Forbes-Robertson b.	Edouard Devrient is director of Karlsruhe Court Theatre
imbaud b. ilde b. Ferrier d. . Corelli b. . Sharp b. ierkegaard d. ogers d. Brontë d.		J. N. Talfourd d.	Sardou's *La Taverne* receives stormy reception at Odéon Ristori performs in Paris
eud b. Haggard b. Harris b. eine d.		Shaw b.	
onrad b. issing b. Musset d.		D. Jerrold d. W. T. Moncrieff d. F. Benson b.	Dingelstedt is director at Weimar Court Theatre

Date	Historical events	Theatrical events	Non-dramatic literary events
1858			G. Eliot, *Scenes of Clerical Life*; Longfellow, *The Courtship of Miles Standish*; Morris, *The Defence of Guinevere and Other Poems*; Trollope, *Doctor Thorne*
1859		Charles Kean concludes his management of the Princess's	Darwin, *On the Origin of Species*; Dickens, *A Tale of Two Cities*; G. Eliot, *Adam Bede*; Fitzgerald, *The Rubaiyat of Omar Khayyam* Meredith, *The Ordeal of Richard Feverel*; J. S. Mill, *On Liberty*; Tennyson, *Idylls of the King* (begins)
1860	Abraham Lincoln elected President of US		Collins, *The Woman in White* Dickens, *Great Expectations* (begins); G. Eliot, *The Mill on the Floss*; Peacock, *Gryll Grange*; Ruskin, *Unto this Last* (begins); *Essays and Reviews*
1861	US Civil War begins; Prince Albert d.	Charles Fechter's revolutionary *Hamlet*; Edwin Booth's first English tour	G. Eliot, *Silas Marner*; Mayhew, *London Labour and the London Poor* (begins); Palgrave, *The Golden Treasury*; Trollope, *Framley Parsonage*; Mrs H. Wood, *East Lynne*
1862		Phelps ends his management at Sadler's Wells	G. Eliot, *Romola* (begins); Meredith, *Modern Love*; Trollope, *Orley Farm*; Hugo *Les Misérables*
1863			E. Gaskell, *Sylvia's Lovers*; Kinglake, *History of the Crimean War* (begins); Reade, *Hard Cash*; Renan, *Vie de Jésus*

...ths and deaths ...on-dramatic ...ters	First performances of notable UK plays	Births and deaths of notable UK playwrights	Continental theatrical events
			Production of *Le Fils naturel* by Dumas fils at Théâtre Gymnase; Rachel d.; André Antoine b.
Doyle b. Ellis b. Grahame b. E. Housman b. ⟨.⟩ Jerome b. Thompson b. Quincey d. ⟨⟩nt d. ⟨⟩caulay d.	Boucicault, *The Octoroon*		
W. Rolfe b. ⟨⟩openhauer d.	Boucicault, *The Colleen Bawn*	Barrie b.	Début of the elder Coquelin at Comédie Française
⟨⟩vo b. ⟨⟩gore b. ⟨⟩. Browning d. ⟨⟩ugh d.			Scribe d.
⟨⟩Henry b. ⟨⟩eterlinck b. ⟨⟩Wharton b. ⟨⟩oreau d.			Bernhardt's first appearance at Comédie Française, in Racine's *Iphigénie*
⟨⟩tayana b. ⟨⟩ackeray d.	Taylor, *The Ticket-of-Leave Man*	C. Selby d. J. Martin Harvey b.	Stanislavski b.

Date	Historical events	Theatrical events	Non-dramatic literary events
1864			Browning, *Dramatis Personæ*; Dickens, *Our Mutual Friend* (begins); E. Gaskell, *Wives and Daughters* (begins); Le Fanu, *Uncle Silas*; Meredith, *Sandra Belloni*; Newman, *Apologia pro Vita Sua*; Trollope, *The Small House at Allington*
1865	US Civil War ends; Lincoln assassinated	Beginning of Bancroft management at the Prince of Wales	Arnold, *Essays in Criticism*; Carroll, *Alice in Wonderland*; Ruskin, *Sesame and Lilies*; Newman, *The Dream of Gerontius*; Tolstoy, *War and Peace* (begins); *Fortnightly Review* begins
1866		Select Committee of House of Commons investigates question of theatrical licences and regulations	G. Eliot, *Felix Holt*; Ruskin, *The Crown of Wild Olive*; Swinburne, *Poems and Ballads* I; Trollope, *The Last Chronicle of Barset* (begins)
1867	Disraeli's Reform Act		Arnold, *Thyrsis*; Marx, *Das Kapital* (begins); Ouida, *Under Two Flags*; Zola, *Thérèse Raquin*
1868		Charles Kean d.; Hollingshead opens the Gaiety	Browning, *The Ring and the Book* (begins); Collins, *The Moonstone*; Morris, *The Earthly Paradise* (begins)
1869			Arnold, *Culture and Anarchy*; Blackmore, *Lorna Doone*; Gilbert, *The Bab Ballads* I; Tennyson, *Idylls of the King* (complete); Trollope, *Phineas Finn*
1870	Franco–Prussian War begins; Vatican Council		Disraeli, *Lothair*; Newman, *The Grammar of Assent*; Rossetti, *Poems*; Zola's Rougon-Macquart series begins

ths and deaths on-dramatic ters	First performances of notable UK plays	Births and deaths of notable UK playwrights	Continental theatrical events
re d. wthorne d. ador d. tees d.	Robertson, *David Garrick*		Monopoly abolished in Paris; Ibsen directs *The Pretenders* in Bergen; Johanne Luise Heiberg's final appearance at Danish Royal Theatre; Offenbach's *La Belle Hélène* produced in Paris
oling b. ats b.	Boucicault, *Arrah-na-Pogue*; Robertson, *Society*		
lls b. ble d. cock d.	Oxenford, *East Lynne*; Robertson, *Ours*		
anett b. wson b. W. Russell b.	Robertson, *Caste*	Galsworthy b.	
Douglas b. rki b.			Dumas fils's preface to *Un père prodigue*
ayon b. acock b. nte-Beuve d.	H. J. Byron, *Uncle Dick's Darling*; Robertson, *School*		
oc b. Douglas b. ain b. Norris b. ckens d. mas père d.	Albery, *Two Roses*; Gilbert, *The Princess*		*In Rome*, Strindberg's first produced play, acted at Dramaten

Date	Historical events	Theatrical events	Non-dramatic literary event.
1871	Paris Commune; University Test Act allows Catholics and Nonconformists to graduate at Oxford and Cambridge	Irving appears in *The Bells*	Darwin, *The Descent of Ma* G. Eliot, *Middlemarch*; Hardy, *Desperate Remedies*; Lytton, *The Coming Race*; Meredith, *Harry Richmond*
1872			Butler, *Erewhon*; Hardy, *Under the Greenwood Tree*; Nietzsche, *The Birth of Tragedy*
1873		Macready d.	Newman, *The Idea of a University* (complete); Pate Studies in the History of the Renaissance; Trollope, *The Eustace Diamonds*
1874			Hardy, *Far from the Madd Crowd*; J. Thomson II, *The City of Dreadful Night*
1875		Tomasso Salvini's Othello at Drury Lane; Ellen Terry's Portia at the Prince of Wales	Meredith, *Beauchamp's Career*; Symonds, *History the Renaissance in Italy* (begins); Tolstoy, *Anna Karenina* (begins)
1876			G. Eliot, *Daniel Deronda*; James, *Roderick Hudson*; Morris, *Sigurd the Volsung* M. Twain, *Tom Sawyer*
1877			
1878	Congress of Berlin	Phelps's last appearance as Wolsey; Irving assumes control of the Lyceum; Mathews d.	Hardy, *The Return of the Native*; Swinburne, *Poems and Ballads* II
1879		Fechter d.	Butcher and Lang, translation of *Odyssey*; James, *Daisy Miller*; Meredith, *The Egoist*; Stevenson, *Travels with a Donkey*

·rths and deaths non-dramatic ·iters	First performances of notable UK plays	Births and deaths of notable UK playwrights	Continental theatrical events
·eiser b. ·oust b. ·léry b.	Gilbert, *Pygmalion and Galatea*; Randall's *Thumb*; L. Lewis, *The Bells*	Robertson d.	
·ardsley b. ·erbohm b.		J. Poole d.	
· la Mare b. M. Ford b. E. Moore b. , Richardson b. · Fanu d. S. Mill d.		Fitzball d. Lytton d.	Zola's preface to *Thérèse Raquin* proclaims naturalism
·esterton b. ·ost b. ·offmansthal b. Stein b.	Taylor, *Lady Clancarty*		The Meiningen troupe succeeds in Berlin and begins its European tours
·ng b. Mann b. ·lke b. ·ingsley d.	H. J. Byron, *Our Boys*		
London b. ·eorge Sand d.	Tennyson, *Queen Mary*		First performance of *Peer Gynt* in Christiania; Wagner's Bayreuth Theatre established; Lemaître d.
·agehot d.	Gilbert, *Engaged*	M. A. Lovell d.	
·asefield b. , Sinclair b. Thomas b.			
·nstein b. ·orster b. ·alin b. ·rotsky b.		J. B. Buckstone d.	World première of *A Doll's House* at Danish Royal Theatre; début of Eleonora Duse at the Teatro Fiorentini in Naples, in Zola's *Thérèse Raquin*

Date	Historical events	Theatrical events	Non-dramatic literary events
1880			Meredith, *The Tragic Comedians*; Ouida, *Moths*; Shorthouse, *John Inglesant*
1881		D'Oyly Carte's Savoy Theatre entirely illuminated by electricity; London appearance of the Saxe-Meiningen Company	
1882			
1884		Gladstone's Reform Act	

~ths and deaths non-dramatic *iters*	First performances of notable UK plays	Births and deaths of notable UK playwrights	Continental theatrical events
›yes b. Strachey b. Eliot d. aubert d.		Planché d. Taylor d.	
	M. A. Jones, *The Silver King*		*Master Olof*, Strindberg's first major play, published and produced by Ludwig Josephson at Nya Teatern in Stockholm; Zola publishes *Le Naturalisme au théâtre*
		C. Reade d.	

A guide to London theatres, 1750–1880

Frederick & Lise-Lone Marker

The theatrical Baedeker which follows is intended as a concise descriptive guide to the principal London playhouses in use during the period 1750 to 1880. The chequered history of these theatres, presented here only in barest outline, constitutes almost a cultural history in miniature. This guide does not pretend to be all-inclusive: some of the more remote and the less important places of entertainment as well as several theatres opened towards the close of our period have been omitted. Theatres outside London proper also fall beyond its scope. Ranging, however, from the august precincts of *Drury Lane* and *Covent Garden* to such popular theatrical haunts as the 'Blood Tub', the 'Dust Hole' and the 'Rickety Twins', this catalogue does embrace all the principal localities where English drama was acted in the capital from the mid-eighteenth to the late nineteenth century. More than a few of these structures have survived until the present day; a small handful of them are still in use as theatres.

Interested readers are referred for further information to the lists and descriptions of theatres found in H. Barton Baker's *History of the London Stage* (London, 1904), Allardyce Nicoll's *A History of English Drama 1660–1900* (Cambridge, 1966), E. B. Watson's *Sheridan to Robertson* (Cambridge, Mass., 1926), and in the relevant volumes of *The London Stage* (Carbondale,

Ill., 1962–8). They are also reminded of Erroll Sherson's *London's Lost Theatres of the Nineteenth Century* and of W. Macqueen-Pope's articles and books on London theatres. Amplifying and sometimes amending these published studies, the superb holdings of the Enthoven Collection, now in the Victoria and Albert Museum and soon to be moved to Somerset House, constitute an invaluable mine of information and memorabilia concerning London's theatre buildings.

Adelphi (Strand). Originally named the *Sans Pareil* and built by John Scott in 1806, this theatre was reopened as the Adelphi on 18 October 1819. Under the managements of F. H. Yates (1825–42) and Madame Céleste-Benjamin Webster (1844–58) it became renowned for the brand of sensational melodrama known as 'Adelphi screamers'. One of the best of the minors, it was rebuilt in 1858. A 'History of the Adelphi Theatre' by E. L. Blanchard was published in *The Era Almanack* (1877).

[Royal] Albert Saloon (Shepherdess Walk, Britannia Fields, Hoxton). Apparently opened at the beginning of the 1840s and offering concerts, ballets, vaudevilles and similar entertainment, this theatre featured two stages built at right angles to each other, one facing an outdoor auditorium and the other opening into a closed theatre.

Alhambra (Leicester Square). This famous music hall, which began as the Panopticon of Science and Art in 1854, obtained a theatrical licence in 1871, and featured *opéra bouffe* and superbly mounted ballets until fire destroyed it in 1882. Subsequently rebuilt, it continued to function as a music hall and variety theatre until 1936.

Astley's Amphitheatre (Westminster Bridge Road). When Philip Astley's old circus-ring theatre burned down in 1803, a new house devoted chiefly to hippodrama and similar spectacles replaced it the following year. Astley's flourished under the management of the colourful Andrew Ducrow (1830–41); it was finally destroyed in 1895.

Britannia (High Street, Hoxton). Distinguished by the variety of its offerings and the permanence of its acting company, this theatre was managed by the Lane family for more than half a century (1841–99).

City of London (Bishopsgate, Norton Folgate). Built by the renowned theatre architect Samuel Beazley and opened on 27 March 1837, this house specialized in domestic and temperance melodramas. It was closed in 1868. 'Three Old London Theatres', published by A. V. Sutherland-Graeme in *The Connoisseur* (August 1936), recalls its history.

City Pantheon. See New City.

Charing Cross. See Toole's.

[Royal] Coburg (Waterloo Road). Built by Dunn and Jones and opened on 11 May 1818, this theatre earned its nickname as the 'Blood Tub' by featuring melodramas of the most sensational sort. Occasionally, however, distinguished performers such as Edmund Kean and Madame Vestris appeared at the Coburg. Renamed the *Royal Victoria Theatre* in 1833, it went on to become one of the most successful of the minors. It is known today as the home of the Old Vic.

Colosseum Saloon (Albany Street, Regent's Park). This originally opened as a variety theatre around 1837, and plays were occasionally presented here during the nineteenth century. (Its activities are distinct from the more refined entertainments and popular panoramas offered at the *Royal Colosseum.*)

Covent Garden (Bow Street). From its opening with *The Way of the World* on 7 December 1732 until its abandonment of drama and its reincarnation as the *Royal Italian Opera House* in 1847, *Covent Garden* remained one of England's foremost playhouses. It continued to be managed by its founder, the celebrated harlequin John Rich, until his death in 1761. The Licensing Act of 1737 had given to it and to *Drury Lane* the only patents for the performance of legitimate drama. During the later eighteenth century Spranger Barry conducted his famous rivalry with Garrick from its stage, and Macklin appeared there as the first authentically costumed Macbeth. The theatre was altered in 1782, increasing its capacity to about 2,500 spectators; the oblong shape of the auditorium drew complaints about poor sightlines. It was rebuilt again by the manager Thomas Harris in 1792, this time in 'lyral form', according to Boaden, in which 'the fronts of the boxes bulged something in the curve of a ship's side'. The size was increased to accommodate 3,013 spectators.

John Philip Kemble joined the management in 1803, inaugurating his most outstanding period as a Shakespearian producer. *Covent Garden* was gutted by fire on 20 September 1808 and a new structure, designed in a pretentiously pseudo–classical style by Robert Smirke Jr at a cost of £150,000, opened the following year. Under the managements of Macready (1837–9) and Vestris-Mathews (1839–42) the theatre again enjoyed periods of significant activity. In 1843 the Theatre Regulation Act dissolved the monopoly held by the patent houses, and four years later *Covent Garden* abandoned legitimate drama to become an opera house. The theatre burned down in 1856, and the present *Covent Garden Opera House* opened on 15 May 1858.

Drury Lane, Theatre Royal. Founded by Thomas Killigrew under a direct charter from Charles II in 1663, *Drury Lane* is the most famous and the oldest surviving of the London theatres. When the original theatre was destroyed by fire in 1672, a new playhouse, designed by Christopher Wren, rose from the ashes two years later. Garrick joined Lacy as joint patentee in 1747 and the theatre continued under Garrick's astute management until his retirement in 1776. Sheridan assumed control the following season; in 1788 John Philip Kemble became the actual manager of *Drury Lane*, remaining its artistic director until 1802, when the difficulties of partnership with Sheridan drove him and his illustrious sister into an association with Thomas Harris at the rival patent house.

During Kemble's management, Christopher Wren's seventeenth-century structure was condemned and a new *Drury Lane* rose on its site, opening on 21 April 1794. Henry Holland's new Lane followed *Covent Garden*'s trend towards increased size, accommodating 3,611 spectators. Both houses became, in Cumberland's words, 'henceforward theatres for spectators rather than playhouses for hearers'. In 1809 *Drury Lane* went up in flames and a new building, designed by Benjamin Wyatt and smaller than its predecessor by some 700 seats, opened on 10 October 1812. During R. W. Elliston's flamboyant tenancy (1819–26) the interior was remodelled and given the appearance which, with minor alterations, it has retained to the present day.

In 1833 the notorious Alfred Bunn gained control of both patent houses, and his two terms of management at the Lane (1833–9, 1843–50) turned it into a concert hall *cum* circus arena. Under Macready's brief intervening management (1841–3) important reforms were introduced. During the second half of the century *Drury Lane*'s fortunes declined until the highly successful impresario Augustus Harris acquired the theatre in 1879.

East London. See **Royalty**.

Gaiety (Strand). Opened by John Hollingshead on 21 December 1868, the old *Gaiety* became famous mainly for its burlesque shows and its Gaiety girls. It closed, tearfully and with a farewell address by Henry Irving, in 1902.

Garrick's Subscription (Leman Street, E). Named for its proximity to the site of the old theatre in Goodman's Fields where David Garrick made his début, this theatre was opened by Wyman and Conquest on 3 January 1831. It burned down and was rebuilt by B. O. Conquest in 1846. The Garrick occupied a lowly position, even among the East End theatres, and records of its activity cease towards the end of our period.

Globe (Newcastle Street, Strand). Built in the slum neighbourhood swept away by the Aldwych alterations, this poorly constructed 1,000-seat theatre was opened by Sefton Parry at the end of 1868. During our period the *Globe*'s principal attractions were the melodramas of H. J. Byron and stage adaptations of Dickens, notably *Bleak House*, in which Jennie Lee's celebrated portrayal of Jo was hailed as 'realism difficult to surpass'. Situated back to back with the *Opera Comique*, the two playhouses earned the nickname the 'Rickety Twins' because of their jerry-built construction. The Globe finally ended its days in 1902.

(A *Globe Theatre* or *Rotunda* apparently opened on Blackfriars Road in 1833, but this playhouse soon became a concert hall.)

Grecian (Shepherdess Walk, City Road, Hoxton). The erstwhile *Eagle Saloon* opened as a variety theatre in 1832 under Thomas 'Brayvo' Rouse. The *Grecian* gave several accomplished actors and singers their start. Under Benjamin Conquest's management (1851–79), it became known for its ballets and lavish Christmas pantomimes. The theatre was rebuilt by Conquest in 1876, and was finally sold to the Salvation Army.

Haymarket (King's Theatre) Opera House. The *King's Theatre* in the Haymarket, the first playhouse constructed in the eighteenth century, was built by John Vanbrugh and opened on 9 April 1705. It underwent little change during Garrick's time, but in 1789 it was destroyed by fire and a new theatre was erected the following year. Used regularly for opera under a variety of managements, it was occasionally occupied by the homeless patent companies during periods of rebuilding. Renamed *Her Majesty's* at the accession of Queen Victoria, the house was again gutted by fire in 1867. Rebuilt in 1872, *Her Majesty's* was finally demolished in 1892.

Haymarket, Theatre Royal. The *Little Theatre* in the Haymarket, erected by John Potter in 1720, is the second oldest London playhouse still in use. Its history is a colourful one. During our period it entered a new phase when the resourceful Samuel Foote acquired it in 1747. At the cost of a leg – broken and amputated as the result of a prank played by noble friends who, to make amends, interceded with the king on his behalf – Foote gained a royal patent in 1766 which permitted performances in the summer months. Under the subsequent managements of the elder George Colman and his son (1777–1820) the theatre prospered, and many outstanding performers, including Henderson, Elliston, Charles Mathews the elder and Liston, made their débuts there. The old playhouse was demolished in 1820, and the stately *Haymarket Theatre* we know today opened on 4 July 1821. The management of Benjamin Webster (1837–53) marked a brilliant period during which all the great actors of the day appeared at the *Haymarket*. Webster's successor, the comedian John Buckstone, maintained its position as the foremost comedy house in London during his tenure there. His ghost is still said to haunt the theatre. In 1880 the *Haymarket* passed into the control of the Bancrofts.

Holborn (Holborn). Opened by Sefton Parry in 1866, this theatre passed through the hands of a number of managers, including Barry Sullivan and Horace Wigan, and was known by several names, including the *Mirror*, the *Curtain* and the *Duke's Theatre*, during its brief career. It burned down in 1880.

Lyceum (Strand). Originally built in 1765, the *Lyceum* housed exhibits, entertainments, phantasmagoria and waxworks during the first half century of its existence. In 1809 Samuel Arnold gained a licence to present opera and musical drama and renamed the theatre the *English Opera House*. Six years later he rebuilt the theatre at a cost of £80,000, opening his lavish new playhouse on 15 June 1816. In 1830 this theatre too was razed by fire; a new *Lyceum*, designed by Samuel Beazley and with its main entrance now in Wellington Street, was opened on 14 July 1834. When the monopoly of the patent houses was broken in 1843, the *Lyceum* branched into legitimate drama. The management of Vestris and Mathews (1847–55) was highlighted by the scenic marvels created for the staging of Planché's extravaganzas. Under Fechter's regime (1863–7) revolutionary methods of staging and acting were introduced. Irving's appearance in *The Bells* signalled the beginning of a momentous new era for the *Lyceum*. With his assumption of the management in 1878 it became one of the most notable of London's theatres.

Marylebone (Church Street, Edgware Road). An unlicensed theatre for crude melodrama, known as the *Royal Sussex* and subsequently as the *Pavilion*, opened in 1831. It was pulled down and rebuilt six years later, opening as the *Marylebone* on 13 November 1837. It operated as a rather undistinguished house for melodrama and pantomime under a variety of managements, including a term by the noted actress Mrs Warner. It was again rebuilt and enlarged in 1864; rechristened the *Royal Alfred Theatre* in 1866, it soon reverted to its old name of the *Marylebone*. Towards the end of the century it became the *West London Theatre*. Damaged by enemy action in the Second World War, the building was finally destroyed by fire during its demolition in 1962. Its history is recorded in Malcolm Morley's two publications, *The Old Marylebone Theatre* (St Marylebone Society Publication No. 2, 1960) and *The Royal West London Theatre* (St Marylebone Society Publication No. 6, 1962).

Mirror. See Holborn.

New City (Milton Street [formerly Grub Street], Fore Street). The *City Pantheon* ('late City Chapel') was operating in a disused Grub Street chapel in 1829. On 4 April 1831 it was opened by John Kemble Chapman as the *New City*, then altered and reopened by him on 26 December 1832. This respectable minor theatre featured performances of a generally higher quality: Fanny Clifton (Mrs Stirling) made her début here, and Kean acted Shylock in 1831. The theatre was closed in 1836

New Royal Brunswick (Wellclose Square). When the *East London Theatre*, formerly the *Royalty*, burned down in 1826, it was rebuilt and reopened as the *New Royal Brunswick* on 25 February 1828. So poor was the workmanship, however, that the entire structure collapsed three days later, during a rehearsal of *Guy Mannering*. Fifteen people were killed and twenty injured in the tragedy.

New Royal West London. See Prince of Wales's.

New Royalty. See Soho.

New. See Prince of Wales's.

Olympic (Wych Street or Newcastle Street, Strand: no trace of the theatre's location remains after the Aldwych rebuilding). Built by Philip Astley from the timber of the old French warship 'Ville de Paris' (the deck was used for the stage), the *Olympic Pavilion* opened on 1 December 1806. The venture proved a failure for Astley, and the redoubtable Robert William Elliston took over in 1813, rebuilding the theatre at considerable expense in 1818. The management of the *Olympic* by Madame Vestris (1831–9), marked by a series of significant artistic and managerial reforms, constituted a highpoint in the theatre's history. 'There was introduced for the first time in England that reform in all theatrical matters which has since been adopted in every theatre in the kingdom', observed Charles Mathews, who made his début at the *Olympic* in 1835 and married Vestris three years later. 'Drawing-rooms were fitted up like drawing-rooms, and furnished with care and taste.' After Vestris and Mathews departed for *Covent Garden* in 1839 the *Olympic*'s fortunes declined. It burned down in March 1849 (arson was suspected) and was rebuilt by its manager Walter Watts the following year – only to be closed again when Watts was arrested for fraud and forgery. It enjoyed its greatest long-run success in 1863, when Tom Taylor's melodrama masterpiece *The Ticket-of-Leave Man* took London by storm. Manager Horace Wigan was the first Hawkshaw in Taylor's play, and he went on to create an improved reputation for the *Olympic*. The theatre finally closed at the end of the century.

Opera Comique (Strand). Located in the same disreputable neighbourhood as the Globe, the *Opera Comique* opened in October 1870. Built back to back with the *Globe*, this flimsy and draughty playhouse was as badly constructed as its sister; together they were known as the 'Rickety Twins'. Long narrow tunnels from three thoroughfares formed the *Opera Comique*'s entrance, for which reason it was often called *Theatre Royal, Tunnels*. A fire would have proved a holocaust, but fortunately none occurred. Ristori and the company of the *Comédie Française* made guest appearances here, but the theatre's heyday came at the close of our period with the first productions of Gilbert and Sullivan's *HMS Pinafore*, *The Pirates of Penzance* and *Patience*. The *Opera Comique* closed in 1899.

Pantheon (Oxford Street). Built by James Wyatt and opened in 1772, the *Pantheon* was a popular location for balls and masquerades. It was used in place of the *Haymarket* when the latter burned down in 1789. The *Pantheon* itself burned down in 1792 and, although rebuilt by Wyatt, it enjoyed little further use as a playhouse. Reopened as an opera theatre in 1812, its owners lost £50,000 in just over a month, and the building was sold two years later. Subsequently serving for over seventy years as the offices of Gilbey's the wine merchants, the structure was pulled down in 1937.

Pavilion. See Marylebone.

[Royal] Pavilion (Whitechapel Road, Mile End). Opened by Wyatt and Farrell on 10 November 1828, this playhouse was known for 'Newgate melodrama'. Fanny Clifton (Mrs Stirling) scored her first success there. The theatre was destroyed by fire in 1856 and rebuilt. It continued into the present century as the home of Jewish drama in the East End.

Prince of Wales's (Tottenham Street). Regarded throughout most of the nineteenth century as London's most contemptible playhouse and consequently nicknamed the 'Dust Hole', this building progressed from a concert hall and riding ring to a theatre, known as the *New*, about 1810. Renamed the *Regency* and, after considerable alterations, the *Regency Theatre of Varieties*, it achieved little distinction. Considerably 'improved', it reopened as the *New Royal West London* at the end of 1820, 'the smallest of these places devoted to the drama', as one contemporary source describes it, and 'of too humble pretensions to create jealousy'. Visiting French companies appeared here during this period. Known also for a time as the *Tottenham Street Theatre*, the playhouse, altered and redecorated, reopened as the *Queen's* on 3 February 1831. During the 1830s a series of managers, including Madame Vestris, failed to succeed with it, and after 1839 it declined into its most disreputable 'Dust Hole' period. All the more striking, then, was its renaissance during the management of the Bancrofts (1865–79) when, rechristened the *Price of Wales's* by royal permission, it became one of London's most important and fashionable theatres.

During our own century the old theatre, closed from 1882 to 1905, has been known as the *Scala*. It should not be confused with the *Prince of Wales's* in Coventry Street, which opened in 1884 and treated London audiences to their first view of *A Doll's House*, altered almost beyond recognition as *Breaking a Butterfly*.

Prince's. See **St James's.** (The *Prince's* was also the first name given to the *Prince of Wales's* in Coventry Street.)

Princess's (Oxford Street). Built by a silversmith named Hamlet, this playhouse began its career as a bazaar and exhibition hall. Converted by Hamlet into a theatre in 1840, it specialized in promenade concerts and opera. Charlotte Cushman and Edwin Forrest made their London débuts here in 1845. During Charles Kean's management (1850–9) his luminous series of Shakespearian revivals made it London's most brilliant playhouse. Fechter's revolutionary *Hamlet* was seen at the *Princess's* in 1860. From the mid-sixties until the close of our period the theatre became famous for its thrilling melodramas, extending from Boucicault's fabled sensation, *The Streets of London* (1864), to the classic of them all, *The Silver King* (1882), with which manager Wilson Barrett enjoyed a run of nearly 300 performances.

The theatre that Hamlet built ultimately ended its days as a warehouse.

Queen's (Tottenham Street). See **Prince of Wales's.**

Queen's (Long Acre). Originally St Martin's Hall, this house was opened as a theatre in 1867. Its stage was spacious and well equipped, and during its brief life such notable performers as Irving, Charles Wyndham, Phelps, Ellen Terry and Salvini acted there. It closed as a theatre in 1878.

Regency or **Regency Theatre of Varieties.** See **Prince of Wales's.**

Royal Alfred. See **Marylebone.**

Royal Circus. See **Surrey.**

Royal Clarence (Liverpool Street, King's Cross New Road, WC1).
Started in 1830 as the *Royal Panharmonium*, this house became a regular
theatre, known as the *Royal Clarence*, in 1831 or 1832 (*The Tatler* for
8–9 May 1832 calls it 'small, neat, well-filled'). Closed for a time as disreputable, this playhouse was known by several names, including the
Regent, Argyll, King's Cross and *Cabinet Theatre*, during the years from
1852 to 1867.

Royal Italian Opera House. See **Covent Garden.**

Royal Kent (Kensington High Street). Enjoying the patronage of the Duke
of Kent, this small, fashionable 250-seat playhouse functioned between
1834 and the early 1840s.

Royal Manor House (King's Road, Chelsea). Managed for a time by E. L.
Blanchard, this obscure theatre seems to have been in operation from
1838 to about 1841,

Royal Sussex. See **Marylebone.**

Royalty (Wellclose Square). In unsuccessful defiance of the patent theatres
John Palmer, a *Drury Lane* actor, opened the *Royalty Theatre* on 20 June
1787, but his plans for establishing a rival playhouse for legitimate drama
were short-lived. Under Macready, his successor and the father of the
celebrated tragedian, the *Royalty* offered burlettas and pantomimes with
little success. The theatre's existence remained precarious; in 1816 it was
completely renovated and opened as the *East London Theatre*, only to
be consumed by fire ten years later.

See also the **New Royal Brunswick,** erected on the site of the old
Royalty in 1828.

Royal Victoria. See **Coburg.**

Sadler's Wells (Rosebery Avenue). One of the most interesting of the
minors, the history of *Sadler's Wells* dates back to the seventeenth
century, when Sadler operated a popular – and rowdy – pleasure garden
on the site of a medicinal spring. In 1765 Rosoman (who lent his name
to a nearby street) pulled down the old wooden 'Musick House' used by
Sadler, and replaced it with a stone theatre which he built in seven weeks.
He retired with a comfortable fortune in 1772. During the tenure of his
successor, the *Drury Lane* actor Thomas King (1772–82), the theatre
was ably managed, but the managers who followed King relied on a very
mixed bill of fare ranging from performing dogs to children's recitations
(including, it is believed, a declamatory recital by the young Edmund
Kean). The nineteenth century saw *Sadler's Wells* devoted to a repertory

of sensational aquatic melodramas staged with the help of a large tank (90 feet by 24 feet and 5 feet deep) flooded with water from the New River. *The Siege of Gibraltar*, featuring a full naval bombardment, was the first of these popular spectacles.

   After the abolition of the monopoly, however, *Sadler's Wells* entered a lengthy period of artistic brilliance under the management of Samuel Phelps (1844–62), whose programme of Shakespearian revivals made it one of London's most noteworthy playhouses. After Phelps its glory faded, and in 1878 it was closed as a dangerous structure. It was subsequently reconstructed, and its history has continued to our own day.

St James's (King Street, St James's). Opened by John Braham on 14 December 1835, the early history of this minor theatre is unillustrious. It was known for a short time as the *Prince's*; in 1842, under its original name, it became the home of French plays and visiting French companies. It was not until the close of our period, under the management of John Hare and the Kendals, that it rose to prominence. The renowned tenancy of Sir George Alexander began in 1891.

Sans Pareil. See Adelphi.

Sans Souci (Leicester Place, Leicester Square). A small playhouse built by Charles Dibdin in 1796 to house his one-man entertainments, the significance of the Sans Souci is slight. It accommodated foreign troupes and amateur groups until it fell into disuse after 1834.

Soho (Dean Street, Soho Square). Opened as 'Miss Kelly's Theatre and Dramatic School' in 1840, the *Soho* (sometimes called the *Royalty* and the *New English Opera House*) remained a principal centre of amateur activity during much of the period. It was reconstructed in 1861 and 1863; as the *New Royalty* it later gained fame as the site of the Independent Theatre's private productions of *Ghosts* (1891), *Charley's Aunt* and *Widowers' Houses* (both 1892).

[Royal or New] Standard (Shoreditch High Street). Opening in 1835 as the *Royal Standard*, this north-east suburban playhouse was one of the most capacious theatres in London, seating over 2,000 spectators. It was remodelled and reopened as the *New Standard* in 1845. In 1866 it was gutted by fire and rebuilt on a larger scale, opening two years later. The quality of its stock company was high, and it attracted visiting stars from the West End. Like many theatres of its kind, the *Standard* ended its days as a cinema. It was destroyed during the Second World War.

Strand (Strand). Having transformed a former panorama house to a theatre, the Yorkshire comedian L. B. Rayner opened his *New Strand Subscrip-*

tion Theatre in 1832. The playhouse had no licence, and tickets were sold off the premises (hence its designation Subscription Theatre). The *Strand* quickly became the focal point of the legal battle between the patent theatres and the minors, and its early period is marked by continual litigation. Ingenious efforts were made to evade the Patent Laws – including the not uncommon practice of selling tickets through a confectioner's, with a box ticket included in the purchase of 1 oz of lozenges for 4*s.* and admission to the pit offered for $\frac{1}{2}$ oz of peppermint drops at 2*s.* The *Strand* was ultimately licensed as a minor and was formally opened under the management of Douglas Jerrold and James Hammond in 1836. Dickens's novels were adapted and acted there. The *Strand*'s varied career includes a period of popularity under the direction of William Farren the Younger (1848–50), but its fortunes generally declined until the advent of W. H. Swanborough in 1858. During the long Swanborough management (1858–72) the *Strand* flourished as the 'house of burlesque', featuring the texts of H. J. Byron and the popular comic acting of Marie Wilton (the future Lady Bancroft). The *Strand* was condemned and rebuilt in 1882; it was finally demolished to make way for the Aldwych Underground Station.

Surrey (Blackfriars Road). This theatre, one of the most famous of the minors, originated as a riding school and exhibition established by Charles Hughes in 1771 and operated in competition with Philip Astley. In 1782 the enterprise obtained a licence, and Hughes went into partnership with Charles Dibdin. Together they built the *Royal Circus*, an elaborate theatre in which the pit was replaced by a circus ring, at a cost of £15,000. This structure burned down in 1803 and was replaced the following year. Under Robert Elliston's management (1809–14) the circus ring was eliminated and the playhouse became the *Surrey*. When the Great Lessee left for the *Olympic*, the building returned for a time to its circus ways, but under Thomas Dibdin (1816–23) it again became a theatre.

The *Surrey* flourished once more during Elliston's second tenure (1827–31), scoring one of its greatest successes with Douglas Jerrold's nautical melodrama *Black-Eyed Susan*, which starred T. P. Cooke as William, the honest seaman. 'All London,' declares the *Athenaeum*, 'went over the water' (the theatre was on the south side of the Thames), and on the 300th night of the run 'the walls of the theatre were illuminated and vast multitudes filled the thoroughfare'. Transpontine melodrama became the *Surrey*'s stock-in-trade. During the long and prosperous Shepherd-Creswick management (1848–69) the sensational and spine-tingling 'Surrey pieces' were again in high favour. The versatile George Conquest took over the theatre in 1880. It later became a cinema, and was finally pulled down in 1934.

Toole's (William IV Street). Opened as the *Charing Cross* in 1869, this small playhouse was of little significance until J. S. Clarke's revival of *The Rivals* in 1872. Later renamed *Toole's Theatre*, it flourished chiefly after 1880.

Tottenham Street. See Prince of Wales's.

Vaudeville (Strand). Built during the great boom in theatre construction that began in the late 1860s, the Vaudeville opened on 16 April 1870. It registered an early success later the same year with the production of James Albery's *Two Roses*, which featured Henry Irving in the role of Digby Grant. The history of the *Vaudeville Theatre* extends to our own day.

Vauxhall Gardens (Vauxhall). Known in the seventeenth century as the *Spring Gardens*, *Foxhall*, and frequented by Pepys, dramatic spectacles and later a few operettas and vaudevilles were occasionally staged here. Frequent riots led to its closing in 1859. The site was built over, but the name persists.

West London. See Marylebone.

Westminster Subscription (Tothill Street). Built in 1832 and first managed by T. D. Davenport, this theatre never succeeded in obtaining a licence. During the four years of its existence, however, several players of note got their start there.

I The social and literary context
Michael R. Booth

1 The theatre and its audience

The middle of the eighteenth century does not mark a watershed in theatrical affairs. It is not possible to draw a line at 1750 and declare that the theatre on the one side is markedly different from the theatre on the other: one can do this easily in 1660 but not ninety years later. The London theatre was extremely stable in the years following 1750, more stable than it had been earlier in the century or was to be again until the actor-manager oligarchy of Irving, Harris, Tree, Alexander, Wyndham and Hare dominated the *fin de siècle* theatre and the Edwardian decade. In 1750 Garrick and Lacy completed their third season as managers of Drury Lane, an immensely successful partnership lasting until 1776. In 1750 John Rich had been manager of Covent Garden for eighteen years and was to remain so until his death in 1761, after which his son-in-law John Beard ruled the theatre until 1767. The Licensing Act of 1737 had effectively suppressed competition with the patent theatres; their operation was consistently profitable; the nature and class structure of their audiences relatively unchanging; and patterns of dramatic taste firmly established. It is not to these years that we should look for radical change and theatrical upheaval.

Yet such change and upheaval were soon to come. By the end of the eighteenth century, London, a city of 900,000, was on the edge of a population explosion that sent this figure up to nearly 3 million in 1850 and nearly 4 million in 1880. Until late in the eighteenth century provincial immigration had been the only means for London's increase in population, since the death rate regularly exceeded the birth rate. Now, however, the improvements in medical knowledge, sanitation and hygiene, the widespread use of pottery dishes instead of pewter, the introduction of washable cotton clothes, all combined to raise life expectancy and make a substantial increase in population possible. Emigration from rural areas accelerated, especially in the bad times for agriculture in the 1820s and 1830s. London's role as clearing house for Britain's import and export trade expanded enormously after 1815; large working- and lower middle-class districts were established in the East End and directly south of the Thames – districts in which the kind of theatrical entertainment demanded was quite different from that offered by the patent theatres of the eighteenth century. The rapid growth of the industrial towns in the Midlands and the north, such as Manchester, Liverpool, Leeds, Sheffield and Birmingham, eventually created a type of provincial theatre patron who had to be catered for, not only with London successes, but also with plays especially written for local provincial audiences. In London the new playhouses of the East End and South Bank – the Britannia, the Grecian, the City of London, the Surrey, the Coburg (later the Victoria), the Pavilion, the Bower, among others – had their own plays, playwrights and neighbourhood clientele. The function of the eighteenth-century Town as arbiter of taste disappeared; playwriting embraced a confused anarchy of forms in a vastly increased output, and the traditional norms of critical judgement could no longer be applied.

The effects on theatrical taste of the changing nature of audiences and the reflection of this taste in the repertory are important matters, but, before they can be discussed, the audience itself, its composition, habits and development during the period 1750–1880, needs examination. In 1750 and for many years thereafter, the class divisions among audiences were directly related to the seats they occupied in the auditorium, as had been the case a long time before 1750. The upper classes still sat in the front and side boxes; the 'critics' and professional men, civil servants, tradesmen and a general cross-section of the middle class in the pit and lower gallery; the working class, including servants, journeymen, apprentices, sailors and their womenfolk, in the upper gallery. In 1762 the practice of seating spectators on stage, particularly at benefit performances, was abolished at Drury Lane, but it lasted perhaps twenty years longer at Covent Garden. These divisions cannot be firmly drawn: there is evidence that wealthy tradesmen sat in the boxes, once the sole preserve of the aristocratic and the fashionable; the lower middle class and their families were sometimes found, for economic reasons, in the second gallery, and members of the *beau monde* sat occasionally in the pit. Precise evidence on the composition of the audience in the various parts of the house is lacking in the eighteenth century, but much can be deduced from prologues, epilogues, the plays themselves and contemporary comment. In 1809 the Earl of Carlisle, comparing the theatre of the 1760s to that of his own day (to the latter's detriment), described the boxes and pit of the former time:

> The side boxes were few in number, and very incommodious, especially when the frequenters of those boxes appeared in them in full dresses, the women in hoops of various dimensions, and the men with swords and habiliments all calculated to deny convenient space to their neighbours. Frocks were admitted into the front boxes, but they were not usually worn by gentlemen in the evening; women of the town quietly took their stations in the upper boxes, called the green boxes; and men whom it did not suit either to be at the expense of dress, or who had not time to equip themselves, as before described, resorted to the pit. This of course comprehended a large description of persons, such as belonged to the inns of court, men of liberal pursuits and professions; and who, by a uniform attendance at the playhouse, became no incompetent judges of the drama. Their situation in the pit enabled them to hear and observe. Their habits of life led them to an acquaintance with the authors and the actors of the day; the latter were not ignorant – they were continually before a tribunal that makes itself respected.[1]

The well-known prologue by Miles Peter Andrews to Frederick Reynolds's *The Dramatist*, performed at Covent Garden in 1789, vividly describes crowded boxes:

> What an overflowing House, methinks I see!
> Here, Box-keeper, are these my Places? No,
> Madam Van Bulk has taken all that Row;
> Then I'll go back – you can't – you can, she fibs,
> Keep down your Elbows, or you'll break my Ribs;
> Zounds, how you squeeze! Of what do you think one made is?

[1] *Thoughts upon the Present Condition of the Stage* (1809), quoted in Watson Nicholson, *The Struggle for a Free Stage in London* (2nd ed., New York, 1966), pp. 182–3.

Is this your Wig? No, it's that there Lady's.
Then the Side-Boxes, what delightful Rows!
Peers, Poets, Nabobs, Jews, and 'Prentice Beaux.

In 1792 Richard Tickell described the pit in a prologue to Joseph Richardson's *The Fugitive*, comparing it with the pit of older days:

And yet, in modern Times, the aspiring Wit
Braves but few perils from the well dress'd pit.
Not as of old, when, train'd to frown and fret,
In murky state the surly synod met.
Vain of half learning and of foreign rules,
Vamp'd from the jargon of the antient schools.
In black full-bottom'd wig, the Critic God
Shook his umbrageous curls, and gave the nod!
The pit was then all men – how shrunk the muse
From those bleak rows of overhanging yews!
Unlike the gay parterres we now salute,
That shines at once with blossoms and with fruit;
With chequer'd crowds that mingled taste dispense;
With female softness join'd to manly sense.

The traditional division of audiences in this way persisted well into the nineteenth century. In 1809 John Dallas commented in the Preface to his farce *Not at Home*, 'In saying the PUBLIC I am glad of this opportunity of stating what I mean by that word at a Theatre. I mean that cultivated Company who usually occupy the circle of dress boxes; I mean those judicious Critics who take their station in the Pit; I mean my worthy friend John Bull, who is to be found in either Gallery.'[1] In 1831 Planché could still address the house, in the finale to *Olympic Revels*:

Ye belles and ye beaux
Who adorn our low rows,
Ye gods, who preside in the high ones;
Ye critics who sit
All so snug in the pit,—
An assemblage of clever and sly ones.[2]

[1] Quoted in Allardyce Nicoll, *A History of English Drama, 1660–1900*, IV (2nd ed., Cambridge, 1955), pp. 11–12.
[2] Ibid., IV, 12.

Both these descriptions applied, not to the patent houses, but to minor theatres in the West End: the Lyceum and the Olympic respectively, the Olympic, however, being an unusually fashionable theatre for the 1830s. Thus the organization of audiences according to social tradition and price structure extended beyond the bounds of Drury Lane, Covent Garden and the Haymarket.

Throughout the last half of the eighteenth century the patent theatres were largely the preserve of the aristocratic, the fashionable, the educated, the gentry and the middle-class tradesman. The lower classes were confined to the upper gallery, if they could afford it, for theatregoing was much more expensive in relative terms than it was in the nineteenth century. 1s. for the upper gallery was a substantial sum when weekly wages for day-labour and for journeymen throughout much of the eighteenth century varied, depending upon the kind of work, between 10s. and a guinea.[1] The upper gallery was certainly all the workman could afford, and in the patent houses he was in a minority, although carefully catered to by the make-up of the repertory, especially in the matter of farce, pantomime and entr'acte entertainment. Nevertheless, the predominant pattern of taste was that of an educated middle-class audience leavened with aristocratic spice, and the repertory on the whole was constructed accordingly.

The period 1792–1812, during which Covent Garden and Drury Lane underwent enlargement and rebuilding, and when the minor theatres started to challenge the monopoly of the major houses, can be regarded as the beginning of a period of social and theatrical change which meant the end of an old and established order and the development of new patterns of patronage, taste and drama that transformed the theatre. Whether, by 1812, the rise of the new Covent Garden and the new Drury Lane necessitated spectacle, performing animals and coarsened acting styles in order that spectators distant from the stage could see and hear properly[2] – as has often been argued – or whether a new type of audience came into the theatres about that time and demanded fare of this sort, the fact remains that audience

---

[1] For a detailed discussion of the relationship between wages and attendance at the theatre, see H. W. Pedicord, *The Theatrical Public in the Time of Garrick* (2nd ed., Carbondale, 1966), pp. 22–36.

[2] 'The public are no longer to be attracted by a certain round of established plays, and a certain number of stock scenes; at theatres where they can neither hear nor see, they must have the stimulus of perpetual and expensive variety to make them come at all, and to keep them in tolerable good humour when they are there; their sense of hearing is only to be gratified by noise, and their sense of seeing by glare' (Dramaticus, *An Impartial View of the Stage*, 1816, p. 3). This is only one of many such contemporary views.

tastes and habits of attendance did alter. The new Drury Lane, which opened in 1812, was soon in serious financial difficulties, and was joined a few years later by Covent Garden. The minor theatres commonly did no better.

The cause of the financial trouble is linked with the endlessly discussed matter of the so-called 'decline of the drama', which every critic and historian of the period has pondered.[1] The question is such a large one and embraces so many areas of theatrical practice, playwriting and social life that it cannot be considered properly here. My own opinion is that the word 'decline' is misleading and unacceptable. Those who use it are almost always referring to the literary quality of staged drama, and their judgements are entirely based upon a perusal of printed texts. This is one criterion, admittedly an important one, and the vast majority of nineteenth-century plays fail to meet it (a truth surely relevant to the total output of drama in any age). Yet it is neither the only criterion, nor the most significant one; nor can canons of literary criticism ever be applied to purely theatrical and obviously non-literary forms such as nineteenth-century melodrama, farce and pantomime. It is a criterion that ignores the actor in a century of great and individual acting, that ignores the scene-painter in the greatest age of English scene-painting, that ignores the stage machinist, carpenter and lighting man at a time when technological developments in stage machinery, trapdoors, sets, the controlled use of gas, limelight and stage fire, all contributed to a visual excitement, a mechanical ingenuity and a sense of theatrical effect not known on the English stage before or since. To judge nineteenth-century drama fairly, we must judge it as theatre, not as text, and we cannot do this by looking at it only in terms of dramatic literature. I have said elsewhere that 'drama did not so much "decline", as within new social and cultural contexts, radically change its nature'.[2] I believe that this approach is a far better starting point for an examination of nineteenth-century drama than the traditional, literature-oriented one, as long as it also recognizes theatrical contexts as valid grounds for evaluation.

To return to audiences in the nineteenth century, there is no doubt that managers found boxes and frequently the pit poorly attended, while the galleries were full. This would indicate a falling-off in theatregoing by the aristocratic, the fashionable and the middle class; such indeed was the case.

[1] See *A History of English Drama*, IV, and E. B. Watson, *Sheridan to Robertson* (Cambridge, Mass., 1926). Almost all those in the nineteenth century who wrote on the stage took up the question in one way or another.
[2] *English Plays of the Nineteenth Century*, ed. Michael R. Booth, I (Oxford, 1969), p. 6.

Charles Kemble complained in 1832 that theatres were on the whole 'never above one-half full',[1] and unfortunately the cheaper seats were the occupied ones. Prices of admission, which until about 1820 had been slowly on the rise for a century, with long periods of stability, now started to fall as managers attempted to bring their prices within the means, not of the fashionable, who could afford high prices,[2] but of people who previously could not afford to sit anywhere but the gallery. If the house could not be filled one way, it must somehow be filled another. During the years following 1750, prices for Drury Lane and Covent Garden were steady at boxes 5s., pit 3s., lower gallery 2s. and upper gallery 1s. Lesser theatres were cheaper: the entertainments at Sadler's Wells, for instance, were half as much. The venerable institution of half price permitted anybody to pay that sum after the conclusion of the third act of the mainpiece; from 1825, half price began at nine o'clock, no matter what was happening on stage. By the time of its rebuilding in 1809, prices at Covent Garden had risen to boxes 7s. 6d., pit 4s. and galleries the same as before at 2s. and 1s. Significantly it was the rise in the pit price and the number of private boxes that roused the anger of the OP rioters, and their riot in 1809 on the reopening of Covent Garden, a series of nightly disturbances originating in the pit over a two-month period during which the rioters shouted, blew catcalls, sounded rattles, jeered, danced, waved banners and battled the management's hired bruisers, was a certain indication of class antagonism operating in the theatre auditorium.[3] The rioters triumphed, and the prices were reduced. Stephen Kemble substantially lowered prices at Drury Lane in 1818, and in Osbaldiston's Covent Garden management of 1835–7 they were 4s., 2s. and 1s., as they were under E. T. Smith at Drury Lane as late as 1852. A thorough economic study of nineteenth-century theatre has yet to be written, but even a random sampling of admission prices in the first half of the nineteenth century shows a general downward trend. At the minor theatres prices were even lower. In 1799 at Sadler's Wells they were 4s., 2s. and 1s. – high in comparison with

[1] *Report from the Select Committee on Dramatic Literature* (1832), p. 52.
[2] This class did not at all mind paying half a guinea for a pit seat at the opera and 4s. for the gallery. The popularity (or fashionableness) of the opera among the upper classes was one of the main reasons for the financial difficulties of the theatres. Ironically, the various managers of the Haymarket opera were financially in serious difficulties, in spite of the high prices, because of substantial production costs and the large salaries paid to imported stars.
[3] There had been strong indications of class antagonism in the *Chinese Festival* riots that wrecked Drury Lane in 1755, when the boxes fought the pit in defence of the French dancers. The half-price riots at Drury Lane and Covent Garden in 1763 were rooted in economic anger at the attempt to abolish half price.

the minor theatres of the mid-nineteenth century. By 1850 one of the leading East End theatres, the Britannia, charged 1s. 6d. for stage boxes, 1s. for other boxes, 6d. for the pit, 4d. and 3d. for the galleries. In the same year a spectator could witness a performance at the Victoria for 1s., 6d. and 3d.; and at the Bower Saloon, a low South Bank theatre, for 6d., 4d. and 2d.

After about 1820, therefore, admissions were considerably cheaper than during the last half of the eighteenth century. Such prices must have meant at least an influential increase in attendance from the lower middle and working classes, and an inevitable effect upon the repertory. Times were hard after 1815, which did not help attendance and may have spurred price reductions, but these did not enable the patent theatres, at least, to achieve prosperity: the absence of box patrons in goodly numbers was a fatal blow. The existence of neighbourhood theatres such as the Victoria and the Britannia, which catered especially, at low prices, for the very classes that either comprised a minority of patent theatre audiences in the eighteenth century or did not attend at all, meant that dramatic fare appropriate to their taste – simple melodrama, low farce, jolly pantomime – had to be provided in immense quantities. Once again, the effect of such theatres upon the content and style of nineteenth-century drama was very great. Changes in audience composition and class structure were everywhere dictating changes in the drama itself.

The absence from the theatre of persons of fashion and the respectable middle class was commonly noted in contemporary accounts. It was frequently argued that the lateness of the dinner hour in the best society and the comforts of a good book by the domestic fireside kept these classes away from the theatre. There may be something to the first argument, but the second is untenable when one considers that at the end of the century domestic comforts and good reading matter were generally diffused, yet the theatre prospered. However, this argument was popular: Macready propounded it to the Select Committee on Dramatic Literature in 1832,[1] and in 1863 Henry Morley was of the same opinion.[2] Certainly the indifference of that portion of theatregoers who formerly sat in the boxes was damaging. Hazlitt belaboured them even when they were there, being compelled on one occasion in 1816 to sit in the boxes when he could not find a seat in the pit:

> It is unpleasant to see a play from the boxes. There is no part of the
> house which is so thoroughly wrapped up in itself, and fortified against

[1] *1832 Select Committee Report*, p. 135.
[2] *Journal of a London Playgoer* (1866), pp. 294–5.

any impression from what is passing on the stage; which seems so
completely weaned from all superstitious belief in dramatic illusion;
which takes so little interest in all that is interesting. Not a cravat nor
a muscle was discomposed, except now and then by some gesticulation
of Mr Kean, which violated the decorum of fashionable indifference.[1]

The upper classes may have been repelled by the cruder sort of entertainment now offered in the patent theatres, but in view of the general level of
theatrical taste in the first half of the nineteenth century this is unlikely.
More probably, the theatre for them simply became unfashionable, as it had
in the 1730s when Farinelli was singing in London. Imported dancers were
making the ballet most fashionable, and opera was at the height of its vogue
and brilliance at the very same time that theatres suffered. This was the time
when Catalani, Braham, Grisi, Malibran, Mario, Rubini, Tamburini, Pasta,
Lablache, Sontag and Jenny Lind sang in London; it was obvious where
the upper classes were. One critic, writing in 1815, certainly knew, although
in his comment idealising the past:

> Fifty years ago the drama was supported and the theatres frequented,
> by the first circles of fashion, and the social meal of dinner was previ-
> ously enjoyed that they might not miss a single scene of that spirited
> and instructive drama, which was then the attraction, but such animated
> dialogue would melt into thin air . . . upon our present magnificent
> edifices, where our Lords and Ladies scarcely condescend to take an
> occasional half an hour's lounge, to see some new actor or actress,
> previously to the more delightful and edifying amusement of the Italian
> Opera.[2]

The respectable middle class were not at the opera, however. The patent
theatres were thought to be altogether too much for them, and of course they
would rarely be found in the working-class theatres. Dramaticus, a useful
observer, assigned causes for their absence:

> That part of the community which comprehends men of letters and
> research, merchants, and respectable tradesmen, people of quiet manners
> and a certain time of life, who never think of encountering the noise,
> bustle, crowd, and glare of our present enormous theatres, would be
> very constant attendants with their families, if they could hear, as
> formerly, a good play and entertainment, throughout, without the
> interruption of dancing, mimicry, and show.[3]

[1] *A View of the English Stage* (1818), p. 243.
[2] *An Impartial View of the Stage*, p. 3.   [3] Ibid., p. 21.

Where previously this class could be fairly sure of sitting in a part of the house occupied by their own kind, as in the pit or the lower gallery, they now ran the risk of being cheek by jowl with undesirables who were formerly safely out of the way in the upper gallery. Dutton Cook quotes a letter written in 1827 to Elliston, then manager of the Surrey, complaining of chimney-sweeps in the theatre wearing 'the very dress' of their occupation:

> This not only incommodes ladies and gentlemen by the obnoxious odour arising from their attire, but these sweeps take up twice the room of other people because the ladies, in particular, object to their clothes being soiled by such unpleasant neighbours. . . . People will not go, sir, where sweeps are. . . . It is not a week ago since a lady in a nice white gown sat down on the very spot which a nasty sweep had just quitted, and, when she got up, the sight was most horrible, for she was a very heavy lady and had laughed a great deal during the performance; but it was no laughing matter to her when she got home.[1]

An aspect of the patent theatres that helped to keep the respectable classes away was the number of prostitutes who used the saloons and lobbies for their trade. In the eighteenth century prostitutes frequented the theatre, but they kept largely to the green or upper boxes and did not intrude obviously upon the audience. Now the public rooms outside the auditorium became their area of operation. In 1819 Sir Walter Scott objected strongly to the practice: 'The best part of the house is openly and avowedly set off for their reception; and no part of it which is open to the public at large is free from their intrusion, or at least from the open display of the disgusting improprieties to which their neighbourhood gives rise. . . . No man of sense would wish the female part of his family to be exposed to such scenes.'[2] On his tour of England in 1826 Prince Pückler-Muskau noted that the patent theatres were 'the resort of hundreds of these unhappy women with whom London swarms':

> They are to be seen of every degree, from the lady who spends a splendid income, and has her own box, to the wretched beings who wander houseless in the streets. Between acts they fill the large and handsome 'foyers', and exhibit their boundless effrontery in the most revolting manner. . . . The evil goes to such an extent, that in the theatres it is often difficult to keep off these repulsive beings, especially when they are drunk, which is not seldom the case.

[1] *A Book of the Play* (1876), I, 23.
[2] 'Essay on the drama', *Essays on Chivalry, Romance, and the Drama* (1888), pp. 225–6.

According to the prince, such circumstances were a cause of the absence of respectable families from the theatre.[1] In 1833 another commentator fulminated against 'the glaring indecencies of our playhouse lobbies and saloons' and complained that 'while we are blessed with a Censor, who scrupulously changes "damn it" into "hang it", and cannot allow the public ear to be polluted with "my angel!" we have theatres where open profligacy revels with a freedom scarcely known in other civilized lands, and which the wives and daughters of our citizens can scarcely enter without a blush'.[2] This source of complaint was of long duration. The first person to do anything effective about it seems to have been Macready when he undertook his Covent Garden management in 1837: in 1842, when he was manager of Drury Lane, he issued orders that women of the town were to be refused admission to the theatre altogether.[3]

Macready's two tenures of management marked the beginning of a deliberate attempt, painfully protracted though it was, to bring the fashionable, the educated and the respectable back into the legitimate theatre. When he vacated Drury Lane in 1843 and it reverted to the indestructible Bunn, and when Covent Garden became an opera house in 1847, it appeared that this cause was for ever lost. However, Samuel Phelps, at Sadler's Wells from 1844 to 1862, engaged himself in the formidable project of turning that theatre from an unruly melodrama house into a home for Shakespeare and the legitimate drama. His achievements during his long term there were substantial, and not the least of them was the way in which Sadler's Wells was transformed into a predominantly working- and lower middle-class theatre of the utmost respectability. Henry Morley noted in 1857 that 'there sit our working classes in a happy crowd, as orderly and reverent as if they were at church, and yet as unrestrained in their enjoyment as if listening to stories told them by their own firesides'.[4] The analogy with worship was also used by a later writer, who remembered that 'in the boxes, the pit, and even in the gallery, numbers almost amounting to a majority of those present, were nightly to be seen checking the text as it fell from the actor's lips by reference to their open Shakespeare, with as much devotion, and perhaps more, than if they had been at church'.[5]

Yet the working classes were not the solution of the theatre's financial

[1] *Tour of a German Prince* (1832), III, 128.
[2] *Edinburgh Review* (July 1833), p. 296. The licenser was George Colman.
[3] *The Diaries of William Charles Macready*, ed. William Toynbee (1912), II, 154.
[4] *Journal of a London Playgoer*, p. 162.
[5] Richard Lee, 'Samuel Phelps', *Theatre* (September 1886), p. 142.

problems: the drive towards respectability and status was designed to attract the moneyed and educated classes. The exact middle of the century is an important date in this respect, for it was in 1850 that Charles Kean began a nine-year management of the Princess's Theatre, a management that really marked the beginning of the end of a drama based upon the support of popular audiences, without significant participation from the fashionable, the socially respectable and the intellectually cultured segments of the population. This participation, when it occurred, led ultimately to the problem play, the middle- and upper-class settings and themes of Jones, Pinero, Wilde and Shaw. After the 1850s the theatrical tide turned, and the success of the Bancrofts in drawing society to the Prince of Wales's from 1865 to 1879 was only a confirmation and extension of an earlier trend. Macready, in large and financially burdened theatres, had tried and apparently failed; Charles Kean had more success at the smaller Princess's. Here, in scenically spectacular and archaeologically elaborate productions of Shakespeare, together with well-mounted and restrainedly acted adaptations of romantic French melodrama, Kean significantly raised contemporary standards of rehearsal, acting and production. All this attracted those very classes the theatre desperately needed.

Kean's accomplishment at the Princess's would have been impossible without public support,[1] and he was also assisted by Queen Victoria. Her relationship to the theatre was an important one,[2] and it has received scant attention. She loved drama; she was frequently seen at the theatre (until the death of Albert); she built a stage at court and brought the best performers of the day to play on it; at the end of her reign she knighted actors (Irving in 1895 and Bancroft in 1897) and thus gave the profession the kudos of social status. What the queen thought significant society valued and the church commended; audiences both grew in numbers and increased in respectability. Thus her involvement in theatre was not negligible, and no account of the English stage in the nineteenth century can afford to omit her. Although a devotee of opera and visiting French dramatic companies, she recognized the dangers of fashionable patronage of these amusements alone. In a letter to the King of Prussia in 1849, she said that 'Chevalier Bunsen has been helping us in an attempt to revive and elevate the English drama

---

[1] Kean was also lucky enough to run his first season through the summer of the Great Exhibition. The result was a net profit of £7,000. J. W. Cole, *The Life and Theatrical Times of Charles Kean* (2nd ed., 1859), II, 3.

[2] See *A History of English Drama*, V (1959), pp. 9-10, and *Sheridan to Robertson*, pp. 16-19.

which has greatly deteriorated through lack of support by Society'.[1] The reference was to the command performances at Windsor Castle. In 1848 she appointed Kean, an actor to whom she was partial and one of great professional and social decorum, as a sort of Master of Revels, responsible for bringing a company to Windsor at least once a year: a stage was erected for the purpose in the Rubens Room. With occasional interruptions these performances, mainly of Shakespeare and the modern drama, lasted until the year of Albert's death, 1861.

Contemporary comment was fully aware that Queen Victoria's prime intention was not merely to amuse herself and her court, but to awaken higher society to the necessity of supporting English drama. *The Times* drew attention to the matter:

> When the highest patronage in the land considers that an English dramatic performance is such an entertainment as to merit the construction of a stage in her own drawing-room, with all the appurtenances of a regular theatre, the opinion that the native drama is unfashionable receives an authoritative rebuke. . . . A certain elevated class of the public, by shunning English theatres and skipping English critiques, might soon lose sight of the native drama altogether. But now, the plays and the actors are forced upon the attention of the higher orders from another point. He who studies the proceedings of the Court, has an English theatrical programme thrust into his view; and the same course of reading which tells him that her Majesty took an airing, also informs him that Mr. and Mrs. Kean play *Hamlet* and *Ophelia*. The crowded state of the principal theatres would seem to indicate that an awakened interest for theatricals is already taking effect.[2]

Kean himself made much the same point, albeit more lyrically, in a speech to a General Theatrical Fund dinner in 1849:

> By selecting the drama for their hours of private relaxation, by introducing it into the chosen circle of their domestic privacy, by permitting the royal children, in their earliest budding youth, to become familiar with the magic verse of Shakespeare, her Majesty and her royal consort have stamped an importance and impressed a sterling value on the stage, that will be long felt and most thankfully appreciated. Covered by the protecting shield of royal favour, assisted by the powerful influence and

[1] *Further Letters of Queen Victoria*, ed. Hector Bolitho (London, 1938), p. 14.
[2] 26 January 1849.

commanding prestige of royal taste, and heralded, as I may say, by a patent of precedency, our art and its professors resume their position with increasing hopes and redoubled energy.[1]

J. K. Chapman, the author of *A Complete History of Royal Dramatic Entertainments*, published in 1849 or 1850, declared that the country would applaud the queen 'for the step she has already taken towards promoting the revival of the drama',[2] and that 'the patronage of the drama by HER MAJESTY at Court was the first streak of welcome light breaking through the darkness of the dramatic horizon'.[3] Chapman's effusiveness is perhaps suspect, since the book was dedicated to Victoria, and the latter statement is undoubtedly exaggerated, but his general tenor was everywhere repeated. Two more references may serve as a final illustration of this point. J. W. Cole, Kean's biographer, commented that 'it was manifest to all, except the discontented minority who can find good in nothing, that this was a great step towards the restoration of fashion to the once crowded but now almost abandoned temples of dramatic worship'.[4] And in Planché's extravaganza *Mr. Buckstone's Ascent of Mount Parnassus* (1853) there is the following dialogue between Buckstone and the Spirit of Fashion:

FASHION: Why you must surely know
    Fashion has long ceased to the play to go,
    Except by fits and starts.
BUCKSTONE: That is too true.
    But now a fresh start's given the drama to
    By royal patronage – 'The play's the thing.'
    And goes to court. If that won't Fashion bring
    Back to the play – why nothing will.

Naturally Kean benefited in his Princess's management from the queen's concern with theatre, and she attended the Princess's with some regularity.[5] What she had started he continued through the 1850s. Henry Morley's demand in 1866 that 'our model manager should take for standard of the

---

[1] *The Life and Theatrical Times of Charles Kean*, I, 352.
[2] *A Complete History of Royal Dramatic Entertainments*, n.d., p. 6.
[3] Ibid., p. 86.
[4] *The Life and Theatrical Times of Charles Kean*, I, 347.
[5] For a fuller account of Queen Victoria's concern with the theatre, see my article, 'Queen Victoria and the theatre', *University of Toronto Quarterly*, XXXVI (April 1967), pp. 249–57. I am indebted to the *UTQ* for permission to incorporate material from the article into this chapter.

people he would please an honest Englishman of the educated middle class' was already on its way to at least partial fulfilment. [1]

The next management after Charles Kean's to attract society consistently was the Bancrofts' at the Prince of Wales's. When Marie Wilton, later Squire Bancroft's wife, decided to take the Queen's Theatre off Tottenham Court Road, it was a low melodrama house in a run-down neighbourhood; nothing, she was told, could make it fashionable. Her description of the audience there is interesting in the knowledge of the audience she was soon to attract:

> Some of the occupants of the stalls (the price of admission was, I think, a shilling) were engaged in devouring oranges (their faces being buried in them), and drinking ginger-beer. Babies were being rocked to sleep, or smacked to be quiet, which proceeding, in many cases, had an opposite effect! A woman looked up to our box, and seeing us staring aghast, with, I suppose, an expression of horror upon my face, first of all 'took a sight' at us, and then shouted, 'Now then, you three stuck-up ones, come out o' that, or I'll send this 'ere orange at your 'eds.' [2]

The theatre was redecorated, and the lessee was proud of her carpets and curtains and white lace antimacassars on the stalls seats. The antimacassars were not put down for the former clientele of the Queen's: the audience Marie Wilton was aiming at was a high-class West End audience, and she was completely successful. So confident were the Bancrofts of their class of patronage that Bancroft was in 1874 the first manager in London to charge 10s. for the stalls, a precedent soon followed, according to Bancroft, by every other manager in the West End; the prices of all other seats in his theatre rose correspondingly. [3] When the Bancrofts took over the Haymarket in 1880, this confidence was again demonstrated by the entire replacement of the pit by 10s. stalls. Their action caused a noisy demonstration on the opening night – begun by cries of 'Where's the pit?' – but nothing more; the contrast with the success of the prolonged OP riots of 1809 sufficiently illustrates the changed character of audiences. Bancroft justified himself at the box office. In the Haymarket's six-month opening season a profit of £5,000 was made on a revival of Bulwer-Lytton's *Money*, and £10,000 on a revival of Robertson's *School*. After five years at the Haymarket the Bancrofts retired from management with a net profit of over £180,000 in twenty years at two

[1] *Journal of a London Playgoer*, p. 24.
[2] Squire and Marie Bancroft, *Mr. and Mrs. Bancroft on and off the Stage* (1888), I, 178–9.
[3] Squire and Marie Bancroft, *The Bancrofts* (1909), p. 255.

theatres.[1] Such an achievement would have been impossible before the return to the theatre, in large numbers, of the upper and middle classes. From 1815 to 1850 the theatre was largely unprofitable and frequently bankrupting for investors; during the next fifty years it became possible for astute managers, like the Bancrofts and the actor-managers who came after them, to amass considerable profits. The prosperity of later Victorian England was an important aspect of these profits: better attendance at theatres was a consequence of better economic conditions as well as other factors. Theatre building, which had halted in central London since 1843, started again in 1866 with the Holborn and boomed until the end of the century. The Bancrofts in particular were fortunate to open the Prince of Wales's in the most prosperous decade of the century so far. They were also lucky in possessing Tom Robertson as their dramatist. Robertson's comedies are mostly concerned with the upper middle class and the lesser aristocracy, and Robertson was sensitive to his audiences. When one considers the elevation of the lowly, working-class Queen's into the elegant and fashionable Prince of Wales's, the successful absorption of Esther Eccles in *Caste* into the aristocratic D'Alroy family can be regarded as a dramatic analogue of the social achievement of the Bancrofts in the theatre.

An economic footnote concerning the matter of the stalls in Victorian playhouses is illustrative of the social direction of the theatre. Although stalls had been introduced before 1850 – according to Watson in 1828 at the Lyceum,[2] and according to Dutton Cook in 1829 at the King's Theatre[3] – they were still uncommon. Their introduction at the Lyceum occurred during the visit of a French company; the King's Theatre in the Haymarket was of course London's main opera house. In other words, stalls were originally for the comfort of the fashionable. Their prices were higher than pit prices since they were the nearest seats to the stage and the best in the house: generally one did not see as well from the boxes as from the pit. After 1850 managers were not slow to reap the financial advantage of turning part of the pit into stalls; they would not have done this, however, if a wealthier class of audience had not been willing to pay the higher prices. By 1866 19 per cent of the 49,818 seats available in twenty-seven London theatres, excluding opera houses, were listed as 'stalls',[4] and the pit was pushed steadily back from its ancient position of privilege until finally its suffering

[1] Squire and Marie Bancroft, *The Bancrofts* (1909), p. 275.
[2] *Sheridan to Robertson*, p. 87.
[3] *A Book of the Play*, I, 147.
[4] *Report of the Select Committee on Theatrical Licences and Regulations* (1866), p. 295.

occupants ended up, airless, dark and badly sighted, under the low overhang of the first balcony. A letter of complaint at the end of our period vividly illustrates the difficulties of pittites, once the proud and feared judges of deferential authors:

> As soon as the curtain rises the stalls begin to come in, and for the next ten minutes we are annoyed by the passing to and fro and the sitting down of the late comers; perhaps we lose the thread of the play and get careless and fidgety. The pit is not a particularly comfortable place now-a-days, pushed away as it is under the dress-circle, and generally consisting of bare backless benches; and, perhaps, this helps to keep away the elder men who might steady us. Then, if managers are so greedy as to pack people into seats behind pillars, and in corners where they cannot see, they are dull, and will most certainly become noisy.[1]

The climax came when Bancroft abolished the pit altogether at the Haymarket. An era had passed in the theatre.

The 1866 Report of the Select Committee on Theatrical Licences and Regulations is a useful storehouse of information, not only on the number of stalls seats in London theatres, but also on the composition of audiences. John Hollingshead testified that the nightly audience was 'largely composed of country people; the old metropolitan playgoer lives out of town, and does not go so much to the theatre as he used to do; the provincial people come up to town, and fresh audiences are created every night'.[2] The fact that provincials could come up to town easily was due to improvements in railway transportation: the same technological progress that was spreading London suburbs far and wide and enabling the suburbanite to commute daily to the City also made dinner in town and an evening at the theatre possible for the suburban family, and a visit to town possible for the provincial family. Thus the potential theatre audience was enormously increased, and long runs became common. In the 1850s only 15 productions of all kinds ran for 100 consecutive nights or more; in the 1860s there were 45 and in the 1870s 107. The longest run of the fifties was 150 nights for *A Midsummer Night's Dream*; in the sixties *The Ticket-of-Leave Man* ran for 407 performances, *Our Boys* in the seventies for 1,362.[3] Such long runs were an indication of growing patronage from the fashionable and middle classes as well as of an

[1] *Theatre* (January 1883), p. 47.
[2] *1866 Select Committee Report*, p. 191.
[3] *Who's Who in the Theatre*, ed. John Parker (11th ed., London, 1952), pp. 1805–36.

increase in the potential audience. Significantly, it was during Charles Kean's tenure of the Princess's that mainpieces on an evening's bill began to have consecutive runs of any length: *Henry VIII* ran for 100 nights in 1855, *The Winter's Tale* for 102 nights in 1856 and *A Midsummer Night's Dream* for 150 nights in 1856–7. There is no doubt that 'country people' were now coming up to London in greater numbers than ever before in search of edification and amusement: the summer of the Great Exhibition was proof of that. Thomas Purnell, writing several years after the Select Committee, can be cited in support of Hollingshead's testimony; his description of the theatre audience is more comprehensive, though perhaps not comprehensive enough:

> The chief supporters of our theatres are country people, incited by the advertisements and criticism they have seen in the London papers; those of the nobility afflicted with *ennui*, who have no engagement for the night; busy professional men who come at fixed intervals with their families . . . men who go to the theatres from habit, just as they take tobacco, and a large number of green-grocers and other shopkeepers, who have received orders for displaying play-bills in their windows.[1]

The Select Committee of 1866 was told by John Green, the lessee of Evans's Rooms (a music hall), that 'there are 40,000 people go to theatres and places of entertainment in London every night'.[2] Many thousands of these went to music halls and pleasure gardens: the rapid spread of music halls in London during the 1860s was representative of their general multiplicity and popularity in the last half of the century. In 1868 the *Era Almanack* listed thirty-eight large and small music halls as open in London.[3] With its sentimentality, domesticity, patriotism and completely satisfying light entertainment, the music hall must have considerably encroached upon theatre attendance by the working and lower middle classes. The manager of the Alhambra music hall estimated in 1866 that half his audience was working class.[4] The development of the halls and the powerful attraction

[1] Thomas Purnell, *Dramatists of the Present Day* (1871), p. 14.
[2] *1866 Select Committee Report*, p. 201. In 1866 Henry Morley estimated average daily attendance at twenty-five theatres (excluding music halls) at 15,000 (*Journal of a London Playgoer*, p. 17). If this figure is correct, it would mean that theatres were playing to about one-third capacity; 15,000 is probably too low an estimate. Pedicord calculates a daily average of 2,000 for Drury Lane and Covent Garden about 1760 (*The Theatrical Public in the Time of Garrick*, p. 16).
[3] R. Mander and J. Mitchenson, *British Music Hall* (London, 1965), p. 19.
[4] *1866 Select Committee Report*, p. 59.

they held for their audiences meant, on the whole, that West End theatres became more and more the preserve of the middle and upper middle class. By 1880 the middle-class conquest of the theatre auditorium, and consequently of the drama itself, was complete.

The behaviour of audiences during the period 1750–1880 was informative, not only about class origin and seating position, but also about the matter we have been concerned with, the social direction of the theatre. Broadly speaking, audiences were relatively well behaved in the last fifty years of the eighteenth century, especially in the years preceding the opening of the new Drury Lane and the greatly enlarged Covent Garden in the 1790s, though there were savage (but infrequent) outbursts of rioting. In the first three or four decades of the next century the auditorium was the scene of much coarseness, vulgarity and tumult, as well as a great deal of noisy good spirits. After 1850 behaviour improved, and complaints were eventually made, not of uproar in the pit and gallery, but of stolid indifference in the stalls. By 1880 theatres were reasonably quiet and well-mannered places.

Much attention has been paid to disturbances in eighteenth-century playhouses, so much so that the whole period has seemed, in the lurid view of some commentators, one long riot. Actually, as Pedicord has pointed out,[1] such riots were infrequent and only occasionally involved the general public in a real sense. More common, and indeed a standard feature of audience behaviour until at least the middle of the nineteenth century, was, during a performance, talking, laughing (but not at the stage), flirting, eating, drinking, walking about, condemning and praising with equal vociferousness, inattention and a dozen other practices that gave life and colour to the house but were sometimes the despair of authors, actors, managers and critics. Boswell in 1763 was indulging in a popular pastime when he resolved with two friends to go to Drury Lane to damn a new play, in this case Mallet's tragedy *Elvira*:

> Just as the doors opened at four o'clock we sallied into the house, planted ourselves in the middle of the pit, and with oaken cudgels in our hands and shrill-sounding catcalls in our pockets, sat ready prepared, with a generous resentment in our breasts against dullness and impudence, to be the swift ministers of vengeance. . . . The prologue was politically stupid. We hissed it and had several to join us. . . . We did what we could during the first act, but found that the audience had lost

---

[1] *The Theatrical Public in the Time of Garrick*, pp. 51–7.

their original fire and spirit and were disposed to let it pass. Our project was therefore disconcerted, our impetuosity dampened.[1]

Boswell was merely exercising the honoured right of the critic in the pit to render judgement in whatever way he chose. The prologue to *The Fugitive*, quoted above, indicates that towards the end of the century the pit, under feminine influence, was kinder to the author and his new play than it had been earlier:

> Not as of old, when, train'd to frown and fret,
> In murky state the surly synod met.

However, that instrument of terror and justice, the catcall, was still in use (as it was in the OP riots); the gallery had their sticks and disposable fruit, and it was still a fearsome thing for an author to face the verdict of his audience, as the prologue to Thomas Holcroft's *Duplicity* (1781) shows:

> Well fare the bard, whose fortitude, sedate,
> Stands, unappall'd, before impending fate;
> When cat-call-pipers, groaners, whistlers, grinners,
> Assembled, fit to judge of SCRIBBLING SINNERS!
> What mortal mind can keep its terrors under
> When gods sit arm'd, with awful-wooden thunder?
> What heart, so brave, can check its palpitation
> Before the grave dispensers of damnation?

The behaviour of gallery audiences came in for a greater share of disapprobation than did the conduct of their betters in the pit. Their rowdiness seems to have increased considerably after the opening of the new Covent Garden in 1809 and the new Drury Lane in 1812 – perhaps, at least in part, because they could neither hear well nor see well and must have suffered from heat and overcrowding. Charles Kemble told the Select Committee of 1832 that the shilling gallery was 'commonly very riotous'.[2] Class antagonism was at the root of some of the criticism: a correspondent of the *Theatrical Inquisitor* in 1818, who described himself as an habitué of the pit at Covent Garden and Drury Lane, wrote to complain of the 'uproar and disturbance' in the galleries, an annoyance that often prevented a word of the play from

---

[1] *Boswell's London Journal*, ed. F. A. Pottle (London, 1950), pp. 154–5. Boswell's mooing like a cow in the pit of Drury Lane, and the gallery's cries of 'encore', is a well-known Boswell anecdote. It is recounted in *Boswell's Journal of a Tour to the Hebrides*, ed. F. A. Pottle and C. H. Bennett (London, 1936), p. 387.
[2] *1832 Select Committee Report*, p. 55.

being heard and frequently stopped its progress altogether. This noise usually occurred in the upper gallery, '*particularly* after the entry of the second price visitors. The smallness of the price of admission to this gallery, at that period of the evening, enables the most worthless and profligate to be there.' Therefore, he suggested, half price should be abolished for the upper gallery, which would prevent 'at least two thirds of the noise and disturbance'.[1] In 1826 the fastidious Pückler-Muskau was horrified at the conduct of an English audience in a patent theatre, and apportioned most of the blame to the galleries:

> The most striking thing to a foreigner in English theatres is the unheard-of coarseness and brutality of the audiences. The consequence of this is that the higher and more civilized classes go only to the Italian Opera, and very rarely visit their national theatre. English freedom here degenerates into the rudest licence, and it is not uncommon in the midst of the most affecting part of a tragedy . . . to hear some coarse expression shouted from the galleries in a stentor voice. This is followed, according to the taste of the bystanders, either by loud laughter and approbation, or by the castigation and expulsion of the offender. . . . Such things happen not once, but sometimes twenty times, in the course of a performance, and amuse many of the audience more than that does. It is also no rarity for some one to throw the fragments of his 'goutè', which do not always consist of orange-peels alone, without the smallest ceremony on the heads of the people in the pit, or to shoil them with singular dexterity into the boxes.[2]

A year later the prince saw Macready in *Macbeth* at Drury Lane, a visit that confirmed his opinions as to why 'the English theatre is not fashionable, and is scarcely ever visited by what is called "good company"', since he found that 'the interest was generally so slight, the noise and mischief so incessant, that it is difficult to understand how distinguished artists can form themselves, with so brutal, indifferent, and ignorant an audience as they have almost always before them'.[3]

The galleries were not alone in creating disturbances, for the boxes could sin in ways other than their usual clattering, chattering and ogling. In 1755 gentlemen from the boxes battled with the pit in an unsuccessful attempt to save the *Chinese Festival* performances, and an angry gentleman with a sword

---

[1] *Theatrical Inquisitor* (November 1818), p. 368.
[2] *Tour of a German Prince*, III, 126–7.
[3] Ibid., IV, 248.

could be a dangerous person in an eighteenth-century theatre. Early in the next century, behaviour in the boxes could be almost as boorish as behaviour in the gallery, and occasionally riotous. When Catalani did not appear as advertised in *Enrico IV* at the King's Theatre in 1813, gentlemen rioters poured on to the stage in protest, struggled with soldiers, disarmed some of them and threw their weapons into the orchestra.[1]

It is difficult to generalize, however, about the behaviour of audiences at any given date in the nineteenth century, since so much depends upon the neighbourhood, the theatre, the performance – a pantomime audience on Boxing Night was not at all the same as an audience for Shakespeare, even at the same theatre – the prices, the management and the popularity of main-piece and after-pieces. The nobility, for instance, were attracted to any theatre offering something exceptional: in 1805 the press of British and foreign nobility for places at Sadler's Wells to see the aquatic melodrama *An Bratach, or the Fairy Flag* was immense, rows of coroneted carriages lining the streets near the theatre.[2] Master Betty in 1804 at Covent Garden was a similar attraction, as were *Black-Eyed Susan* at the Surrey in 1829, Ducrow's horses, and Van Amburgh's lions. It is safe to say that probably by the 1840s, and certainly in the next decade, the manners and general behaviour of audiences began to improve: a natural consequence of the middle-class takeover of the theatre and the increasing sobriety of Victorian middle-class habits. Reports of disorders in the pit and missiles hurled from the gallery dwindle away to almost nothing; in the former case, since the best seats in the pit were now stalls and had entirely different and staider occupants, it is not hard to see why. First-night demonstrations of hostility to a new play were still common, but otherwise the chief complaints against the stall holders with regard to disturbing others were the fairly trivial ones – considering what norms of behaviour *had* been like – of coming in late and conversing during a performance: the same complaints, in fact, as were heard about the boxes earlier in the century, and before.

It is curious to reflect that a cause of critical concern in the last half of the nineteenth century was not the rowdiness of audiences, but their passivity. As early as 1855 W. B. Donne commented that society had 'reached a period of refinement incompatible with strong and natural emotions. We are become, in all that regards the theatre, a civil, similar, and impassive generation.'[3] At the very end of our period Donne's statement was enlarged

[1] *Theatrical Inquisitor* (June 1813), pp. 278–84.
[2] *The Memoirs of Charles Dibdin the Younger*, ed. George Speaight (London, 1956), p. 67.
[3] W. B. Donne, *Essays in the Drama* (2nd ed., 1863), p. 206.

in the *Theatre*: 'English audiences are painfully cold, and in fashionable theatres indifference is *chic*. The passionate enthusiasm of an Italian or Viennese house would be voted absurd by our languid youths and insipid maidens of the gilded order, and therefore it is to the pit and gods that the artists look for appreciation.'[1] With the stalls in possession of the phlegmatic middle class and the first balcony, now the 'dress circle', the resort of the fashionable, the relationship between actors and audience inevitably changed. In 1880 Clement Scott declared that 'nervous and impulsive acting, a bright and enthusiastic style, plays of passion and interest, exciting plots and ideal touches become impossible when everything is reduced to a drawing-room level, and the tone of the acting of the day is turned to the bored listlessness and polished coldness of the times in which we live'.[2] Scott attributed list-lessness and coldness in the theatre to the disappearance of the old pit audience, and it is unnecessary to repeat that such a change in audiences caused a significant theatrical revolution. 'The pit once removed or curtailed,' said Scott, 'the pit once banished upstairs, the pulse of interest which once vibrated through the theatre ceases to beat. The hum is hushed. The applause is deadened. The entertainments cease to fizz.'[3] The majority of contributors to a symposium conducted by the *Theatre* in 1880 on the question 'Is the Pit an Institution or an Excrescence?' agreed that Bancroft had a perfect right to turn the Haymarket pit into stalls if he wished to, but also agreed that the consequences of this change in particular, and of the universal shrinkage of the pit in general, were harmful to the theatre. Three years later the *Theatre* returned to the subject of modern audiences:

> Is the audience of a West-End theatre ever emotionally excited in these days, save such audiences as collect at the Princess's or the Adelphi who are all emotion, and applaud sentiment, no matter who utters it? It is a melancholy but undoubted fact that an ordinary, every-day theatrical audience is chiefly composed of a very dull set of people, stupid, yet captious, who only ask to be amused, and object to being emotionally excited, and who go to see Shakespeare at the Lyceum because it is the fashion, but think it a bore and sure to be slow. It would have been difficult for Siddons herself to excite such as these.[4]

[1] Emily Faithfull, 'The duty of an audience', *Theatre* (September 1879), p. 77.
[2] *Theatre* (March 1880), p. 141.
[3] 'A plea for the pit', *Era Almanack* (1874), quoted in *Theatre* (March 1880), p. 138.
[4] *Theatre* (October 1883), p. 206.

The effect of the new audiences has been noted elsewhere.[1] Both Watson and Nicoll regard the results, in the form of a quieter, more realistic acting style, as beneficial to the theatre, but the writers of the 1870s were not so sure. Clement Scott's opinion has already been noted; Frank Marshall, writing for the symposium on the pit, was of a similar mind, and his point of view was widely representative of traditionalist critical opinion:

> I hold it to be absolutely necessary for the actor's art that he should have in front of him an audience able and willing to express audibly their approbation and disapprobation. In this respect I think most persons, who have observed carefully the behaviour of those who occupy the ten-shilling stalls and those who occupy the two-shilling pit, will admit that the latter have the decided advantage. . . . Granted that the ten-shilling audience will pay as much attention to the acting as they will to the dresses and stage decorations, their inability to express the enthusiasm which, doubtless, they feel at the artistic representation set before them, paralyses the artists' energies and inclines them insensibly to exaggeration when they wish to produce an extraordinary effect.[2]

The fashionable and middle-class West End audience did not, of course, embody the entire theatregoing public of London, as any examination of the auditoria of the neighbourhood theatres would have shown. These theatres were noisy but not disorderly, and their patrons were more absorbed in the stage than their West End equivalents. Benjamin Webster testified to the Select Committee of 1866 that he found such audiences just as appreciative of good acting as West End audiences, and declared, 'I have played at the Standard, and a better audience I have never acted to, or a more discreet audience. At the Standard, the City, and Surrey Theatres, I found my audience rather better and more attentive than at the West End; they do not converse during the performance.'[3] After a visit to the Britannia in the 1850s, Dickens noted the presence of many family groups. In the boxes and stalls they 'were composed of persons of very decent appearance, who had many children with them'. The spectators' clothes were commonly greasy and shabby, fustian and corduroy 'neither sound nor fragrant'. Nevertheless, it was a good audience:

[1] *Sheridan to Robertson*, p. 89, and *A History of English Drama*, IV, 12–13.
[2] *Theatre* (March 1880), pp. 130–1.
[3] *1866 Select Committee Report*, p. 166.

Besides prowlers and idlers, we were mechanics, dock-labourers, costermongers, petty tradesmen, small clerks, milliners, stay-makers, shoe-binders, slop workers, poor workers in a hundred highways and byeways. Many of us – on the whole, the majority – were not at all clean, and not at all choice in our lives or conversation. But we had all come together in a place where our convenience was well consulted, and where we were well looked after, to enjoy an evening's entertainment in common. We were not going to lose any part of what we had paid for through anybody's caprice, and as a community we had character to lose. So, we were closely attentive, and kept excellent order.[1]

Dickens went to the Victoria in 1850 and observed that 'the company in the pit were not very clean or sweet-savoured' and contained many 'good-humoured young mechanics', their wives and sleeping infants. The boxes 'were of much the same character (babies and fish excepted) as the audience in the pit'.[2] He also noticed 'some young pickpockets of our acquaintance' in several parts of the house. Around 1860 Thomas Erle, who was given to witty sneers at the working-class theatres, said that the Victoria was 'largely graced by the presence of embryo and native convicts, and of gentlemen on tickets of leave'.[3] Dickens and other commentators marked, in the Britannia and theatres like it, the huge and suffocating galleries packed with coatless youths who expressed approval and disapproval with shrill whistles, cheers and united sound effects of massive volume; the consumption of fried fish, porter, sausages, ham sandwiches, cakes, oranges and pig-trotters; the babies in the pit; the general spirit of enjoyment; the immense popularity of stage favourites and comic songs; and the intense interest in the business of the stage.

Any account of the nineteenth-century London theatre audience and its tastes that confined its purview to the West End and omitted this very substantial audience would be seriously defective. And it *was* a substantial audience. An appendix to the Report of the 1866 Select Committee shows that of the total number of places available in metropolitan London theatres – excluding opera – 28, 933, or nearly 60 per cent, were in twelve theatres outside the West End: Astley's, the Britannia, the Bower, the City of London, the Effingham, the Grecian, the Marylebone, the Pavilion, Sadler's Wells,

[1] 'Two views of a cheap theatre', *The Uncommercial Traveller* (London, 1907), p. 39.
[2] *Household Words*, 30 March 1850.
[3] *Letters from a Theatrical Scene Painter* (1880), p. 101.

the Standard, the Surrey and the Victoria.[1] Such a mass audience of the working and lower middle classes had not existed in the eighteenth century, although its embryo was present in the spectators of rope-dancing and tumbling at Sadler's Wells and interludes at the theatrical booths of the great fairs. It was, however, a minority audience in relation to the development of the mainstream of the drama after 1850, although its influence had both directly and indirectly dominated the drama in the first half of the century. By 1880 the drama of this mainstream was a middle-class product, catering to middle-class audiences, seated in theatres designed for middle-class convenience. In a sense the wheel had come full circle again. Although the term 'middle-class', referring to audiences, could not comprehend the same kind of people in both 1750 and 1880, it is roughly correct to say that in terms of class the theatre was in much the same relationship to its West End audience in 1750 as in 1880. The intervening years had seen the theatre pass, for the first time since the medieval period, under a rule that was essentially popular; it then passed out again into middle-class control, and all aspects of class composition, behaviour and taste among theatre audiences, as well as of the drama itself, must be related to this primary sequence of events.

[1] *1866 Select Committee Report*, p. 295. This list antedates the theatre-building boom that began in 1866, which was a West End boom.

2 Public taste, the playwright and the law

The eighteenth and nineteenth centuries were full of critics decrying the taste of the times, the corruption of the stage, the decline of the drama, and the ignorance of the public. They chose as objects of haughty wrath or sorrowing pity the managers, actors, audience, dramatists, theatres, the French, the opera, morality, social habits and a dozen other things, all of which, singly or in combinations, were at one time or another to blame for the sad state of the theatre. Even during one of the most stable and prosperous periods of the eighteenth-century theatre, Garrick's management of Drury Lane from 1747 to 1776, the prophets of doom were never silent, and during the nineteenth century, when ink on the topic of 'the decline of the drama' flowed from a thousand pens, the voice of the critic was indeed heard in the land. But people kept coming to the theatre, and one cannot safely take the opinion of a critic lashing his age as to the merits of public taste. The best thing to do is examine the repertory and relate it to its audiences; the critics may then be invited to comment.

For the purposes of a brief examination of what audiences saw and why, Garrick's management at Drury Lane is a good place to start for several reasons: it begins at about the beginning of our period; it covers a wide span of time, thirty years, and is thus thoroughly representative of dramatic taste; and it is well documented by modern scholars.[1] There is little point in traversing their ground, but a summary of their conclusions might be helpful.[2] In tragedy the order of popularity ran, in total number of perform-ances: pathetic – Shakespeare – pseudo-classic – heroic – pseudo-romantic; in comedy: manners – sentiment – Shakespeare – intrigue – humours (these all being Nicoll's categories, with unavoidable overlapping).[3] Comedy was nearly half again as popular as tragedy, and in both genres Shakespeare was easily the most commonly performed single dramatist (both these facts were also true of Covent Garden). However, farce and especially pantomime were proportionally far more popular than either tragedy or comedy, and many a Shakespearian mainpiece was bolstered by *The Anatomist* or *Queen Mab* as an after-piece. No mainpiece was played as often as the most popular pantomimes at Drury Lane and Covent Garden, except for *The Beggar's Opera*, an indication of the enduring appeal of the ballad opera form. What is apparent from the most casual study of the playbills of the period and the information compiled in the *London Stage* is the range of fare offered by the managers and no doubt demanded by the audience. Not only could its members watch a regular programme of a tragedy, or a comedy, or a ballad opera, followed on the bill by a farce or pantomime – revivals being judiciously mixed with new pieces – but they also enjoyed entr'acte songs, dances and other speciality numbers, processions and pageants, orchestral music before, during and between the individual pieces, and an ingenious variety of prologues and epilogues. No matter how serious or austere the tragedy, there were bound to be jolly comic dances between the acts, and nobody saw anything unusual or incompatible in this mixture.

What impresses, then, is the eclecticism of dramatic taste in the second half of the eighteenth century, an eclecticism that lasted into the next century and to the end of our period in 1880. The bewildering anarchy of

---

[1] Chiefly in three works: *Drury Lane Calendar, 1747–76*, ed. Dougald Macmillan (Oxford, 1938); *The London Stage, 1660–1800*, IV, ed. G. W. Stone, Jr (Carbondale, 1962); and *The Theatrical Public in the Time of Garrick*. Nicoll, *A History of English Drama*, III (1955), has also analysed the repertory of 1750–1800.

[2] See in particular *The Theatrical Public in the Time of Garrick*, pp. 134–51, and *The London Stage*, IV, clix–clxxv. The following summary is based on *The London Stage*, IV, clxii–clxvi.

[3] The order at Covent Garden was the same in tragedy, except for a reversal in the positions of pseudo-classic and heroic; in comedy it was manners – intrigue – sentiment – Shakespeare/humours. The choice of repertory at both theatres was heavily dependent upon what performers were available and when.

dramatic forms and blends of forms in the nineteenth century – Nicoll has formulated, or tried to formulate, eighty-five categories of dramatic writing – suggests a wide variety of attempts by playwrights to hit upon the right prescriptions for success. With the influx of new audiences, the absence of the fashionable, the increase in population, the growing number of minor theatres playing the 'illegitimate' drama, and the huge size of the new patent theatres, the kinds of drama offered reflected changing patterns of taste. Melodrama, spectacle, farce, Shakespeare, verse tragedy, pantomime, light opera, sentimental comedy and the whole field of entr'acte entertainment – these were the main types of theatre in the first thirty years of the nineteenth century, and they all had roots in the previous century. In most of these types there is little doubt of a coarsening of taste, of a new vulgarity, of the most obvious appeal to sensation and spectacle, of a greater delight in low comedy and outrageous costume. These were not necessarily unfortunate developments; they merely expressed the theatrical times and imparted to early nineteenth-century theatre its distinctive colouring and flavour.

Precisely when these changes in taste occurred is hard to say. Both the large patent theatres were staging characteristically nineteenth-century entertainment, particularly melodrama and spectacle, in the 1790s, and in the same decade the Royal Circus (later the Surrey) began exhibiting dumb-show melodrama. The opening of the huge new Drury Lane in 1794 is an important date in this regard; so, too, is 1809, the year of the new Covent Garden and the OP riots. The length and success of the riots were a sign that the elements of mob rule were no longer a minority in the dictation of theatrical policy. The year 1811 is also significant: Covent Garden audiences first saw Astley's stud of horses in an equestrianized *Blue-Beard*. According to Boaden they 'were received with immense applause' on their initial appearance, and later 'the audience were in raptures, as at the achievement of a wonder'.[1] As a result Covent Garden had its best season financially until it became an opera house – £98,000 – *Blue-Beard* alone producing over £21,000 in forty-one nights.[2] In 1803 the dog Carlo brought Drury Lane great profit in *The Caravan* by jumping into the water to save a child.[3] A host of such entertainments followed *Blue-Beard*, and the taste for

[1] James Boaden, *Memoirs of J. P. Kemble* (1825), II, 542.
[2] *The Life and Times of Frederick Reynolds* (2nd ed., 1827), II, 404.
[3] Reynolds, the author of *The Caravan*, asked contemptuously, 'What would they [his detractors] have called me, had they known, that I cleared three hundred and fifty pounds simply by a dog jumping into a small tank of water!' (Ibid., II, 351.)

equestrianized drama lasted well into Victorian times,[1] and indeed to the end of the century in the presentation of patriotic spectacles. Dog drama was also enjoyed at the Bower Saloon and other theatres in the fifties and sixties. Ducrow's horses and Van Amburgh's lions together in *Charlemagne* in 1838 far outdrew legitimate drama; the queen went six times in six weeks to see the lions at Drury Lane, and the nobility (including the Duke of Wellington) streamed into the theatre every day to watch the lions being fed and to observe Van Amburgh's control over them.

The point here is that too many critics have assumed that the Regency and early Victorian theatre was entirely the preserve of the uneducated rabble, and that all dramatic taste sank to their level. While it is true that large sections of the fashionable class and the respectable middle class stayed away from the theatre then, it is also true that the melodrama, low farce, physical spectacle, wild sensation and triumphant morality so beloved of the urban masses were acceptable to their class superiors in the best theatres. Even contemporary critics fell into this error. Richard Hengist Horne, one of the most acute observers of the drama in his time, was torn between the life and vitality of the 'illegitimate' and the higher claims of the 'literary' theatre. His prejudices in favour of the latter should make us wary of totally accepting statements like the following, although there is much truth in it: 'The drama has sunk from the educated and the tasteful to the uncultivated, and those of coarser pleasures – from the refined gentleman to the intelligent trader, and from him to the small shop-keeper, the inferior class of operatives, the ignorant and the degraded.'[2] There is enough evidence, however, to demonstrate three things: firstly, that the gentleman who stayed away from the theatre did not mainly do so for reasons of taste; secondly, that gentlemen – I use the word in its social-class sense – did indeed go to the theatre, but not in sufficient numbers to keep it economically viable; thirdly, that there still existed, and continued to exist, a considerable taste for a theatre of refinement, elegance and intellectual significance, as witness the managements of Vestris and Mathews at the Olympic, Covent Garden and the Lyceum in the thirties and forties, and Macready's tenure of Covent Garden and Drury Lane around the same time. Even as Horne wrote, Phelps was beginning his respectable and thoroughly legitimate seasons at Sadler's Wells, and

[1] In 1856 and 1857 William Cooke staged at Astley's elaborately equestrian versions of *Richard III*, *Macbeth* and *1 Henry IV*. Charles Kean introduced horses with great success into his *Richard II* and *Henry V* at the Princess's in 1857 and 1859 respectively. See A. H. Saxon, 'Shakespeare and circuses', *Theatre Survey*, VII (November 1966), pp. 59–79.

[2] *A New Spirit of the Age* (1844), II, 98–9.

Charles Kean's management at the Princess's was only a few years away. To be fair to nineteenth-century audiences in the matter of taste, this kind of evidence must be set off against the other.

The general movement of nineteenth-century dramatic taste was from the romantic to the realistic, from the illusionist to the solidly physical, from the poetic to the prosaic, these tendencies applying to all aspects of theatre: acting, costuming, scenery, staging and the content of the drama. Such a movement occurred on all class levels of taste in all types of drama. Melodrama, for example, was simultaneously popular in the 1790s at the patent theatres and the lowly minors; it appealed to all classes. Its content then and until about 1820 was primarily Gothic, and its settings the forests of Bohemia, the wilds of Calabria, the heaths of Scotland, the palaces of Eastern potentates. This kind of thing represented the Romantic movement in the theatre, and it was not by chance that adaptations of Scott and Byron flooded the stage: both the literary and the popular growths were nourished by the same stream. When the romantic light faded in poetry and the novel, it faded in the theatre also, and Gothic melodrama was largely replaced, first by the nautical, which although possessing a strong element of the domestic was still romantic in its depiction of naval glories and the heroic individualism of the brave sailor, and then by the domestic proper, this at a time when the major novelists of the period – with the partial but notable exception of the Brontës – were domestic in emphasis. By 1843 the main East End theatres had been built, and melodrama was the staple food of them all, as it was on the South Bank. Although played all over England, its real home was in working-class areas. This is not surprising, considering that the urban working class led a hard and dirty life at best, and melodrama offered them thrills, escapism, ideal friendship and love, perfect human beings, their very own heroes and heroines, supreme individualism, an inexorable code of justice, ultimate happiness and rewards to the virtuous poor – little of which they met with in daily work and life. Melodrama was anti-aristocrat, anti-employer, anti-landlord, anti-landowner and anti-wealth, often violently so. All this is perfectly explicable in terms of nineteenth-century economic and social developments. While it was escapist and wish-fulfilling, melodrama was also realistic in that it presented not only the daily life of London streets and homes, but also a considerable number of serious social problems, including drink, poverty, urban life, homelessness, class antagonism and industrial strife. The continued popularity of the village setting in domestic melodrama can be explained only when one realizes that the majority of workers in London and the industrial towns before 1850 were emigrants

from the country; the predominant note of village melodrama is nostalgia
for a lost rural heritage, a lost simplicity, a lost innocence, a gentle past for
ever gone. Indeed, domestic melodrama was always socially relevant in one
form or another – surely one factor in its enormous popularity – in an age
when other types of drama, such as verse tragedy, were not. Melodrama's
appeal, its very nature, cannot be fully appreciated without some understanding of its social context.

The movement from the romantic to the domestic meant that all the
paraphernalia of living had to be put on the stage: by 1880 exact reproductions
of familiar streets, squares, bridges and public buildings, as well as exact
domestic interiors from the third floor back to the ballroom, drawing room
or conservatory, could be seen in the theatre. Domestic drama of all types
was thoroughly Victorian, accurately reflecting the importance in everyday
thinking and living of the surface of life, of acquisitiveness and business 'go',
of home life and the marriage ideal, of the pulse of great cities and their
teeming humanity, of the variety of everyday existence, of the sense of a
huge world in ceaseless busy motion to a preferably ideal and happy end.
Thus it perfectly suited the taste of the times, and it was useless for George
Stephens, an advocate of the superiority of the 'unacted drama', to complain
that his dramatic inspiration was 'damped and oppressed by the apathy of
the iron and material age we have fallen upon', an age too full of 'mammon-
worship and go-ahead mania that recognize their sordid objects in milloc-
racies and railocracies'. What should happen, according to Stephens, is that
'the superstitious rage of this generation for the gathering of *impedimenta*,
as even the heathens styled wealth, yield to severer, nobler, and purer
tastes'.[1] Victorian tastes, however, were not on the whole severe, noble and

---

[1] 'Advertisement' to *Dramas for the Stage*, 1846. What Stephens presumably was offering
as examples of the right kind of taste were his own plays. In one of them, *Forgery*, the
villain Elrington goes mad and utters the following speech:

> Spread sail!
> Over the crimson billows. Favouring gales
> Now murmur, and, inviting, curl the deep!
> Black o'er the furrowed main blow hurricanes!
> (*He suddenly starts: his eyes fix. After some time he proceeds.*)
> What tamed the restiff blast? My lone sail flaps
> As on a slumberous stronde. The silent sea
> Her shivering surface parts!
> Ah! Drops the world?
> Whither, my soul? What grand assize awaits thee?
> Great Judge, I plead me guilty!
> Mercy! Mercy!
> (ELRINGTON, *raving, falls dead into the arms of* GRIMLOCK.)

1a The audience in the gallery at Astley's

1b 'At the pit door', 1873

Riot at Covent Garden Theatre, in 1763, in consequence of the Managers refusing to admit half-price in the Opera of Artaxerxes.

2b 'Actresses dressing in a barn', 1738

3a View of the auditorium of the Georgian Theatre, Richmond, Yorkshire, built in 1788, as reconstructed (under the direction of Richard Southern) in 1962

3b The restored stage of the Georgian Theatre, Richmond, set with a woodland scene of *c.* 1820

4a The two remaining sets of grooves on the stage right of the Eagle Opera House, Marshall, Michigan, viewed from the front of the stage

4b The grooves on the stage right of the Eagle Opera House viewed from the opposite side of the stage

5a The upstage set of grooves on the stage left, Eagle Opera House

5b The downstage set of grooves on the stage left, showing also the proscenium door and part of the auditorium side

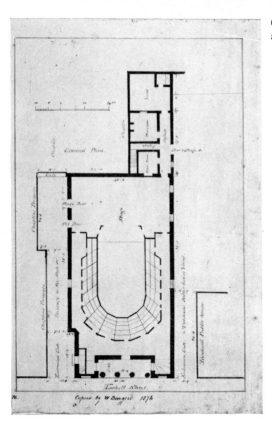

6a Plan of the theatre at Ipswich as it was about 1809

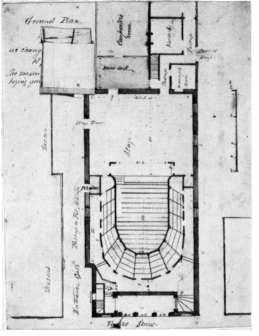

6b Plan of the Ipswich Theatre in 1815, showing increased stage, shortened auditorium and widened proscenium opening

7a Water colour by W. Burgess, resident scene-painter, of the Ipswich Theatre interior in 1882 showing rounded-off stage box

7b Plan of the Ipswich Theatre in 1887 showing removal of all but the five boxes facing the stage

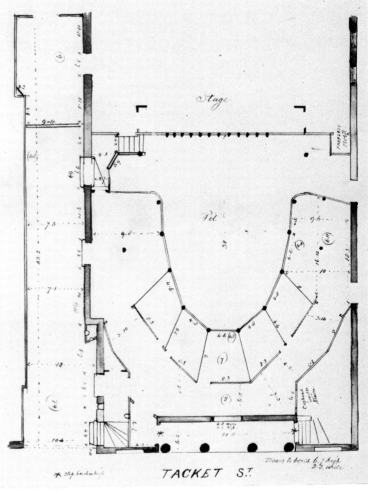

7c Elevation of the auditorium side at Ipswich in 1889, showing effect of removing the side boxes

8a Theatre Royal, Bristol, built 1766, based on Wren's Drury Lane of that period. The fore-stage originally came out to the left-hand great pilaster

8b Typical provincial theatre at Scarborough, 1813, drawn by J. Green and 'etched' by Rowlandson

9a Holland's Covent Garden in 1804

9b Smirke's Covent Garden in 1815

10a A view of Smirke's Covent Garden dated 1833

10b Wyatt's Drury Lane in 1815

11a Wren's Drury Lane as altered by the Adams in 1777

11b The Haymarket Theatre, London, retaining the old Georgian arrangement of auditorium as late as the 1800s

12 A model reconstruction by Richard Southern of an English corner trap, based on Contant's *Parallèle des théâtres*, 1859

13a A Harlequinade at Covent Garden about 1770

13b The Royalty Theatre, Wellclose Square, London, 1787

14a Theatre Royal, Bath, in 1824, showing the pit floored over on the occasion of a fête on George IV's birthday

14b Wren's Drury Lane (altered by the Adams in 1777, and redecorated by Greenwood and Capon in 1783) as it was before its demolition in 1792 to give place to Holland's larger theatre

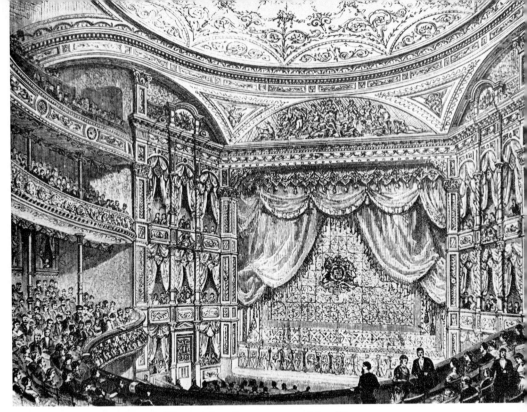

15a The Princess's Theatre, London, as reopened in 1880

15b The Coburg Theatre (later to become the Old Vic) at its opening in 1818

16a An example of Frederick Fenton's scenery: *The Winter's Tale*, 1854

16b An example of William Capon's architectural scene designs for Kemble at Covent Garden, 1808

pure, and plays that attempted to embody these virtues only were usually failures. The dramatist Shirley Brooks said contemptuously that 'the present generation go for a full year together to see a house on fire, or a lady thrown into a pond'.[1] Of course he was right: a stage fire was both real and sensational; the pond (Brooks was probably thinking of *The Colleen Bawn*) was also real and the villainous deed a sensational act. Realism and sensation were essential ingredients of nineteenth-century dramatic taste; the public loved them and managers and authors would go to any lengths to provide them. Shakespeare was staged with increasing realism from Macready through Charles Kean to Irving and Tree; again, this was what the vast majority of the theatregoing public wanted. In this regard a comment on the spectacular presentation of Cleopatra's barge and the battle of Actium (both on stage) in Drury Lane's *Antony and Cleopatra* of 1873 is enlightening, and here the matter can rest:

> There are in a miscellaneous public, such as Drury Lane is filled with, many whose imaginations are not to be kindled by merely verbal delineations, and are best pleased when the eye is made interpreter to the sense. What may be called the childish part of the public, and it is a large one, must be conciliated if success on a large scale is aimed at, and for these Shakespeare's magic verse . . . requires for the full satisfaction of their thought the aid of bodily images to eke out and complete what to them are but imperfect hints.[2]

I have emphasized melodrama because it contained just about everything that appealed to nineteenth-century dramatic taste: sensation, spectacle, violence, true love, romantic fantasy, strong narrative, fine sentiment, rhetoric, courage, low comedy, domestic realism, home and family, eccentric characters, patriotic spirit and a happy ending. All this can also be found in the nineteenth-century novel, and in this sense the novel can be closely related to the stage; they are not so far apart as critics complaining of the separation of literature from the drama would have us believe. This dramatic taste became slowly more sophisticated as the century wore on and better-educated audiences came to the theatre in greater numbers than before. Significantly, the burlesques of melodrama that authors like H. J. Byron and F. C. Burnand wrote increased greatly in the 1860s; such burlesque, eventually destructive of melodrama itself, presupposed an audience thoroughly familiar with melodramatic conventions yet willing to mock them.

[1] *1866 Select Committee Report*, p. 162.
[2] Charles Kenney, *Poets and Profits at Drury Lane Theatre* (1875), p. 43.

Such an audience did not exist, at least in any strength, earlier in the century. Nevertheless, the growth of an educated and serious public was a slow business, and the prospects seemed as gloomy to some critics in the 1890s as they had to Horne in the 1840s. William Archer declared in 1882 that 'a frivolous public calls for frivolous plays, and frivolous plays breed a frivolous public',[1] and summed up the matter of middle-class taste as it appeared to him:

> Modern Englishmen cannot be got to take the drama seriously. The theatre is supported by the most Philistine section of the middle class, and by the worse than Philistine, the utterly frivolous section of the upper class. People of intellect or culture go at long intervals to one or two theatres, and are perfectly in the dark as to what is really good and bad. A theatre supported mainly by people who have taste and thought for everything except the drama, cannot be expected to take a serious hold of life. Pleasure, and that of the least elevating sort, is all that the public expects or will accept at even our best theatres. People talk of the theatre as an instrument of culture, but they take very good care that it shall be nothing of the sort. A drama which opens the slightest intellectual, moral, or political question is certain to fail. The public will accept open vice, but it will have nothing to do with a moral problem. It likes to go to the theatre to-night, and to forget the name, plot, and characters of the piece tomorrow. It will laugh always, cry sometimes, shudder now and then, but think – never. Especially it will have nothing to do with a piece to whose theme the word 'unpleasant' can be applied.[2]

To audiences of 1882 'unpleasant' meant sexually suggestive (in a non-comic way), throwing an unflattering light on a marriage relationship in a play without a happy ending, or studying men and women analytically without the rose tint of Victorian stage idealism. Such audiences were rigidly moral in this respect: Archer's comment on the public accepting open vice probably refers to French farce. Nicoll suggests that since hostile attitudes to the theatre within the church were meliorating, churchgoers no longer stayed away from the theatre, but brought their moral outlook with them.[3] Certainly it is true that church opposition to the stage was lessening, but then nineteenth-century audiences, despite their broad sense of humour,

[1] *English Dramatists of To-day* (1882), p. 17.
[2] Ibid., pp. 8–9.
[3] *A History of English Drama*, V, 14–18.

had always been prudish about the content of their plays. They loved to see Madame Vestris in a breeches part, or smile at ribald comic songs, or roar at a suggestive bit of low comedy acting, or enjoy the Gaiety girls in provocative costumes, or laugh at Gallic mores, but woe betide an actor who had to utter a serious speech with a suggestion of immorality or impiety in it. Charles Rice noted hissing at the expression 'O Lord of Hosts' in Bulwer-Lytton's *The Duchess de la Vallière* (1837).[1] In Boucicault's *Old Heads and Young Hearts* (1844), Charles Mathews knelt during a love scene and said to his lady, 'I came to scoff, but I remained to pray.' The audience hissed because they thought the line came from the Bible, whereas it was actually from Goldsmith.[2] Some performers did not lead especially moral lives, and on the part of the public this was generally expected of the acting profession. But if they became notorious in any public sense, audiences could turn on them savagely. In 1807 a Mrs Johnston appeared at Covent Garden after a two-year absence; she was married to Henry Johnston, an actor in the same company, and had children. Their marital disputes caught the public attention, and her two years away from the stage had apparently been spent, as Boaden delicately put it, 'under the protection, as it is called, of wealth and fashion'. Upon her appearance on stage, 'a perfect yell of fury burst out', but she struggled through the evening as best she could after imploring the mercy of the house. A few days later she acted again: 'the uproar was terrific.' While personally sympathetic to the erring actress, Boaden concluded of her circumstances:

> These are facts as well known as the theatre which they sully . . . is a public to be told, that it has in such a case no jurisdiction; that its sole duty is to enjoy its amusements, whether to weep or laugh, while it encourages infamy in its course, and makes harder by its indifference even the callous heart . . . are you to fawn upon the talent, while you loathe its possessor? Are you to worship, by the glare of the stage, that WANTON, whose exploits, in the public journals, cannot be read by decency at your breakfast table?[3]

Boaden's language was mildness itself compared to the tumult that greeted Edmund Kean on his first two appearances at Drury Lane in 1825 after being found liable for damages on a suit for criminal conversation by Alderman Cox, a suit brought on account of Kean's prolonged liaison with Cox's

[1] *The London Theatre in the Eighteen-Thirties*, ed. A. C. Sprague and Bertram Shuttleworth (London, 1950), p. 13.
[2] *1866 Select Committee Report*, p. 142.
[3] *Memoirs of J. P. Kemble*, II, 445–6.

wife. The case attracted a great deal of publicity and scabrous comment. A considerable faction of the press and public determined to drive Kean off the stage, at least temporarily, and *The Times* thundered loudly against him, declaring that Kean 'is advanced many steps in profligacy beyond the most profligate of his sisters and brethren of the stage. . . . It is of little consequence whether the character of King Richard and Othello be well or ill acted, but it is of importance that public feeling be not shocked, and public decency be not outraged.'[1] The attempt to suppress Kean failed (it did, after a trying time in the provinces, drive him to America, where he underwent the same sort of reception on his first performance in New York and a tremendous riot on his only venture into Boston), but it showed what moral outrage could do in the theatre.

Eighteenth-century audiences were also firmly, though not riotously, moral. A study of the drama of the time shows that morally it was entirely inoffensive; even so the licenser sometimes decreed the rephrasing of dialogue for moral reasons. The moral taste of the period is interestingly reflected in the attitude to Restoration comedy. After 1750 the Restoration dramatists were performed only in morally acceptable versions. Garrick's popular adaptation of *The Country Wife* appeared as *The Country Girl* in 1766 and drove Wycherley's original off the stage until the twentieth century.[2] In these adaptations, morally objectionable characters, such as Sir Jasper Fidget and his ladies, were removed; indecent allusions and dialogue were cut out or 'improved', and Restoration irony and cynical wit became prettified sentimentalism. So infrequently were even these adaptations played in the nineteenth century that Leigh Hunt, in his edition of 1840, found it necessary to present the plays of Wycherley, Congreve, Vanbrugh and Farquhar to his readers as if they were virtually unknown. Macaulay reviewed Hunt's edition in a famous denunciatory essay, and his moral attitude to the Restoration playwrights was much more typical of his century than Hunt's. To Macaulay, 'this part of our literature is a disgrace to our language and our national character'.[3] His main objects of attack were indecency and cynicism. Actually, he had room to review only Wycherley and Congreve, finding the latter the superior

[1] Quoted in Giles Playfair, *Kean* (2nd ed., London, 1950), p. 239.
[2] For a discussion of moral attitudes to Restoration comedies in the eighteenth century, see E. L. Avery, '*The Country Wife* in the eighteenth century', *Research Studies of the State College of Washington*, X (1942), pp. 142–58, '*The Plain Dealer* in the eighteenth century', ibid., XI (1943), pp. 234–56, 'The reputation of Wycherley's comedies as stage plays in the eighteenth century', ibid., XII (1944), pp. 131–54, and *Congreve's Plays on the Eighteenth-Century Stage* (New York, 1951).
[3] Thomas Babington Macaulay, *Critical and Historical Essays* (London, 1907), II, 414.

dramatist and not so 'gross' as the former: 'Wycherley's indecency is protected against the critics as a skunk is protected against the hunters. It is
safe, because it is too filthy to handle and too noisome even to approach.'[1]
All through the nineteenth century and well into the twentieth, Restoration
comedy was barred from the stage on moral grounds.

In the eighteenth century the Examiner of Plays struck out offending
passages or demanded rewording, but refused to license only three plays,
all apparently for political reasons.[2] During the first half of the nineteenth
century, however, he was strenuously active on political, moral and religious
grounds, occasionally to the disgust of managers and the public. There is
no reason, however, to believe that his conservatism was really at odds with
public taste. Charles Kemble commented that 'such is the improved state
of education, and the moral and religious feeling, that in any theatre I do
not think that the audience would suffer anything that was licentious to be
heard on the stage. I have frequently seen things . . . that have been suffered
to pass by the licencer, which have not been suffered to pass by the audience.'[3] An anecdote about George Colman, then Examiner of Plays, recalls
him as saying of a scene he thought 'a little too free', 'Depend upon it, if I
do not cut it out, the audience will cut it out for me.'[4] Testifying before the
same Select Committee, Davidge, the proprietor of the Coburg, believed
not only that audiences could be entrusted 'with the care of preserving the
theatre from licentiousness', but also that 'it would never be to the benefit
of any theatre to meddle with political matters generally, because what you
might derive from the representation of plays which might give pleasure to
one party, you would lose by giving offence to the other'.[5] This latter view
was commonly imparted to the committee by other proprietors and managers. Davidge's questioner, however, thought that 'political allusions appear
to be much more popular to the frequenters of the theatres than any licentiousness', and the dramatist James Kenney believed that 'the real ground
. . . for the necessity of a licenser, is with reference to the political allusions
which may act upon the feelings or passions of an audience'.[6] Colman's petty
tyranny as licenser was frequently complained of; Lords Chamberlain were
usually more lenient than he when for various reasons they dealt personally
with the licensing of scripts. His greed for fees was notorious; he struck out
any address to the deity, any mention of heaven or hell, any 'damn' (even

---

[1] Thomas Babington Macaulay, *Critical and Historical Essays* (London, 1907), II, 435.
[2] *The London Stage*, IV, clxxi.   [3] *1832 Select Committee Report*, p. 51.
[4] Ibid., pp. 229–30.   [5] Ibid., p. 85.
[6] Ibid., p. 230.

though his own plays had been full of these things, and he swore constantly himself); a lover could never call his mistress 'angel'.[1] W. T. Moncrieff told the committee that Colman objected to 'thighs' and 'goblin damned' in his own work. Such instances were numerous with Colman and with other licensers to a lesser degree, and irritating to dramatists, but their moral and political control over the drama was not actively challenged until the 1890s. Majority opinion at nineteenth-century Select Committee hearings on the theatre favoured the retention of the Lord Chamberlain's authority in dramatic affairs. Naturally such authority was inhibiting; it stopped play-wrights from commenting seriously upon sexual matters – if they had wished to, which is doubtful – and it also prevented the drama from openly depicting, satirically or otherwise, the vigorous political life of the times.

In a very real way, then, the Lord Chamberlain and his Examiner of Plays acted throughout our period as governmental arbiters of taste, which is basically why the English drama from 1737 until nearly the twentieth century has not been, and could not be, concerned with sex, politics and religion. As well as being constituted a regulator of the content of the drama, the Lord Chamberlain was also controller and licenser of the theatres them-selves, and determiner of what type of drama they could perform. After 1843 any theatre could play any kind of dramatic piece, but for the remainder of the century the Lord Chamberlain still retained the power of veto over the performance of any play or part of a play, be it scene, song, line, phrase or word, in the public theatre. His powers derived from the Licensing Act of 1737, and the history of his use of these powers and the manner in which they affected the development of the theatre from 1737 to 1843 has been carefully documented by Watson Nicholson in *The Struggle for a Free Stage in London*. For the nineteenth century in particular E. B. Watson has included a substantial chapter on the theatrical monopoly in *Sheridan to Robertson*; most historians of eighteenth- and nineteenth-century theatre have touched in some measure upon the effect of the law upon theatrical affairs.

A brief summary of the situation may, however, be helpful here. During the second half of the eighteenth century the Licensing Act served to confirm the monopoly of the two patent theatres, Covent Garden and Drury Lane. Evasions of the law, which were widely attempted in the years following the passage of the Act, dropped off after mid-century to almost nothing. A further Act of 1752 allowed local magistrates in London and Westminster and within twenty miles thereof to grant licences to places of amusement and

---

[1] R. B. Peake, *Memoirs of the Colman Family* (1841), II, 429–49. See also *A History of English Drama*, IV, 17–20.

public entertainment in their jurisdictions. Under this Act Sadler's Wells received a licence for its special kind of summer fare, which then consisted of singing, dancing, tumbling and pantomimic entertainments. Astley's in 1777 received such a licence for equestrian shows, and so, later, did the Royal Circus for dumbshow melodrama and other light fare. It was never thought that this kind of licence, authorizing entertainments quite different from those at the patent theatres, and usually in places remote from the centre, could ever infringe upon and threaten the monopoly, but eventually this is what happened. Summer theatre at the Haymarket was regularized with a grant of letters patent to Samuel Foote in 1766. This theatre did not compete with Drury Lane and Covent Garden, being open only when they were closed; indeed, the Haymarket struggled under serious disadvantages when the patent theatres chose to extend their own seasons. The only real challenge to the monopoly in the eighteenth century came when John Palmer, armed with a licence from a local magistrate, attempted in 1787 to open the Royalty (near the Tower) as a theatre for legitimate drama, in open defiance of the monopoly. Despite the distance of the Royalty from the West End, the patent theatres took immediate legal action; Palmer was forced to revert to singing, dancing and dumbshow, and abandoned the Royalty at the end of one season. Another Act of 1788 extended local licensing to the rest of the country, at the same time offering the equivalent of London patents to theatres in selected provincial towns; this Act in no way encroached upon the privileges of Drury Lane and Covent Garden. Thus at the end of the century these two theatres appeared unshaken in their monopoly, and they interpreted the Licensing Act to mean that this monopoly would be for ever guarded by the majesty of the law – an interpretation that could hardly have occurred to Walpole in 1737.

If in the eighteenth century the patent theatres' monopoly triumphed, during the period from 1800 to 1843 this monopoly declined until it lay gasping on its deathbed. As Nicholson has pointed out, so contradictory, vague and confusing were the various Acts and regulations governing the theatres that much depended upon the individual Lord Chamberlain and the way he chose to interpret the law.[1] In the eighteenth century the men holding this office had rigorously protected the patent theatres. In the early years of the nineteenth century the Lord Chamberlain was the Earl of Dartmouth. He was not an ally of the patentees, and was obviously friendly towards the efforts of the minor theatres to challenge the monopoly; to this end he granted licences to new theatres himself, as he was empowered to do. By 1807

[1] Watson Nicholson, *The Struggle for a Free Stage in London* (1906), pp. 138–40, 160–5.

he had issued at least seven such licences, among them being those to the Olympic and the Adelphi, soon to become two of the most important minors in London. At first the spoken word could be legally heard only at the patent theatres. As matters stood later, the minors were permitted to play the 'illegitimate' drama, a term of inexact meaning generally signifying melodrama, pantomime, spectacle, burlesque and anything – which could be a great deal – with some musical accompaniment and a few songs; this last, in practice, being what the much disputed and legally vague word 'burletta' meant. They could not perform the 'legitimate' drama: regular tragedy, comedy and farce; these were reserved to the patent theatres. On the other hand there was nothing to stop the patent theatres from producing the illegitimate, a course they pursued vigorously as soon as it proved good box office – a clearly unjust state of affairs. The minors fought to enlarge their privileges, and the majors resisted doggedly, although the tide of events was turning against them. At the Surrey from 1809 to 1814, Elliston had comedies and tragedies rewritten in doggerel rhymed verse and played to a piano accompaniment. Several years later at the same theatre classic plays like *Douglas* were performed with the addition of songs and spectacular effects, as well as original legitimate works. Thus was the term 'burletta' extended. However, the minors had to watch their step. The patent theatres eagerly prosecuted obvious violations of their rights, and even liberal Lords Chamberlain could not push the law too far.Occasionally a minor theatre would get away with Shakespeare or something equally legitimate, but this did not happen often.

The rapid spread of minor theatres over the face of London and the increasingly generous interpretations of what constituted burletta and the illegitimate were paralleled by attempts to challenge the monopoly inside and outside Parliament. The king was petitioned in 1810 to establish a third theatre for the regular drama, and that year the same petitioners argued for a third theatre before the Privy Council. In 1811 a London Theatre Bill was introduced into the Commons, and in 1812 and 1813 a similar bill was put before the House. In the face of entrenched opposition from the patentees and their parliamentary allies, and the legal doubts of the crown, all these efforts to break the monopoly failed. Nevertheless, the ranks of the protesters were steadily augmented, notably by a group of dramatists, and the matter did not rest there. A Select Committee of the House of Commons to investigate theatrical affairs was proposed by Edward Bulwer, as he then was, and began hearings with Bulwer as chairman in 1832. Out of the committee report came the Dramatic Performances Bill, which would allow any licensed theatre to play the legitimate drama and would gather into the hands of the Lord Chamberlain all authority over theatres. Introduced in 1833, the bill easily passed the Commons (in spite of the energetic efforts of the patentees) but was narrowly defeated in the Lords. After this, efforts to attack the monopoly in Parliament temporarily ceased, but the war continued on other fronts. The Lyceum and the Haymarket were allowed in 1833 to open in time for Easter; in 1837 the same permission was extended to the new St James's, the Adelphi, and the Olympic. These extensions all represented encroachments upon the business of Drury Lane and Covent Garden, the last three being granted by a new Lord Chamberlain, Conyngham, who had little sympathy with the patent monopoly. By the late 1830s Drury Lane and Covent Garden were in such a bad way financially that even they could see little advantage in a continuation of their much abused monopoly rights. For example, they had recently been limited to spoken dialogue only, and could not – while the minors could – perform the drama on Wednesdays and Fridays during Lent. Finally, in 1843 the Theatre Regulation Bill was introduced and passed both Houses in three weeks with little opposition; this bill repealed all previous Acts treating of the control of the stage and in effect abolished theatrical monopolies and special privileges. However, the Lord Chamberlain's authority over the content of the drama was increased: any piece performed anywhere 'for hire' in Great Britain had to be sent to him for approval, and his power to forbid performance of the whole or any part of the piece submitted was absolute – a power not removed by legislation until 1968.

It is difficult to see any significant effect of the Licensing Act and the powers of the Lord Chamberlain on the nature of drama throughout most of the eighteenth century, except to banish from the stage political satire, which in the 1730s was taking on a particular form, as evidenced by Fielding's *Pasquin* and *The Historical Register*. Moral standards were certainly maintained by edict, but these would have been enforced by post-1750 audiences in any case, and were not relevant to the *form* of the drama, which traditionally manifested itself in comedy, tragedy, pantomime, farce and ballad opera. Late in the eighteenth century, however, and during that part of the next century prior to the passage of the Theatre Regulation Bill, the law was of great importance in determining the form and content of drama, and not merely in ways relating to the censorship of offending dialogue. E. B. Watson has shown that the law prevented managers like Macready and Vestris from playing the legitimate drama in small theatres where they could make a profit, rather than in the financial tombs of Drury Lane and Covent Garden;

he also suggests that by 1843 the older dramatists, like Jerrold and Planché, were too schooled in the accepted traditions of playwriting to offer anything new to the freed stage, and thus in a sense had been prevented from realizing their artistic abilities fully under the legal conditions prevailing when they wrote most of their plays.[1] The first argument is undoubtedly correct; the truth of the second is doubtful. But the main point to establish here is that because the minor theatres were forced by legal fiat into dumbshow, spectacle, melodrama, burletta and burlesque, the law shaped the whole course of nineteenth-century drama. For these types of drama were extremely popular with the new audiences of a fast-growing city; the patent theatres borrowed them to prop up their own legitimate offerings, and at a later date sometimes fell into them entirely. When theatres were freed from the monopoly in 1843 the character of their entertainments did not change: the minors knew what the public wanted and stuck to it, venturing rarely into the formerly forbidden ground of the legitimate. It is going too far to say that had there been no theatrical monopoly these forms of the illegitimate drama would not have developed, yet much of the vigour, vulgarity, colour, excitement and sense of life in the drama of the first half of the nineteenth century was, in part at least, attributable to the Licensing Act of 1737.

The Lord Chamberlain's powers of censorship were only trivially restrictive to the great majority of authors; they well knew the established legal boundaries of taste and subject matter, which were also very much those of their audiences. The class movement of theatre audiences from the fairly gentlemanly to the more uncouth resembled a similar movement in the authorship of the drama. Just as many literary gentlemen tried to get plays accepted in the nineteenth as in the eighteenth century, but playwrights on the whole tended to be workaday theatre practitioners rather than educated members of the middle class. Significantly, whereas eighteenth-century literature contributed to the stage Steele, Addison, Fielding, Gay and Goldsmith – all successful dramatists – the nineteenth-century stage could make successes only of Bulwer-Lytton and possibly Tennyson. There was no lack of effort: Lamb, Coleridge, Wordsworth, Keats, Shelley, Byron, Scott, Hunt, Dickens, Browning, Swinburne and others wrote plays, but the results were generally not happy and often unacted. It is not my intention here to discuss the reasons why. The writers themselves and their contemporaries blamed the managers, the theatres, the audiences, the actors and the age. A few later critics and historians have agreed with them; others, notably Allardyce Nicoll, have pointed out the low opinion many writers held of the stage, and

[1] *Sheridan to Robertson*, pp. 50–6.

questioned their willingness to learn the fundamentals of the dramatist's craft. Whatever the reasons, and whatever the apportionment of blame – if one can even use 'blame' in this context – there undoubtedly was a separation between literature and drama, or to be more precise a separation between men of letters and the occupation of the dramatist. Such a separation had not occurred before the nineteenth century, for the drama was a primary artistic mode for Elizabethans, Jacobeans and poets and wits at the court of Charles II. For many critics, nineteenth-century and modern, this dichotomy was the root cause of 'the decline of the drama'; the drama simply was bad because the playwrights were not good enough. I have touched upon the alleged badness and decline of the drama above: suffice to say here that one of the things seriously wrong with nineteenth-century drama was that it frequently tried to be 'literary', which meant imitating the great Elizabethan dramatists and the Romantic poets' imitation of them. There is no nineteenth-century play quite so bad to read as one of those products of the 'unacted drama', represented for instance by the plays of F. G. Tomlins and George Stephens, who proudly proclaimed the superiority of their own work to the daily rubbish of the stage. It may be argued that these men were merely poor writers; so they were, but their attitude was symptomatic of a malaise deeply affecting nineteenth-century drama.

Byron was the Romantic who dabbled most in the drama: he wrote several plays, only one of which, *Marino Faliero* (1821), was performed (not successfully) in his lifetime, although Macready adapted *Werner* in 1830 and through his own acting made it a standard work in the repertory; Byron's address reopened Drury Lane in 1812; Byron was also a member of the Drury Lane committee of management in 1815, and a great admirer of Kean. Yet he treated the theatre like a child's toy, throwing it aside when he was weary of it. He told Charles Bucke that he was sick of theatres, adding 'Besides – should I not be a fool, and a confounded fool too, to risk my reputation in a place where any rascal may hiss me for a shilling.'[1] His membership of the Drury Lane committee was 'really very good fun, as far as the daily and nightly stir of these strutters and fretters go', and he asked Thomas Medwin, 'Who would condescend to the drudgery of the stage and enslave himself to the humours, the caprices, the taste or the tastelessness of the age?'[2]

Ever looking to past ages for dramatic inspiration, Byron's contemporaries and those who followed him refused to recognize the rich and varied life of

[1] Preface to *Julio Romano* (1830).
[2] Samuel C. Chew, *The Dramas of Lord Byron* (Baltimore, 1915), p. 35.

their own times as valid material for the stage. This attitude was of course a sterile one and could not be productive even if the talent was there. Fortunately it was an attitude not held by the lesser mortals who turned out the melodramas, pantomimes, farces and burlesques that are far more interesting and expressive of the age than the literary imitations. Yet had the men of letters thought differently about the relation of their own age to the drama, and had they resolved really to work at the theatrical trade till they mastered it, nineteenth-century drama might have run in new channels.

Such a view is idealistic, however, since for the greater part of the nineteenth century working at the theatrical trade was not profitable, and one could not in fairness expect the major poets, novelists and essayists to abandon their own lucrative writing to struggle with an unfamiliar form for scanty rewards, even presuming they had both interest and desire to do so, which many did not. The economic aspect of playwriting in the eighteenth and nineteenth centuries has received very little attention,[1] but it is important because the remuneration involved partially determined the quality of the drama and was also a sign of the economic health or sickness of the theatre generally. An illuminating comparison can also be made between the income of a popular dramatist and the income of a best-selling novelist or poet, a comparison that places the financial gulf between them, in the nineteenth century at least, in sharp perspective.

Before the 1790s it was not unusual for an author to receive between £100 and £200 for the copyright of a five-act play or three-act comic opera.[2] His other source of income, benefit nights, varied widely, depending upon the degree of success or failure of each play. A reputable author, like Murphy or O'Keeffe, could make a steady though not princely income from the theatre. With the 1790s and the enlargement of Drury Lane and Covent Garden we are still in a period of good theatre attendance, and the earnings of the most successful playwrights rose considerably. At about the same time the system whereby an author took his benefit on the third, sixth, ninth and twentieth nights of his play, after the deduction of house charges, was altered to one of fixed payments of £33 6s. 8d. for each of the first nine nights and £100 on the twentieth night: if a play ran twenty nights he would receive £400. For the fortieth night – a rare event then – another £100 was added. Frederick Reynolds claimed he was the first author to make such an

---

[1] For the nineteenth century I know only of a brief appendix in *Sheridan to Robertson*, pp. 434–6, and a short treatment in *A History of English Drama*, IV, 51–6, and V, 68–71.
[2] A. S. Collins states that the usual price given for the copyright of a play in 1750 was £100; in 1771 it was £150. (*The Profession of Letters*, London, 1928, p. 25.)

arrangement with a manager, for *The Rage* at Covent Garden in 1794.[1] However, the same claim was made for Cumberland;[2] at any event the new system was in effect at both Drury Lane and Covent Garden in the 1790s. Forty years later the same method of payment obtained at the same rate, as testimony to the Select Committee of 1832 demonstrates, but there was no signed contract between author and manager. These amounts were given for mainpieces; much less was offered for after-pieces, which were evidently paid for not at a nightly rate but in a lump sum. In the season of 1813–14 Isaac Pocock received £100 from Covent Garden for the immensely popular melodrama *The Miller and His Men*. For his farce *The Irish Ambassador* (1831) James Kenney was to have received 100 guineas from Covent Garden and £25 more if it was performed twenty nights.[3] These two examples appear to represent about the top of the financial scale for the after-piece.

By the 1830s, however, the income of dramatists was appreciably diminishing; their halcyon days were over. In 1801 George Colman got £400 for *The Poor Gentleman* and an identical sum in 1805 for *Who Wants a Guinea?*, plus an extra £150 for each copyright; in 1803 his comedy *John Bull* ran forty-seven nights at Covent Garden to average receipts of £470 a night, and Colman received a total of £1,200 for the play.[4] In 1797 Mrs Inchbald obtained £800 for *Wives as they Were and Maids as they Are*, and in 1807 Thomas Morton got £1,000 for *Town and Country*.[5] Thomas Dibdin was house dramatist for Covent Garden in the season 1799–1800 at £5 a week; in addition he made £200 from a comedy, including the copyright, and £50 from a farce; his total income that season was £543. Four seasons later Dibdin was still house dramatist at the same salary, but his income had risen to £1,515. He was therefore able to 'lay out a considerable sum on furniture, books, pictures, &c.'[6] and had already invested £1,400, with his brother Charles, in a quarter share of Sadler's Wells. Reynolds was another dramatist who regularly reported accounts of his income. By 1796, after ten years of writing for the stage, his 'usual dramatic income' for a comedy was £500; he exceeded this substantially in 1793 with £620 from *How to Grow Rich*, in 1804 with £600, including £200 for the copyright, from *The Blind Bargain* and in 1810 with £700 (again £200 for the copyright) from *The Free Knights*, an opera. Reynolds proudly estimated his total income over

[1] *The Life and Times of Frederick Reynolds*, II, 182.
[2] *Memoirs of the Colman Family*, II, 413.
[3] *1832 Select Committee Report*, p. 232.
[4] *Memoirs of the Colman Family*, II, 413.
[5] *The Life and Times of Frederick Reynolds*, II, 282.
[6] *The Reminiscences of Thomas Dibdin* (1827), I, 371.

forty years as a dramatist (1785–*c.* 1825) at above £19,000, 'a sum hitherto unequalled in the history of dramatic writing'.[1]

Such golden times for the leading dramatists did not endure beyond the 1820s, and by then both Drury Lane and Covent Garden were in serious financial trouble. James Kenney in 1832 had received only £50 out of the sum owing to him from *The Irish Ambassador* at Covent Garden, and he had been paid nothing so far of the £400 owing to him for *Masaniello* at Drury Lane because of the bankruptcy of the manager, Price, despite the fact that the piece had played there for 150 nights and was still playing.[2] The Select Committee proceedings of 1832 contain many complaints from playwrights of managers depriving them in various ways of a part or the whole of fees legitimately earned. Macready testified that the amount a publisher would now offer for the copyright of a play had drastically declined from a high point thirty years before: '100 l. was a low price for a play then, but now frequently 10 l. is offered, and sometimes even that is considered a hazard.'[3] In contrast to the high fees regularly received by Reynolds, Colman and others around the turn of the century, the only dramatist to do at all well during the 1830s and 1840s was Bulwer-Lytton. Macready gave him £600 for *Richelieu* at Covent Garden in 1839 (after he had refused to accept any payment for *The Lady of Lyons*), and Webster £200 more for the rights to represent *Richelieu* in London (at the Haymarket) for three years. Bulwer-Lytton also received from Webster £600 for *The Sea-Captain* (1839) and £600 for *Money* (1840). Except for *The Sea-Captain*, these were all great successes.[4] No other author could command either Bulwer-Lytton's literary prestige or his fees. The most eminent dramatist of the twenties and thirties was Sheridan Knowles, whose highest fee was £600, received from Vestris and Mathews of Covent Garden for *Love* (1839). About 1840 Charles Kean offered him £1,000 for a play not yet written, but it was not forthcoming. In contrast to Reynolds's earnings from playwriting of over £19,000, Knowles – the leading and most admired dramatist of his time – made only £4,600 in his career.[5] Webster had contracted with Bulwer-Lytton on the basis of a flat payment for the rights of representation for a certain period. This was a new system and appears to have been widely introduced in the forties. Under it, depending on the theatre and the nature of the piece, the author was paid according to the number of acts he had written – at £50 or

[1] *The Life and Times of Frederick Reynolds*, II, 421.
[2] *1832 Select Committee Report*, p. 226.
[3] Ibid., p. 135.
[4] These figures are from Charles H. Shattuck, *Bulwer and Macready* (Urbana, 1958).
[5] L. H. Meeks, *Sheridan Knowles and The Theatre of His Time* (Bloomington, 1933), p. 54.

£100 an act at the better theatres – and no more. This method of payment further reduced the potential income of dramatists, since it did not take into account the length of a run. Ironically, the new system coincided with the increasing frequency of the long run, yet resulted in authors being paid far less than at the beginning of the century when runs were immeasurably shorter.

These figures all relate to the patent theatres, as well as the Haymarket, which was relatively prosperous. For the minor theatres, easily the biggest market for playwrights, the remuneration was much less, and they usually paid a fixed sum, even in the early days. Davidge of the Coburg told the 1832 Select Committee that the highest fee he ever gave was 50 guineas, the average fee being £20. A Coburg author could also be paid at a nightly rate, never exceeding a guinea, and only on the first run of a new piece.[1] Charles Dibdin in 1797 received the highest price Astley's paid for a new pantomime: 5 guineas. It had taken him six weeks to write. His brother Thomas received £5 a week all the year round to write for Covent Garden; Charles was given a guinea and a half a week (and half a guinea for his wife's acting) to write thirty-six pieces a year for Astley's, and that sum only when the theatre was open.[2] In 1800 his salary for the same job at Sadler's Wells, combined with the duties of manager, was 2 guineas a week.[3] Douglas Jerrold got £5 a week from the Surrey in 1829 to serve as house dramatist, having left the Coburg because of the low salary for the same post. In that year Elliston gave him £50 for the enormously successful *Black-Eyed Susan*, which ran 150 consecutive nights at the Surrey alone, another 250 elsewhere in London the same year, as well as runs in many provincial towns. That £50 and another £10 for the copyright was all Jerrold had for one of the most popular plays of the century. The highest minor theatre payments rarely seem to have exceeded about £70 for a three-act play. In 1839 J. B. Buckstone wrote to Yates of the Adelphi (a minor theatre of the first class) offering to write a three-act drama on 'my old terms' for £70.[4] Buckstone, however, was at the top of his profession and commanded the highest prices. The

[1] *1832 Select Committee Report*, pp. 77–8.
[2] *Memoirs of Charles Dibdin the Younger*, pp. 18–20. Vincent Crummles paid Nicholas Nickleby about £1 a week – 'nearly double' if houses were good – for his services as house dramatist and actor in Portsmouth, with the dramatic talents of Smike thrown in. W. T. Moncrieff did rather better at Drury Lane about 1823, being paid £10 a week and writing four to six pieces a season; sometimes he had to produce something in twenty-four hours (*1832 Select Committee Report*, p. 175).
[3] *Memoirs of Charles Dibdin the Younger*, p. 41.
[4] Edmund Yates, *His Recollections and Experiences* (1884), I, 33.

great majority of dramatists were less fortunate, and if they depended for their living solely upon writing for the stage, their situations could be most precarious. In 1832 W. T. Moncrieff concluded that 'as the drama is at present constituted, it is impossible for any man, whose misfortunes may oblige him to resort to that species of writing, to obtain a fair remuneration for his labour and talent'.[1] And Moncrieff, too, was a popular and well-known dramatist.

The consequences of the low market value of drama after about 1820 or 1830 were obvious. Authors either had to turn out great quantities of material very quickly or abandon the drama entirely, as did Jerrold and Knowles. Since the copyright value of a play had fallen off to almost nothing, this source of income, lucrative in the past, was not to be thought of. If a playwright was fortunate he could obtain a regular position with a theatre as house dramatist, as did the Dibdins, Jerrold, Moncrieff and Boucicault, but the salary was usually low and the workload heavy. During Charles Dibdin's engagement at the Surrey as 'Acting Manager, Author, and *Contriver*', he wrote twenty-one new pieces, 'chiefly of three Acts each', in twenty-eight weeks for the 1825 summer season.[2] Reference has been made above to his earlier contract to write thirty-six new pieces a year for Astley's. This sort of thing was common for a house dramatist. In 1845 George Dibdin Pitt wrote seventeen melodramas and a pantomime for the Britannia, and two years later nineteen melodramas and a pantomime, as well as six pieces produced at other theatres.[3] Concerning his twenty-one plays for the Surrey in 1825, Dibdin noted that eight were based on French plots and the remainder 'British Manufacture'. Of course the only way an author could keep up the monetary pace at the low rates prevailing was feverishly to adapt French plays, work to a few stereotyped situations and characters, steal from popular novels, dramatize newspaper reports of crimes, rewrite his own old plays and borrow liberally from his fellow dramatists. Careful and original work was not encouraged by the prevailing financial circumstances; dramatists *had* to be hacks, willy-nilly.

The reasons for the decline in playwrights' income were largely economic. As I have already mentioned, theatre management from about 1815 to the 1860s was generally unprofitable at majors and minors alike. Many managers went bankrupt, and naturally the income of authors declined. It was also a period when the leading stars could ask and get up to £50 a night from a

[1] *1832 Select Committee Report*, p. 176.
[2] *Memoirs of Charles Dibdin the Younger*, p. 148.
[3] *A History of English Drama*, IV, 373-5.

London manager: more than one contemporary critic felt that stars were making money at the expense of writers. The payroll of the patent theatres was extremely high, since virtually separate companies had to be maintained for tragedy, comedy, opera and ballet. None of this would have mattered if rising revenues had run ahead of rising expenses, but they did not; on the whole, West End theatre attendance did not pick up again until the 1850s at the earliest. A further consideration of these matters properly belongs in a study of the economics of the theatre itself, but clearly dramatists could not obtain adequate remuneration from their work until three things happened: firstly, that managers entered into contractual arrangements fair to authors; secondly, that the theatre generally became more prosperous; thirdly, that the existence of a reading public for drama and protective copyright legislation would ensure for the dramatist a good income from his published plays. When these conditions were fulfilled in the 1880s and 1890s, the financial lot of the dramatist was vastly improved.

Meanwhile, by the time the Select Committee on Theatrical Licences and Regulations sat in 1866, monetary returns for playwrights were little better. Buckstone gave Tom Taylor £150 for *Our American Cousin* in 1861; owing to Sothern's Lord Dundreary, it ran for a year at the Haymarket, made Sothern a star and netted Buckstone £20,000. Taylor, too, received only £200 for *The Ticket-of-Leave Man*, which reached over 400 consecutive performances at the Olympic in 1863–4 and was one of the most popular melodramas of all time. Taylor and authors like him would have made something from provincial rights collected on their behalf by the Dramatic Authors' Society, but these did not as yet amount to very much. The Bancrofts raised actors' salaries at the Prince of Wales's and no doubt believed themselves to be doing handsomely by their leading author, Tom Robertson. For *Society*, *Ours* and *Caste* Robertson received £1, £2 and £3 a night respectively,[1] which would have meant £165, £300 and £468 respectively on the first runs of these plays; the Bancrofts, however, also paid for revivals and eventually gave Robertson £5 a night.[2] In 1869 Robertson received his maximum, £10 a night for *Home* at the Haymarket, or £1,330.[3] Compared to his fellow playwrights, then, Robertson at the end of his career (1869–70) was doing very well: he recorded his income for 1869 as about £4,300, and for 1870 about £4,000.[4] But this was the same decade in which Taylor was

[1] T. Edgar Pemberton, *The Life and Writings of T. W. Robertson* (1893), p. 221.
[2] *The Bancrofts*, p. 91.
[3] Francis C. Burnand, *Records and Reminiscences* (4th ed., 1905), p. 315.
[4] *The Life and Writings of T. W. Robertson*, p. 283.

being paid a straight £50 an act, and it must also be remembered that the Bancrofts treated authors with comparative generosity. At the lesser theatres there was no improvement at all. Shepherd of the Surrey told Burnand in 1866 that the best he could manage was 10s. a night, and said that only a West End theatre might pay the 3 guineas a performance Burnand had asked for his burlesque.[1] Burnand also related that the top price anywhere for a popular author was then £100 an act, that a farce from the French never fetched more than £20 or £30 and that an original farce might have obtained £50 from a generous manager.[2] Charles Reade estimated his income from the drama at £35 a year, and H. C. Newton recalled being asked in 1882 to write a pantomime for the Elephant and Castle (whose house dramatist, George Roberts, was getting 30s. a week) for £3; at about the same time Astley's paid him £10 for a new version of *Mazeppa*.[3]

A playwright's income from publishers was still ludicrously low. No longer was there a market for the octavo play at 3s. or 5s., and almost the only plays printed were in cheap acting editions designed for stage use and impossible to read for pleasure. These acting editions, which completely dominated the printed play market after about 1830, were issued by several publishers over varying periods, and include Dolby's *British Theatre* (1823–5), Cumberland's *British Theatre* (1826–61) and Cumberland's *Minor Theatre* (1828–43), Duncombe's *British Theatre* (1828–52), Richardson's *Minor Drama* (1828–31), Lacy's – later French's – *Acting Editions* (1851–   ) and Dick's *Standard Plays* (1883–1908).[4] The publishers of these editions bought the copyright from the author, usually for a few pounds, and then collected acting fees from both amateurs and professionals for all plays on their list, other than those on which the copyright had expired.

One ray of light illuminated the 1860s, however. It was in this decade that Boucicault, by making a sharing agreement (instead of accepting the

---

[1] *Records and Reminiscences*, p. 293.
[2] Ibid., p. 295.
[3] H. C. Newton, *The Old Vic* (1923), p. 36.
[4] The dates of the editions are from *A History of English Drama*, IV, 248, and V, 231. The two great collections of plays in manuscript for the period 1750–1880 are the Larpent collection (1737–1824) in the Huntington Library and the Lord Chamberlain's collection (1824–   ), now in the British Museum. For the eighteenth century performances of plays are exhaustively catalogued in the volumes of *The London Stage, 1660–1800*, and in special studies such as *Drury Lane Calendar, 1747–76* and C. B. Hogan, *Shakespeare in the Theatre 1701–1800*, 2 volumes (London, 1952–7). For the nineteenth century Nicoll's Hand-lists of Plays in *A History of English Drama*, IV and V, are the only authoritative source for performance dates; there is also a Hand-list in III for 1750–1800.

usual lump sum payment) with Webster of the Adelphi for *The Colleen Bawn* and *The Octoroon* in 1860 and 1861, profited to the extent of thousands of pounds (the exact figure is unknown). In 1866 the Select Committee was told that Boucicault continued to make such sharing arrangements with both London and provincial theatres; Boucicault himself testified that he took half the profits, and in the provinces 'that drama going around the country acts as a star; and I receive a clear half of the net profits in all those theatres, by which means it sometimes appears in five or six theatres at the same moment'.[1] By these means Boucicault netted several hundred pounds a week, but his contractual methods were aggressively unorthodox and he himself an exceptionally big-name dramatist and box office attraction. Other authors were slow to make similar arrangements, although Burnand did, most profitably, for *Black-Eyed Susan* (1866) and other burlesques. In 1879 Burnand was calling for a general 10 per cent royalty arrangement, since 'at present authors are underpaid, and it suits them better, far better, to adapt foreign plays provided by the managers than to devote time and labour to original work'.[2] In a few years most authors were following Boucicault and Burnand, royalty and sharing agreements were common, a reading public again existed for the drama, and comfortable fortunes could be amassed from writing for the stage.[3] Naturally, good money attracted good talent, and men of letters returned to the theatre.

A brief comparison between the earnings of playwrights and the earnings of writers in other branches of letters clearly illustrates the relative poverty of the former. Even when the most popular dramatists were prospering, their rewards were much lower. Fanny Burney, for instance, received £3,000 in subscriptions for *Camilla* (1796). Scott obtained £4,000 for *The Lady of the Lake* (1810), £4,500 for *Kenilworth* (1821) and by 1818, Lockhart said, was making £10,000 a year. A minor novelist, Susan Ferrier, received £1,000 from Blackwood for *The Inheritance* (1824) and £1,700 from Cadell for *Destiny* (1831). Murray gave Byron £2,000 for the third canto of *Childe Harold's Pilgrimage* in 1816 and £1,575 for the first two cantos of *Don Juan*. Henry Hart Milman received 500 guineas in 1822 for his poem *Belshazzar*. Writing for periodicals was also not unprofitable. Southey at one time got 100 guineas an article from the *Quarterly*, and in Waverley-novel days

---

[1] *1866 Select Committee Report*. In New York Boucicault's profits had been even greater.
[2] 'Authors and managers', *Theatre* (February 1879), p. 17.
[3] To cite two examples only: under a royalty system Henry Arthur Jones made £18,000 from *The Silver King* (1882) and Pinero over £30,000 from *The Second Mrs. Tanqueray* (1893). These figures may have included royalties from the published plays.

Constable paid the unprecedented sums of 10 and 20 guineas a sheet for reviews in the *Edinburgh Review*.[1] In the forties, when the income of dramatists had generally been declining for several years, that of novelists and short story writers was rapidly rising. In 1840 Chapman and Hall agreed to pay Dickens £3,000 for a six-month copyright on *Barnaby Rudge* (they had already given £4,500 for *Nicholas Nickleby*), and in 1869 agreed on £7,500 for the first 25,000 of *Edwin Drood*, profits beyond that figure to be equally divided. As an editor Dickens could in the sixties offer £1,000 for a short story in *All the Year Round*.[2] From 1860 Thackeray was making £7,000 a year from his work as author and editor,[3] and Trollope listed his earnings as a novelist as totalling about £61,000, the highest individual amount being £3,525 for *Can you Forgive Her?* (1864).[4] Finally, George Eliot's account book shows a steady progression: £1,705 for *Adam Bede*, £3,985 for *The Mill on the Floss*, £6,000 for *Felix Holt*, £8,783 for *Middlemarch* and £9,236 for *Daniel Deronda*, all these figures representing earnings over several years for each novel. Thus in about twenty years as a novelist alone, beginning in the late 1850s, she made about £30,000.[5]

The position of dramatists under the copyright laws was also important in determining their financial status. During the eighteenth century there was no such thing as a copyright, or an author's proprietary right, in a dramatic performance. His play, if it reached a third, sixth or ninth night (and later a twentieth), realized sums entirely dependent on attendance on those nights and the amount of house charges to be deducted, unless his benefit was 'clear', in which case he received the whole amount, an unusual privilege for an author. Revivals afforded the author no further payment; neither did later performances at another theatre. If his play was printed the publisher paid for the copyright, which was protected for fourteen years and a further fourteen if the author was still alive. In 1814 this period of protection was altered to twenty-eight years from publication or for the life of the author, whichever was longer. When there were only two or three theatres in London and few in the provinces, performances of a new play from which the playwright received nothing could only be occasional and not financially damaging. However, with the spread of theatres in London and the provinces

---

[1] For all these figures, except for those relating to *Kenilworth* and Lockhart, which come from the *DNB*, I am indebted to Collins, *The Profession of Letters*.

[2] The figures concerning Dickens are from Edgar Johnson, *Charles Dickens: His Tragedy and Triumph* (New York, 1953).

[3] Gordon N. Ray, *Thackeray* (London, 1955–8), II, 392.

[4] *An Autobiography* (1883), pp. 325–6.

[5] *The George Eliot Letters*, ed. Gordon S. Haight (London, 1955), VII, 358–64.

in the nineteenth century, the law was quite inadequate for the protection of a dramatist's rights. Before 1833, once a play was printed it could be performed anywhere without fees, as there was still no legal right in a dramatic presentation; furthermore, an author got nothing from provincial performances of even an unpublished London success. (The ways and means of obtaining copies of unprinted plays were about the same as in Elizabethan days.) A manager could accept a play, postpone production indefinitely or else not produce it at all, with no recompense to the author. In France this was impossible, and from 1791 no piece could be performed anywhere in the country without the written consent of the author. French playwrights received royalty payments on the night's receipts at every theatre in France, in varying percentages depending on the number of acts and the status of the theatre: at the Comédie and the Odéon, in the highest class, $12\frac{1}{2}$ per cent for a four- or five-act play, $8\frac{1}{3}$ per cent for two or three acts, $6\frac{1}{4}$ per cent for one act, after deduction of a fixed one-third from the gross receipts for house charges. A French playwright also received extra payment should his work form the whole evening's entertainment at any theatre, and had legal perquisites such as selling a certain number of tickets for every performance. Thus the most popular French dramatists lived royally on ample fortunes.[1] In England organized agitation among dramatic authors led to the Dramatic Copyright Act of 1833, which gave the author sole property in an unpublished composition and the exclusive right to have it represented on stage. His rights in a printed play now terminated twenty-eight years from publication or at the end of his life – as before – and were made retroactive to 1823. In 1842 an extension was made to seven years after the author's death or forty-two years from publication, whichever was the longer.

The Act of 1833 certainly improved the dramatist's position, but there were many loopholes. The Act was legally interpreted to mean that a publisher who held the copyright of a play could collect the acting fees, and not the author. This interpretation was at least partly responsible for the virtual disappearance of plays well printed for reading pleasure, although the value of dramatic copyright had been declining for some years, and it was hardly worthwhile for a playwright to see his work through the press. Conjunctively, the reading public for drama in the eighteenth century, generally well educated and interested in the drama as literature, dwindled

---

[1] The best account of comparative conditions prevailing for English and French dramatists shortly before the passage of the Dramatic Copyright Act is T. J. Thackeray, *On the Rights of Dramatic Authors* (1832). See also J. R. Planché, *Recollections and Reflections* (revised ed., 1901), pp. 138–47.

away through a lack of interest in perusing the printed record of what in the nineteenth century became far more of a theatrical product, rather than a literary one, than it had been. Its place was *not* taken by a far less literate public – given the popular nature of drama in the first half of the century – simply not interested in reading plays. In all this there was little financial comfort for the dramatist. Evasions of the Act of 1833 in the provinces were commonplace; in short, there was still little to encourage a dramatist to print his plays, and in the growing American theatrical market there was no legal protection for the English author. Plays were stolen and performed in America with no payment to the English writer, who was powerless to remedy the situation; his only American income could come from an arrangement with an honourable manager. In return, however, he could of course steal American plays when necessary, and much more relevantly the French drama still lay wide open for theatrical plunder. A further Act of 1852 protected the copyright of foreign authors, but was easily evaded under a section stating that nothing so far enacted should 'prevent fair Imitations or Adaptations to the English Stage of any Dramatic Piece . . . published in any Foreign Country'.

After the Act of 1833 the Dramatic Authors' Society was formed to guard the interests of dramatists and collect their provincial fees. Its secretary in 1866, J. Stirling Coyne, gave testimony before the Select Committee that usefully illuminates the dealings of authors with London and provincial managers:

> A dramatic author receives from the manager of a London theatre a certain sum for the right of acting a piece in London, either for a limited number of years, or for the entire copyright, and that piece belongs to the manager in London during the term of the arrangement . . . but the copyright belongs to the author in the provinces. The author gives . . . permission to the managers of theatres in the provinces to play all the pieces on the list of the Dramatic Authors' Society for a certain sum per year or per month, according to the duration of the season. He sells the London right, and the London manager reserves the piece for his own theatre, but the provincial right is in all cases reserved by the author himself.

An author made independent arrangements with a London manager, but the income from provincial fees was collected by the society 'in bulk, and it is distributed among the authors *pro rata* according to the number of pieces that each author may have had acted each year at that theatre'.[1] Although established in 1833, the Dramatic Authors' Society had been a regular working society with a fixed system of operation only since approximately 1860. It was of great benefit to many playwrights, but its fees were low, and authors like Boucicault and Burnand, who could do much better for themselves acting independently, would not allow their plays to be placed on the society's list. However, it had improved matters: Buckstone in 1833 was offered only £10 by Yates for a year's acting copyright in the provinces of a comedy, *The Rake and His Pupil*;[2] John Maddison Morton, whose playwriting stretched from the thirties to the eighties, was reported to have collected, under the society, £500 a year from provincial fees – but at what period in his career these amounts were made is not specified.[3]

Further improvements in the laws governing dramatists lie after 1880 and beyond our period. By the 1880s, as has already been pointed out, dramatists themselves were securing far better terms, on the basis of royalties, from managers. In 1886 the Berne Convention gave the authors of subscribing states basically the same legal rights internationally as they were afforded in their own countries. Incidentally, it also expressly forbade the 'fair Imitations and Adaptations' permitted in the Act of 1852, so that the flood of free French adaptations was legally prevented: the impetus thus given, of necessity, to original English drama was considerable. In 1891 the passage of a new American copyright law in effect allowed English authors to print their own plays without fear of piracy, and a more cultivated reading public re-created the market for well-printed plays that existed before 1830. The next domestic Copyright Act, which cleared up anomalies in previous Acts, was not passed until 1911. Thus the position of the English dramatist was made legally more secure and financially more profitable – two essential conditions for the health of the drama and theatre after 1880.

[1] *1866 Select Committee Report*, p. 209.
[2] *Recollections and Experiences*, I, 33.
[3] Arthur à Beckett, *Green Room Recollections* (1896), p. 254.

II Theatres and actors

1 Richard Southern

2 Frederick & Lise-Lone Marker

1 Theatres and stages

In the matter of theatre architecture, the period 1750 to 1880 contains the whole development in form that led from the stage of the Elizabethan-plus-Restoration pattern to the birth of the picture-frame proscenium 'arch' that survives generally today. This development is fortunately well documented. Our first evidence comes from the year 1766.

(i) The lost remains at King's Lynn

In this year there was erected within the large, empty, medieval guildhall of St George at King's Lynn a complete Georgian theatre interior. This fact is sufficiently interesting in itself, but the further point that certain very informative vestiges of this adaptation survived for our inspection as late as 1948 (when they were removed) makes King's Lynn an especially suitable subject from which to begin a study of mid-Georgian theatre architecture.[1]

The remains were such that we can trace the construction of the theatre almost step by step. The process may be resumed in diagrammatic form as follows.

[1] *Theatre Notebook*, III (October–December 1948), p. 6.

In Figure 1 is shown a simplified representation of the hall with the most notable feature of the surviving evidence specially stressed. This was the remains of a group of eight timber posts, some 9 inches square, planted firmly on the floor of the hall and reaching their chamfered tops to fit snugly against the sloping rafters of the pitched roof above. These posts were paired in two rows some 20 feet apart; three of the pairs – A, B and C in the diagram – belong to one specific assembly; the fourth pair, D, are relatively independent.

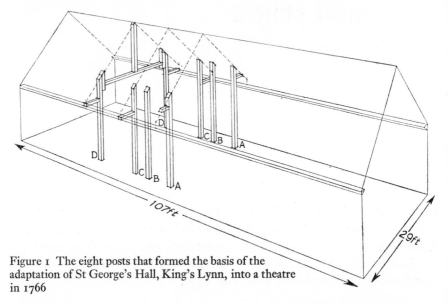

Figure 1   The eight posts that formed the basis of the adaptation of St George's Hall, King's Lynn, into a theatre in 1766

The pairs of posts were not spaced equally, and the difference is significant; the space between the A-pair and the B-pair was some 7 feet 9 inches, and the space between the B-pair and the C-pair only 4 feet. In all these vertical timbers certain cuts, mortices and traces of paint showed the existence formerly of further elements. Beside these signs there was one piece remaining in much more substantial form, and that was the element indicated in the next figure.

Figure 2 shows it in its relation to the three pairs of posts. It was a continuous ceiling at a level a little below where the posts joined the timbers of the original roof. In extent it was bounded by the four posts A and C. Its underside was plastered and bore clear traces in the peeling paint of a decoration, based on a circular motif.

This figure also shows diagrammatically that the lower parts of all these posts, the D-pair as well as the three other pairs, had once been whitewashed up to some 4 or 5 feet from the floor. The line of demarcation, E to F in Figure 2, showed a slight slope upwards towards F. The slope was entirely consistent with the angle of rake of a stage floor; and the indication was that the parts under the floor had been whitewashed and the parts above painted with some dark colour, now impossible to determine.

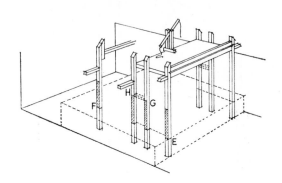

Figure 2 The proscenium ceiling and rain machine, with stage and proscenium doors reconstructed

Between posts B and C on either side there were marks, some 8 feet 6 inches above the presumed stage level, of a cross-member (indicated at GH) which suggested a door-head.

Above the edge of the ceiling over the A-pair of posts there was a vertical fascia, bearing traces of moulding.

Finally, on the floor in the loft over the ceiling there was one unmistakably theatrical object, a rain machine in the form of a wooden cylinder containing shot or the like, and pivoted in the centre like a seesaw between two uprights. Traces of a rope remained at the ends of the cylinder for working it up and down, and it still produced a perfectly credible sound of rain.

Figure 3 shows a first step in the reconstruction, with the stage now indicated and the door-head timbers shown in place and also extended, at the same level, between the posts at B and A. It may be noticed that the stage floor is not continued to the back of the hall. This is probably because, at some point no longer specifiable, the stage itself gave way to space for dressing rooms. Whether they would have been at floor level with an approach up steps to the stage, or on the level of the stage itself, is not certain.

Figure 4 shows the development of the appearance of the original walls planted on the inner sides of the three principal pairs of posts. Of this some explanation must be given.

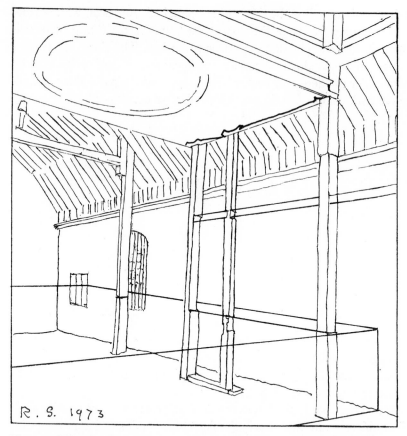

R. S. 1973

Figure 3 View showing posts and underside of ceiling, indicating in thicker line the signs of the pilaster capitals

In the remains of the ceiling decoration, at the two ends adjacent to the posts, the paint does not quite reach the limits of the plaster, but leaves a strip 2 inches or more wide, stretching from post A to post C (see Figure 3). Two particular features mark this strip. First, its edge between posts A and B is exactly parallel with the side of the ceiling, but between posts B and C its edge is raked slightly inwards until at post C it is some 5 inches wide. Second, above the posts themselves in each case, an apparently irregular patch breaks the strip, running into the field of the ceiling. These unpainted patches correspond exactly in shape with the plan-shape of the top of a pilaster capital of the Corinthian type. It is practically certain, therefore, that these posts were originally faced with just such pilasters as those lining

Figure 4 Reconstruction of the appearance of the original proscenium unit
(compare with Figure 5 and Plate 8a)

the sides of the proscenium walls in Wren's sectional drawing of a playhouse,
or those on the proscenium sides of his Dorset Garden Theatre.[1]

Suppose that these three pilasters are back in position. There would be,
between the two at A and B, a wide space, in which, as the ceiling-signs
above it show, there had once been some sort of partition running squarely
up-and-down-stage; and between the two pilasters at B and C a narrower
space, which had similarly contained some sort of partition but now running
not exactly up-and-down-stage, but slightly raked inwards towards the back.
Since the two spaces are very different in width and even slightly different
in angle, they probably originally contained different kinds of element; one

[1] Cf. Vol. V of *The Revels History of Drama in English, Part II* (1).

of these would pretty certainly have been an entrance door and it would have taken its place naturally in the narrower, upstage space, and would have been set at the slight angle partly for better display and partly to give some vestige of the traditional perspective effect.

As for the element in the wider space; we know from Colley Cibber[1] that Wren's original Drury Lane proscenium had had two doors of entrance removed about 1700, and their space converted into stage boxes (a new door being added upstage of these). A stage box is, then, likely to have occupied the wider space in the King's Lynn proscenium.

We can therefore provide, with some confidence, a door in the narrow space between pilasters B and C, and a proscenium box, or stage box, between pilasters A and B. Some verification for both was found in the signs remaining on the posts.

We turn to the traces of moulding, already mentioned, which can still be discerned along the vertical fascia above the front of the ceiling, and ask what they signify. Two remarkably fortunate pieces of evidence came to help here. First, a photograph in the records of a previous owner of the hall (reproduced in the *Industrial World*, October 1932) showed that formerly the simple mouldings had been surmounted by a row of dentils, since fallen away. The second was the discovery of a drawing from a still earlier date, in the King's Lynn Museum, where not only the mouldings and the row of dentils were indicated but also the fact that above them there had been a plastered cove, sweeping up to a flat ceiling over the pit.

Returning now to the gutted hall. It was possible to find, still fixed to the original timbers of the roof, a few of the curved, eighteenth-century, wooden 'formers' that had served to shape this cove, and to note that they had been present on either side of the hall in two lines, running from the proscenium to a certain point over the auditorium. Further examination showed that, beside these formers, the downward-facing surfaces of the roof timbers bore, in certain areas, many signs of nailheads and laths, and in other areas, no such traces. From this could be read (1) the extent of a certain section of the auditorium ceiling that had been flat, and flanked at the stage end and the two sides by a cove and moulding, and (2) another section, more distant from the stage than the first, that had been undecorated at the sides, and had sloped up instead of being horizontal. From these two sections it was possible to estimate the areas of, first, the pit and, second, the gallery.

A further hint about the shape of the auditorium remained in traces of whitewash on the roof timbers. They suggest that the two side boxes most

[1] Colley Cibber, *An Apology for his Life*, Chapter 12 (Everyman's Library ed., p. 212).

distant from the stage were not in line with the other side boxes but turned in, diagonally, to cross the corner and meet the centre box at the back. Curiously enough, this would give us an auditorium with seven boxes and might thus illustrate that otherwise rather puzzling number of seven boxes which Brunet gave in his description of the interior of Dorset Garden in 1676.[1]

Finally, to the above information may be added the fact that in a Georgian theatre the auditorium side boxes ran round at the same level as the stage box, while above them there might be either another tier of boxes with the gallery above that or, in a small theatre, only the open gallery itself, extending unpartitioned down the sides of the house over the side boxes, in what was termed 'the slips'. It is pretty certain that here the Georgian builders, confined as they were by the roof of the medieval hall, could not have erected an auditorium three storeys high; and thus the arrangement shown in the figure can with some confidence be offered as a probable impression of the original theatre.

One remark is worth adding to the statement above that Georgian side boxes were on a level with the stage box. There was a reason for this. In those days theatrical entertainment in an ordinary town was not continuous; it went by seasons, and during the off-seasons the theatre building might, for economical reasons, have to be turned to other uses. One such use would be to house dances, routs and balls. This *dual purpose* in the function of a theatre building is not entirely unknown to us today; but instead of building, as we do now, a hall with a flat floor for dancing and adding to it seats and a stage to make a theatre, the Georgians were more civilized and gave precedence the other way; that is, they built a proper theatre but in such a manner that a line in the architecture always ran round the auditorium at the level of the stage. No feature of the theatre above was allowed to drop below this line, and no feature of the pit below was allowed to project above it. Thus it became possible to *floor over the pit* on occasion and create one large dancing surface continuous with the surface of the stage, and admirably flanked with places for viewing and sitting out (compare Plate 14a). So it is that one can presume the side boxes of the King's Lynn playhouse were built level with the box reconstructed on the stage.

In neither of the two surviving Georgian theatres, at Bristol or at Richmond, can the proscenium element be seen in the same integrity as at King's Lynn; here there had actually been that essential acting area which the Restoration theatre men had developed out of the *proscaenium* of the Elizabethans – that transparent 'hall', giving off from the auditorium, continuous

[1] Vol. V, Part II (1).

with it and embraced by it, where the action of the show took place. At Lynn there was lacking the height of Davenant's Dorset Garden where the proscenium sides were tall enough to include, over the balconies, a third storey of an attic character, in which tapestries appear to have hung and which was level with the music room over the stage. But Lynn was probably closely like Wren's Drury Lane, save that it embodied one development (or regression) – its lower door is lost and instead the stage box has been born.

(ii) Scenery in the late eighteenth century

It is probably because the proscenium element at King's Lynn was so complete and self-sufficient that the rest of the remains were disappointingly negative so far as concerns information about scenery or machinery. It seems most likely that there was some kind of groove-and-shutter system, perhaps like that in the Lincoln's Inn Fields tennis court theatre for Davenant's *Siege of Rhodes*.[1] As for the scenery, we may suppose that the majority of shows would have been set from stock. Stock scenery was natural in any system that necessitated touring but employed only primitive transport. A circuit company travelling by cart, or at worst on foot, on eighteenth-century roads could not burden itself with special scenery. And since at that date the individual setting of a scene in a play did not exact that particular consideration it receives today (among other reasons because it was so much less conspicuous under the dim candle-lighting), so it would pay the manager of a circuit to furnish each of his theatres with its own stock of most gener-ally useful scenes. These would not need to be very various – a Temple, a Tomb, a City Wall with a gate, a Palace Exterior, a Palace Interior, a Street Scene, a Chamber Scene, a Prison, a Garden and some rural prospects of Woods, etc. These were all that were specified in a typical list published in 1758 in a pamphlet entitled *The Case of the Stage in Ireland*. And the attitude of the time is emphasized by an observation added to the list that such scenes should be painted by a master scenic artist if one could be found, but 'otherwise they should be as simple and unaffected as possible to avoid offending a judicious eye. If for some particular purpose, any other scene is necessary, it can be got up occasionally.'

It was the mark of a manager of exceptional quality to retain, as for instance Garrick did, a scene-painter to decorate particular shows, like Philip James de Loutherbourg (1740–1812), or as Kemble did in William Capon (1757–1827). Some of de Loutherbourg's scenic models survive today (at, for

[1] Vol. V, Part II (1).

instance, the Victoria and Albert Museum in London) and they show a very accomplished facility in romantic landscape painting. Particularly does his work show a courageous attempt to break away from the rigid, repeated wings, and to incorporate the irregular shapes of cut scenes and high groundrows.

Capon was one of the first to make detailed studies of past styles of architecture and to combine them in settings for revivals of historical plays that pretend to some specific attempt at a sense of period. Boaden, in his *Life of J. P. Kemble* (1825), especially notes that for the Drury Lane of 1799 'Capon painted a very unusual pile of scenery, representing a church of the fourteenth century with its nave, choir and side aisles, magnificently decorated; consisting of seven planes in succession. In width this extraordinary elevation was about 56 feet, 52 in depth and 37 feet in height. It was positively a building.' The reference to the 'seven planes' is interesting as an example of how far the 'relief scene' of Inigo Jones had developed in the course of a century and a half.

(iii) The machinery of an eighteenth-century stage

It seems that in the last quarter of the eighteenth century the techniques of theatrical staging had at length reached a sort of temporary stability. The planning of theatres had become regularized, so that not only had almost every small town in England acquired a theatre for itself, but almost all these theatres, from Yorkshire to Cornwall, were of like dimensions and similar structural pattern.

But, since artists in any medium arise unaccountably and not simply because there are opportunities for them, so the increase in the number of theatres unfortunately did not lead to an equal increase in the number of highly inventive and dedicated managers to follow in the footsteps of a Davenant or compete with a David Garrick, and the amount of slipshod and makeshift setting soon became a target for general criticism. But before turning to see something of this criticism, it will be useful to look at the two surviving theatres of the eighteenth century, each of which presents a different aspect of the times.

The Theatre Royal, Bristol, preserves (though in a form that has suffered mutilation in Victorian and modern days) the character and main dimensions of Wren's Drury Lane. It was thus unusual for its size among provincial theatres, as befits a town of Bristol's relatively large population (see Figure 5 and Plate 8a). It still shows today two pairs of the 'great pilasters' that Wren

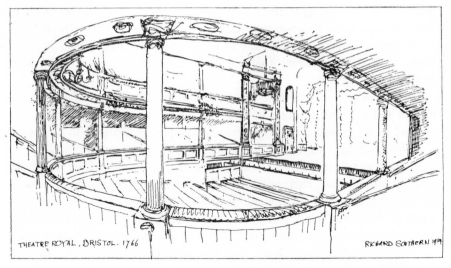

THEATRE ROYAL, BRISTOL. 1766

RICHARD SOUTHERN 1971

Figure 5 Sketch reconstruction of the probable appearance of the original Theatre Royal, Bristol, showing fore-stage (compare with Plate 8a)

lined his proscenium sides with, but its fore-stage is now cut back from in front of the nearer of the two pilasters (where a sign of the original edge of the stage can still be seen) to behind the farther pilaster, and the proscenium doors are now blocked. The ceiling has been raised, the gallery extended and much Victorian plaster decoration added to the fronts of the boxes, underneath which there still exists, concealed entirely from sight, very simple but dignified Georgian panelling with gilded mouldings.

The Bristol Theatre Royal till recently possessed a nearly unique collection of stage machinery, though it has now been done away with as a hindrance to modern productions. The system was almost exclusively concerned with visible scene change, that is, transformation under the eyes of the audience. This, in the eighteenth century, meant that every single scenic piece on the stage had to be connected with a machine of some sort to enable its changing to take place without visible human assistance; everything had to move apparently of its own accord, simultaneously and as nearly as possible instantaneously. The main part of every Georgian stage was equipped for this purpose and for this purpose alone; it was not equipped to aid the actor in his relation to the audience, for the very good reason that the Georgian actor (or at least his Restoration forebears) did not use the 'main' stage; he used the fore-stage, and from thence his relation with the audience was already assured and his job was merely to make the most of it. What we now call the 'stage proper' behind the actor had no other function originally than to facilitate transformation of scenery.

But as the Georgian period developed and the fore-stage dwindled, entrances 'within the scene' became more frequent; verisimilitude in interior furnishing and in behaviour became more admired (just as classic perspective splendour had formerly been admired), and the complication in scenic elements grew so great that ultimately the whole system of visible scene change was to break down because of the sheer impossibility of supplying machinery capable of handling it without concealment – or unless such gigantic and spectacular equipment was installed as outweighed the dramatic action of the play. But that comes later. The Georgian scenic system was an excellent one, but only for the Georgian production of a play.

Though no two stages were necessarily planned exactly alike, the machinery of an English stage of this period can be described generally as follows.

The stage floor behind the curtain may be divided into two areas. In each the actual floorboarding, as distinct from the joists underneath, was almost entirely removable to allow of various effects; and sometimes even parts of the joists themselves were made to lift out. The area in front contained *traps* and the area behind *cuts* (Figure 6). A trap is a squarish opening, varying from about 2 feet by 2 feet to about 6 feet by 3 feet according to its purpose. A cut is some 30 feet long, varying from some 4 inches wide to 3 feet wide, and running normally right across the acting area. The traps were chiefly intended for an actor to rise or sink through; the narrow cuts were for certain elements of scenery to rise or sink through, and the wide cuts for both scenery and grouped tableaux of actors together. The method of opening either a trap or a cut was to drop the floorboards normally covering it and slide them away under the adjacent floor. To allow this, every portion of the stage floor covering an opening had to be provided with a system of sloping grooves cut in the joists beneath it, and an arrangement of levers by which the floorboard could be dropped just below stage level for withdrawal, or raised back to stage level upon closure (see Figure 7).

Generally, the plan of a stage included two 'corner' traps at the front; then behind those a central rectangular 'grave' trap; behind again possibly two further corner traps. Additionally there might be a larger square central trap farther back, called a 'cauldron' trap, traditionally associated with *Macbeth* as the grave trap was associated with *Hamlet*. This completed the front area of the stage.

A further type of trap may conveniently be mentioned here, though it was a type that was usually built into a piece of scenery, not into the structure

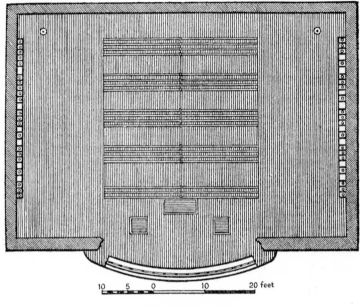

PLAN OF STAGE FLOOR

Figure 6 A typical stage floor (above), with the joists beneath (opposite), showing three traps near the front and four sets of 'cuts' behind

of the stage. It was called the 'vamp' trap. Its name is derived from a device first used in the melodrama called *The Vampire; or, the Bride of the Isles*, written by J. R. Planché and produced at the English Opera House (later the Lyceum) in 1820. The vamp trap consisted of a rectangular opening cut and framed in the particular piece of the scenery, and filled in with two vertical flaps, spring-hinged like a double door, so that the actor could quickly push through between them and leave them to swing immediately into place again, giving the effect of his walking through a solid wall.

Behind the stage traps came a succession of narrow cuts and wide cuts. A typical arrangement in a medium-sized theatre might be two narrow cuts and one wide cut, repeated twice again behind.

Though the above is a typical arrangement for a medium-sized stage it already includes fifteen openings, all of which had to be associated with their slider mechanisms below, for working the openings. The slider mechanism in every single instance had to include the means for dropping the trap door, sliding it aside, sliding it back, raising it again to its orginal position and holding it firmly when in place. Not only this, but beneath each opening

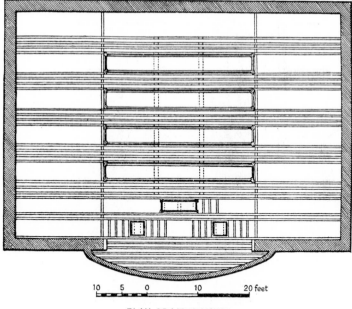

10   5   0   10   20 feet

PLAN OF MEZZANINE

there had to be the additional mechanism essential to the working of the theatrical effect that the opening was planned to accommodate.

This was usually a lifting and lowering device. Beneath a corner trap it would be a small platform just big enough to raise the standing figure of an actor. Such a platform might be worked fairly slowly by a winch; but frequently the appearance of the actor had to be instantaneous, or such that he seemed to shoot through the stage (Plate 12). Then the platform had to be precisely counterweighted and the trap opening fitted for the occasion with a special covering, for example the 'star' trap, and the actor had to be a highly trained specialist, preferably one of a family hereditarily accustomed to this dangerous work. A star trap was a special 'door' fitted in and containing a circular opening with a number of triangular segments all hinged to fly up from pressure below and return to place the instant the figure had shot through. A typical problem facing the carpenter with a star trap was how to deal with the impact of the heavily counterweighted platform as it shot up and reached the level of the stage; one ingenious solution to this problem was to make the counterweight out of a succession of iron balls vertically

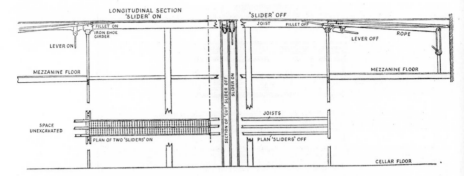

Figure 7 Diagram illustrating the working of the 'sliders' by means of which the cuts in the stage could be opened

linked together. This chain of balls descended as the trap rose, and at a given moment the lowest ball reached a bed or stop-level below; an instant later the next ball, then the next, until in a fraction of a second, the trap being now at the limit of its ascent, all counterweight balls had come to rest on the bed below, and were no longer exerting their pull on the platform. There remained one further necessity: to lock the trap instantaneously in its position at stage level, or alternatively to insure that the actor, at the limit of his leap upwards, so controlled himself that he did not descend again on the platform of the trap, but on the firm floor to one side of it.

The grave trap was far simpler in use, and merely needed to offer a player some firm bed to step down on. But the arrangement beneath a narrow cut was again very complicated. Here, some three or four upright posts had to be arranged in the stage basement beneath the upstage side of the cut. These posts were hollow, and in the face of each an open slit ran down from top to bottom. In the hollow interior of the post a vertical timber was fitted to slide up and down, with a rope attached to the bottom end running up in a groove within the post and over a pulley in the side. On pulling the rope, the 'tongue' rose up out of its slot something like the tray sliding out of a matchbox held end-up. This arrangement was called a *sloat* or *slote*. When three or four such sloats were positioned under a cut, a scenic groundrow could be fixed across, attached to the moving piece in each sloat; if the ropes actuating the tongues were all carried to one winch, the turning of the handle would raise the groundrow steadily up through the stage floor into position in the scene above. The lower portions of transformation scenes were usually worked in this way.

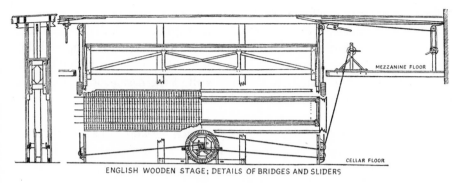

ENGLISH WOODEN STAGE; DETAILS OF BRIDGES AND SLIDERS

Figure 8 Diagram illustrating the working of a 'bridge' below the slider cuts

Under the wider cuts the system was even more involved. What had now to be raised was a platform (called a 'bridge') of considerable length and weight, bearing not only scenery but possibly rostrums and a tableau of grouped actors (see Figure 8). The long platform had to be understrutted to keep it from sagging, accommodated between four corner posts, counter-weighted and connected with a winch mechanism sufficiently powerful to enable the whole weight to be handled. This mechanism usually involved use of the *drum and shaft* system (see lower part of Figure 8). In this, a number of ropes could be wound round a longish cylinder of relatively small diameter called the shaft. Built into the shaft at some convenient point was a much shorter cylinder of considerably greater diameter called the drum, round which a master working-line could be wound in the opposite direction to the first group of ropes, and then led to the actuating winch. On turning the winch, the drum acts as a lever, rotates the shaft and winds all the ropes on or off. At any point on the shaft a rope wound in the opposite direction could be led to a counterweight to ease the load.

When, in addition to all the above, it is remembered that the stage floor itself had to be rigidly enough supported, by a still further system of posts, to stand the weight of mass dancing or, if called upon, of a procession in-cluding elephants, it will be realized that in the basement, or *mezzanine*, of an eighteenth-century stage there was a pretty complicated forest of timbers. To top all the problems was the fact that, although any post could be held in its upright position by side bracing, it could *not* be supported in the forward–backward direction, since any permanent brace for that purpose would cut across the path of the traps and prevent their use. But the stage floor above was itself not level; it raked, or sloped down, towards the audience. It thus tended in time to creep forwards and pull all the supporting posts gradually out of true. To prevent this, every vertical support below the stage had to be kept upright by a removable iron hook linking it to the one behind, and ultimately to the back wall of the basement. These hooks could be dropped when a cut had to be used, and replaced when the cut was finished with.

To turn now from the basement to the machinery on and above the stage itself. Here a condition operated which had very considerable effect on the history of eighteenth-century scenery; the situation needs to be visualized in some detail.

The flat scenes of the Jacobean masque had worked in grooves grouped all together near the back of the stage and behind the last pair of wings. At some date (probably quite early) in the Restoration public theatre, not only could flat scenes be worked near the back of the stage but a few pairs could be run across nearer the front, that is to say between the second and third pairs of wings, or even immediately behind the first pair.

This possibility of closing in a flat scene at other parts of the stage than the back was dramatically an advantage, and made possible variations from deep to shallow scenes, as well as increasing the facilities for discoveries, but it did involve an additional obstacle because the big grooved timbers holding the flats had now to cross the stage (both at floor level and above) at several points, instead of at one point only at the back. And since the space between the front pair of wings was substantially greater than the space between the back pair, the front upper grooves had to be longer and more cumbersome than the back had been, and they suffered greater risk of sagging in the centre. In addition, their presence downstage would ruin the appearance of any scene with arched borders by cutting across the opening of the arch.

But of even greater practical importance were two problems caused by the lower grooves on the floor when they were used downstage. The first was that they had to be most carefully related in position to the slider openings or they would encroach upon them or cover them – and a typical lower groove was likely to be as much as 18 inches wide. Secondly, since such groove-timbers had to be at least $1\frac{1}{2}$ inches thick, it followed that any actor walking forward from the back of the stage had to pick his way over three, or more, obstacles like railway sleepers in his path. Such a situation was likely soon to be found intolerable.

The solution was to do away with the centre parts of all the flat grooves,

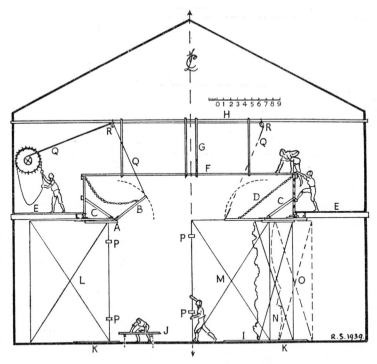

Figure 9 Diagram of the working of flats and wings in grooves. The black
shape at A represents the discovered groove-part shown in Figure 10

leaving the closed flats supported only by their offstage halves. Now, of
course, a gap was visible under the joined flats in the interval between the
left and right grooves. Moreover, the remnants of the grooves still projected:
those below into the sides of the acting area, and those above into the space
in the borders. The next step, then, was to make the visible remnants of the
lower flat-grooves temporarily removable, and only to resort to them when
they were needed (see J, Figure 9), and to hinge the projecting arms of the
upper grooves so that they could be pulled up like a row of drawbridges
when arched borders were used (see B and D, Figure 9). Both these jugglings
had to be capable of being worked under the eyes of the audience, and
worked so accurately that the smooth sliding of the flats was in no way
affected. All these disadvantages were patiently borne with at first. We even
read that, as late as 1845–50, a lower groove might have to be pushed in
from between the wings at the side of the stage, furnished with a wooden

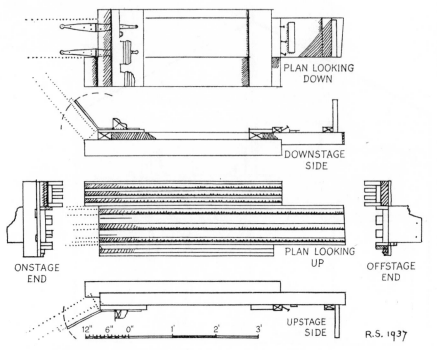

PLAN LOOKING
DOWN

DOWNSTAGE
SIDE

ONSTAGE
END

PLAN LOOKING
UP

OFFSTAGE
END

12" 6" 0"   1'   2'   3'

UPSTAGE
SIDE

R.S. 1937

Figure 10 Measured drawing of the surviving 'fixed' part of one set of grooves
discovered at the Theatre Royal, Bristol

pin at either end which could be dropped into a couple of square holes in
the stage floor to keep the groove steady.[1]

Above the stage, running along either side wall, was a gallery called the
fly floor (E, Figure 9). To the underside of this gallery the fixed part of the
upper grooves (see Figure 10) was braced, and to the rail of this gallery the
hinged parts of the upper flat-grooves were linked by check-chains so as to
prevent their dropping below the horizontal, and thus fouling the movement
of the flats. Both the 'flopping over' of these groove-arms in use, and the clank
of the chains that checked them are remarked on by contemporary writers.[2]

Between the fly rails on either side stretched a series of *catwalks* (F,
Figure 9), along which fly-men could creep out to free any details of the
complex which caught and jammed. Sometimes the fly floors also accommodated a number of long shafts, to one of which all the sky borders were
rigged, to another all the arch borders, to a third all the beam borders, and

[1] See the Ipswich manuscript referred to on p. 83.
[2] e.g., *Magazine of Art*, volume for 1889, p. 94.

so on. Thus any set of borders could be taken up, and another dropped in, in no more than a few seconds.

Fairly close above the fly floor (probably about 30 feet above the stage) was the *grid* (H, Figure 9), stretching over the whole acting area and carrying the suspension pulleys for the hanging lines. The lines were tied off at cleats on the fly-rail or led to shafts. The grid was never high enough in an eighteenth-century theatre to permit the flying of a complete backcloth without folding or 'tumbling'. Indeed cloths were rarely used at first because no way of getting rid of them was practicable without the use of relatively cumbersome rollers.

Above the grid were the drums and shafts for working the lines to the cloud machines below. The actors made their way out to such cloud machines by walking along the catwalks from the fly floor.

The detailed working of the groove system, with some review of its history, is described in the present writer's *Changeable Scenery* (1952). It is worth adding that since that account was published a few other actual examples of grooves have been found. One such is especially interesting not only in confirming that grooves were used in America, but because four groove units were actually discovered in position in the theatre. The theatre was the old Eagle Opera House in Marshall, Michigan, opened in 1868. The find consisted (see Plates 4a, 4b, 5a and 5b) of two pairs of groove units; one pair at the back of the stage and one pair at the front. The evidence shows that there had originally been four pairs on this stage (two pairs are now lost). The stage itself was 23 feet 9 inches deep; the proscenium opening was 27 feet 6 inches wide and some 12 feet to 15 feet high.

The upstage pair of groove sets contained four fixed grooves, 7 feet long, for wings, and immediately behind four similar grooves but with hinged 5-feet extensions for flats. The downstage sets had two 7-feet wing grooves and four grooves with 5-feet hinged extensions. The height above the stage floor of the downstage set was 11 feet. These grooves have now been removed and preserved.

(iv) The Georgian theatre at Richmond, Yorkshire

The second surviving provincial theatre, the Georgian Theatre at Richmond, Yorkshire, shows its original 1788 features almost perfectly. By mere chance in the decisions of the local council, it survived with only one major alteration: its pit was floored over about 1850 and the whole structure below the floor, throughout the building, was removed without disturbing the stage and auditorium above (which is something of a tribute to the skill of the local craftsmen at that time), and replaced by a vaulted wine cellar. This was removed after the Second World War, again without disturbing the stage and auditorium above (this also was done purely with local labour and is an equal tribute to the craftsmen, and town clerk, of the time). And, with the aid of a local trust, by 1962 the pit, the pit passages, the understage space, the two dressing rooms and incidentally the whole of the interior decoration were restored according to the signs surviving in the original fabric, and the theatre was made suitable for performances once again (Plate 3a).

This theatre, besides affording a unique opportunity to savour the atmosphere of a small British theatre of 1788, illustrates a particular development of the auditorium characteristic of the period: namely, that the fore-stage is now cut back so that the stage stops only an inch or two in front of the proscenium doors (Plate 3b).

A very significant change in the development of the technique of theatrical presentation is reflected in this shrinking of the fore-stage at Richmond. In the first place it is apparent that the actor is beginning to have a different relation with the scenery: he is henceforward to make fuller use of entrances 'within the scene' which formerly had been rare. But, in the second place, what is perhaps less immediately evident from the above is that in the sweep of progress the final link with the technique of Elizabethan fore-stage acting – or 'proscaenium' acting – is now almost entirely broken. Theatre architecture has kept step with this progress. The actor is beginning to be part of a unified picture – one may say, as one watches it happening, of an *illusionistic* picture. No longer does he enter a playhouse fore-stage and act against a dim scenic background that occasionally opens or closes in the intervals of his action, but he now enters a woodland grove from between the trees at the side, or enters a room from another room just beyond. In short, there is now an implication that he enters not from our theatre but from a hidden extension of the scene, and that the scene is thus part of a larger world extending like ours beyond the walls of the playhouse.

Improvements in lighting during the later decades of the eighteenth century help this impression. Oil burners come to replace candles and thus the details of the scene-painting become less obscure.

A concrete example of this general tendency is found in a play written for the circuit to which Richmond belonged. It was *The Lady's Dream* by George Jefferson, presented at Harrogate in September 1822. The printed edition contains a specific 'Explanation' of stage directions wherein we read that RH signifies Right Hand; LH, Left Hand; SE, Second Entrance; UE,

Upper Entrance; RHD, Right Hand Door; and LHD, Left Hand Door. But 'doors' are no longer the principal means of coming on to the stage – 'entrances' (that is the spaces between wings) are equally, or more, important. There are four scenes in this play which deserve our particular notice. The first is an exterior, 'A Grove'. The second is a room in a house with a character discovered at breakfast. The third is another 'Apartment' in the same house. The fourth is again an exterior, 'A Public Road with a view of Hambiton Hills in the distance'.

In the first scene all entrances are marked simply LH or RH: therefore no character enters this exterior by the proscenium doors. The logic of illusion is beginning to work.

In the second scene, despite the fact that it is on the contrary an interior, all entrances are still marked LH or RH. But it is to be especially noticed that no character in this scene enters *as from the outside world*; all come in from neighbouring rooms in the same house. All are members of the household.

But in the third scene, although it is again an interior and simply another room in the same house, we have a notable change. Now, certain characters do enter who are not members of the household, but visiting, and coming from the outside streets (one imagines them in hats and cloaks). All these characters are specifically directed to use the doors, to enter LHD or exit RHD. Yet there is one particular exit in this scene that is differently treated: on a certain occasion one of the characters says, 'Show the gentleman down the back stairs, Lucy'. And the direction follows, '*Exeunt* Lucy *and* Flash R.H.U.E.'. They do *not* go to the street; therefore they do not make use of the entrance doors by which they came into the house, but go out instead through the Right Hand Upper Entrance, or the entrance between the right-hand upper wing and the back-scene. Apart from the exit described above, all the 'normal' entrances and exits in the third scene of *The Lady's Dream* are by the doors.

In the last scene, again an exterior, no reference to doors is found at all; all entrances are marked RHUE or RHSE.

What is happening, among other things, is that the Romantic movement is beginning to have effect. The romance of a figure strolling into a grove between the profiles of trees, or entering a chamber between pensive columns, all now a little more clearly lit than before, and with the shadows perhaps a little more effectively painted, is beginning to appeal. The actor is, at this moment, a sleekly costumed figure in a romantic world of illusion, not any longer a motley fellow coming in on occasion to a platform in one's own normal, social world.

(v) Regency and early Victorian

If word labels are of any use we may call this transition a transition from the 'Georgian' to the 'Regency' (soon to move on again to the 'early Victorian'). The distinction is in this instance not un-useful for it gives us a name for certain very considerable developments in theatre arrangement that can be called *Regency*.

One of these was a move to reform the Georgian auditorium by abolishing the very characteristic rows of boxes that distinguished it. Another was the sudden increase in theatre buildings of the new form that took place in London in the 1830s. To take the abolition of the boxes first:

The pioneer theatre in this respect was the Sans Pareil (later the Adelphi) in the Strand, opened in 1806. A very clear illustration of the effect of the change is offered in a print published about a decade later (see Plate 17). The innovation is the extension of the width of the pit. In a Georgian theatre the pit had been very securely nested in the embrace of the first tier of boxes (see Plates 3a, 7a, 8b, 13b and 14b), so closely that an occupant of the pit was able to stand up and converse intimately with the occupant of a box; this conformation had still obtained at Richmond in 1788, and later. But to extend the pit meant abolishing the boxes and replacing them by an open, overhead 'circle' or gallery. The change was apparently motivated by a desire to increase the revenue from pit takings. For a decade or so an uncertainty seems to have ruled about the change, but it was to become accepted (Plates 9b and 15b).

Coupled with this change was a very considerable increase in the rate of new theatre building in London. Taking the period of this chapter in decades, we find that no new theatres were built in the 1750s; in the sixties, the seventies and the eighties there were two in each decade; in the 1800s three; in the 1810s one; in the twenties three. And – and this is the point of making this list – in the 1830s there were no less than fourteen new theatres opened in London. The forties and fifties saw three and two respectively, the sixties seven and the seventies eleven. There occurred, then, a tremendous surge in theatre building in the 1830s, outnumbering any other decade in the period under consideration. There were certain social and legal reasons for this which do not especially concern a history of staging, but the very fact of this sudden and unprecedented increase in the thirties does affect the history and does indicate that the innovations of Charles Kean, Samuel Phelps and others came at a moment when a burst of expansion had affected the whole London scene. Curiously enough, in the provinces, the

1820s, 1830s and 1840s had seen a decline in the prosperity of the many theatres that had sprung up all over the land in the preceding half century. But these had been Georgian theatres of the 'perfected' type that the Restoration had been leading up to. The London theatres of the 1820s and particularly the 1830s were of a different type with different techniques available to them, and different aims in the complex relationships between the actor, the spectacle and the audience. There remains to us a document from one particular provincial theatre that gives some opportunity to understand the strains of transition that theatrical presentation was suffering over this period. It is worth a brief review before going on to follow the pursuit of scenic illusion.

The document is a richly illustrated manuscript scrapbook (now in the Ipswich Public Library) made by the manager of the Theatre Royal at Ipswich, in which he records the history of the building from its erection in 1803 to its abandonment in 1890, a period reaching only just outside the limits of this chapter.[1]

The Theatre Royal, Tacket Street, Ipswich, was built very much on the same lines as the Richmond Theatre had been in 1788 (Plate 6a). It had some improvements: the house was wider, some 40 feet as against Richmond's 24 feet. In length the auditorium was some 42 feet from stage-front to back of boxes, as against Richmond's 26 feet. It had seventeen boxes in the first tier as against Richmond's eleven. But its stage was at first 27 feet deep, like Richmond's. The chief difference was that, while the layout of Richmond's auditorium had been strictly rectangular with four boxes either side and three across the back, that at Ipswich had five boxes on the sides, but facing the stage a sweeping curve of seven boxes with their fronts on the chords of a semicircle. In short, a move towards a house with a shallower stage in proportion to the auditorium.

This beginning proved unsatisfactory. In 1815 the plan of the house was altered (Plate 6b): two boxes on either side were done away with, and the stage extended to become 30 feet deep; the proscenium opening widened to 21 feet.

The method of widening the proscenium opening brings to attention a particularly characteristic feature of the Regency auditorium. In Georgian theatres the side boxes had run straight and unbroken to the proscenium door; the consequence of widening the space between the two doors meant, of course, that in effect each of these two stage boxes seemed now to project into the proscenium opening. The characteristic feature was to round off

[1] *Architectural Review* (August 1946), p. 41.

the square corner of each stage box in a sweep towards the side wall of the theatre, so that the box was now open not only towards the pit, but also towards the stage (see Plate 7a). This allowed the proscenium opening to be widened by a matter of some 8 feet. Furthermore, the proscenium doors, now drawn back in their new positions, might now be set directly up-and-down-stage instead of on the splay, so adding some further inches to the opening. This curved stage-corner to the front box is never seen until the nineteenth century and it adds to the growing sense of separation between auditorium and scene. It makes the auditorium a sort of fenced viewing place from which to look out at the stage, instead of a room into which the players come to bring their entertainment to you.

In consequence of these changes the manager at Ipswich was able to claim, in the scrapbook noted above, that the 'Theatre has been greatly improved, in consequence of a judicious alteration more room is gained to Senic [*sic*] representations and an excellent view of the stage is afforded from every part of the boxes'.

A quite remarkable detail of this early stage was the wing machinery. Up to 1857 there had been four changes of wings available, Palace Interior, Wood, Cottage Interior and Rock. These wings, the manuscript informs us rather cryptically, 'had four on each barrel'. It goes on to say that the wings 'were worked by means of a spindle passing through the stage[;] at the end was a grooved wheel around which passed a rope connected with another wheel situated on the prompt side of the stage, so when a scene required changing a man had only to turn the wheel changing the whole number at once'. Whatever this implies, it was 'converted into the modern style' in 1857. This modern style is a variant of the normal groove system.

With further regard to wings, we learn something that settles a possible doubt. At Ipswich proscenium wings, typically painted to represent crimson draperies, were used in front of the scenic wings. A plan shows these as a pair of separate 'book-wings' behind the proscenium opening, serving to mask the sides very efficiently. Since they were 'booked' (that is, hinged up the centre), they could be stood on their own, like a part-open book on end, and consequently did not need grooves. They remained for all scenes. Behind them the first wing-grooves were set some 12 feet back from the front of the stage; behind these again came three other sets of wing-grooves. Flats could be run on behind either the first, the second or the third wing-grooves.

In 1858 the two upstage corner traps were taken out and in their place was built a special 'Corsican' trap (of which more, in a later part of this section, see pp. 89–90). Eighteen years later two particularly important developments took place. They are recorded as follows: until 1876 the stage 'did not have properly constructed "flies", but in this year they were put in by a stage carpenter from the Adelphi Theatre London who also put in "gas Battens" with coloured "mediums" for moonlight and other effects'. It is significant to find that these 'properly constructed flies' do not by any means imply what we would understand by full flying space: in fact the words possibly meant only a better system of suspension pulleys, for in 1884 other alterations were made which 'enabled the "borders" to be drawn up higher'.

Returning now to 1877, we find two other indications of progress: first, that the Corsican trap was no longer needed and so was done away with and its mechanism removed from the stage cellar; second, that the boxes and pit were reseated with 'backed seats' as opposed to the earlier benches. Then in 1883 the gallery was reseated and 'brought out 18 inches over the upper boxes, the floor of the back part of the gallery being raised 2 feet giving a better rake to the seats'.

All these notes are vivid indications of the cares accumulating on the shoulders of the manager of a provincial theatre in the nineteenth century, and reflect the need for constant attempts at improvement and keeping up to date. But the theatre at Ipswich was fundamentally of late Georgian type, and this character lay deep in its bones. It could never aspire to the genuine, early Victorian airiness of the widened pit.

Yet it tried. In 1887 the manager removed all the lower side boxes (Plates 7b and 7c), retaining only the five facing the stage, and supported the tier above on iron columns, so that the theatre gives, as a contemporary photograph of the interior shows, a rather pathetic air of doing its best – but ineffectually – to keep up with the times.

In 1888 came the most ambitious step of all so far as scene handling was concerned. The stage 'roof was taken off, the walls carried up 10 ft. higher and a high pitched "mansard" roof instead of the old "hip" form put on which with the new "flies" and "grid" floor made the stage one of the best in the provinces the scenes being made 16 ft. high'.

Of these scenes (a few of which could now, because of the improved flying system, be *drops* instead of flats) we have some record in coloured replicas inserted in the scrapbook. They 'did duty for any ordinary pieces', and included a Palace Arch and backing a two-door Flat, a Cottage Flat, a Prison Flat, a Front Wood, Front Chamber, Front Street, Back Wood, Back Street, Horizon and so forth.

But all this effort was unavailing to make a really Georgian playhouse into a truly Victorian theatre; and in 1890 the Ipswich Theatre Royal had to be closed, to give in to a modern competitor.

Scenery continued to be a problem throughout this whole period. We may see the sort of thing that destroyed the 'illusion' if we go back a few years, when in 1844 an amusing and instructive letter appeared in a paper called the *Great Gun* (No. 7, 28 December). In it a correspondent signing himself 'David Groove' wrote:

> I am by profession a scene-shifter . . . . A few evenings ago . . . the two halves of a scene, from mere perverseness, refused to come into that close contact which is requisite for a perfectly good effect. In short, sir, I and my colleague on the opposite side produced this sort of thing:-

Figure 11

> . . . we drew the two halves off, and dashed them on again, hoping thus to attain the wished-for junction, and produced this effect:-

Figure 12

. . . Again, sir, did my colleague and I draw off the 'pair of flats' and, as I thought, we at last brought them together close as wax. What was my horror when I discovered that I had, in my tremor, exchanged one scene for another, and that this effect was the consequence :-

Figure 13

There is plenty of evidence to show that this joke was no extravagant flight of fancy but a dry comment on a situation that was of not infrequent occurrence.

Even in the epoch-making productions of Charles Kean at the Princess's Theatre a year or two later, the system of scenery was physically the same, and open to similar objections to those exposed in the above letter. But these Kean productions call our attention at the moment for another reason.

Kean's productions at the Princess's between 1850 and 1859 became notable in the history of presentation for several reasons. They came at a time when a still better source of lighting had been recently made available to the theatre – coal gas. They are the first body of productions of which a very considerable coloured pictorial record was made at the time, which now survives for our study (in the theatre collection of the Victoria and Albert Museum). They came at the crest of the wave of the new Victorian expansion as it swept over the Romantic movement. They came after two decades of unprecedented increase in London theatre building. They came at the period of the Great Exhibition when a new attitude towards education was spreading, and when such brilliant developments in scene-painting as the moving panorama and diorama had comfortably coupled instruction and art. They were earnestly supported by the new young queen. They were eminently 'respectable' and could be safely attended by a 'family' audience. And Charles Kean had been educated at Eton and became a Fellow of the Society of Antiquaries.

His productions over the decade were very varied: they ranged from a sort of gentlemanly melodrama (such as *Pauline*, *The First Printer* and *The Corsican Brothers*) to the more suitable plays of Shakespeare. A very great point was made of the research that was put into ensuring the accuracy of historical details, or of the architecture, foliage and flora of a foreign country. Lavishness of display, of effects and of learning was added to Shakespeare, and much of his text was cut or transposed to make way for it. Most of the leading scenic artists of the day were employed (Cuthbert, Grieve, Lloyds, Telbin) not only on painting the scenery but on designing the properties and furniture, and on extensive voyages abroad to collect sketchbooks of reference to ensure the accuracy of their designs. After the shows had been presented, a further body of skilled watercolourists was set to paint representations of the stage as set, and the effects as seen, and even of the costumes and the properties down to drinking cups and wands. All these are available to us today at the Victoria and Albert Museum.

In the designs it is very notable that despite the new care to import historical accuracy into almost every detail, the general impression is consistently and unescapably early Victorian. The phrase '*almost* every detail' is significant, since even Charles Kean's historical advisers could not prevail upon Mrs Kean or the other ladies of the company to part with their voluminous petticoats and corsets when in period dress, and the silhouettes of their figures are quite unmistakably mid-nineteenth-century. This is (in a manner) as it should be, for no artist can be a proper mirror of his times if the characteristics of his times are not reflected in his work. The indictment here should not be against Kean so much as against the belief that archaeological accuracy is possible in a living theatre anyway.

Kean introduced a moving panorama behind the lovers walking in the wood in *A Midsummer Night's Dream*. He presented a fine effect of surprising dimensions in the destruction of the palace in *Sardanapalus*. He brought a Pyrrhic dance by many warriors into the banquet of *The Winter's Tale*, and a ballet of fairies into the return of Henry V to England after Agincourt. And in his production of Dion Boucicault's first major adaptation from French melodrama, *The Corsican Brothers*, in 1852 (see Plate 43b), he persuaded his carpenters to achieve the seemingly impossible to such effect that by 1858 the device they invented (see below p. 89) had become essential to every production of the play wherever it was acted – and the melodrama itself had become essential to the repertory of every provincial playhouse that had any claim to be with the times. Thus we found the stage floor of the Theatre Royal, Ipswich, being taken up to allow the installation of the device in that year, and by 1877 it had fallen out of fashion and was removed again. This, despite the relatively short popularity of the device in question, is a real example of the modification in theatre structure that could take place solely through the requirements of one given successful play: if the first production is a spectacular success, then immediately the show is in demand by audiences further afield. It comes to them, but it cannot have continued success if it comes without the celebrated effect which made those audiences eager to see it: thus the stages must be adapted to the working of the effect.

In this instance the effect was one that received its name from the play – the Corsican trap. It is worth describing to show the lengths to which the technicians of this period might go. This effect was indeed nothing new (save in one respect) or in advance of what had gone before: it simply involved the slow rising of a ghost through a trap. But the one respect by which this became a national innovation was that Kean saw that the effect of the ghost would be far more eerie if, as he rose slowly through the stage, he drifted slowly across the stage from one side to the other. Another and more picturesque name for it was 'The Ghost Glide'. It may seem a childishly pointless aim to take so much trouble over, but effects in the theatre are curiously outside the normal range of prediction. This one paid its way even as late as Henry Irving's time.

With the slider system the problem was solved. Or more accurately: with the slider system and a working lifetime spent in handling Georgian stage machinery the Victorian stage carpenter could solve it. (Something of this ability to produce solutions still marks the traditional stage carpenter.) The solution was to nest the trap door in the grooves of a slider and attach a line to its understage side and pull it across the stage as the ghost rose. What this, of course, also involved was rigging the rising platform underneath in the same complex, so that as the trap door moved across so did the rising platform below. That meant building the platform on an inclined railway. All this was within the ingenuity of a Victorian stage carpenter. What he had to invent beyond all this, however, was a method of doing the whole of the above without allowing *any aperture in the stage whatever* to be seen during the rising of the ghost.

He brought out two theatrical tricks to achieve this: *scruto* and the 'bristle' trap. Scruto was a long length of flooring made of narrow strips of wood fixed to a canvas back (like the cover of a roll-top desk). This filled the whole of the slider cut at the beginning of the movement, except for the part at the far side where the trap door was. The end of the scruto was attached to this trap door. On pulling the scruto, it slid across the stage, drawing the trap door behind it. It was rolled up offstage, under the stage floor, as it came. Behind the trap door, a duplicate length of scruto, rolled up to begin with, was also attached so that as the trap door moved across and the scruto in front of it rolled up, so the scruto behind unrolled, and kept the aperture of the slider opening filled all the time. Except, of course, for the hole in the trap door itself. It was here that the last touch of ingenuity came in: the edges of the circular opening in the trap door were furnished with a ring of inward-projecting bristles. They bent up as the ghost rose through, brushed his body all the way and never left a glimpse of an opening through the whole procedure.

So, then, with all these new strides in the development of scenic methods during the 1850s, it is strange to read a contemporary of Kean's uncovering another side of the story. The comment comes from the *Art Journal* of 1853, p. 228; though it freely admits that the greatest praise is due for all the innovations, it adds:

> Nevertheless we must be permitted to remark generally, that the mechanism of placing the scenery on the stage, and the mode of throwing light on it are still highly inefficient for artistic illusion, and have not kept pace with other improvements; indeed there has been hardly an advance at all for the last half century. The scenes are still in two slides, and where they meet in the centre the most delicately painted landscape is presented to the public eye, divided by a cutting line, which is also frequently disfigured with dirt from the handling of the sceneshifters.

At the same time as Kean's Princess's productions, a rival in the person of Samuel Phelps at Sadler's Wells was following developments in his own way. His shows, again including many Shakespeare revivals, were perhaps less elaborate than Kean's but contained some interesting innovations and were probably better Shakespeare. The scenic artist for Phelps was Frederick Fenton (for whose style see Plate 16a), and he has left a vivid reminiscent account of the smell of oil and sawdust which infested theatres in the days when Phelps first took over management of the Wells. Fenton obtained permission to introduce gas, and it was first used there in 1853 for *A Midsummer Night's Dream*. To increase the illusion Fenton ordered from Glasgow a special seamless piece of blue net, the size of the act drop, and used it to give a sort of transparency effect through the fairy scenes.

Furthermore he used, as a travelling background in the wood, a diorama which he helpfully describes for us as 'two sets of scenes moving simultaneously', the front set representing nearby foliage and tree trunks, with the intervals cut out to reveal slowly drifting clouds moving on the second plane behind.

Among the reminiscences in this passage (which can be read in an edition-de-luxe of *A Midsummer Night's Dream* compiled by J. Moyr Smith and published in 1892) Fenton interestingly reminds us that before 1850 very few theatres were enabled to have gas, and that when Phelps had taken over the Wells the lighting had been from side lamps of which there were only six behind each wing. To dim them, the lamps were simply turned away from the stage on pivots and shone out into the wing space. Chief of all the interesting points is that there were actually no lights above at all – and thus all the borders in those days hung in darkness. The effect might certainly have been conducive to mystery but not to any illusion of naturalism.

Only four years after Kean ended his great period of management at the Princess's Theatre, a magazine called *All the Year Round*, under Charles Dickens's editorship, published in 1863 an article entitled 'A new stage stride'. It comments pertinently but critically on all the survivals of the scenic technicalities of the Restoration theatre. Some insight is given on what observers felt about the general situation in scenery at the time. The claim is made that many were beginning to wish that something be done to 'render the illusion of the stage more complete'.

Here we find, singled out, this idea of 'complete illusion' as being one of the purposes for which scenery stands. This rendering of 'the illusion of the stage more *complete*' is a new conception. It had not been previously demanded of scenery that it should supply a 'complete illusion'. Scenery had been hitherto a mere painted accompaniment to the action of 'painted' players – possibly not irrelevant to the site of the dramatic action, but never more. Now, in the increased lighting, with the reduced fore-stage, and the frequent entries in the scene, we begin to hear of this motive of 'complete illusion' imputed to scenery

A typical instance of the failure in illusion is quoted in the use of those wings 'by which the stage has hitherto been bounded on the right and left'. Entrances made between wings are said to give an impression such as to leave the audience in a state of uncertainty as to whether the player was supposed to be walking through a wall or whether the room 'had been left, for the sake of ventilation, with no walls at all at the sides'. The slightly facetious sarcasm of contemporary criticism creeps in here, and the writer goes on to complain of another evil of the wings in grooves, in that it was apparently a common fault to fail to withdraw the used wings sufficiently outwards to be completely hidden behind the new wings when they slid on, and thus it 'would continually happen that in the midst of a dark forest . . . we were rendered unbelieving, and our young illusions were crudely checked, by a glimpse of a bit of pilaster with a gorgeous curtain. . . .'

The borders too came under the same criticism. Many spectators were said to be not satisfied with 'those strips of canvas . . . in parallel lines across the top of the stage'. Much of their pleasure, we read, was 'sacrificed' in 'resisting' the impression made by glimpses of architectural borders in forest scenes, and in 'ignoring' the sight of stage hands, with the traditional paper caps, standing ready in the wings.

These are clearly very legitimate criticisms; if scene changing was really so slipshod it was proper to attack it, and it is interesting to realize that even at that time people did feel it to be slipshod. The article now turns to describe how scenery was handled in Parisian theatres of the time and how Charles Fechter had recently introduced something of their system into the Lyceum. Briefly, in this system the wings were supported against masts projecting through slits in the stage floor and carried in wheeled chariots running on rails in the mezzanine floor under the stage. The observation is made that such 'slits, unlike raised grooves, can be carried completely across the stage, and, accordingly, any scene or piece of a scene can be pushed anywhere'.

Such a facility was clearly an advantage over the limitations of grooves – those grooves which, the writer adds, 'could never be carried far on to the stage, lest the actors should tumble over them'. And yet it is a fact that, despite this limitation and despite a number of isolated experiments, the continental system of *chariots* running under their slits in the stage was never widely adopted in England. It remained to serve the branch of theatre for which it was really invented, namely the spectacular continental presentation of opera.

Perhaps one of the most surprising references in this article is to the method by which furniture was shifted in the days when scene changing took place under the eyes of the audience. It was done quite frankly by uniformed servants of the theatre behaving much as the 'invisible' assistants who work so effectively on the Japanese stage. Their presence is criticized but the precision with which they did their work is warmly acknowledged, and one supposes they must have been quite neat to watch. But the interesting question is: how does the above writer hope to replace these stage-furniture-movers in the improved theatre to which he is looking? The reply is that 'in future their work will be accomplished by means of trap-doors and other simple contrivances'. Thus it is borne in upon us that no conception ever arose, at that date, of the revolution that was to be effected by Irving in 1881 – that is to say, the concealment of scene change altogether by the dropping of a front curtain. But that innovation comes outside the scope of the present chapter.

Two other innovations of the future were, however, accurately foreseen in this article of 1863. The first is that interior scenes were conceived as being 'shut in above with a ceiling', instead of being crowned with those distracting borders. Much controversy still exists about the origin of the 'box set'. The controversy is aggravated when no clear definition is offered of what is meant by the term. Either of two kinds of set may be intended: first, the more old-fashioned kind in which the side walls are not made up of a series of wings, but by flats arranged edge to edge, thus presenting a continuous surface. The important distinction, however, is that this type is still masked in at the top by the traditional borders, now either lowered in and 'trapped' (as it was called) between the flats of the side walls, or hung a little higher and merely touching the tops of the flats. Such is probably the kind of arrangement used in most of the earlier occasions which are offered by historians as examples of the original box set.

But the other kind of set is the only one that can fairly claim the name of 'box set', according to modern usage. Here no borders are used at all but the top of the scene is masked by a large, horizontal piece lying over the whole scene and appearing from the front exactly like the flat ceiling of a room. It is this latter kind that was envisaged as an innovation in 1863. As a matter of interest, the term which was used to describe the first kind in Victorian promptbooks was a 'chamber with "raking flats" ', never a 'box set'.

The other innovation in the article of 1863, the most modern of all, is a new method of constructing exterior scenes. Here

> the sky will close the scene in overhead: an unbroken canopy extending from a certain point behind the proscenium and high above it, over the stage, and away to where, at the extreme backward limit of the theatre, it mingles softly with the horizon . . . this great arched canopy, spanning the stage from side to side, and from front to back, will lend itself to all sorts of beautiful and truthful effects.

Thus was the coming of the cyclorama heralded as early as 1863.

The tendency is clearly towards a sort of scenery where 'there shall be really no flaw or weak place about it, no unfinished gaps to which the scrutinising eye can wander in the confident hope of ascertaining "how the trick was done" '. A new world of theatrical illusion is opening.

One last step remained to be taken to complete this illusionistic phase of scenic history. It was taken by Sir Squire Bancroft at the renovated Haymarket Theatre of 1880; it amounted to the final withdrawal of the forestage, the complete discarding of the entrance doors, and the confining of the action entirely within the scene. But Bancroft did more than this: he perfected a picture. The way in which he did it can be read in a pamphlet printed for the opening.[1]

There we find first an interesting admission that 'the Auditory still retains the distinguishing feature of the old Theatre [that is, the one which Nash had designed in 1821] in having the Balcony nearly level with the stage' (compare Plate 11b). In other words, the level of Nash's first tier of Regency boxes round the pit had been retained in a form of open seating now called a 'balcony', but which did not follow the innovations of the Sans Pareil and the Coburg (see Plate 15b) in being raised one storey above the level of the pit. In this, the announcement says, it was 'original and unlike any other Theatre in the Country'.

Next comes the real innovation, namely that 'The Proscenium . . . is a massive and elaborately gilded frame complete on all sides, the lower part forming the front of the Stage and concealing the Orchestra'. This, Bancroft wrote, was 'simply perfection', and quoted 'an eminent French comedian' as remarking that '*le spectateur est devant un tableau dont les personnages parlent et agissent. C'est parfait pour l'illusion et pour le plaisir artistique.*' But it provokes thought to notice that a writer in the *Graphic* of 7 February 1880 found that 'the new proscenium taking the form of a broad massive gold frame with four sides . . . seems to reduce what is going on upon the stage to a mere picture overpowered by a heavy and elaborate setting'.

It would almost seem, if the announcement in the Bancroft pamphlet was correct, that its sponsors believed that a brave new world had begun in the theatre: a world that was 'almost perfect for illusion'!

[1] *Theatre Notebook*, V (April–June 1951), p. 59.

2 Actors and their repertory

Lamented, scolded, or ignored by those critics whose attention is focused solely on the literary aspects of the drama, the period between 1750 and 1880 is nonetheless among the richest eras in English theatre. It introduces us to David Garrick at the height of his powers at Drury Lane, and carries us through an unparalleled succession of outstanding actor-managers to the threshold of Henry Irving's regime at the Lyceum.

The pages that follow attempt to suggest four unified blocks of time within this period: the reign of Garrick, the dominant centrality of John Philip Kemble and his illustrious sister Sarah Siddons around the turn of the century, the various reactions against 'the Kemble religion' which set in with the 'lightning' of Kean, the 'familiarity' of Macready, and the drawing rooms of Madame Vestris, and, finally, the movement towards a new school of realistic acting.

Any such division is in part misleading. The history of pre-naturalistic acting conveys a strong sense of continuity, both in terms of specific stage traditions and in terms of a wider, shared aesthetic. Also, in a very real sense this period of richness is, almost by definition, one of astonishing flux and interaction of so-called stylistic 'opposites'. It is sometimes forgotten that Garrick appeared on the same stage with Quin, and Kemble with Cooke, and Kean with Macready.

A by-product of the great performances of this age has been the writing of some of our finest dramatic critics. Viewed through such contemporary eyes, rather than in the distorting light of preconceptions acquired through the modern theatre, the history of acting in this or any age also has much to say, by implication at least, about the styles, popular tastes and kinds of drama that held sway.

(i) The Garrick era: 1750–1776

In the decade before 1750, the emergence of David Garrick (1717–79) on the London stage had brilliantly accelerated a stylistic revolution in English acting. Garrick's thirty-five-year association with the theatre made his name synonymous with an era that was remarkable not only for his unique fame as an actor, which extended throughout Europe, but also for his important contribution as co-manager, together with James Lacy, of Drury Lane between 1747 and his retirement in 1776. Following the triumph of his formal début as Richard III at Goodman's Fields in 1741, Garrick quickly became the outstanding representative of a style which reflected the growing emphasis, evident in all phases of theatrical endeavour, upon a picturesque, heightened emotionality.

The statuesque dignity and weighty solemnity represented by the tragic acting of James Quin (1693–1766), a dominant figure on the London stage until his retirement in 1751, failed to satisfy the demand for striking and vigorous exhibitions of the passions which was making itself felt. The rhetorical force and majesty with which Quin invested characters such as Addison's Cato and Shakespeare's Brutus evoked the admiration of his contemporaries. 'No man every arriv'd at an equal perfection in speaking the sublime with Mr. Quin', wrote John Hill in 1750.[1] In comedy, his Falstaff was regarded as a masterpiece. 'Quin, in characters of singular humour and dignified folly, of blunt and boisterous demeanour, of treacherous art, contemptuous spleen, and even of pleasing gravity, had no equal', emphasized Thomas Davies, Garrick's first biographer.[2] Nevertheless, there is ample evidence that the powerful pathos which characterized Quin's acting in some tragic roles tended in others to develop in the direction of an overwhelming, sonorous declamation which not only eclipsed inner passion, but also precluded all but the most formal and deliberate movements on the stage.

In an article from 1754 comparing the old and the new styles of acting,

[1] John Hill, *The Actor* (London, 1750), p. 99.
[2] See his *Memoirs of the Life of David Garrick, Esq.* (London, 1780), I, 30.

The Connoisseur stressed that such rhetorical immobility represented a tendency quite common among pre-Garrick performers: 'The tragedians of the last age studied fine speaking; in consequence of which their action consisted in little more than strutting with one leg before the other and waving one or both arms in a continual see-saw.'[1] Similarly, Davies noted that before Garrick's time audiences 'had long been accustomed to an elevation of the voice with a sudden mechanical depression of its tones, calculated to excite admiration, and to intrap applause'. Furthermore, he adds, 'to the just modulation of the words, and concurring expression of the features from the genuine workings of nature, they had been strangers, at least for some time.'[2]

In contrast, Garrick's acting style was revolutionary in its emphasis on a far more varied and intense scheme of expression, highlighting and strengthening the pathos and picturesque emotionalism for which the sentimental drama of the period provided the literary basis. Davies specifically singled out Garrick's 'look and action' while speaking Cibber's lines as Richard – 'Off with his head! So much for Buckingham' – because of the actor's 'visible enjoyment of the incident'.[3] Numerous contemporary accounts stress Garrick's great mobility and fundamental physical expressiveness. He was 'alive in every muscle and in every feature', marvelled Richard Cumberland, who witnessed the clash between the old and the new when Quin and Garrick performed together at Covent Garden in 1746.[4] Garrick amply compensated for his short stature and rather heavy features with his physical grace and elasticity, his plastic mimicry and his startlingly penetrating eyes. This plasticity of expression was a decisive factor in the attainment of that amazing vitality and protean quality continually mentioned in evaluations of his art. Visiting Paris during a prolonged stay on the Continent from 1763 to 1765, Garrick entertained his foreign audience with a virtuoso pantomimic display. Among those whom he inspired was Denis Diderot, who used Garrick's art as an illustration of his own thesis in *Paradoxe sur le comédien* that acting is the art of expression, and thus depends on the degree of self-possession (rather than emotional identification) with which the performer is able to convey stage emotion.[5]

---

[1] *The Connoisseur*, ed. A. Chalmers, *British Essayists*, XXV (London, 1817), p. 193.
[2] Davies, *Garrick*, I, 40.
[3] Ibid., I, 41.
[4] *Memoirs of Richard Cumberland* (London, 1806), p. 60.
[5] 'Garrick will put his head between two folding doors, and in the course of five or six seconds his expression will change successively from wild delight to temperate pleasure, from this to tranquillity, from tranquillity to surprise, from surprise to blank astonishment, from that to sorrow, from sorrow to the air of one overwhelmed, from that to

Everything in Garrick's behaviour contributed to the total effect of vivaciousness. 'He moves to and fro among other players like a man among marionettes', wrote one of his most astute observers, Georg Christoph Lichtenberg. The German traveller also emphasized the extent to which this movement fulfilled the prevalent ideals of balletic grace and the beautiful form:

> When he turns to someone with a bow, it is not merely that the head, the shoulders, the feet and arms, are engaged in that exercise, but that each member helps with great propriety to produce the demeanour most pleasing and appropriate to the occasion. . . . In the scene [as Abel Drugger] in *The Alchemist* where he boxes, he runs about and skips from one neat leg to the other with such admirable lightness that one would dare swear that he was floating in the air. In the dance [as Benedick] in *Much Ado about Nothing*, also, he excels all the rest by the agility of his springs.[1]

The French ballet reformer Jean Georges Noverre (1727–1810) singled out for special praise the element of idealization which permeated Garrick's art: 'A faithful worshipper of nature, he knew the value of selection, he preserved that sense of propriety which the stage requires even in the parts least susceptible of grace and charm.'[2]

Although equally successful in tragic and comic parts, Garrick had a particular genius for moving an audience to share in more violent emotions. 'He was master of all the passions, but more particularly happy in the exhibition of parts where anger, resentment, disdain, horror and despair and madness predominated.'[3] Pantomime and total physical co-ordination highlighted this charged, dramatic quality in his acting. A related feature was the ceaseless change and fluctuation in his expressions of emotion. The players of the preceding era had come to seem 'unnatural' because the monotony of their gesticulation and declamation tended to make their emotions appear static. The key words now were vigour, enthusiasm and fire. Violent transitions in moods and attitudes, reflected in speech, in movement and in every feature

---

fright, from fright to horror, from horror to despair, and thence he will go up again to the point from which he started,' wrote Diderot in *The Paradox of Acting* (New York, 1957), pp. 32–3.
[1] *Lichtenberg's Visits to England as described in his Letters and Diaries*, trans. M. L. Mare and W. H. Quarrell (Oxford, 1938), pp. 6–7.
[2] Jean Georges Noverre, *Letters on Dancing and Ballets* (London, 1951), p. 83.
[3] Davies, *Garrick*, I, 80.

of his face, were Garrick's speciality. 'He falls from fury into tears with a breath; and is pure and entire in both sensations', wrote one astonished reviewer.[1] Genest described Garrick's Richard in similar terms: 'The passions rose in rapid succession, and, before he uttered a word, were legible in every feature of that various face – his look, his voice, his attitude changed with every sentiment.'[2] Chaumont in Otway's *The Orphan* became one of the actor's celebrated roles precisely because 'the quickness and fire of look, as well as expression and gesture, which so eminently distinguish Mr. Garrick from all of his contemporaries, nowhere operate more happily' than in this part.[3] In the scene between Jaffier and Belvidera in the fourth act of another Otway play, *Venice Preserved*, conflicting dramatic emotions were once again vividly depicted by Garrick through 'the mad confusion which is seen in his visage, the pangs which heave his breast on representing to himself his friend in tortures, the resolution of stabbing Belvidera, prevented by the gleam of love, which for a moment may be seen to glow in his face, but afterwards eclipsed by returning rage'.[4] These 'whirlwinds of conflicting passions', exerting an intense appeal to the compassion and sentimental engagement of the audience, constituted the foundation of Garrick's remarkable success in the wide range of nearly 100 parts, Shakespearian and otherwise, which he played during his long career. His gliding in and out of madness made his overpowering King Lear the outstanding achievement of that career. Depicting 'violent starts of amazement, of horror, of indignation, of paternal rage, excited by filial ingratitude' and progressing through 'the deepest frenzy' to the final picture of 'the parent, the sovereign, and the friend [shining] out in the mildest majesty of fervent virtue', his Lear was, in the enthusiastic language of Dr James Fordyce, 'such a picture as the world never saw anywhere else, yet such a one as all the world must acknowledge perfectly true'.[5]

No other actor at this time seems to have excelled in sudden transitions with the same brilliance as Garrick. Nevertheless, accounts of his fellow players also dwell upon plasticity in mimic expression as the major criterion of their art. Garrick's leading lady, Mrs Hannah Pritchard (1711–68), was

---

[1] *The Literary Magazine*, III (1758), p. 20; cited in B. L. Joseph, *The Tragic Actor* (London, 1959), p. 113.
[2] John Genest, *Some Account of the English Stage from the Restoration in 1660 to 1830* (Bath, 1832), IV, 14.
[3] Francis Gentleman, *The Dramatic Censor, or, Critical Companion* (London, 1770), II, 57.
[4] Samuel Derrick, *The Dramatic Censor* (London, 1752), pp. 8, 68.
[5] *The Private Correspondence of David Garrick*, ed. James Boaden (London, 1831–2), I, 157–9.

a dignified but versatile actress talented both in comedy and tragedy. Notable as Gertrude, as Queen Katharine in *Henry VIII* and in the title part of Johnson's *Irene*, Pritchard's outstanding role was as Lady Macbeth. Snatching the daggers from Macbeth 'she presented to the audience a picture of the most consummate intrepidity in mischief'; in this scene, Davies recalled, 'their looks and action supplied the place of words. You heard what they spoke, but you learned more from the agitation of mind displayed in their action and deportment.'[1] The majestic Mrs Mary Ann Yates (1728–87) won critical acclaim as Mandane, the role created for her by John Hoole in *Cyrus*, for her intense and skilful use, 'through every change of tenderness, rage, fear, affection and distraction', of the 'judicious transitions of voice, happy variations of countenance, and picturesque attitudes' which she employed to move her audience.[2]

Eloquent transitions from one emotion to another were accomplished not only through facial expression and gesture but also by means of strong bodily movements. Some, among them the actor Theophilus Cibber (1703–58), scorned Garrick's 'studied tricks, his overfondness for extravagant attitudes [and] frequent affected starts'.[3] Charles Macklin (*c.* 1700–97), himself a heavy and far less mobile performer whose serious Shylock had created a sensation by breaking with the established tradition for the part in 1741, disliked Garrick's specially contrived death speeches and 'his strange manner of dying and griping [*sic*] the carpet; his writhing, straining and agonizing (all of which he has introduced into the profession of acting)'.[4] Generally, however, the younger actor's 'starts' were widely admired. One of the most celebrated of them, at the moment when the Ghost appears to Hamlet, is vividly recaptured in Lichtenberg's description:

> Garrick turns sharply and at the same moment staggers back two or three paces with his knees giving way under him; his hat falls to the ground and both his arms, especially the left, are stretched out nearly to their full length, with the hands as high as his head, the right arm more bent and the hand lower, and the fingers apart; his mouth is open: thus he stands rooted to the spot, with legs apart, but no loss of

[1] Davies, *Garrick*, II, 184, and *Dramatic Miscellanies* (Dublin, 1748), II, 93.
[2] Gentleman, I, 237.
[3] *Theophilus Cibber to David Garrick, Esq., with Dissertations on Theatrical Subjects* (London, 1759); cited in Frank A. Hedgecock, *David Garrick and his French Friends* (London, 1912), p. 55.
[4] James Kirkman, *Memoirs of the Life of Charles Macklin, Esq.* (London, 1799), I, 246–9, 259, 260; see also Lily B. Campbell, 'The rise of a theory of stage presentation in England during the eighteenth century', *PMLA*, XXXII (1917), p. 188.

dignity, supported by his friends, who are better acquainted with the apparition and fear lest he should collapse. His whole demeanour is so expressive of terror that it made my flesh creep even before he began to speak.[1]

Dramatic starts and animated attitudes were by no means peculiar to Garrick alone. The same observer's description of Macklin's Shylock clearly indicates the relationship to Garrick's technique, and gives little suggestion of the so-called subdued realism with which Macklin is sometimes credited: 'In the scene where he first misses his daughter, he comes on hatless, with disordered hair, some locks a finger long standing on end, as if raised by a breath of wind from the gallows, so distracted was his demeanour. Both hands are clenched, and his movements abrupt and convulsive.'[2] Churchill's *The Rosciad*, published in 1761 to describe the famous actors of the day (invidiously, for the most part, in order to produce a panegyric upon Garrick, the Roscius of the title), satirized the latter's only real rival, the tall and strikingly handsome Spranger Barry (1719–77), for exaggerated attitudinizing:

> Some dozen lines before the ghost is there
> Behold him for the solemn scene prepare:
> See how he frames his eyes, poises each limb,
> Puts the whole body into proper trim: –
> From whence we learn with no great stretch of art,
> Five lines hence comes a ghost, and, ha! a start.[3]

Normally, however, Spranger Barry, who made his début at Smock Alley in Dublin in 1746, was admired for his easy and graceful movements and deportment. He played together with Garrick at Drury Lane in Otway's *Venice Preserved* and *The Orphan* and Rowe's *The Fair Penitent*, and at various times there each acted Hamlet and Othello (one of Garrick's few decisive failures). When Barry went to Covent Garden in 1760, he appeared in competition with Garrick in such roles as Richard III, Lear and Romeo. The latter became a kind of endurance contest between the two houses during the 1750–1 season, lasting for twelve consecutive nights. Well-informed connoisseurs took to watching Barry for the first three acts, in which he was reputed to be superior to his competitor, and then rushing to Drury Lane to catch the two final acts, in which Garrick shone. (A lesser controversy raged over the Juliets, pitting the lovely George Anne Bellamy [*c*. 1727–88] at

---

[1] *Lichtenberg's Visits*, p. 9.
[2] Ibid., p. 40.
[3] *The Poetical Works of Charles Churchill*, I (London, 1844), p. 92.

Drury Lane against the grander and more tragically forceful Mrs Susanna Maria Cibber [1714–66] at Covent Garden.) Whatever the relative merits of the two male performers, however, Barry, who excelled in roles of romantic heroes and lovers, was ideally suited as Romeo. His 'deportment' was widely praised: 'It were hard to say whether it were more graceful or more expressive, and his broken voice in the last scene, the scarce articulate utterance of despair, chill every heart that hears him.'[1] 'He was a Nightingale – such a voice was never heard', the actress Frances Abington (1737–1815) assured Henry Crabb Robinson many years later.[2]

The fiery Henry Mossop (1729–74), popularly considered next to Garrick and Barry during this period, was by contrast 'utterly void of grace in deportment and dignity in action'.[3] Gaining wide approval as Richard III, as Othello and as Pierre in *Venice Preserved*, Mossop's outstanding part remained Zanga in Edward Young's *The Revenge*. In this role his forte, the expression of tempestuous emotionality, was allowed to dominate; 'his wild bursts of perfidy acknowledged, and justified, in the fifth act of the play, struck every auditor with a degree of astonishment.'[4] Mossop's Macbeth, however, was regarded as inferior to Garrick's for interesting reasons. The *London Chronicle* castigated Mossop for his mechanical movements and gestures, 'whereas every attitude of Macbeth requires boldness and freedom'. Garrick's portrayal, on the other hand, displayed 'such a commanding air in every movement, and such a graceful horror, if we may so express it, as has hardly been equalled even by himself in any other performance'.[5] The impression of such 'graceful horror' lives perhaps most vividly in the iconographic material recapturing moments in Garrick's roles as Macbeth, as Hamlet and as Richard III. The furious intensity of his reaction in these pictures is carefully counteracted and balanced in each case by the conscious gracefulness of his attitude. Comparing, in turn, the range of pictures of the great actors from Garrick to Irving in particular scenes, one must be struck by a remarkable similarity – the result both of a conscious cultivation of prevalent ideals of the beautiful form and of a continuous tradition of gesture and business in specific situations.[6]

Pantomimic business and reactions were intended to illuminate not only

[1] William Cooke, *Memoirs of Charles Macklin* (London, 1804), p. 161.
[2] Henry Crabb Robinson, *The London Theatre 1811–1866*, ed. Eluned Brown (London, 1966), p. 37.
[3] Davies, *Garrick*, II, 230.
[4] Ibid., I, 161–2.
[5] *London Chronicle*, XLVII (1757), p. 375.
[6] See Plates 26a–39b.

lines of dialogue but also the pauses between. Physical eloquence was a major factor in the effectiveness of Garrick's comic by-play in such roles as Sir John Brute in Vanbrugh's *The Provoked Wife* and as Archer in Farquhar's *The Beaux' Stratagem*. Audiences watching the latter play were treated to a brilliantly mimed scene between Garrick's Archer and the Scrub of Thomas Weston (1737–76), an able comedian whose Abel Drugger surpassed, in the opinion of some, even the work of Garrick:

> Garrick throws himself into a chair with his usual ease of demeanour. . . . Weston sits, as is fitting, in the middle of his chair, though rather far forward and with a hand on either knee, as motionless as a statue. . . . When Archer at last with an easy gesture crosses his legs, Scrub tries to do the same, in which he eventually succeeds, though not without some help from his hands, and with eyes all the time either gaping or making furtive comparisons. And when Archer begins to stroke his magnificent silken calves, Weston tries to do the same with his miserable red woollen ones, but, thinking better of it slowly pulls his green apron over them with an abjectness of demeanour, arousing pity in every breast.[1]

This example represents an ideal. There was, by contrast, always the danger that actors when not directly engaged in the dialogue would lapse into the absent inattentiveness which was a frequent critical target throughout the eighteenth century. One critic disgustedly described a *Hamlet* performance in which the much admired Mrs Cibber, seated with Hamlet at her feet during the play scene, 'rose up three several times, and made as many courtesies, and those very low ones, to some ladies in the boxes'.[2] Other beauties of the age – Mrs Bellamy, Catherine ('Kitty') Clive (1711–85) and that vivacious mistress of 'breeches parts' Margaret ('Peg') Woffington (*c.* 1714–60) – were likewise found guilty of touring the boxes with their eyes when not involved in the action, to the great dismay of their demanding manager.[3] In this capacity Garrick undoubtedly exerted considerable personal authority to improve standards of discipline, casting and rehearsal attendance. Perhaps the most radical change which he introduced concerned the practice of seating audiences on the stage itself. This custom was attended by innumerable distracting incidents that ranged from spectators getting up to

[1] *Lichtenberg's Visits*, pp. 26–7.
[2] *Theatrical Review* (1763), p. 213; cited in Joseph, p. 131.
[3] See *An Apology for the Life of George Anne Bellamy* (London, 1785), II, 113, and also Kalman A. Burnim, *David Garrick, Director* (Pittsburgh, 1961), p. 43.

embrace particular favourites among the actors, to their handing fallen hats and articles of clothing back to the performer who had dropped them, whether intentionally or otherwise. Practical as well as aesthetic problems were created by these stage spectators. 'The battle of Bosworth Field has been fought in a less space than that which is commonly allotted to a cock-match', Davies declared.[1] Garrick banished spectators from the Drury Lane stage in 1763, four years after their removal at the Comédie in Paris. This accomplishment, in conjunction with the brighter illumination also introduced about this time, had two results: greater enhancement of the possibilities for stage pictorialism, thus opening up the path which the theatre would follow in the coming decades, and placement in bolder visual relief of the picturesque attitudes, starts and transitions of the performer himself.

When the actor took the stage at Garrick's theatre, he did so largely as a sovereign craftsman not much disposed to take advice about his art from the manager or anyone else. This sometimes raised difficulties. When Jonson's *Every Man in his Humour* was revived at the beginning of 1750, a star cast, headed by Garrick as Kitely, included the gifted Harlequin Henry Woodward (1717–77) in one of his comic masterpieces as Captain Bobadill and Richard Yates (1706–96) at his most engaging as Brainworm. Garrick, anxious for a successful production, apparently expected from the cast greater acquiescence in his instructions than was the case. Such an assumption was, however, 'a compliance, after all, which could not be expected from men of great professional abilities, such as Yates and Woodward. All that can be expected from genius is, to take the out-line and to observe a few hints towards the colouring of a character; the heightening, or finishing, must be left to the performer.'[2] It is an often quoted fact that Mrs Pritchard played Lady Macbeth initially without ever having seen anything but her own part.

Fundamentally, Garrick's art, like virtually every view of acting promulgated before the emergence of naturalism, was strongly influenced by the basic premise that nature is comprised of ideal and absolute forms which the actor must imitate. 'Every passion has its peculiar and appropriate look, and every look its adapted and peculiar gesture', Aaron Hill had declared. In his *Essay on the Art of Acting*, which first appeared in 1753 and was continually rearranged, pirated and reissued anonymously until the end of the nineteenth century, Hill recognized ten dramatic passions. These, from which all others derive, were distinguished by their 'outward marks, in action'.[3] The actor's

---

[1] Davies, *Garrick*, I, 339.
[2] Davies, *Dramatic Miscellanies*, II, 43.
[3] *Works of the late Aaron Hill, Esq.* (London, 1753), IV, 357. Cf. Part III, p. 154.

province being to portray human emotions in a convincing manner, a thorough knowledge of the full plastic vocabulary for the various passions was the main prerequisite for his profession. Garrick's contribution was his remarkable ability to create exciting emotional transformations, 'discovering where in all his characters, the writer had intended any change of passions' and making that discovery the springboard for a startling transition from one emotion to the next.

In Garrick's acting, pantomimic reactions and forceful attitudes virtually exploded the flow of the declamation and led to a de-emphasis of controlled cadences of speech. The actor himself admits that 'at my first setting out in the business . . . I endeavoured to shake off the fetters of numbers, and have often been accused of neglecting the harmony of the versification from too close a regard to the passion and the meaning of the author'.[1] Predominant weight was placed on intensified dramatic 'effects' which emphasized a passion through the whole range of speech and actions, playing on the emotions of the audience through continual, artful variations. The breaking up of speeches was accompanied by a rapid succession of expressive attitudes, gestures and mimicry. When as Richard III Garrick

> started from his dream; he was a spectacle of horror – he called out in a
> > manly tone
> Give me another horse;
> > he paused, and with a countenance of dismay, advanced, crying out in a
> > tone of distress
> Bind up my wounds,
> > then, falling on his knees, said in a most piteous accent
> Have mercy, heaven![2]

The practice of dividing a soliloquy up into its emotional components, punctuating and interrupting its flow with frequent pauses to indicate transitions of thought, was not confined to Garrick alone. It accounted as well for much of the 'natural' impression evoked by Charles Macklin's Shylock: 'In the third act scene, where alternate passions reign, he breaks the tones of utterance, and varies his countenance admirably', declared the *Dramatic Censor*.[3] The 'silver-toned' Spranger Barry too won praise for the moving effect of his broken tones of speech. David Garrick, however, remained the representative *par excellence* of this technique: 'No man,' wrote Francis

[1] *Private Correspondence*, I, 92.
[2] Genest, IV, 14.
[3] Quoted in E. A. Parry, *Charles Macklin* (London, 1891), p. 67.

Gentleman, 'ever did, nor possibly ever will, speak . . . broken sentences, and make transitions with such penetrating effect.'[1]

Garrick's retirement in 1776 and the transfer of his interest in Drury Lane to young Richard Brinsley Sheridan ended a distinct era. In an artistic sense, Garrick's contributions as an actor and manager would continue to influence the art of his successors. In the most literal sense, however, the 1770s saw the ranks of the older actors thinned by the deaths of Mossop, Weston, Woodward, Barry and Garrick himself. The previous decade had witnessed the passing of Peg Woffington, Mrs Cibber, Quin and Mrs Pritchard. Macklin, practically a centenarian, was virtually the last survivor of an age. The year following Garrick's leavetaking marked, in many ways, a new stage of development. *The School for Scandal* resuscitated English comedy: Mrs Abington was the first Lady Teazle, 'Gentleman' Smith (1730–1819) was Charles Surface, and John Palmer (1742–98), remembered with such nostalgia by Charles Lamb in his essay 'On the Artificial Comedy of the last Century', succeeded in making Joseph the hero of the play. Two new actors made their London débuts, John Henderson (1743–85) and the elegant and fashionable Elizabeth Farren (1759–1829). The interregnum was brief, however, for the Kembles were already waiting in the wings.

(ii) 'The Kemble religion': 1776–1812

The rise of John Philip Kemble (1757–1823) from the precarious existence of a provincial stroller to the undisputed position he enjoyed for more than a quarter of a century as the overlord of England's foremost theatrical dynasty is a fascinating saga to which only the briefest allusion can be made here. Kemble's illustrious sister Sarah Kemble Siddons (1755–1831), described quite simply by Brander Matthews as 'probably the greatest actress the world has ever seen',[2] had an unpromising début as Portia at Drury Lane in the closing days of 1775. She was as unsuited to this part as the versatile comic actor Thomas King (1730–1804), who played opposite her, was to the character of Shylock, and the production miscarried. After a number of appearances opposite Garrick during the last months of his management, her services were dispensed with and she was compelled to spend the following six years practising her art in the provinces, chiefly at York and Bath.

The reappearance of Siddons at Drury Lane in October 1782 was, by

---

[1] Gentleman, I, 55–6.
[2] Brander Matthews, *Papers on Acting* (New York, 1958), p. 70.

contrast, a sensation. Sentimental and tear-compelling roles as Isabella in Southerne's *Fatal Marriage*, as Jane Shore, as Belvidera in *Venice Preserved* and as Euphrasia in Arthur Murphy's *The Grecian Daughter* (a part in which Fanny Kemble recalled her aunt 'in piles of powdered curls, with a forest of feathers on top of them, high-heeled shoes, and a portentous hoop')[1] established her as the leading theatrical celebrity of the day. Already in her second season Sir Joshua Reynolds painted her as the Tragic Muse (and, exceptionally for him, signed the painting, having 'resolved to go down to posterity on the hem of your garment'):

> When I attended him for the first sitting . . . he took me by the hand, saying 'Ascend your undisputed throne and graciously bestow upon me some good idea of the Tragic Muse.' I walked up the steps, and instantly seated myself in the attitude in which the Tragic Muse now appears. This idea satisfied him so well, that without one moment's hesitation he determined not to alter it.[2]

Not unaided by his sister's stunning success, John Kemble bowed as an actor at Drury Lane in September 1783 as a solemn and deliberate Hamlet – a part which Hazlitt later asserted that he played 'like a man in armour, with a determined inveteracy of purpose, in one undeviating straight line'.[3] It was not, however, until 23 September 1788 that Kemble recorded in his private journal the proud words: 'This day I undertook the Management of D. L. Theatre.'[4] As the first of the succession of great actor-managers dominating the English stage in the nineteenth century, his managerial programme is fully as important as his personal contribution as an actor. Moved by the recognition that 'much was yet to be done in the representations of Shakespeare's plays', he determined, in the words of his indefatigable biographer James Boaden, 'when he should acquire the necessary power, to bend every nerve to make them perfect beyond all previous example'.[5]

The strength of this determination is evident even in the repertory of Kemble's first period of management, from 1788 until the closing of Drury Lane in 1792. In this first season he produced, more or less according to his own ideas, *Henry VIII* and *Coriolanus, or The Roman Matron* – the latter a

[1] Frances Ann Kemble, *Records of a Girlhood* (New York, 1879), p. 190.
[2] Thomas Campbell, *Life of Mrs. Siddons* (London, 1834), I, 242.
[3] *Hazlitt on Theatre*, ed. William Archer and R. W. Lowe (New York, n.d. [originally published 1895]), p. 127.
[4] See Herschel Baker, *John Philip Kemble, the Actor in his Theatre* (Cambridge, Mass., 1942), p. 122.
[5] James Boaden, *Memoirs of the Life of John Philip Kemble, Esq.* (London, 1825), I, 157.

combination of Shakespeare and James Thomson designed to enhance his own statuesque portrayal and the majestic power of Mrs Siddons's Volumnia (whom the actor and Kemble protégé Charles Young recalled 'coming down the stage . . . marching and beating time to the music; rolling (if that be not too strong a term to describe her motion) from side to side, swelling with the triumph of her son. Coriolanus, banner, and pageant, all went for nothing to me, after she walked to her place').[1] Revivals of *Henry V*, *The Tempest*, *The Two Gentlemen of Verona*, *1 Henry IV* and *King John* followed in due course.[2]

Drury Lane was condemned in 1792, and an enlarged and completely remodelled building was opened in 1794 with Kemble's *Macbeth*, featuring Siddons in one of her most famous roles as Lady Macbeth and introducing Charles Kemble (1775–1854), youngest member of the dynasty, as Malcolm. (A little boy named Edmund Kean was one of the impish sprites.) During John Philip Kemble's control of the new theatre from 1794 to 1802, he continued to pursue his 'avowed passion' for Shakespeare, until the difficulties of partnership with Sheridan drove him to join Thomas Harris at Covent Garden in 1802, taking Siddons and Charles Kemble with him. From 1803 to the burning of Covent Garden in 1808, he presented no fewer than six of the tragedies, five of the histories and two of the comedies. His final phase, the palmy years from the reopening of the new Covent Garden in 1809 until his retirement in 1817, was marked by renewed efforts that included the 1811 revival of *The Winter's Tale*, in which Mrs Siddons's Hermione provided her most celebrated personification of the 'classical' dress and manner cultivated by the Kemble school. In all, this pioneering Shakespearian producer brought before the public twenty-seven revivals of Shakespeare in twenty-nine years – eight of the tragedies, all the histories except *Richard II* and *Henry VI*, and thirteen of the comedies.[3]

Despite confrontations and personality clashes, Kemble succeeded in developing an impressive programme of reform at Drury Lane. His attention to detail extended to every aspect of production. 'It is a *literal* and *positive* fact', asserted the *Morning Post* (16 October 1788), 'that not a *Lady's petticoat* is *trimmed* without first consulting Mr. Kemble.' In addition to important

[1] Related in Percy Fitzgerald, *The Kembles* (London, [1871]), I, 285–6.
[2] Cf. George C. D. Odell, *Shakespeare from Betterton to Irving* (London, 1920), II, 50.
[3] Harold H. Child, 'Shakespearian productions of John Philip Kemble', *Shakespeare Association Papers*, XIX (Oxford, 1935), p. 4, appears to be incorrect in his totals (twenty-five revivals, including only eleven of the comedies); Baker, p. 334, simply takes over the error. Kemble's published versions, collected in his *Select British Theatre*, 8 volumes (London, 1815), clearly total twenty-seven plays.

reforms of scenery and costuming, he undertook to coach the younger actors and even organized theatrical drill squads behind the scenes. Nonetheless, he could do little without the express permission of Richard Brinsley Sheridan. Pressed by the capriciousness and laxness of Drury Lane's irresponsible patentee, who was too engrossed with politics at this time to do more than clean the theatre's treasury of all he could lay his hands on, Thomas King had resigned his position as stage manager in 1788 with the ominous statement that he lacked 'sufficient authority to command the cleaning of a coat'.[1] For fourteen years, until Kemble left Sheridan's theatre in desperation, he too was subjected to the financial negligence and exasperating carelessness of the autocratic, domineering patentee.[2]

Kemble's customary methodical care also marked his term as manager of Covent Garden, where he now owned one-sixth of the enterprise (the patentee, Thomas Harris, controlled one-half of the shares). Boaden indicates that the duties of Kemble's predecessor here, the actor William 'Gentleman' Lewis (1749–1811), had included the casting and arranging of plays, daily attendance at rehearsals and a frequently uncomfortable intervention between Harris and his authors and actors. Kemble brought to these traditional duties the same remarkable precision and discipline which had distinguished his management of Drury Lane.

The trend during John Philip Kemble's career towards larger theatres and the consequent decline of theatrical intimacy are familiar facts, and the evidence concerning the details of these larger playhouses has been presented frequently. Twice, in 1782 and 1792, both Covent Garden and Drury Lane were entirely altered and remodelled. Once, in 1808 and 1809 respectively, both houses were consumed by fire – through divine intervention, in the opinion of some pious minds – and rebuilt from the ground. Influenced by Sheridan's financial difficulties, the 1794 reopening of Drury Lane increased its capacity from 2,500 to 3,611 spectators. Similarly, the new Covent Garden erected under Kemble's management in 1809 – a house damned by Boaden as having 'not a particle of taste' and branded by the OP rioters as 'the house that Jack built' – included an auditorium of more than 3,000 seats.

[1] Boaden, II, 405–6.
[2] See Baker, p. 124. Boaden recalls one of the tense moments in Kemble's strained association with the capricious 'Sheri'. At a dinner party, following a prolonged and stony silence during which Kemble 'looked unutterable things', he rose 'like a pillar of state and addressed the astonished Sheridan: "I am an EAGLE, whose wings have been bound down by frosts and snows; but now I shake my pinions and cleave into the general air, unto which I am born." He then deliberately resumed his seat, and looked as if he had relieved himself from insupportable thraldom' (Boaden, II, 75–6; Fitzgerald, I, 300).

In the immense playhouses of Harris and Sheridan, it would hardly be correct to assume that Kemble's Shakespearian performances reigned as the sole, or even the chief, attractions. Kemble may be credited largely with making Shakespeare palatable to the public of this age, but in fact a broad spectrum of the popular taste clamoured for melodramatic spectacle and animal extravaganza. The vogue of Gothic strangeness and the supernatural on the stage was immense, and prodigious hits such as James Cobb's *The Haunted Tower* and M. G. Lewis's *The Castle Spectre* enjoyed innumerable performances. Similarly, the mania for Kotzebue saw twenty of his plays produced in England between 1796 and 1801. Kemble's portrayal of the title role in *The Stranger* (from *Menschenhass und Reue*) was reckoned by contemporary critics alongside his best Shakespearian performances: 'His person was moulded to the character', wrote Hazlitt. 'The weight of sentiment which oppressed him was never suspended; the spring at his heart was never lightened – it seemed as if his whole life had been a suppressed sigh!'[1]

Little or nothing, however, could surpass the popularity of 'the new performers', the four-legged stars of the animal extravaganzas that flooded the stage. 'Splendid dresses, elaborate conflicts on horseback, in which the "highly trained animals" simulated all the agonies of death, with the capture of towns, were spectacles that filled the theatres for many a night', observed Percy Fitzgerald.[2] The most cursory glance through Oulton's *History of the Theatres of London* amply confirms this view. In the 'grand Romantic Melo Drama' *Timour the Tartar*, concocted by M. G. Lewis and staged at Kemble's Covent Garden in 1811, 'a splendid combat scene exceeded all that ever had been witnessed of the kind' and 'the new performers (*the horses*) displayed wonderful ability.' For the Christmas pantomime in 1812, even Kemble and Harris outdid themselves with 'the introduction of a much-talked-of new performer from the banks of the Ganges, his first appearance on any stage! – this was an elephant, and he was highly applauded'.[3]

Showmanship strongly coloured what is commonly thought of as Kemble's austere and 'formal' artistic persuasion. A popular sensation comparable to his animal dramas in its wide appeal was the Master Betty craze in the season of 1804–5, during which the 13-year-old 'Infant Roscius' William Henry West Betty (1791–1874) was permitted to bellow and declaim the leading classical roles, driving even Kemble and Siddons from the field in defeat.

[1] *Hazlitt on Theatre*, p. 125.
[2] Fitzgerald, II, 141.
[3] W. C. Oulton, *A History of the Theatres of London . . . from the Year 1795 to 1817 inclusive* (London, 1817), II, 266, 274.

The flush of success was brief, however; public favour soured, and the prodigy was banished.[1] Nor was John Kemble above attempting to sustain the
rage by bringing out an 8-year-old actress, a certain Miss Mudie, in the leading role of Garrick's *The Country Girl* (a bowdlerized version of Wycherley's
The Country Wife) the following season. In spite of Kemble's dignified rem-
onstrances from the stage, the unfortunate child was hissed off by the audience
and mercifully prevented from finishing the part. The familiar words ap-
propriated by him to signify submission on this occasion embody, in many
ways, a guiding principle of his management: 'The Drama's laws the Drama's
patrons give.'[2] On only one occasion, during the sixty-six nights of OP rioting
and jingoism, did Kemble directly oppose the drama's violent British patrons
– and on that occasion 'Black Jack', as his detractors sometimes called him,
was eminently unsuccessful.[3]

In general, however, though in a moment of irritation the *Examiner* (19
December 1813) might complain that Kemble never looks twice at a play
that cannot 'be converted into a pageant, but bring[s] forward with much
pretence any drama that has its proper capabilities of ostentatious spectacle',
the view of most of Kemble's contemporaries, as exemplified in *Bell's
Weekly Messenger* (19 December 1813), had usually quite a different ring:
'We question, whether Greece, in all her elegance, and Rome, in all her
luxury, possessed a stage which could rival Covent Garden, in pure refinement, and classical splendour.' Although his managerial activity revolution-
ized stage practices and techniques in a wide variety of ways, it is useful in
the present context to consider the kind of influence which such a manager
might have upon specific aspects of performance.

The actor at this time, as we have seen, was largely a sovereign craftsman
who prepared his role independently, on the basis of established conventions

[1] Not permanently, however. After three years at Cambridge, Betty made an unsuccessful
effort to regain his theatrical footing in 1812. The dignified Mrs Siddons disdained to
act with him, and Crabb Robinson, after seeing him in the title role of *Alexander the
Great*, by d'Egville and Kemble, declared him to be 'a fat fair ranting screaming fellow
who might much better represent a Persian Eunuch than a Macedonian conqueror' (*The
London Theatre*, p. 49). Hazlitt, 'a sneaking admirer', recounts a meeting with him later
in life (see *Hazlitt on Theatre*, pp. xii–xiii), but in general the Infant Roscius passed his
adult life in obscurity.

[2] John Ambrose Williams, *Memoirs of John Philip Kemble, Esq.* (London, 1817), p. 40.
Kemble was quoting from Dr Johnson's Prologue, spoken by Garrick at the reopening
of Drury Lane in 1747.

[3] *The Covent Garden Journal*, 2 volumes, ed. J. J. Stockdale (London, 1810), provides a
fascinating account of the events surrounding the OP riots. See also Part I above, p.
9.

and traditions, without the participation of a director in the modern sense. 'In the getting up of old plays', writes Boaden in connection with the duties of the stage manager, 'or such as have lain aside even for a few years, the first question asked upon a stage is, "How is the *business* done; who knows it?" The acting manager should, therefore, be a person of long experience or have served himself under able generals.'[1] Characteristic of this system was the manner in which Kemble, before becoming manager, had been 'rehearsed' in the role of King John by Thomas Sheridan (1719–88), an actor and specialist in stage declamation and elocution who was a key figure in the transition from Garrick's style to the declamatory 'grand style' of the Kembles.[2] 'Old Mr. Sheridan came to [Kemble's] lodgings, with great kindness', writes Boaden concerning this typical instance of the passing on of stage tradition, 'and read the character over to him; I suppose very nearly as he used to play it.'[3]

Actual stage rehearsals remained remarkably few in number by modern standards, a fact closely connected with the actor's independence. On one occasion Mrs Siddons recalled having acted Belvidera in *Venice Preserved* 'without ever previously having seen the face of one of the actors; for there was no time for even one rehearsal'.[4] For certain new plays, somewhat greater preparation was afforded. Thus Cumberland's *The Jew* received four full rehearsals and six rehearsals of individual scenes before its production in 1794. 'Furthermore,' a contemporary source informs us, 'all these rehearsals were at the most only two hours long, and sometimes less', providing 'for a full-length, five-act, brand-new comedy a grand total of about fifteen hours'.[5] In the same year another Cumberland play, *The Wheel of Fortune*, in which Kemble's portrayal of Penruddock was hailed as 'one of his most correct and interesting performances and one of the most perfect on the modern stage',[6] received a total of nine rehearsals of about one hour each. Even this preparation seems considerable, however, when we reflect on the fact that *Measure for Measure* was revived by Kemble after a nine-year pause on the basis of only two rehearsals. His promptbook for this play, preserved in the Players Club in New York, clearly suggests the nature of static, convention-

---

[1] Boaden, II, 370–1.
[2] On this significant theatrical figure, see Lily B. Campbell, pp. 191–4, and Esther K. Sheldon, *Thomas Sheridan of Smock-Alley* (Princeton, 1967).
[3] Boaden, I, 133.
[4] Fitzgerald, I, 211.
[5] See Edwin Duerr, *The Length and Depth of Acting* (New York, 1962), pp. 284–5, and Charles B. Hogan, 'An eighteenth-century prompter's notes', *Theatre Notebook*, X (1952), p. 39.
[6] *Hazlitt on Theatre*, p. 125.

alized blocking that made such a feat possible; only exits and entrances are noted, and these are, without exception, made through the first or second wing openings at either side, guiding the actors into the semicircle traditionally formed at the footlights.

Discipline at these few rehearsals seems to have been extraordinarily lax. George Colman the Younger, in his notorious preface to his melodrama *The Iron Chest* (1796), in which he rains invective on Kemble's head for the manager's treatment of his play, laments: 'They yclep it a rehearsal, I conjecture, because *they do* NOT *rehearse*.' By the shade of Garrick, swears the embittered author, there was never a single rehearsal

> wherein one, or two, or more, of the Performers, very essential to the piece, were not absent: and *all* the rehearsals which I attended, so slovenly, so irregular, that the rugged master of a theatrical Barn, might have blushed for the want of discipline.

Although the polemical tone here must be taken into account, Colman's complaint is closely echoed nine years later in Thomas Holcroft's more sweeping plea for a disciplinarian, in his *Theatrical Recorder* of 1805.[1]

Anecdotes illustrating the spontaneous situations that could arise in an unrehearsed performance are plentiful, though the majority are probably spurious.[2] One such anecdote, no doubt credible, concerns the renowned *Othello* at Covent Garden in 1807–8 and introduces us to Kemble's erratic rival, the fiery and temperamental George Frederick Cooke (1756–1812). Cooke's impassioned abandon was the very antithesis of Kemble's measured grandeur. His speciality was craft: Leigh Hunt once called him 'the Machiavel of the modern stage'.[3] The contrast between his personal attack and the decorous reserve of the Kemble style led Charles Lamb to remark that 'he is always alive to the scene before him and by the fire and novelty of his manner he seems likely to infuse some warm blood into the frozen declamatory style into which our theatres have for some time past been degenerating'.[4] The production which pitted Cooke's Iago against Kemble's Moor provides a vivid object lesson in the concept of independent role preparation. 'Kemble

[1] Selections from the *Theatrical Recorder* are reproduced in A. M. Nagler, *Sources of Theatrical History* (New York, 1952), pp. 419–22.

[2] The curious reader is referred to Fitzgerald, I, 189, on Mrs Siddons as Constance in *King John*; to ibid., II, 188–9, on Siddons as Mrs Beverley and as Queen Katharine; and to Baker, p. 71, on Kemble as Richard III.

[3] Leigh Hunt, *Critical Essays on the Performers in the London Theatres* (London, 1807), p. 216.

[4] *Morning Post*, 2 January 1802.

had sent for Cooke to rehearse with him at his room, but Cooke would not go', runs the story in Fitzgerald's version:

> 'Let Black Jack,' so he called Kemble, 'come to me.' So they went on the boards without previous rehearsal. In the scene in which Iago instils his suspicions, Cooke grasped Kemble's left hand with his own, and then fixed his right, like a claw, on his shoulder. In this position, drawing himself up to him with his short arm, he breathed his poisonous whispers. Kemble coiled and twisted his hand, writhing to get away, his right hand clasping his brow, and darting his eye back on Iago.

Later, when Cooke was in New York, where he ended his life in 1812, Washington Irving spoke to him about the famous scene. 'Didn't I play up to Black Jack!' exclaimed the brilliant but eccentric Cooke. 'I saw his dark eye sweeping back upon me.'[1]

Kemble made at least some effort to introduce greater discipline and precision in the conduct of rehearsals. Because he insisted on such essentials as promptness, he gained a reputation for 'uncommon asperity'. He objected strongly to the neglect of smaller parts, and secondary players were required to perform their roles exactly as rehearsed. He paced off his own blocking, and any unexpected alteration would disconcert him 'through the rest of the scene'. Actions were carefully planned, causing Leigh Hunt to record that 'he never pulls out his handkerchief without a design upon the audience'.[2] His care in handling stage groupings and processions prefigured the crowd scenes of Charles Kean and, still later, the Meininger, and directly shaped the technique of an American counterpart like Thomas Hamblin.[3] He 'always spent as much time at rehearsal in marshalling and disciplining the corps dramatique as in any other occupation' – hence the unusual effectiveness, according to John Finlay's *Miscellanies*, of his mob in *Julius Caesar*, which Finlay saw in Dublin in 1815. In this production two excellent actors, the comedian William Farren Jr (1786–1861) and Henry Johnston (1777–1845), 'shewed their good sense' by taking part in the crowd scenes, without thinking it beneath their dignity, and Finlay accords special praise to the work of Farren (the matchless Peter Teazle of his day) as leader of the mob.[4]

[1] Fitzgerald, II, 339; A. C. Sprague, *Shakespeare and the Actors* (New York, 1963), p. 194; Pierre Irving, *Life and Letters of Washington Irving* (New York, 1862–4), IV, 241.

[2] Leigh Hunt, *Dramatic Essays*, ed. William Archer and R. W. Lowe (London, 1894), p. 8.

[3] See F. J. Marker, 'From Covent Garden to the Bowery: Kemble and Hamblin promptbooks for *Henry VIII*', *Theatre Survey*, IX (November, 1968), pp. 72–87.

[4] Finlay's *Miscellanies* (Dublin, 1835), cited in A. C. Sprague, *Shakespearian Plays and Performances* (Cambridge, Mass., 1953), pp. 53, 252.

Walter Scott found, however, that Kemble's 'anxiety as a manager made him sometimes too busy; he was apt to be drilling the performers even during the time of the performance. . . . We ourselves remember to have seen a very pleasing-looking young person much disturbed by Kemble's directions about lifting and lowering the sword in the scene betwixt princess Anne and Richard' in the first act of *Richard III*.[1] Kemble's instructions to his supporting players sometimes directed them 'to forego all exertion for fear of interfering with his proper effect'. Leigh Hunt was outraged that one actress was 'expressly forbid to go near him when he falls, to assist him when he rises, to kneel to him, or to embrace him; in short, she is obliged to appear as an automaton'.[2] Kemble and his illustrious sister held centre stage, both figuratively and literally, and the rest of the cast were not expected to interfere with that ordained ascendancy.

Critics have been fairly uniform in their choice of labels to describe the Kemble school of acting. A host of commentators have spoken of his 'splendid formalism'; the 'grand style' of Kemble and Mrs Siddons, 'akin to the classical romanticism of English literature'; the 'ideal beauty' sought for in their emphasis on elocution and propriety of pronunciation; the 'classical style of the majestic Kemble'; his adherence to the 'teapot school' of Mossop – one hand on the hip, the other extended and moving in curved lines; and his studied artfulness as 'the Euclid of the Stage':

> Lo Kemble comes, the Euclid of the stage;
> Who moves in given angles, squares a start,
> And blows his Roman beak by rules of art;
> Writhes with a grace to agony unknown,
> And gallops half an octave in a groan.[3]

Similarly, an almost endless array of distinguished observers in Kemble's own time – Scott, Lamb, Hazlitt, Leigh Hunt, Horace Walpole, Macready and others – added their voices in allegiance to, or violent rejection of, the Kemble religion. Hunt in particular waged a fanatical campaign against Kemble's 'vicious' system of pronunciation, declaring that some of the

---

[1] Walter Scott, 'Revue of Boaden's *Memoirs of the Life of Kemble*', *Quarterly Review*, XXXIV (1826), pp. 230–1.

[2] Quoted in Fitzgerald, II, 362.

[3] Sprague, *Shakespearian Players*, chapter 3, *passim*; Lily B. Campbell, pp. 194–200; Duerr, pp. 278–85; Nagler, pp. 451–3; Marvin Rosenberg, *The Masks of Othello* (Berkeley and Los Angeles, 1961), p. 43; *The Thespiad* (1809), pp. 16–18.

sounds issuing from his mouth were as unintelligible as Coptic or 'Hindos-tanee'. (The oddities of Kemble's pronunciation are preserved in full: 'vargin' for 'virgin', 'hijjus' for 'hideous', 'infaremity' for 'infirmity', 'bird' for 'beard', and so on.)[1] Hazlitt's view of Kemble was dictated in large measure by his avowed preference for the volatile and passionate Edmund Kean (1787–1833). In general he found the older actor 'cold and artificial', 'dry, hard, and pedantic', a performer working 'according to the book of arith-metic', 'as shy of committing himself with nature as a maid is of committing herself with a lover', and best suited to 'parts involving the development of some one solitary sentiment or exclusive passion'.[2]

Yet this torrent of uniform-sounding epithets has often obscured the im-portance of the ingredient in this style which also caused Hazlitt to assert that, in summary, 'the distinguishing excellence of his acting may be summed up in one word – *intensity*; in the seizing upon some one feeling or idea, in insisting upon it, in never letting it go, and in working it up, with a certain graceful consistency, and conscious grandeur of conception, to a very high degree of pathos and sublimity'.[3] An awareness of this aspect of Kemble's approach led Alan Downer, in his classic study of eighteenth-century acting, to observe wisely: 'Kemble's style of acting was better fitted to the high sounding melodramatics of [Rolla in] *Pizarro*, than the tall, preternaturally solemn character studies of Sir Thomas Lawrence would indicate.'[4]

Staggering dramatic pathos and intensity were, of course, the very hall-marks of the art of Sarah Siddons. Her Lady Macbeth was to Hazlitt 'little less appalling in its effects than the apparition of a preternatural being'.[5] William Charles Macready (1793–1873), who as a young player in Newcastle appeared opposite her ('with fear and trembling') as Beverley in Moore's *The Gamester* and as Norval in Home's *Douglas*, has left a striking description of her violent emotionality as Mrs Beverley and Lady Randolph. In the former role

> the climax to her sorrows and sufferings was in the dungeon, when on her knees, holding her dying husband, he dropped lifeless from her arms. Her glaring eyes were fixed in stony blankness on his face; the powers

[1] For a full account of Kemble's artificial pronunciation, complete with Hunt's 'little lexicon', see Fitzgerald, II, 353–64.

[2] *Hazlitt on Theatre*, pp. 90, 111, 125, 128.

[3] Ibid., pp. 129–30.

[4] See his 'Nature to advantage dressed: eighteenth-century acting', reprinted in *Restora-tion Drama*, ed. John Loftis (New York, 1966), p. 344. The article originally appeared in *PMLA*, LVIII (1943), pp. 1002–37.

[5] *Hazlitt on Theatre*, p. 122.

of life seemed suspended in her; her sister and Lewson gently raised her, and slowly led her unresisting from the body, her gaze never for an instant averted from it; when they reached the prison door she stopped, as if awakened from a trance, uttered a shriek of agony that would have pierced the hardest heart, and, rushing from them, flung herself . . . on the prostrate form before her.

Macready's recollection of her, leaning over her dead son at the close of *Douglas*, conveys the same sense of her passionately heightened mimic and vocal technique:

> The anguish of her soul seemed at length to have struck her brain. The silence of her fixed and vacant stare was terrible, broken at last by a loud and frantic laugh that made the hearers shudder. She then sprang up, and, with a few self-questioning words indicating her purpose of self-destruction, hurried in the wild madness of desperation from the scene.[1]

The declamatory classicism of John Kemble and especially of Mrs Siddons was deliberately broken up (if somewhat less frequently than in Garrick's acting) by skilful and conscious use of pantomime and stage business. These 'points', part of what Arthur Colby Sprague has recognized as a continuous tradition of Shakespearian stage business, were often remarkably popular moments in the production. In *Henry V*, Kemble's celebrated 'starting up from prayer at the sound of the trumpet, in the passage where he states his attempted atonement to Richard the Second, formed one of the most spirited excitements that the stage has ever displayed'.[2] Kemble's revolutionary stage business in *Hamlet* was also the object of much admiration, discussion and imitation. Commenting on the innovation, introduced at his début, of kneeling at the descent of the Ghost, the *Public Advertiser* (7 October 1783) remarked: 'In such Doating is John Bull for Novelty, that six Barbary horses shall be impawned, that if Hamlet, whether right or wrong, will kneel, on the first shutting of the Trap-Door, he shall get a thundering *Clap of Applause!*' 'The *kneeling* at the descent of the Ghost was censured as a *trick*', recorded Boaden, 'I suppose merely because it had not been done before; but it suitably marked the filial reverence of Hamlet, and the solemnity of the engagement he had contracted.'[3] John Henderson, a highly esteemed actor of the Garrick

[1] Sir Frederick Pollock (ed.), *Macready's Reminiscences* (London, 1875), I, 55–6, 57.
[2] Boaden, II, 8.
[3] Ibid., I, 98; cf. the very complete description of Kemble's Hamlet in *A Short Criticism on the Performance of Hamlet by Mr. Kemble* (London, 1789), pp. 12–14 (quoted at length in Downer, p. 331).

school who until his untimely death shared honours with Kemble as the popular tragedian of the age, saw and adopted this 'point' – as did generations of Hamlets after him.

Hamlet's requisite 'start' upon first catching sight of the Ghost was, in Kemble's interpretation, a model of boldly conceived yet classically harmonious movement. Gilbert Austin's *Chironomia; Or, a Treatise on Rhetorical Delivery* (1806), which outlines a system of 'notation for gesture', observes (p. 421) that at this moment Kemble moved suddenly into the strong position

$$\frac{\text{Bvhf}}{\text{st. Li. x}}$$

i.e., he stretched both hands horizontally forward, with the palms vertical, the fingers pointing upwards (Bvhf); he started (st.); and his left foot was advanced, his weight clearly on his right, and his feet far apart (Li. x).[1] Other items of business from Kemble's performance of the play confirm the impression of studied dignity. In the grave scene even he thought himself 'too studiously graceful'.[2] He broke the tradition of leaping into the grave, and his duel with Laertes was criticized for being 'too mechanical and artificial'. Such dignified reserve was, however, freely contrasted with moments of impulsive, romantically coloured business. One example is a 'point' recorded by the visitor Ludwig Tieck at the close of the play: at Hamlet's line, 'Here, thou incestuous, murderous, damned Dane, Drink off this potion; – Is thy union here?' Kemble violently 'thrusts the poisoned chalice to the king's mouth, and forces him, as he dies, to drink it, which I take to be the right thing'.[3]

This mixture of statuesque repose and sudden emotional shock in Kemble's

[1] Cf. Sprague, *Shakespeare and the Actors*, p. 139.

[2] Boaden, I, 103.

[3] Theodore Martin, 'An eye-witness of John Kemble', *The Nineteenth Century* (February 1880), p. 9.

The spicing of Kemble's dignified reserve with another sort of variety is seen in the presence of the venerable tradition of the grave-diggers' waistcoats in his Covent Garden production in 1811; Louis Simond explains:

After beginning their labour, and breaking ground for a grave, a conversation begins between the two grave-diggers. The chief one takes off his coat, folds it carefully, and puts it by in a safe corner; then taking up his pickaxe, spits in his hand, – gives a stroke or two, – talks, – stops, – strips off his waistcoat, still talking, – folds it with great deliberation and nicety, and puts it with the coat, – then an under-waistcoat, still talking – another and another. I counted seven or eight, each folded or unfolded very leisurely, in a manner always different, and with gestures faithfully copied from nature (*Journal of a Tour and Residence in Great Britain* (New York, 1815), II, 121–2).

art appears at its most effective in his Coriolanus, the role for which he was probably most ideally suited and in which he took his leave of the stage in 1817. Hazlitt has described 'the vehemence with which he moved forward increasing every instant, till it hurried him on to the catastrophe', but Walter Scott has captured the clearest impression of the realistically conceived emotion in Kemble's death scene:

> The Volscian assassins [approached] him from behind . . . [and] seemed to pass their swords through the body of Coriolanus. There was no precaution, no support; in the midst of the exclamation against Tullius Aufidius, he dropped as dead and as flat on the stage as if the swords had really met within his body. We have repeatedly heard screams from the female part of the audience when he presented this scene, which had the most striking resemblance to actual and instant death we ever witnessed.[1]

Mrs Siddons, a more temperamental as well as a more gifted performer than her brother, epitomized this blend of harmonious control with skilfully heightened, almost demented dramatic passion. Her unparalleled power is conveyed by Hazlitt's assertion that 'she did the greatest things with child-like ease; her powers never seemed tasked to the utmost, and always as if she had inexhaustible resources still in reserve. The least word she uttered seemed to float to the end of the stage; the least motion of her hand seemed to command awe and obedience.'[2] Even her greatest roles, however – Lady Randolph in Home's *Douglas*, Mrs Beverley in Moore's *The Gamester*, Belvidera in *Venice Preserved*, Constance in *King John*, Queen Katharine in *Henry VIII* – were eclipsed by her legendary portrayal of Lady Macbeth. Her analysis of this role, 'Remarks on the Character of Lady Macbeth', affords an interesting basis for comparison with the eye-witness transcription of her acting that has come down to us from G. J. Bell.[3] The actress's analysis of the part is dispassionate and even rather feeble when seen in the light of her dynamic and fiercely independent creation of the character on the stage. Its comments on the celebrated Siddonian sleepwalking scene ('Behold her now, with wasted form, with wan and hagged countenance . . . the smell of innocent blood incessantly [haunting] her imagination') provide only a hint

---

[1] *Quarterly Review*, XXXIV (1826), p. 224.
[2] *Hazlitt on Theatre*, p. 151.
[3] Siddons's role analysis is printed in Campbell's *Life*, II, 10–34; Bell's reconstruction of her performance and comments on its original publication are printed in Brander Matthews, pp. 75–114.

of the spirit of her performance. For her actual entrance on the stage, observed Bell,

> she advances rapidly to the table, sets down the light and rubs her hand, making the action of lifting up water in one hand at intervals. Later, she speaks the words 'One, two' while 'listening eagerly,' and the sigh which follows the realization that 'all the perfumes of Arabia will not sweeten this little hand' is 'a convulsive shudder – very horrible. A tone of imbecility audible in the sigh.'

The action in this scene, which established a tradition for subsequent Lady Macbeths, met with a storm of indignation at its introduction. Sheridan came to Siddons's dressing room, she recalled, to express

> the greatest surprise and concern that I meant to act without holding the candle in my hand; and when I argued the impracticability of washing out that 'damned spot' that was certainly implied by both her own words and those of her gentlewoman, he insisted, that if I did put the candle out of my hand it would be thought a presumptuous innovation, as Mrs. Pritchard had always retained it in hers.

The strong-willed actress persisted, however, adding that 'Mr Sheridan himself came to me after the play, and most ingenuously congratulated me on my obstinacy.'[1]

Unlike Kemble, who found powerful rivals for ascendancy in actors like Cooke and Henderson, Sarah Siddons tolerated no challengers and left no immediate successors to her title as the Tragic Muse. Eliza O'Neill (1791–1827) seemed, after an overwhelming success as Juliet in 1814, to promise, with her 'tenderness and sensibility and the simple force of passion', a renewal of the Siddons grandeur. Hazlitt, Shelley and the German visitor Pückler-Muskau all paid eager tribute to her art, but an early retirement in 1819 abruptly terminated her career and the hopes which it had raised.

Siddons's position in the comic vein was considerably less sovereign. In the highly popular 'breeches parts' she was notorious, even in her own time. As Rosalind in *As You Like It*, 'the town was not a little amused at her dress – mysterious nondescript garments that were neither male nor female – devised to satisfy a prudery which in such a play was wholly out of place.'[2] A similar puritanical reserve marked her portrayal of Imogen in *Cymbeline*. 'A taste which I will neither censure nor examine on the present occasion', pronounced Boaden solemnly, 'calls upon females, who assume the male

[1] Fitzgerald, I, 242, 243.   [2] Ibid., I, 248.

habit, for a more complete display of the figure, than suits the decorum of a delicate mind.'[1] It is perhaps not too unkind to remember that the Siddonian figure was not ideally suited to complete display: towards the end of her career, when she knelt to the Duke in *Measure for Measure*, two attendants had to come forward for the express purpose of helping the corpulent star to rise.

For a large public with less 'delicate' minds than Boaden's, the favourite exponent of these erotically provocative breeches parts and tomboy roles was the delightful Dorothy Jordan (1761–1816). From her début as Peggy in *The Country Girl* (DL 1785) to her retirement in 1814, she continued to charm audiences in such high-spirited roles as Miss Hoyden in Sheridan's *A Trip to Scarborough* and Sir Harry Wildair in Farquhar's *The Constant Couple* – while preserving her stamina to bear ten children as the mistress of the Duke of Clarence, later William IV.

Sarah Siddons's farewell to the stage in 1812, rather than John Philip Kemble's belated retirement in 1817, marked the end of the predominance of the Kemble style. Charles Kemble carried on its classical spirit: 'in comedy he was without a rival,' commented Macready; 'in tragedy he was first-class in second-rate parts.'[2] His most significant contribution remains his collaboration with J. P. Planché in the historically authentic revival of *King John* at Covent Garden in 1823. Stephen Kemble (1758–1822) is remembered, if at all, as the man who played Falstaff without the necessity of padding. Hazlitt was revolted when he witnessed the feat in 1816: 'We see no more reason why Mr. Stephen Kemble should play Falstaff, than why Louis XVIII is qualified to fill a throne, because he is fat and belongs to a particular family.'[3] By that time, however, the début of the tempestuous Edmund Kean in 1814 had stolen from the Kembles most of their former lustre. 'We wish we had never seen Mr. Kean,' wrote Hazlitt in the *Examiner* (8 December 1816). 'He has destroyed the Kemble religion; and it was the religion in which we were brought up. Never again shall we behold Mr. Kemble with the same pleasure that we did, nor see Mr. Kean with the same pleasure we have seen Mr. Kemble formerly.'

(iii) Forces of change: 1814–1843

Three major reactions against the established Kemble style shaped the course of English theatre during the years between 1814 and 1843: the passionate intensity of Edmund Kean, the trend towards greater familiarity represented

[1] Boaden, I, 343.   [2] *Macready's Reminiscences*, I, 225.   [3] *Hazlitt on Theatre*, p. 104.

by William Charles Macready, and the drawing-room manner of Madame Vestris at the Olympic.

Kean, in Leigh Hunt's opinion, 'did extinguish Kemble: at all events we hold it for certain that Kean hastened his going out. It was as sure a thing as Nature against Art, or tears against cheeks of stone.'[1] The overwhelming vitality and power of Kean's acting during his brief but brilliant period of triumph until the mid-1820s, when scandals in his private life, alcoholism and ill-health all contributed to his decline, place him beside Garrick and Mrs Siddons among the conspicuously great English actors. The éclat and intensity of his style endeared him to the romantic temperament. Coleridge's famous statement that his acting was 'like reading Shakespeare by flashes of lightning' felicitously captures the irregular and sometimes uneven splendour of his genius.[2] It also touches upon a central feature of his art: he was uniquely capable of establishing an explosive, immediate communication with his audience, of moving them with seemingly irresistible force to a paroxysm of feeling. 'He stirred the general heart with such a rush of mighty power, impressed himself so vividly by accent, look and gesture', wrote G. H. Lewes, that 'no audience could be unmoved; all defects were overlooked or disregarded, because it was impossible to watch Kean as Othello, Shylock, Richard, or Sir Giles Overreach without being strangely shaken by the terror, and the pathos, and the passion of a stormy spirit uttering itself in tones of irresistible power.'[3]

Small and unimpressive of stature, but with extremely flexible limbs and features, and large, dark, singularly expressive eyes, Edmund Kean possessed none of John Philip Kemble's classical repose and dignity of form. Kemble, Hazlitt pronounced, 'is the very still-life and statuary of the stage; a perfect figure of a man; a petrification of sentiment, that heaves no sigh, and sheds no tears; an icicle upon the bust of tragedy'.[4] By contrast, Kean seemed to be all cyclonic energy, all fire, all intensity. Although he appeared in some few comic roles, among them Abel Drugger, his vein was tragic. He was, as Lewes remarked, nothing if not passionate.[5]

The animation, vigour and force with which Kean created an emotional part, using the physical resources of mime, movement, gesture and speech to

[1] *Tatler* 278 (25 July 1831).
[2] This descriptive simile was not meant by Coleridge as undiluted praise, however, for he adds that Kean's transitions, 'though sometimes productive of great effect, are often unreasonable'. See *Table Talk*, ed. T. Ashe (London, 1888), p. 25.
[3] George Henry Lewes, *On Actors and the Art of Acting* (London, 1875), pp. 2–3.
[4] *Hazlitt on Theatre*, p. 91.
[5] Lewes, p. 16.

convey a series of emphatic transitions, are epitomized in his portrayal of Zanga in Young's *The Revenge*:

> He had all the wild impetuosity of barbarous revenge . . . . He was like a man stung with rage, and bursting with stifled passions. His hurried motions had the restlessness of the panther's: his wily caution, his cruel eye, his quivering visage, his violent gestures, his hollow pauses, his abrupt transitions, were all in character. . . . The whole character is violent; the whole expression is in action.[1]

This turbulence of character and violence of emotion made a part like Sir Giles Overreach in Massinger's *A New Way to Pay Old Debts* one of his most celebrated. The intensity with which Kean personified fury in the last act had an audience impact which has become legendary. 'The effect of this powerful playing', runs one colourful account, 'was such, that one of the actresses on stage . . . fainted; Byron at the same time was seized in his box by a convulsive fit; whilst women went into hysterics, and the whole house burst into a wild clamour of applause.'[2] Kemble, who also played Overreach in 1816, seemed with his coolness and aloofness totally miscast in comparison.

Kean's Sir Edward Mortimer in *The Iron Chest* was similarly constructed of a series of swift, picturesque plastic actions, fluently melting into one another. 'The transitions in this play, from calmness to deep despair, from concealed suspicion to open rage, from smooth decorous indifference to the convulsive agonies of remorse, gave Mr. Kean frequent opportunities for the display of his peculiar talents', wrote Hazlitt in the *Examiner* (1 December 1816), emphasizing that in 'the picturesque expression of passion by outward action' he was simply without a rival.

The lion-like power (to borrow Lewes's phrase)[3] of Kean's talent was complemented by a singularly graceful beauty of appearance and deportment which made their bearer the perfect embodiment of this period's ideal. His romanticism was not the mere outpouring of passion. His acting style, like that of his predecessors, depended to a very great degree upon the use of physical poses and attitudes composed to underscore, in a pictorially pleasing manner, a given dramatic passion. It is no coincidence that his Richard III should be described by Hazlitt as 'a perpetual succession of striking pictures'. A memorable moment in his performance was, according to Hazlitt's perceptive review in the *Morning Chronicle* (15 February 1814), the courtship

[1] *Hazlitt on Theatre*, p. 54.
[2] J. Fitzgerald Molloy, *The Life and Adventures of Edmund Kean* (London, 1888), I, 248.
[3] Lewes, pp. 4, 6.

scene with Lady Anne, in which Kean's 'attitude in leaning against the side of the stage before he comes forward . . . was one of the most graceful and striking we remember to have seen. It would have done for Titian to paint.' Unlike Cooke, whose approach had been 'more violent, hurried, and full of anxious uncertainty', Kean's attack presented, in the words of the same reviewer, 'an admirable exhibition of smooth and smiling villainy. The progress of wily adulation, of encroaching humility, was finely marked throughout by the action, voice and eye. He seemed, like the first tempter, to approach his prey, certain of the event, and as if success had smoothed the way before him.'

Consummate pathos as well as consummate beauty constituted Kean's force as an artist. 'He always gives you the grace and the nature too – the ideal with the common – the charm of the thought with the energy of the passion', remarked Leigh Hunt.[1] When Kean attempted to vary and improve upon his effects, as he evidently did at least during his first seasons, the result was sometimes the destruction of what had originally been built up with such care.[2] By nature, however, he was not an impulsive artist. What appeared to be spontaneous effusions of genius were in fact, as astute observers realized, rooted in the detailed and methodical approach of a conscious craftsman. Frequently his performances were criticized for their unevenness. Yet no actor has equalled his talent for projecting an overall emotional impression which exploded into flashes of overwhelming pathos. His delivery of the curse in *King Lear* crystallized into one such single sustained effect: 'He threw himself on his knees, lifted up his arms like withered stumps, threw his head quite back, and in that position, as if severed from all that held him to society, breathed a heartstruck prayer, like the figure of a man obtruncated!'[3] In the same passage, Crabb Robinson was astonished by the effect produced 'by his manner of bringing out his words with the effort of a man nearly exhausted and breathless – rather spelling his syllables than forming them into words – "how sharp – er–than a– serpent's tooth–it– is" etc. etc. . . . He does not need vigour or grace as Lear, but passion which never fails him.'[4]

Kean's foremost performances were remarkable not only for their intensity of passion and the vehemence of the transitions which cast them into bold

[1] *Tatler* 165 (15 March 1831).
[2] Best illustrated by Hazlitt's three reviews in 1814 of Kean's Richard: *Morning Chronicle* (15 February and 21 February) and *The Champion* (9 October).
[3] *Hazlitt on Theatre*, p. 194.
[4] Crabb Robinson, *The London Theatre*, p. 92.

relief. Another notable quality derived from his ability to express subsiding emotion. 'His instinct taught him', commented G. H. Lewes,

> that a strong emotion, after discharging itself in one massive current, continues for a time expressing itself in feebler currents. The waves are not stilled when the storm has passed away. There remains the ground-swell troubling the deeps. In watching Kean's quivering muscles and altered tones, you felt the subsidence of passion. The voice might be calm, but there was a tremor in it; the face might be quiet, but there were vanishing traces of the recent agitation.[1]

Related to Kean's technique of showing subsiding emotion was his novel treatment of death scenes, as noticed by Henry Crabb Robinson. 'Hitherto actors when they died thought they had only bodily suffering to represent – And he who could strain the muscles of the throat the most frightfully was the hero', recorded the indefatigable diarist. Kean, however, introduced a new conception: 'he has performed dying scenes on this principle that even in the last moments the ruling passion and the personalities of the character are not to be lost in the general idea of human suffering.' Putting this principle into practice, Kean's mortally wounded Macbeth 'poises himself for a second, totters and falls. He revives, crawls after his sword and as his fingers reach it he dyes [*sic*].' Similarly, ebbing passion continued to activate Kean's stricken Richard: 'when his sword is beaten out of his hands he continues fighting with his fist as if he had a sword.'[2]

Kean's Othello, termed by Hazlitt his 'best character', was nonetheless criticized by him for being 'too often in the highest key of passion, too uniformly on the verge of extravagance, too constantly on the rack'.[3] The opening acts were passed over quickly by Kean; in a situation such as Othello's address to the Senate (I, iii) he was ineffective: 'He had little power of elocution unless when sustained by a strong emotion; and this long simple narrative was the kind of speech he could not manage at all.'[4] But in the third act he reached – too quickly, according to some observers – his celebrated peak of jealousy and passion. Leigh Hunt's description of Kean's 'Farewell' speech (III, iii) offers an exceptionally clear example of this style of romantic acting:

> The whole passage would have formed an admirable study for a young actor, in showing him the beauty of sacrificing verbal painting to a

[1] Lewes, pp. 8–9.   [2] Crabb Robinson, p. 60.
[3] *Hazlitt on Theatre*, p. 70.   [4] Lewes, p. 5.

pervading sentiment. . . . Mr. Kean gave no vulgar importance to 'the plumed troop' and 'the big wars', as commonplace actors do; because the melancholy overcomes all; it merges the particular images into one mass of regret.[1]

'His voice in the farewell apostrophe to Content,' noted Hazlitt elsewhere, 'took the deep intonation of the pealing organ, and heaved from the heart sounds that come on the ear like the funeral dirge of years of promised happiness.'[2] One of Kean's early Iagos was Junius Brutus Booth (1796–1852), an imitator whose début as Richard was 'an exact copy or parody' of the Kean manner, and whose Ancient was likewise 'a very close and spirited imitation' of the star. In a comparison of these two actors by Junius Brutus's son, the great American tragedian Edwin Booth (1833–93), Kean's 'Farewell' speech is again singled out for comment. It sounded, Booth had told his son, 'like the moan of ocean or the soughing of wind through cedars. His peculiar lingering on the letter "l" often marked his delivery; but here, in the "Farewell," the tones of cathedral chimes were not more mournful.'[3] The same speech ('the music of a broken heart', John Vandenhoff called it),[4] marked, not unfittingly, the end of Kean's own career: after delivering it in 1833 to his last Iago, his son Charles Kean, he collapsed on the stage and died less than two months later.

Edmund Kean's closest rival throughout his career and his undisputed successor after his death was William Charles Macready, whose long professional life on the London stage extended from his début at Covent Garden in 1816 to his retirement thirty-five years later. The artistic development of the 'Eminent Tragedian' has been charted by the best theatrical critics of the age – Hazlitt, Hunt and Lewes have all written persuasively about him – and their descriptions are supplemented by the copious diary notes (totalling half a million words in the 1912 edition) left by this unusual personality.[5] Macready's acting, according to his own avowed aim, was a blend of the styles of Kean and the French tragedian François Joseph Talma (1763–1826).[6]

[1] Hunt, *Dramatic Essays*, pp. 207–8.
[2] *Hazlitt on Theatre*, p. 33.
[3] Brander Matthews, p. 248.
[4] See his *An Actor's Notebook, or The Green-Room and the Stage* (London, 1865), p. 21.
[5] Pollock's *Macready's Reminiscences* (1875) was followed by William Toynbee's edition of *The Diaries of William Charles Macready, 1833–1851*, 2 volumes (New York, 1912 and London, 1912); a recent abridgement is J. C. Trewin's *The Journal of William Charles Macready 1832–1851* (London, 1967).
[6] *Athenaeum* (1851), p. 252.

Talma, Macready felt, was 'the most finished artist of his time, not below Kean in his most energetic displays, and far above him in the refinement of his taste and extent of his research, equalling Kemble in dignity, unfettered by his stiffness and formality'.[1] Inspired by Kean's methods (although revolted by his personal life), Macready sought to evolve an equivalent of the fiery transitions and 'picturesque plastic action' of the older performer. The result became the insertion of the melodramatic and domestic touches that are the hallmarks of Macready's contribution as an actor.

Hazlitt's reviews of Macready's earliest appearances in London set the tone for what was to come. Writing in the *Examiner* (22 September 1816), the critic felt that the young actor's début as Orestes in Ambrose Phillips's Racine translation *The Distressed Mother* established him as 'by far the best tragic actor that has come out in our remembrance, with the exception of Mr. Kean'. As Mentevole in Jephson's *Julia, or The Italian Lover*, however, Macready was criticized by the *Examiner* (6 October) for a trait that was to become a characteristic: 'Mr. Macready sometimes, to express uneasiness and agitation, composes his cravat, as he would in a drawing-room.' As Othello in his initial London season, Macready was the first of the century's parade of domestic or 'troubled' Moors that would include the 'intellectualized' Othellos of Charles Kean, Fechter and, not least, the first important black tragedian to appear on the English stage, Ira Aldridge (1804–67).[2] Hazlitt found that Macready as Othello 'whined and whimpered', trying 'to affect the audience by affecting a pitiful sensibility', while others described his portrayal as weak, effeminate, 'deficient in majesty of character and passion' and resembling 'an elderly negress of evil repute, going to a fancy ball'.[3]

These critical reactions identify many of the key aspects of Macready's approach as an actor. Peculiarly fitted, to borrow Leigh Hunt's phrase, for 'the expression of domestic tenderness', Macready's best roles were not characters of physical or moral grandeur. Lewes saw him as 'radically unfitted for ideal characters – for the display of broad elemental passions'. His

[1] Pollock, I, 238.
[2] On the American actor Ira Aldridge's work, see Herbert Marshall and Mildred Stock, *Ira Aldridge, The Negro Tragedian* (London, 1958).
[3] *Hazlitt on Theatre*, p. 103; William Archer, *William Charles Macready* (London, 1870), pp. 202–3; Lester Wallack, *Memories of Fifty Years* (New York, 1889), p. 132. Macready's Othello is historically important for the warm reception it received in Paris during the famous English performances there in 1827. The English actors, with Edmund Kean, Charles Kemble and Macready in the vanguard, performed from September 1827 to July 1828, and their resounding success marked a triumph for the Romantic movement and a turning point in French theatrical history. See Jean Jacquot, *Shakespeare en France* (Paris, 1964), p. 30.

abruptly inserted 'touches of nature' were often incongruous with the general elevation of a Shakespearian performance. As Macbeth, he stole into the sleeping chamber of Duncan, we are told by Lewes, 'like a man going to purloin a purse, not like a warrior going to snatch a crown', while Leigh Hunt found that his characterization of the same role 'wants the Royal warrant' of conscious ascendancy.[1] Macready's delivery was also distinguished (or blemished, according to one's viewpoint) by the same tendency to juxtapose poetic grandeur with familiarity. Fanny Kemble's explanation of this trait may be vindictive, but it is nonetheless illuminating: she asserts that his 'consciousness of his imperfect declamation of blank verse . . . induced him to adopt what his admirers called his natural style of speaking it; which was simply chopping it up into prose'.[2]

By contrast, Macready's effectiveness as an interpreter of contemporary drama was unrivalled. He created half a hundred roles in new plays, excelling in domestic or melodramatic parts like Bulwer-Lytton's Richelieu, Knowles's Virginius, and Byron's Werner. The writing style of Sheridan Knowles represented the ideal medium for the expression of his art.[3] Writing of the stylistic mixture of 'blank verse and parasols' which Macready combined in his production of Westland Marston's *The Patrician's Daughter* (1842), a blank verse play dealing with contemporary life, this playwright noted that the actor 'was perhaps more anxious than the author to invest the action with every detail of the most modern realism'.[4] His ability to translate emotion into effective pieces of stage business was still, however, in line with the venerable practice of making 'points': Marston remembered him 'as Spinola in [Richard Troughton's] *Nina Sforza*, when, in the fifth act, with foot and sword, he turned over the limbs of the prostrate rival' and the pit howled its indignation at the audacity of the conception.[5] With the example of Edmund Kean clearly before him, Macready strove, in a situation such as the depiction of Lear's growing madness, to present a gradual intensification of the emotional impact. 'He knew well how to raise an emotion by degrees to its

---

[1] See G. H. Lewes's 'Was Macready a great actor?' in his *Dramatic Essays*, ed. William Archer and R. W. Lowe (London, 1896), pp. 126–34, and Hunt's *Macbeth* review, reproduced in Nagler, *Sources*, pp. 471–3.

[2] *Records of a Later Life* (New York, 1882), III, 376.

[3] See also Part III below, pp. 214ff., 223ff.

[4] John Westland Marston, *Our Recent Actors* (London, 1888), I, 285. Joseph's comment on Macready's technique in this respect is illuminating: 'What Macready did in modern plays Kean had done in Shakespeare, treating the text as one in which "more is indicated than is expressed" ' (*The Tragic Actor*, p. 310).

[5] Marston, I, 99.

full height', remarked Lady Pollock, 'and had the skill to fill the cup of anguish drop by drop till it overflowed.'[1]

The influence of the Kemble school continued to be felt, however, throughout the age of Macready. Charles Kemble ('a wretched old coxcomb' in Macready's own estimation)[2] remained popular on the stage throughout a large part of the latter's career. Dignified and forceful, J. M. Vandenhoff (1790–1861) was, in Marston's opinion, 'the last prominent tragedian of the Kemble school'.[2] Macready himself seems to have recalled John Kemble in his emphasis on a clear, single through-line rather than on a series of successive emotional surprises and 'points'. Marston described his 'faculty of grasping the central idea of his part, and making all the lights thrown upon details correspond with that idea'.[4] 'His performances are consequently Wholes,' wrote the *Athenaeum* at the close of his career in 1851. 'His merit is not to be tested by occasional flashes of genius – by partial triumphs achieved in particular scenes – but by the entire conception.'[5]

The performance style of Helen Faucit (1817–98), frequently Macready's leading lady, was at least partly shaped by the Kemble religion and, specifically, by the advice of Charles Kemble. 'Let the expression be genuine, earnest, but not ugly', he had impressed upon her. However sombre the picture may be, 'it must be noble in its outlines; truthful, picturesque, but never repulsive, mean, or commonplace.'[6] Following her début as Julia in Knowles's *The Hunchback* at Covent Garden in 1836, Helen Faucit rose rapidly to stardom in a period not remarkable for its outstanding actresses. No Sarah Siddons, she nevertheless strove, in a part like Belvidera, to merge the statuesque nobility and ideality of the Kemble method with a realistic, almost pathological conception of madness. 'Anything finer than the expression and attitude of Miss Faucit when the death-knell of Pierre sounds', recorded her husband Sir Theodore Martin, 'it would be hard to conceive. The vacant eye, prophetic of the unsettling brain, the dropt jaw, the death-like cheek, the dilated throat, the nerveless rigidity of the extended arms, would have immortalized a sculptor could they have been fixed in marble.'[7]

Fully as significant as his work as an actor is the contribution which Macready made during this period as a manager. The rich source material

---

[1] *Macready as I knew him* (London, 1884), pp. 104 ff.
[2] J. C. Trewin, *Journal*, p. 51.
[3] Marston, I, 22.
[4] Ibid., I, 99.
[5] *Athenaeum* (1851), p. 251.
[6] Helen Faucit, *On Some of Shakespeare's Female Characters* (London, 1899), p. 295.
[7] See his *Helena Faucit* (London, 1900), p. 147.

relating to his two managerships – at Covent Garden from 1837 to 1839 and then at Drury Lane from 1841 to 1843 – allows the student of stage production to investigate his techniques in full measure.[1] The strict attention to detail which had marked Kemble's regimes was carried forward by Macready in his endeavour to achieve 'fidelity and appropriateness' in staging, costuming and the handling of crowd scenes. His campaign to improve rehearsal procedures has been widely discussed and admired. As a young man he discovered that

> it was the custom of the London actors, especially the leading ones, to do little more at rehearsals than read or repeat the words of their parts, marking on them their entrances and exits, as settled by the stage-manager, and their respective places on the stage. To make any display of passion or energy would be to expose oneself to the ridicule or sneers of the green-room.

In disapproval of this custom the young actor attempted 'to rehearse with the same earnestness as I would act'.[2] When, as a manager, Macready finally acquired the power to change the habits of others in this respect, he devoted himself vigorously to the matter of rehearsals. A diary entry for 5 November 1840 notes, for instance, that he spent 'two hours in the rehearsal of one page of the club scene' of Bulwer-Lytton's new play *Money* – though balancing this evidence is the impression of the impermanence of such reforms left by an entry for 16 October 1849 which reads: 'Rehearsed *King Lear* with several characters absent and several not cast: Planché calls the Haymarket "The Patent Self-Acting Theatre". '

Although Shakespearian productions were not nearly as numerous in Macready's managements as under Kemble, the choleric 'Eminent' made a distinct contribution in his restorations of Shakespeare's texts. Most notable, of course, was the memorable revival, for the first time in 150 years, of an accurate *King Lear* that included the Fool – played, due to Macready's misgivings about the actability of the part, by the charming Priscilla Horton, who also delighted her audiences as a flying Ariel.[3] 'Thine is it that our drama did not die': Tennyson's well-known and rather fulsome sonnet to the 'moral,

---

[1] See, for example, Charles Shattuck's promptbook facsimiles, *William Charles Macready's 'King John'* (Urbana, 1962) and *Mr. Macready Produces 'As You Like It'* (Urbana, 1962), and George Scharf's iconographic record, *Recollections of the Scenic Effects at Covent Garden Theatre during the Season 1838–39* (London, 1839).

[2] Pollock, I, 145–6.

[3] Cf. Odell, II, 193–7. See also Dickens's 'The restoration of Shakespeare's "Lear" to the stage' in the *Examiner* (4 February 1838).

17 The Sans Pareil Theatre, London (later to become the Adelphi) as it was in 1816, showing the new convention of a raised 'circle' over a widened pit

18a A fire scene on a transparency, from *The Mirror or Harlequin Everywhere* as designed by Cipriani and Richards at Covent Garden in 1779

18b A maquette by Philippe Jacques de Loutherbourg, inscribed by an unknown hand as being for Garrick's *Richard III*

19 Charles Kean's production of *Henry V*, the Princess's, 1859: the storming of the breach

20a Charles Kean's production of *Macbeth*, the Princess's, 1853: the banquet

20b The same production: the glen near the palace of Forres

21a Covent Garden exterior, 1809

21b Theatre Royal, Covent Garden, *c.* 1861

22a Sadlers Wells, late eighteenth century

22b Theatre Royal, Drury Lane

23 A reconstruction by C. Green of Bartholomew's Fair showing Richardson's 'portable' theatre (1879)

Left Playbill

☞ **Mr. CHARLES KEAN**
In 'RICHARD THE THIRD!'
On which occasion Privileges of every description (except those of the Public Press) will be suspended.

Theatre Royal, Drury Lane.

This Evening, MONDAY, MAY the 14th, 1838,
Her Majesty's Servants will perform Shakspeare's Tragedy (altered by Cibber) of

Richard III.

Henry Sixth, King of England, **Mr. BAKER.**
Prince of Wales, Miss POOLE,   Duke of York, Miss MARSHALL
Richard, Duke of Glo'ster, ... **Mr. CHARLES KEAN.**
Duke of Buckingham, ... **Mr. COOPER,**
Duke of Norfolk, **Mr. DURUSET,**   Earl of Oxford, Mr. HOWELL.
Lord Hastings, Mr. F. SUTTON,   Lord Stanley, Mr. FENTON.
Henry, Earl of Richmond, ... **Mr. KING.**
Sir W. Brandon, Mr. WHETTON,   Sir W. Catesby, Mr. BRINDAL,
Sir R. Ratcliffe, Mr. F. COOKE,   Sir W. Catesby, Mr. BRINDAL.
Sir R. Brackenbury, Mr. MIAN,   Sir W. Herbert, Mr. ROBERTS,
Sir J Tyrrell, Mr. HONNER, Lord Mayor of London, Mr. HUGHES,
Tressel, Mr. H. COOKE,   Sheriffs, Messrs. HEATH & KING.
Lords, Officers, Guards, Archers, Standard-bearers, Pall-bearers, Attendants, &c. &c. &c.
Queen Elizabeth, Mrs. LOVELL,   Duchess of York, Mad. SIMON,
Lady Anne, ... **Mrs. TERNAN**

THE WHITE TOWER   BY-WARD TOWER
VAULTED CHAMBER IN THE WHITE TOWER.
INTERIOR OF OLD ST. PAUL'S,
IN WHICH IS SEEN **THE BODY OF KING HENRY LYING IN STATE.**
STATE CHAMBER in THE TOWER.
GALLERY IN THE TOWER.   THE PALACE.
A STREET IN LONDON.   LANDSCAPE NEAR TAMWORTH.
BOSWORTH FIELD.   RICHMOND'S CAMP.
RICHARD'S TENT!
ANOTHER PART OF BOSWORTH FIELD
THE BATTLE FIELD!

The Evening's Performances will terminate with the Grand Romance of

Blue Beard!

Abomelique, .. (Blue Beard) .. Mr. BAKER,   Selim, ... Mr. TEMPLETON,
Ibrahim, ... Mr. W. BENNETT,   Shacabac, ... Mr. DURUSET,
Hassan, Mr. HONNER,   First Spahi, Mr. F. COOKE,   Second Spahi, Mr. HOWELL,
Third Spahi, Mr. FENTON,   Fourth Spahi, Mr. HATTON,   Slave, Mr. MEARS,
Fatima, ... Miss FORDE,   Irene, ... Miss POOLE,   Beda, ... Mrs. ALLCROFT.

To-morrow, Beardet's Opera of 'The Gipsy's Warning. Deaf as a Post And The Devil on Two Sticks.'
On Wednesday, will be revived Shakspeare's Tragedy of

OTHELLO!

The Part of Othello,   (First Time)   by Mr. CHARLES KEAN.
The Part of Iago,   "   by Mr. TERNAN.
(Whose performance of this took on his First Appearance at this Theatre was received with the utmost favor.)
The Part of Cassio,   "   by Mr. COOPER.
The Part of Desdemona,   (her First Appearance)   by Miss ALLISON,
The Part of Emilia, ... (on this Occasion)   by Mrs. TERNAN.
On Thursday, (delayed till that Day, in consequence of Miss Romer's Indisposition will be produced, a New Opera Buffa) in which

DIADESTE!

OR, THE VEILED LADY.
The Music composed expressly for this Theatre, by M. W. BALFE, who will preside in the Orchestra.   The Principal Characters by
Mr. H. PHILLIPS,   Mr. TEMPLETON,   Mr. GIUBILEI,
Miss ROMER,   Miss FANNY HEALY,   Miss POOLE.
On Friday, a TRAGEDY in which Mr. Charles Kean will perform   And a New Opera Buffa
On Saturday, ...   a New Opera Buffa   And a Variety of other Entertainments.

Miss ALLISON,

of the Theatre Royal, Haymarket, will make her First Appearance on this Stage on Wednesday next, in the Character of Desdemona.

Mr. CHARLES KEAN

on his re appearance on Wednesday was received with the same degree of enthusiasm which attended his previous performances, and having attracted a brilliant and overflowing Audience, will perform **RICHARD THE THIRD** To-Night, and on Wednesday next will perform, for the First Time, Shakspeare's Character of **OTHELLO.**

Right Playbill

PERFORMED but ONCE
At the Theatre Royal in Drury-L
This present Friday, the 9th of May, 17
Will be presented a NEW COMEDY, call'd

School for Scand

The PRINCIPAL CHARACTERS by
Mr. KING,
Mr. YATES,
Mr. DODD,
Mr. PALMER,
Mr. PARSONS,
Mr. BADDELEY,   Mr. AICK
Mr. PACKER,   Mr. FARRE
Mr. LAMASH,   Mr. GAUDR
Mr. R. PALMER, Mr. NORRIS, Mr. CHAP
And Mr. SMITH.
Miss POPE,
Miss P. HOPKINS
Miss SHERRY,
And Mrs. ABINGTO
The Prologue to be spoken by Mr. KI
And the Epilogue by Mrs. ABINGTO
With NEW SCENES and DRESS
To which will be added a Musical Drama, call'd
The DESERTE
Henry by Mr. DAVIES,
Russet by Mr. BANNISTER, Simkin by Mr. CARPEN
Skirmish by Mr. PARSONS,   Flint by Mr. WRIGE
Soldiers by Mr. Legg, Mr. Kear, Mr. Griffith, Mr. Chaplin, Mr. Follet
Jenny by Mrs. DAVIES,
Margaret by Mrs. LOVE,
Louisa by Miss COLLETT,
The Doors will be opened at Half after Five, to begin exactly at Half after Six

25a James Quin, with Peg Woffington and
George Anne Bellamy, in *Coriolanus*

25b Samuel Phelps as
Coriolanus

26a Garrick as Richard III

26b Edmund Kean as Richard III

27a Garrick as Richard III

27b Kemble as Richard III

28a Garrick and Mrs Cibber in Otway's *Venice Preserved*

28b Spranger Barry and Mrs Ann Barry in the same play

29a Hamlet meets the Ghost: Garrick

29b Hamlet meets the Ghost: Henry Irving

30a Garrick and Mrs Pritchard in *Macbeth*

30b Fuseli's rendering of the same characters

31a Later Macbeths:
Edmund Kean

31b Later Macbeths:
Samuel Phelps

32 Later Macbeths: Charles Kean (with Mrs Kean)

grave, sublime' Macready suggests the emotionality with which the literary establishment viewed his stewardship, as the 'last stand' of the legitimate drama.

In contrast to the 'legitimacy' of Macready's contributions, the impact of Eliza Lucy Bartolozzi – better known as the irrepressible Madame Vestris (1797–1856) – was felt mainly in the 'illegitimate' field of burletta and vaudeville comedy to which the minor theatres were confined prior to 1843. After a promising operatic début in 1815 as 'a perfect contralto, possessing a peculiar sweetness',[1] she joined Elliston's troupe at Drury Lane four years later, coincident with leaving her first husband Armand Vestris. Success was quickly hers in the masculine title role of Moncrieff's operatic extravaganza *Giovanni in London; or, The Libertine Reclaimed*. Like Peg Woffington and Dorothy Jordan before her, Vestris excelled in such 'breeches parts': even the fastidious Pückler-Muskau, while recognizing her other talents, realized that 'her great celebrity rests on the beauty of her legs'. Whether in revealing trousers or more conventional attire, her whole appearance exuded vivacious feminine charm, although, as Westland Marston notes in his description, such items as 'a silk skirt, a lace-edged petticoat, a silk stocking, a shoe of satin or patent leather would never have been worn by some of the characters she impersonated'.[2]

Vestris's reputation as an innovator rests, however, not on her acting career but on her managerial accomplishments. At the helm of the Olympic from 1830 to 1838, she created the most significant minor theatre to emerge under the monopoly. 'The little Olympic, the most despised nook in the dramatic world, became not only one of the most popular and fashionable theatres London ever saw', wrote J. R. Planché, 'but [it] served as a life-boat to the respectability of the stage, which was fast sinking in the general wreck.'[3] Planché's enthusiastic summary of her 'reforms' is fairly familiar. Exaggerated promotional devices, inflexible programming and unduly late closings were all abolished. 'The most scrupulous attention' was paid to questions of scenic illusion. Vestris's second husband, comedian Charles Mathews Jr (1803–78), is more informative on the latter point:

> Drawing-rooms were fitted up like drawing-rooms, and furnished with care and taste. Two chairs no longer indicated that two persons were to

---

[1] *The Inquisitor*, cited in E. B. Watson, *Sheridan to Robertson* (Cambridge, Mass., 1926), p. 189, whose chapter on the Vestris management (chapter 9) is one of the first analyses to recognize her significance.
[2] Marston, II, 142.
[3] *The Extravaganzas of J. R. Planché* (London, 1879), I, 286.

be seated. . . . A claret-coloured coat, salmon-coloured trousers with a broad black stripe, a sky-blue neckcloth with a large paste brooch, and a cut-steel eye-glass with a pink ribbon no longer marked the 'light comedy gentleman'.[1]

Improvements in integrated comic acting were achieved by Vestris through a simple expedient: 'her pieces contain but three or four parts altogether, and she always had an equal number of good performers to sustain them.'[2]

The calibre of the company with which she surrounded herself unquestionably explains much of the Olympic success. Planché provided her with a whole series of successful vehicles, beginning with the redoubtable *Olympic Revels* and *Olympic Devils* (in the latter, Vestris was Orpheus, 'a charming musician'). Among the able comic actors whom Vestris gathered around her at one time or another, John Liston (1776–1846) stands out as the greatest low comedian of the age. A veteran of more than three decades on the London stage, Liston's performance in Poole's extraordinary hit *Paul Pry* (1825) became one of the century's renowned comic masterpieces.[3] The style of his acting was 'unconscious and involuntary' – especially marked by an irresistible deadpan that continued to delight audiences until his retirement in 1837. He 'has more comic humour, more power of face, and a more genial and happy vein of folly, than any other actor we remember', thought Hazlitt. 'His face is not caricature: his drollery oozes out of his features, and trickles down his face, his voice is a pitch-pipe for laughter.'[4] Of the younger comedians who performed with Vestris, her husband Charles James Mathews, who made his début at the Olympic in his own play *The Humpbacked Lover* in 1835, is the best representative of the antithesis of Liston's style, the epitome of the elegant light comedy actor. His pantomimic talent was doubtless inherited from his father, Charles Mathews Sr (1776–1835), whose 'At Homes' – one-man shows of character monologues and impersonations – were highly popular during the early years of the century. Grace, ease and elegance remained the hallmarks of the younger Mathews's comic acting. The conversational tone and drawing-room quietness cultivated in the Mathews-Vestris style were indebted to the French influence of the Scribean *comédies-vaudeville*, transferred to English terms by Planché. (The Danish critic and dramatist J. L. Heiberg, in a similar manner but with more startling results,

---

[1] *The Life of Charles James Mathews Chiefly Autobiographical*, ed. Charles Dickens (London, 1879), II, 76.
[2] *The Era*, 30 September 1838.
[3] See also Part III, pp. 216–17.
[4] *Hazlitt on Theatre*, p. 154.

transplanted the same Scribean vaudeville traditions to the Scandinavian theatre, thereby preparing the ground for the future development of Ibsen's art.)[1] In 1875 G. H. Lewes again praised Mathews, who remained on the stage until the close of our period, for his strides in the direction of realistic character acting – although Lewes's conclusion to the essay 'On Natural Acting' surely suggests that, even at that date, the older traditions had in no sense wholly disappeared: 'The nearer the approach to every-day reality implied by the author in his characters and language – the closer the coat-and-waistcoat realism of the drama – the closer must be the actor's imitation of every-day manner; but even then he must idealise, *i.e.*, select and heighten – and it is for his tact to determine how much.'[2]

After relinquishing the Olympic in 1838, Mr and Mrs Mathews took on the management of Covent Garden after Macready ('It is not a fitting spectacle,' fumed the Eminent: 'the national drama in the hands of Mrs Vestris and Mr Charles Mathews!')[3] Here, from 1839 to 1842, and during a later tenure at the Lyceum, they continued to evolve a realistically oriented style of production and performance which represents a third distinct kind of reaction against the Kemble tradition. They presented Dion Boucicault's youthful *London Assurance* in 1841, using 'not stage properties, but *bona fide* realities'.[4] The presence of 'a live dog of mongrel breed' in Vestris's *A Midsummer Night's Dream* extravaganza in 1840 presumably denotes the same penchant for realistic touches.[5] With the dissolution of the monopoly in 1843, a number of other minor theatres were free to make significant contributions to the English theatrical scene. It was not until the 1860s, however, that the direction taken thirty years before by Madame Vestris at the Olympic was pursued in earnest by the Bancrofts at the Prince of Wales's, in their productions of the cup-and-saucer dramas of Vestris's sometime prompter, Tom Robertson.

(iv) New theatres for old: 1843–1880

The 'liberation' of the theatres by the abolition of the monopoly in 1843 produced no sudden wave of new playwrights, rescued from neglect under the old system. The glories of Drury Lane and Covent Garden vanished rapidly

[1] Further information about J. L. Heiberg is available in Henning Fenger's *The Heibergs*, ed. and trans. F. J. Marker (New York, 1970).
[2] Lewes, *On Actors*, pp. 59, 125.
[3] J. C. Trewin, *Journal*, p. 159.
[4] *Theatrical Observer*, 5 March 1841.
[5] See Sprague, *Shakespeare and the Actors*, p. 54.

once their predominance was destroyed. London audiences would have to wait until the final decade of this transitional period before another English actor of the very first rank would again stand before them. The newly legitimized smaller theatres did, however, register positive and significant contributions in the realm of production and stagecraft. Chief among them were three houses, Sadler's Wells, the Princess's and the aforementioned Prince of Wales's.

The actor-manager Samuel Phelps (1804–78) began his remarkable eighteen-year operation of Sadler's Wells in 1844. Seven years earlier, he had made his London début as Shylock at the Haymarket, and his success had 'depressed the spirits' of Macready, ever wary of potential rivals. During the 1840s and 1850s Phelps displayed at the Wells an excellence of production and *mise en scène* which deserves far more scholarly attention than it has yet received. Even in the most obvious terms of repertory statistics, his achievements are impressive. Thirty-four plays by Shakespeare, including such infrequently performed pieces as *Timon of Athens* and *Pericles*, were revived in authentic versions under Phelps's regime. These were supplemented with such noteworthy additions from Stuart drama as Beaumont and Fletcher's *A King and No King* and *The Maid's Tragedy*, Massinger's *The City Madam*, *A New Way to Pay Old Debts* and *The Fatal Dowry*, and Webster's *The Duchess of Malfi*.

The object here, however, is to deal with Phelps's place as an actor. Before engaging him for Covent Garden in 1837, Macready journeyed to Southampton to observe him as Sir Edmund Mortimer in Colman's *The Iron Chest*. 'His level speaking is often very pleasing – always sensible', Macready recorded in his diary, though he found the portrayal lacking in 'finish', in 'depth', and in 'method'. 'There was no *absorbing* feeling *through* the great scenes, no evidence of the "slow fire" "wearing his vitals"; this was particularly manifest in the last act, where he was direct and straightforward even to commonplace. I think he will improve.'[1] Phelps continued, however, to prefer a comparatively controlled and level performance to the ideal of 'absorbing feeling', following the path of 'familiarity' already laid out by Macready. In his Shakespearian *Richard III*, which displaced the popular Cibber version in 1845, he 'did not attempt to make [Richard] a character of points' but acted it 'in the unaffected and level style, so characteristic of this gentleman's performance'.[2] In the same month, as the Priest in Serle's drama *The Priest's Daughter*, his 'imitation of Macready sometimes

[1] J. C. Trewin, *Journal*, p. 101.
[2] *The Times*, 24 February 1845, and *Illustrated London News* (1845), I, 142.

came a little too forcibly, to mar the general excellence of the performance'.[1] Eight years later, in the title role of Knowles's *Virginius*, the *Athenaeum* still found that Phelps's 'pace is equal throughout. The slow movement of the words is invariably the same. Whatever the emotion may be, the pronunciation is not quickened; the tune is varied but the time is uniform.'[2]

The restrained and deliberate quality of Phelps's art suited the portrayal of the more unheroic emotions of pity and pathos. In the domestic world to which *King Lear* has so often been relegated on the stage, 'the apparent absence of histrionic art' in Phelps's portrayal of Lear became 'the greatest merit of his performance; but the pathos, being unmitigated, becomes exceedingly painful'.[3] 'It is seldom that he over-acts', remarked a reviewer of his Brutus, 'but he is always pathetic; in him the most violent emotions excite pity.'[4] The restraint of this style also had, in Henry Morley's opinion, a beneficial effect on the overall co-ordination of a Phelps production:

> The actors are content also to be subordinated to the play, learn doubtless at rehearsals how to subdue excesses of expression that by giving undue force to one part would destroy the balance of the whole, and blend their work in such a way as to produce everywhere the right emphasis. . . . So it is that, although only in one or two cases we may have observed at Sadler's Wells originality of genius in the actor, we have nevertheless perceived something like the entire sense of one of Shakespeare's plays.[5]

A remarkable versatility in Phelps's playing caused the actor-manager Sir Johnston Forbes-Robertson (1853–1937), who trained under him, to assert that he was equally successful in tragedy, character parts and high and low comedy.[6] Such comic characters as Bottom, Peter Teazle, Falstaff, Malvolio and Justice Shallow were among his best roles. Morley's *Journal of a London Playgoer* provides a particularly fine description of Phelps's celebrated interpretation of Bottom. In his initial scene he presented 'a strange, elaborate, and uncouth dream-figure, a clown restless with vanity, marked by a score of little movements, and speaking ponderously with the uncouth gesticulation of

1 *Illustrated London News* (1845), I, 91.
2 *Athenaeum* (1853), p. 1096.
3 *Athenaeum* (1848), p. 346.
4 *Athenaeum* (1846), p. 403.
5 Henry Morley, *Journal of a London Playgoer* (London, 1891), pp. 129–30.
6 See his *A Player under Three Reigns* (Boston, 1925), p. 67.

an unreal thing, a grotesque nightmare character'. Phelps's objective, however, was to create, by means of contrast, a startling comic development in Bottom following his 'translation':

> Throughout the fairy scenes there is a mist thrown over Bottom by the actor's art. The violent gesticulation becomes stillness, and the hands are fixed on the breast. . . . The change of manner is a part of the conception. The dream-figure is dreaming, there is dream within dream, Bottom is quiet, his humour becomes more unctuous, but Bottom is translated. He accepts all that happens, quietly as dreamers do. . . . Not a touch of comedy was missed in this capital piece of acting.[1]

It would be rash to equate the unheroic style of Samuel Phelps with anything approaching a naturalistic performance. He was still part of the older tradition. As an actor he retained the ability to declaim verse with a force and eloquence shared by few of his less talented contemporaries. His approach represents, however, one aspect of the gradual erosion of the older artistic views, the disappearance in the face of increasingly 'realistic' touches, of the points, starts and emotional transitions which had individualized the ideality of neoclassical-romantic acting.

The relatively subdued and less histrionic attack of Phelps was extended still further by such contemporaries as Charles Kean (1811–68), Charles Fechter (1824–79) and Barry Sullivan (1821–91). Kean's important series of Shakespearian productions during his management of the Princess's Theatre from 1851 to 1859 comprises one of the most remarkable efforts in the nineteenth century to evolve a *mise en scène* affording the greatest degree of archaeological accuracy and pictorial splendour.[2] As an actor, however, the younger Kean's début in 1827 had been a singularly unpromising and inarticulate imitation of his father's greatness, a performance which was, according to the *Theatrical Observer* (2 October 1827), 'simply the correct reciting of a well-educated young man'. Returning to London in 1838 following a prosperous tour of America and the provinces, he was more warmly received. Nonetheless, the critic John Forster still found him insufficiently 'familiar in speech and bearing': 'the emotion was prolonged so far beyond the natural point that it seemed at last the appearance of a trick.'[3] Ten years later, however, Kean's style had clearly taken on a new quality. 'He has now

[1] Morley, *Journal*, p. 60. See also A. C. Ward, *Specimens of English Dramatic Criticism* (London, 1945), pp. 127–8.
[2] Cf. Part II (1), pp. 87ff, and Muriel St Clare Byrne, 'Charles Kean and the Meininger myth', *Theatre Research*, VI (1964), 137–53.
[3] *Examiner*, 14 January 1838.

acquired some of that repose, the most rare quality in actors, which he so deeply needed', recorded the *Theatrical Journal* (27 January 1848).

The key to the radical change which took place in Kean's acting lies in his adoption of a new repertory of 'gentlemanly' French melodrama. At the Princess's, where he performed in perfect harmony with his wife and leading lady Ellen Tree (1806–80), Kean's appearances in such French adaptations as Oxenford's *Pauline* and Boucicault's *The Corsican Brothers* and *Louis XI* reshaped his style and 'revealed a first-rate melodramatic actor where hitherto we had known only a bad tragedian'.[1] Even Kean's prominent defects – a weak voice and an expressionless face – seemed to strengthen the impression of quiet intensity which characterized his newly found realism. Lewes, no Kean supporter, waxed eloquent in the *Leader* (28 February 1853) concerning his acting in *The Corsican Brothers*: 'Charles Kean plays the two brothers, and you must see him before you will believe how well and how quietly he plays them, preserving a gentlemanly demeanour and drawing-room manner. . . which intensifies the passion of the part and gives it terrible reality.' Theatrical history of this period affords, it seems, many instances of basically weak actors who made the best of a bad bargain by proclaiming their lack of force as 'realism'.

Both the new repertory of French melodrama and the realistic by-play of the new quiet French comic school contributed to the gradual evolution of a 'new school' of serious English acting.[2] Charles Fechter was himself a French actor who made his début at the *Comédie Française* in 1840 and was, twelve years later, the world's first Armand Duval in *Camille* by Dumas *fils*. He played with equal success and facility, however, in England and America as well. In the 1860–1 season his appearances at the Princess's in such plays as Hugo's *Ruy Blas* and Boucicault's *The Corsican Brothers* climaxed in the legendary 'realistic' *Hamlet* with which his name has become synonymous. The Fechter 'reforms' which drew amazed audiences for five full months disregarded the points, picturesque attitudes and traditional readings which had become inseparable from the role of Hamlet, and replaced them with the style of subdued 'gentlemanly melodrama' already exemplified by Charles Kean. 'It was', as Watson rightly perceives, 'not so much the beginning of a new movement as it was the consummation of a long period of hesitant tendencies in the search for realism.'[3]

[1] Lewes, *On Actors*, p. 15.
[2] On this point, see Alan S. Downer's 'Players and painted stage: nineteenth century acting', *PMLA*, LXI (June 1946), p. 551.
[3] Watson, p. 377.

Barry Sullivan stood out in Bernard Shaw's opinion as the last and one of the 'greatest of the line of British Shakespearian star actors from Burbage and Betterton to Macready'.[1] Although no reformer in Fechter's sense, Sullivan, who made his début as Hamlet at the Haymarket in 1852, impressed his first critics as an adherent of the newer school of subdued acting. Nevertheless, Shaw singled out the qualities of heroic majesty, power and dignity in Sullivan's art which placed him squarely within the older tradition, and which made his Hamlet 'a being of a different and higher order from Laertes and the rest' and his Richard III 'a monster of truculence'.[2] Sullivan's talents as a performer included 'a commanding person, a graceful bearing, a mimetic organization, [and] a powerful and perfectly modulated voice'[3] which afforded him an unusually lucrative career as a travelling provincial star – a career which would, if for no other reason, deserve attention because of Shaw's own provocative assertion that 'I never saw great acting until I saw him; and from him and from Salvini and Adelaide Ristori I learned my stage technique and what great acting can do'.[4]

The Bancroft management of the Prince of Wales's theatre represented, as E. B. Watson has pointed out, another logical continuation of earlier efforts towards realism, rather than something totally new and revolutionary. The work begun in 1865 by the comédienne Marie Wilton (1839–1921) and her future husband Sir Squire Bancroft (1841–1926) at the 'Dust Hole' (as the unattractive Queen's Theatre on Tottenham Street had been known formerly) was substantially in the tradition of Madame Vestris: not only had Robertson served as a prompter for Vestris, but Squire Bancroft's early experience as an actor was significantly moulded by the hints he had received from Charles Mathews.[5] To the staging, costuming and acting of comedy, the Bancrofts applied the taste for domestic familiarity and recognizable 'realism' that had already begun to make itself felt in the performance of serious drama. Their efforts were aided immeasurably by the contributions which their theatrically astute house dramatist Tom Robertson made to the repertory. One notable Shakespearian excursion by these drawing-room realists was their unsuccessful *Merchant of Venice* in 1875, a production

---

[1] See *Shaw on Theatre*, ed. E. J. West (New York, 1958), p. 276. Shaw was a militant champion of Sullivan's reputation on several occasions, notably in his wry review of Allardyce Nicoll's *History of Late Nineteenth Century Drama, 1850–1900* in the *Observer* (29 September 1946).

[2] Ibid., p. 274.

[3] See R. M. Sillard, *Barry Sullivan and his Contemporaries* (London, 1901), II, 163 ff.

[4] *Shaw on Theatre*, p. 277.

[5] Watson, p. 391.

staged on the basis of Venetian pictorial views gathered by the Bancrofts, but remembered for the exquisite Portia of Ellen Terry (1847–1928), a role in which Irving's future leading lady has remained without a rival.

Visits of foreign stars to England were numerous indeed during this period – Rachel, Adelaide Ristori, Charlotte Cushman, Edwin Booth and many others made influential guest appearances – but one such visit in particular throws the transition from romanticism to naturalism into bold relief. The fiery Othello of Tommaso Salvini (1829–1916), one of the greatest of all nineteenth-century actors, created an immense stir at Drury Lane in 1875. A virtuoso playing a heavily mutilated text in Italian and totally ignoring polite cup-and-saucer notions of 'ensemble' playing, Salvini's thunderous performance shocked half the Victorian world. Stunned critics spoke of the Italian 'using Iago as a floor-mop'.[1] Turning on the Ancient, Salvini began the pattern of violence in which audiences saw the image of a great, tormented animal: 'he rushes upon Iago, clutches him by the throat, and forces him down upon his knees . . . at times menacing him with his clenched right hand . . . at times seeming almost to twist Iago's head from his body.'[2] In his very real destruction of Desdemona 'he pounced upon her, lifted her into the air, dashed with her . . . across the stage and through the curtains, which fell behind him. You heard a crash as he flung her on the bed, and growls as of a wild beast over his prey.'[3] The 'terrible and almost excessive demonstration of fury of his last scene' caused timid English actresses to refuse to submit to 'the full fury of his assault'.[4] Henry James was delighted – 'Nothing could be finer than all this; the despair, the passion, the bewildered tumult of it'[5] – but the very considerable critical disagreement over Salvini's Othello reflects more than merely outraged Victorian sensibility. It suggests, too, the kind of change taking place at this time in the English theatre, as it gradually espoused the 'new school' of quieter 'psychological' acting.

As a pro-Salvini observer, it must perhaps be expected that Henry James would find a portrayal like the sentimental and pathetic Shylock of Henry Irving (1838–1905) 'rigid and frigid', 'neither excited nor exciting': 'instead

---

[1] William Winter, *Shakespeare on the Stage*, First Series (New York, 1911), p. 290.

[2] A painstaking transcription of Salvini's performance was made by E. T. Mason, *The Othello of Tomasso Salvini* (New York, 1890): quoted in Rosenberg, *Othello*, p. 110.

[3] J. R. Towse, *Sixty Years of the Theatre* (New York, 1916), p. 163.

[4] Fanny Kemble, 'Salvini's Othello', *Temple Bar*, LXXI (July 1884), p. 376.

[5] Henry James, *The Scenic Art* (New York, 1957), p. 175. Stanislavski, of course, boundlessly admired Salvini, writing of his Othello that 'we were in his power, and we will remain in it all our lives, forever' (*My Life in Art* [New York, 1956], p. 266).

of being "hissing hot", as we have heard Edmund Kean described', he seemed to James to blunt all the points.[1] Although Irving towers as the last of the outstanding actors of the nineteenth century, a full consideration of his contributions as a performer and a manager belongs logically to the period after 1880. His style represents a distinct departure from what had come before. His Mathias in Leopold Lewis's *The Bells*, the part which in 1871 made him a star overnight in a manner that recalled Garrick's Richard and Kean's Shylock, was clearly a psychological study from the moment the snow-covered innkeeper flung open the door: we are asked to believe that he revealed the entire personality of the haunted and pathetic Mathias, without speaking a line, by the way in which he buckled one of his shoes, while in his 'horribly intense' death scene he presented a 'very ugly picture of a dead man's face, convulsed after a dream, in which he thought he was hanged'.[2] In his fine recollection of Irving's Hamlet at the Lyceum in 1874, Clement Scott creates a vivid impression of this complex and subtly detailed psychological portrayal. Irving's Hamlet was 'an artist concealing his art' while 'suffering from moral poison'; he was 'the Hamlet who *thinks aloud*' and who presented in the scene with Ophelia 'the height and delirium of moral anguish, the distraction of the unhinged mind, swinging and banging about like a door'.[3] Irving's Mortimer in the old play *The Iron Chest* again drew a 'picture of mental torture' and caused critics to realize that 'in such characters requiring minute analysis of emotion and sudden vehement out-pourings, Mr. Irving is in the present day almost without a rival'.[4]

The beginning of Irving's sole management of the Lyceum in the first days of 1879 and the commencement of his reign for more than two decades there with Ellen Terry mark the end of our survey of pre-naturalistic acting. This represents a new and distinct theatrical development. The world première in the same year of Ibsen's *A Doll's House* represents another. With the deaths of Phelps, Mathews, Fechter and Ellen Tree all following close upon one another as the 1870s drew to a close, the last of the old actors had passed from the scene and the art of acting had clearly changed. Herman Bang, the Danish novelist, critic and actor, writing in 1880 about the passing of the

---

[1] James, pp. 140–1.
[2] Clement Scott, *From 'The Bells' to 'King Arthur'* (London, 1897), p. 5; Ellen Terry recalled that in this death scene Irving's 'eyes would disappear upwards, his face grow gray, his limbs cold' (*The Story of My Life* [London, 1908], p. 338).
[3] Clement Scott, pp. 61–3.
[4] *Theatre* (1879), II, 228, and *Illustrated London News* (1879), II, 318.

performers and artists of the pre-naturalistic period, touched on something essential which set them apart:

> They began by believing in their merits, our own age begins by worrying about its faults. For our own age, artistic achievement is a matter of intelligence – which therefore demands effort – but for them it was an instinct. They felt that which we must investigate, they saw a unity where we see fragments and contradictions.[1]

(v) Chronology

1741 Drury Lane revival of *The Merchant of Venice* with Charles Macklin as Shylock; début of David Garrick at Goodman's Fields

1747 Garrick is joint patentee at Drury Lane

1750 Spranger Barry leaves Drury Lane for Covent Garden to engage in rivalry with Garrick

1751 James Quin retires

1752 Lewis Hallam leaves with troupe of players for America

1760 Death of Peg Woffington

1763 Garrick clears spectators from the stage, travels on the Continent until 1765

1766 Barry re-engaged by Garrick; deaths of Quin and Mrs Cibber

1768 Death of Mrs Pritchard

1774 Henry Mossop dies

1775 Unsuccessful début of Sarah Siddons as Portia

1776 Garrick retires; Sheridan assumes control of Drury Lane; death of Thomas Weston

1777 Henderson's début at the Haymarket; deaths of Spranger Barry and Henry Woodward

1779 Death of Garrick

1782 Successful return of Mrs Siddons to Drury Lane

1783 John Philip Kemble's début as Hamlet

1785 Dorothy Jordan joins Drury Lane company; Henderson dies

1788 Kemble becomes manager of Drury Lane

1789 Macklin's last appearance as Shylock

1794 Kemble opens enlarged Drury Lane with *Macbeth*, starring Sarah Siddons, with Charles Kemble as Malcolm

[1] See 'Romantikkens Sanger' in his *Kritiske Studier* (København, 1880), pp. 156 ff. Translation by the present authors.

1797　Macklin dies

1800　George Frederick Cooke is Richard III at Covent Garden

1802　Kemble and Mrs Siddons move to Covent Garden

1805　Master Betty craze; Liston's début at the Haymarket

1809　Reopening of Kemble's enlarged Covent Garden

1810　Cooke leaves for America

1811–12　William Charles Macready appears in Newcastle with Sarah Siddons in *The Gamester* and *Douglas*

1812　Siddons's farewell to the stage; Cooke dies in New York

1814　Edmund Kean's sensational début as Shylock at Drury Lane; Eliza O'Neill's début; Dorothy Jordan retires

1816　Macready's London début at Covent Garden

1817　Final appearance of John Philip Kemble

1819　Eliza O'Neill retires prematurely; Madame Vestris in *Giovanni in London* at Drury Lane

1823　Charles Kemble's authentic revival of *King John*; death of John Philip Kemble

1826　Ira Aldridge makes début at the Royalty

1827　Début of Charles Kean; visit of English actors to Paris

1830　Madame Vestris opens the Olympic

1831　Sarah Siddons dies

1833　Edmund Kean dies

1835　Début of Charles Mathews Jr at the Olympic

1836　Début of Helen Faucit at Covent Garden

1837　Macready assumes management of Covent Garden; Liston retires; first London appearance of Samuel Phelps

1838　Vestris relinquishes Olympic management

1839　Macready ends Covent Garden management, assumed in turn by Vestris and Mathews

1841　Boucicault's *London Assurance* at Covent Garden; Macready takes over Drury Lane

1842　Vestris and Mathews relinquish Covent Garden

1843　Macready ends Drury Lane management; theatre monopoly ended by Theatre Regulation Act

1844　Phelps begins eighteen-year management of Sadler's Wells

1845　Charlotte Cushman's guest appearance at the Princess's

1847　Mathews and Vestris begin management of the Lyceum

1850　Charles Kean begins management of the Princess's

1851　Macready's farewell as Macbeth

1852 Début of Barry Sullivan at the Haymarket
1854 Madame Vestris retires; death of Charles Kemble
1856 Death of Madame Vestris
1857 Adelaide Ristori appears in London
1859 Charles Kean ends management of the Princess's; Irving's début at the Princess's
1861 Charles Fechter's revolutionary *Hamlet*; Edwin Booth's first English tour
1862 Phelps ends management at Sadler's Wells
1865 Beginning of Bancroft management at Prince of Wales's
1868 Charles Kean dies
1871 Henry Irving appears in *The Bells*
1873 Death of Macready
1875 Tomasso Salvini's Othello at Drury Lane; Ellen Terry's Portia at the Prince of Wales's
1878 Phelps's last appearance, as Cardinal Wolsey; Irving assumes control of the Lyceum; death of Charles Mathews
1879 Death of Fechter

III Playwrights and plays

Robertson Davies

Introduction

The reader whose idea of the drama of the past does not range beyond the classic repertoire of the present will find little to detain him between 1750 and 1880; few plays from this period continue to hold the stage. In the era that immediately succeeded it, critics and serious students of the theatre derided its artificialities and melodramatic excesses because it was their purpose to sweep them aside in favour of something different and, they were convinced, better. No full and scholarly survey was attempted until 1930, since when Allardyce Nicoll has devoted almost three volumes of his *History of English Drama* to this period; even his sympathetic approach has not fully persuaded a majority of readers that there is much beyond Sheridan and Goldsmith to command their respect in this 130 years.

Such an attitude may be possible to those who think of drama merely as a stepchild of literature; but if we consider the theatre as an art to be understood as a whole and give weight to theatrical value, as well as to the kind of literary worth that looks well abstracted from its context, we know that this stretch of 130 years cannot be ignored. Here is a long period of tragedy, comedy and miscellaneous theatre writing that was taken seriously by audiences and critics whom we dare not dismiss; here is a body of drama in which some of the best players in the history of our theatre delighted to display their art; here is a group of plays of all kinds, some of which held the stage for twenty, some for fifty, a few for more than a hundred years, and some may still be seen. Supposing our interest in the theatre to be serious, and not merely solemn, can it be that there is almost nothing in all this worthy of our attention?

The division of time is arbitrary. Nothing in the drama of 1750 marks it as the birth of an era, but the beginning of Garrick's long and influential reign at Drury Lane in 1747, with the production there of his first very successful farce, *Miss in Her Teens*, is near enough. Nor is 1880 a date that comes at once to mind as the death of a particular period of theatre, though we may recall it as the year in which Henry Irving brought fresh splendour to melodrama in his production of *The Corsican Brothers*, and W. S. Gilbert gave a keener edge to his mockery of melodramatic convention in *The Pirates of Penzance*. But Garrick continued the sort of theatre fare that was popular when he became a manager, supporting it with his gifts as actor and playwright; the melodrama against which forces were strongly marshalled by 1880 continued to be popular at least until 1914, and *The Corsican Brothers* could be seen, movingly acted in the Irving tradition by Martin-Harvey, in 1926. So we are not dealing here with one of those 'ages of drama' so dear to systematizers, but with a long period of theatrical entertainment that took its tone from its audience.

Without some understanding of those audiences we may go astray in our understanding of the plays they took to their hearts. Therefore, without too greatly trespassing on the ground of the other contributors to this volume, it will be necessary from time to time to make reference to the body of play-goers who set the tone of the theatre.

In dealing with the drama it is especially necessary to bear in mind the Protagorean dictum that 'that which is perceived is perceived in the mode of the perceiver'. This is likely to mean that in the theatre the things the audience takes for granted are more influential in shaping the entertainment they are given than the considered aesthetic theories of the best-educated and most thoughtful among them. Watching Garrick, Partridge the schoolmaster and Dr Johnson both bring their notions of what great acting is to the theatre.[1] A great new dramatist might enlarge Partridge's receptiveness, but great dramatists are few in all ages. It was a time of gradual eclipse of the literary element in drama: by 1800 sensation, music, handsome scenes and dresses and a special quality pertaining to melodrama had begun to crowd the theatre-poet off the stage, replacing him with a skilled writer who was but

[1] See *Tom Jones*, Book XVI, chapter 5.

one among a group of theatre-artificers. There was some outcry, much of it in the vein of Mrs Curdle when she assured Miss Snevellicci that 'It's not as if the theatre was in its high and palmy days . . . the drama is gone, perfectly gone'.[1] But the drama was not gone; it was proceeding from strength to strength, noisily, coarsely and, to the dismay of the Curdles, delightfully. It was literature that was gone, and even it had not gone irreparably. It would be truer to say that it was sulking. There was poetry and beauty in this theatre, but it was not poetry of the spoken word; poetic feeling was present, but poetic utterance of the sort that can be separated successfully from other dramatic elements was not.

The reader who seeks comment on particular types of drama such as comedy, tragedy, opera, pantomime and burlesque, considered as coherent wholes, is referred to Professor Nicoll's third and fourth volumes. Revealing and convenient as Professor Nicoll's plan is, there is also something to be learned from a chronological consideration of the plays and playwrights of this period, taking their work as their audiences had to take it. By pursuing a chronological progression we are reminded of the pressure of each theatrical season, the necessity for novelty, and the need to balance comedy against tragedy, which sometimes seems to explain the presentation of manifestly inferior work. In an era where so many playwrights are marked by high professional competence rather than by genius, we must keep in mind the hurly-burly of a theatre in which competition was keen, and the contestants so evenly matched that it is sometimes hard to make revealing distinctions among them. In such a theatre the success or failure of a particular playwright was often a matter of luck, and our period abounds in examples of what seem to be caprice and injustice affecting the fortunes of a play. This is especially true in comedy. Particularly in the first fifty years of our period where there are so many carvers in ivory it is not hard to detect incompetence, but to determine the degree of excellence that raises genius above distinction is not so easy.

Abbreviations

In the following pages the names of certain frequently mentioned theatres are abbreviated thus: CG, Covent Garden (see p. xliv); DL, Drury Land, Theatre Royal (see p. xlv); Hay 1, Haymarket Opera House, in 1837 Her Majesty's (see p. xlvi); Hay 2, Haymarket, Theatre Royal (see p. xlvi; after 1837 abbreviated as Hay). On p. 229, TR Brighton is the Theatre Royal.

[1] *Nicholas Nickleby*, chapter 24. This novel, published in 1838–9, is an admirable guide to the spirit and organization of the provincial theatre during the first forty years of the nineteenth century.

1750–1760

David Garrick was a dominating figure from his assumption of the management of Drury Lane in 1747 until his retirement in 1776. As a playwright
himself, as an actor in search of good parts, as a manager in a theatre that was
professional in the modern sense and as a toucher-up of other men's plays,
he held a position of unique power. The Garrick style is discernible in much
of the comedy and lighter entertainment of his time. Whether he abused his
power is not our theme; there can be no question that he used it profession-
ally. He read countless plays and encouraged many writers; it would have
been strange indeed if he had put his influence behind men whose work did
not appeal to him. He did not attempt to write tragedy, but his ideas about
tragedy may be deduced from the arrangements of Shakespeare he made for
his own use.[1] They are cautious ideas; the Shakespearian sweep of mingled
tragedy and comedy won his intellectual approval, but he did not trust it on
the stage. It is this same caution that puts its mark on his comedy. He was

[1] Garrick's versions of Shakespeare, Jonson, Dryden and others are not considered in
this study; the student is referred to Nicoll, Volume III, 'Hand-list of plays', for their
names and dates. This is not meant to suggest that they are without significance, but is
dictated by the length of this study and the greater importance of Garrick's comedy in
its terms. At least one of Garrick's Shakespeare versions, *Catherine and Petruchio*, was
seen on the stage until 1914.

ingenious, elegant and accomplished within the limitations of his own intellect, which was itself a graceful mirror of the best popular taste of his time.
When his friend Johnson defined comedy as 'A dramatick representation of
the lighter faults of mankind, with an intention to make vice and folly
ridiculous',[1] Garrick might surely feel that he had met all comedy's demands.
It is unjust to call him superficial, but it would be untruthful to say that his
was a probing, strongly individual or arresting mind. His genius was for acting; only his talent was found in his plays.

Garrick's taste in the tragedy of his time is not unfairly indicated by his
choice of *The Roman Father*, by William Whitehead, for production in 1750.
It may detain us briefly because it is so characteristic of its era, and indeed of
the quarter of a century to come. That is to say, it is the work of a man of
letters of no discernible distinction of mind, but of unimpeachable literacy,
for he was a Fellow of Clare Hall, Cambridge, and died Poet Laureate,
succeeding Cibber; his tragedy is classical in theme (the combat between the
Horatii and Curiatii) and leans heavily on Corneille's *Horace*, though it may
be said that where Whitehead seeks to improve on Corneille he botches the
job. He has striven for a classical restraint, and the greater his striving the
more obvious is the mid-eighteenth-century cast of his mind. He has made
sacrifices to that triple-headed hobgoblin of the neoclassical mind, the unities,
but has not quite been able to manage the unity of place. His poetic style may
be sampled in the first speech of Horatius in Act V:

> Thou dost forgive me, then; my dearest boy,
> I cannot tell thee half my ecstasy.
> The day which gave thee first to my glad hopes
> Was misery to this. I'm mad with transport!

The evidence makes clear that *The Roman Father* met the taste of the time;
though Garrick had declared that the stage of Drury Lane was 'sacred to
Shakespeare' he was too shrewd a manager to neglect the tragedy of his age,
which seems often to have been sacred only to propriety.

Borrowing and derivation were of great assistance to contemporary playwrights, both in comedy and tragedy. In an age when reading and travel
were much more restricted than they are now, such dependence was less
likely to be detected, and if detected less likely to be reprehended, than would
now be the case. Garrick's own early success as a playwright, *Miss in Her
Teens* (DL 1747), was drawn from a French original; it is much more than a
translation, and the part of Fribble, the effeminate beau, which the author

[1] *A Dictionary of the English Language*, 1755.

played, was a typical Garrick creation – brilliantly observed and characterized in dialogue that is sufficient without having the rank luxuriance of a puffed-up star part.

As a playwright Garrick shows no growth; he writes as well in his earliest pieces as he does at the end of his career. His construction is as mechanical and perfunctory as it can be without allowing the play to become dull, but his sense of character, over a wide range of men and women in high and low life, is unfailingly acute, and he can always find dramatic speech that is easy and free of padding. He has the true actor's sense of effect; the literary man's faults of getting the point of a speech at its beginning instead of at its end, or of burdening a character with needless though amusing lines, are unknown to him, and he twangs off the wearisome necessities of 'antecedent knowledge' and wraps up the ends of a plot with enviable skill. There is no depth in his work, but he wanted none; he provided pieces in which he and his colleagues could show their art, and as that is all he seems to have desired we may admire the completeness of his success.

We see how good Garrick is when we compare his texts with those of his contemporary Samuel Foote, who wrote more than twenty plays, and a number of revisions, reworkings of old material, and miscellaneous entertainments, during a professional career that lasted from 1747 until 1777. He was a great mimic, and most of his pieces are written to enable him to hit off the eccentricities of someone well known in London life. This being so, it is surprising that they read as well as they do today; even if we know little of the objects of Foote's mockery we feel the bite of his wit. He was sometimes called 'the English Aristophanes' but we may now feel that the name is too complimentary, for he has little scope and no joy. However amusing he may have been as a comedian (and it is said that even the objects of his impersonations were compelled to laugh at them), there is a coarse and jeering spirit apparent in all his work, and his dramatic speech, though sometimes very funny, is equally often rough and grainy.

His little comedy *Taste* (DL 1752) is characteristic. It is a satire on the *virtuosi* and their imitators, who are imposed on by fake pictures, broken statuary and worn coins manufactured by Carmine, Puff and Brush and uttered by them in their disguises as foreign experts; they are unmasked by Lady Pentweazel's oafish son Caleb. A Philistine contempt for all art peeps through the lively speech and, as is usual with Foote's writing, the plot falls to pieces early in the action, and is cobbled up in a hasty, scrambling conclusion.

Like Garrick, Foote shows little growth in art. His long succession of plays is clearly the product of a mind that was completely formed when first he took up the pen, and *The Knights* (Hay 2 1749) and *The Englishman in Paris* (CG 1753) are in his characteristic style, although in the former the scene of courtship between Tim and Sukey gives us a hint of what a much better playwright Foote might have been if he had not been an actor, with a professional interest in providing parts for himself.

Contemporaneous with these works are a handful of tragedies, of which Richard Glover's *Boadicea* (DL 1753) deserves notice because, although it is flat in style and blurred in effect by a too literal adherence to neoclassic precept, it attempts to draw tragedy from British history. Many such attempts were to follow, and none of them were more than fleetingly successful, but they show a consciousness that themes other than those drawn from Greek and Roman sources may be fit for tragedy, and they are hints of the enthusiasm for the picturesque that produced such strange and occasionally powerful effects towards the end of the century.

A truly successful tragedy, with a modern theme and setting, is Edward Moore's *The Gamester* (DL 1753). It is written in prose, which led some critics[1] to deny it dignity, but it achieves the primary aim of tragedy, which is to produce a tragic effect on its audience. Moore came from a working-class home, his education was modest and his mind naïve, but he had strength of conviction. Though his play comes near to bathos in some scenes it is powerful and sustained as a whole, and the sense of doom that hangs over Beverley, the compulsive gambler, is convincing and unrelenting. Garrick from his mastery of stagecraft gave Moore some assistance, and the fine scene between Lewson and Stukely (IV. ii) is from his hand.

Moore has the sense of a mythic world without which tragedy cannot convince. Beverley is a fated man, and the source of his doom is amply clear. We are made to feel that his death is the outcome of his despair, and not a crude retribution for ill-doing. His wife is plainly a personification of his best self, and his destroyer, Stukely, has the compulsive power and attraction of his contrary destiny.[2] The tone of the play reflects Moore's dissenting background: that very rare element in eighteenth-century drama, a prayer addressed unmistakably to the Christian God, is introduced in the fifth act

---

[1] See T. Davies, *The Life of David Garrick, Esq.*, I, 166. *Biographia Dramatica* (London, 1812), under *The Gamester* (II, 257), says: 'Some part of this drama was originally composed in blank verse, of which several vestiges remain.'

[2] For expansion of these concepts, enlightening to the student of drama and melodrama especially, see C. G. Jung, *The Archetypes and the Collective Unconscious*, trans. R. F. C. Hull (London, 1959), pp. 54–72, and *Two Essays on Analytical Psychology*, trans. R. F. C. Hull (New York, 1953), pp. 186–209.

with moving sincerity. Lewson, Beverley's friend, is a successful portrait of a truly good man, and thus achieves what dramatists in all ages have found difficult. Moore does it all by the power of his conviction and native psychological insight, rather than by extraordinary art.

This play reminds us of *The London Merchant* (1731) both in its tearful simplicity and its tragic power. It held the stage at least until 1870, which is a testimony to its effectiveness as a theatre piece, and it must be counted an ancestor of a rabble of anti-vice plays, temperance dramas and so forth that came in the next century. But unlike these feeble children it has a power that springs from something greater than the desire to warn against evil courses of life. Moore's sense of fate and doom cannot be explained by his evangelical opinions alone.

A contrasting tragedy that also enjoyed a long life was John Home's *Douglas* (CG 1757). It bears external marks of neoclassicism: it observes the unities and the catastrophe takes place offstage. But it is of greater interest as a forerunner of Gothic drama, and as a play that seems to say more than its author consciously intended. Lady Randolph is almost Byronic in the sense she gives of an introverted nature feeding upon itself: she contains so much of her own contrary destiny that the play hardly needs the mechanical villain Glenalvon. She asserts that she brings ill-fortune, luckless love, with her, and that melancholy (that rheumatoid arthritis of the romantic drama) has congealed her blood.

What is her trouble? The obvious explanations do not suffice, and the play seems to dally with unexpressed, dangerous emotions. *Douglas* is overhung by a Greek mist that cannot all arise from the author's classical education, and as well as strong hints of *Oedipus* we scent romance afar. The misprized hero, the suggestions but never the corroborations of incest, the role of Death as the settler of all accounts, and particularly the insistence on 'pity' are romantic in evocation.

Pity plays a great part in eighteenth-century tragedy. It was a genteel emotion, and one of the passions that might be freely indulged. Indeed, indulgence in it was a mark of a superior spirit. The second half of the eighteenth century knew precisely what the passions were: William Collins had written *The Passions* in 1750, and this ode was declaimed by actors, read and memorized by readers, for a full century. Fear, anger, despair, revenge, jealousy, hate, hope, pity, love, melancholy, cheerfulness and joy made up the dozen; six are passions from which the mind shrank, and the latter six might be felt keenly, and indeed pleasurably. This certainty and balance were characteristic of eighteenth-century ideas of psychology, and the belief in the autonomy of the passions was equally secure: only one passion could possess the mind at a time. It appears that Home thought that he was remaining true to this received opinion in *Douglas*, but to our eyes it looks as though he were troubled by intimations of mingled and inadmissible emotions in Lady Randolph, and that artistic promptings he could not check had smuggled them into his play.

It seems unlikely that a tragedy so static as *Douglas* appears to be on the surface would have held the stage firmly until 1860, and even have achieved a production in 1950,[1] if there were not more in it than meets the eye at a first reading. A familiar dark fascination is discernible in it. The scene is not merely Scotland, but the closed inner world where time is not reckoned by the clock, where sorrows do not fade and secrets are kept for years, contrary to ordinary probability. Here not pity, but its seductive bastard, self-pity, is a dominating, pervasive passion. This is the twilight world of the psyche, the true landscape of romance.

Garrick contributes three more plays to the first decade of this period, which need not be considered in detail. *Lilliput* (DL 1756) owes only the milieu to Swift; it is a satire on contemporary society which derives much of its undoubted charm from the fact that it was written to be played by children. We may think some of the dialogue rather gamy for very young players, but the eighteenth century did not. *The Male Coquette* (DL 1757) is a perceptive study of a homosexual: Daffodil, the male coquette, cultivates a reputation as a gallant, although he really dislikes women. The eccentric sexual atmosphere of this play is emphasized by the introduction of a 'breeches' part for Sophia, who assumes male dress in order to observe Daffodil when he is off his guard. The clubroom scenes of fashionable life are excellent satire, and the piece shows no signs of having been composed and produced in less than a month, which was the case. *The Guardian* (DL 1759) strikes a more sentimental note. Miss Harriet, an heiress, loves her middle-aged guardian Heartly, but as he thinks himself too old for her it is some time before he understands her hints. This piece is enlarged from Barthélemy Christophe Fagan's *La Pupille* (1734), and is of interest because it flirts with the theme of renunciation, which was to achieve great proportions as romance gained in power.

A characteristic Foote farce, *The Author* (DL 1757), should be noted here. In it an acquaintance of Foote's, a Welsh gentleman named Ap Rhys, was ridiculed as Cadwallader, and succeeded in securing suppression of the play.

[1] At the Lyceum, Edinburgh, and subsequently at the Citizens' Theatre, Glasgow, with Dame Sybil Thorndike as Lady Randolph, August 1950.

It begins promisingly but by the second act has become almost incomprehensible, and is capriciously and arbitrarily concluded.

Arthur Murphy, whose career begins at this time, was at first a protégé of Foote's, but when Foote stole the best of his *The Englishman from Paris* and used it before Murphy's play could be produced, the relationship became one of rivalry. *The Apprentice* (DL 1756) is an undistinguished farce, ridiculing the pretensions of London apprentices who sought to be amateur actors. It is of some interest because of the ejaculatory style of speech affected by the character of Wingate, one of the many irascible fathers in eighteenth-century comedy to speak in this way. We can only assume that this mannerism was widely observable at the time. *The Upholsterer* (DL 1758) is a better piece, satirizing the concern about national affairs shown by a group of tradesmen who neglect their own businesses. But *The Orphan of China* (DL 1759) is a signal that Murphy took himself seriously as a playwright, for it is a full-scale tragedy.

The tragedy of this decade, except for the two plays which have been considered at some length, makes heavy reading. Crisp's *Virginia* (DL 1754), Whitehead's *Creusa* (DL 1754), M'Namara Morgan's *Philoclea* (CG 1754), Dr Philip Francis's *Constantine* – the title 'Doctor' becomes, unhappily, a warning of classical dullness among these writers – (CG 1754), Dr John Brown's *Barbarossa* (DL 1754), John Moncrieff's *Appius* (CG 1755), Dr Brown's *Athelstan* (DL 1756), John Home's *Agis* – a disappointing successor to his first tragedy – (DL 1759) and Robert Dodsley's *Cleone* (CG 1758) are not productions to which one can turn with pleasure, nor, having once read them, is one likely to read them again. They are listed here only to show the persistence of the managers of the two patent houses in presenting contemporary writing. Every season Drury Lane and Covent Garden each brought forward two new tragedies, and sometimes good acting and the patience of audiences gave them a modest success. But they were sickly children, fathered by men anxious to be known as writers of tragedy, rather than writers with any strongly tragic sense of life, any freshness as poets or any true feeling for the stage. During the discussion of the remaining part of this fifty years, such lists cannot be avoided. They are a part of the climate of the theatre, the moonless nights of Covent Garden and Drury Lane.

Murphy's *Orphan of China* is no better than these, but it is interesting because in it Murphy rose above his mechanical farces to a mechanical tragedy, and was to go beyond this to better things. It is drawn from Voltaire's *Orphelin de la Chine* (1755) and it seems to be a Roman drama in an unconvincing Chinese setting. The rightful heir to the throne, Zaphinni, has been reared by the mandarin Zamti and his wife Mandane as their son, called Etan; their own son Hamet has been foisted on the Corean tyrant Timurkan as the prince; Timurkan conquers China and is slain by Zaphinni, after Zamti and Mandane have died by the tyrant's hand. There is much nobility and mother-love in the play, and the verse is heavy with pinchbeck splendours. The Epilogue is curious, for it undercuts the play and jeers at the Chinese in a manner that seems extreme, even in an era when epilogues were expected to be light in tone and mildly amusing about what had gone before. This play doubtless owed some of its acceptance to the contemporary enthusiasm for Chinoiserie in art and decoration.[1]

The close of this decade is distinguished only by the appearance of the Reverend James Townley's farce *High Life Below Stairs* (DL 1759) which held the stage until 1895. Its theme was the pretension and dishonesty of servants, and was so keenly resented by that class of society that some footmen rioted at the second performance and had to be subdued by their masters before the play could proceed. Whether the indignation it provoked sprang from a sense of injustice, or chagrin at being found out, is impossible to determine, for the two emotions (not having the autonomy of passions) can exist simultaneously.

[1] For more information on 'the Chinese taste', see *The Dictionary of English Furniture*, ed. Ralph Edwards (London, 1924–7), II, 72–3. This vogue appeared several times, one period of popularity lying between 1750 and 1765.

1760–1770

This decade brings us first a characteristic piece by Foote, *The Minor*, at his own theatre (Hay 2 1760). The plot suffers from the necessity to provide the author with three parts, in addition to which he mimicked George White-field, the Methodist leader, in Shift's final speech. It was admired in its time, but the cruelty of the basic plot makes it distasteful now. A sequel called *The Methodist*, attributed to Foote but in reality from the pen of Israel Pottinger, bookseller, madman and hack, was printed in 1761 but never acted.

A popular production in a form that gave great pleasure was Isaac Bicker-staff's *Thomas and Sally* (CG 1760), set to music by Thomas Augustine Arne. Such operettas – diminutive even for that modest form and playing about half an hour – were much in vogue as after-pieces. This one is notable because of its early use of a plot worn to threads in the century and a half to come: Sally is a virtuous country girl who resists the dishonourable proposals of a dissolute squire until her sailor lover Thomas returns from sea and puts the squire to rout. The verse is pleasing and has some unexpected felicities, as when the squire puts his case:

> Perhaps you're afraid of the world's busy tongue:
>> But know, above scandal you then shall be put;
> And laugh, as you roll in your chariot along,
>> At draggle-tail Chastity walking afoot.

Arne has set these words to a tune of delightful insouciance, and indeed his music adds a comic dimension all through the piece – something that must be borne in mind whenever this sort of drama is considered.

A prose after-piece of merit is George Colman's *Polly Honeycomb* (DL 1760). It gives an insight into one of those received ideas mentioned earlier as basic to the drama of any age: Polly's frailty is that she can read and write, and in the eyes of her father this gives access to dangerous notions; when Polly says, 'If it was not for novels and love-letters, a girl would have no use for her writing and reading', we can understand, if not sympathize, with Honeycomb's final dictum that 'A man might as well turn his daughter loose in Covent Garden as trust the cultivation of her mind to a Circulating Library'. We may bear this in mind when Sir Anthony Absolute fifteen years later describes a circulating library as 'an ever-green tree of diabolical knowledge'.

Arthur Murphy's *The Desert Island* (DL 1760) is of interest only as an example of the sort of thing on which Garrick was prepared to risk money. Adapted from Metastasio's *L'Isola disabitata* (English translation 1760), it tells of Constantia and her daughter Sylvia, who live on a desert island where they were abandoned by the husband and father Ferdinand when Sylvia was an infant; Ferdinand returns with a friend, Henrico; he did not desert them but was carried away by pirates while Constantia slept; Sylvia immediately falls in love with Henrico.

However, Murphy abandons such foolishness in *The Way to Keep Him* (DL 1760; expanded to five acts, DL 1761). The author contrasts the marriage of the Lovemores, who are at odds because Mrs Lovemore is a dull woman and a high-minded complainer, with that of Sir Bashfull and Lady Constant, in which the husband is so devoted to his wife that he plays the tyrant lest he be laughed at for his unfashionable constancy. The play was commended for its 'natural and easy dialogue',[1] which does indeed do much to compensate for a silly plot.

Plays about marriage were welcome to the eighteenth century, during which many provocations to dissatisfaction were not balanced by easy divorce. George Colman's *The Jealous Wife* (DL 1761) was a popular example; it held the stage until 1892, and was successfully played at the Old Vic in 1930. In it Mrs Oakly's jealousy makes her husband's life a burden until he takes the advice of his brother, the Major, and subdues her by a show of courage; Harriet, the heroine of the underplot, runs away from home to escape a forced marriage, is almost ravished by Lord Trinket who has the assistance

[1] *Biographia Dramatica* (1812 ed.), III, 392.

of the odious Lady Freelove, but is at last happily married to Oakly's ward Charles.

It is when reading such plays as this, good but not of the first rank, that we are most reminded of the differences between eighteenth-century audiences and ourselves. What seem to us to be stock characters – and in this play the comic Irishman and the comic sailor are combined – had a validity for them that we do not recognize in an era when differences of regional speech and specialized profession have been almost rubbed smooth. The accomplished but too copious speech suggests that these audiences picked up the point of a joke more slowly, and relished it longer, than do we; some reading in jestbooks of the period supports this opinion that their humorous pace was slower than ours.[1] Perhaps most extraordinary is the sudden and complete reform of Mrs Oakly: is this because theirs was a shallow and contrived psychology? It seems more likely that one of the satisfactions they expected from a comedy was a happy release to the mainspring of the plot. Nothing we read that comes from the best minds of the period suggests that the intellectual tone of the time was naïve, and we cannot suppose that the tone changed completely when people went to the theatre. We can but conclude, therefore, that they expected observation of nature to be applied to character, but preferred plots to be frankly artificial; the mirror was held up to nature but, like one of the convex mirrors of the period, was required to recompose the elements it reflected in a pleasing pattern, some things being brought very much into the foreground and others diminished almost out of existence. Comedy was a matter of convention, and prologue and epilogue left the audience in no doubt that nature must not trespass upon the politenesses of art.

There is a philistinism inherent in this attitude that shows clearly in Colman's next play *The Musical Lady* (DL 1762) in which a penniless wooer persuades an heiress to marry him by pretending to share her taste for Italian music; once he has secured her, and her fortune, he mocks her out of her enthusiasm, to the delight of his father. 'This passion for music is but one of the irregular appetites of virginity', he declares. In considering all comedy of this period we must remember that the Married Woman's Property Act of 1882 put a brake on several hundred years of fortune-hunting and the brutalities that sprang from it. *The Musical Lady* shows a growth in Colman's mastery of stage speech, which is markedly more witty and nervous in this piece than in its predecessor. He holds the ground thus gained, and improves

---

[1] *Joe Miller's Jests: or, the Wit's Vade-Mecum* (London, 1739), for example: notice jests 25, 79 and 167.

on it, in *The Deuce Is In Him* (DL 1763), though the plot, about a Colonel Tamper who pretends to have lost an eye and a leg in battle to test the 'truth, constancy and affection' of his Emily, is rough in substance. Emily discovers the trick, and turns the tables by pretending to be in love with Mlle Florival, who is disguised as a man. Sexual ambiguity of this sort is common in much comedy during this fifty years.

We need not stop long over Garrick's successful little interlude *The Farmer's Return from London* (DL 1762), with its simple fun about the 'crownation' and the Cock Lane Ghost. Foote, in *The Lyar* (CG 1762), is uncharacteristically coherent, for he took his plot from several sources, of which he acknowledges only Lope de Vega, and it includes none of the grotesqueries he devised for his own playing. It was a failure, unlike *The Orators* (Hay 2 1762), in which Foote sets up a school of oratory, and plays Peter Paragraph, a satirical portrait of George Faulkner, the one-legged Dublin printer. Foote himself had lost a leg, and regarded other one-legged men as his natural prey. One of his greatest successes was *The Mayor of Garratt* (Hay 2 1763), which long held the stage because of the well-conceived character of Jerry Sneak, a worm who turns, and some salty comment on the caprice of elections. But in *The Patron* (Hay 2 1764) and *The Commissary* (Hay 2 1765) he is as diffuse as ever; the latter play contains an ill-natured caricature of Arne as Dr Catgut; Foote was nettled by the success of others.

It should be said that at this time Mrs Frances Sheridan, mother of Richard Brinsley Sheridan, brought forward *The Discovery* (DL 1763) and *The Dupe* (DL 1763): the former enjoyed some success but the latter, unaccountably to modern taste, was condemned as indecent.

Two of Foote's most financially successful wooden-leg plays are *The Devil upon Two Sticks* (Hay 2 1768) and *The Lame Lover* (Hay 2 1770). The first is a satire on the medical profession, and in it Foote caricatured the President of the College of Physicians, Sir William Browne. The touch of magic borrowed from Le Sage's original lifts this piece above Foote's usual level, though the scenes are static. The second play strikes at the legal profession, and the invention and wit are better than is usual in this author.

If the theatrical fare of this decade seems of little worth, we may agree with Foote's stricture, in *The Devil upon Two Sticks*, that 'the several arts of the drama . . . are directed by the Genius of Insipidity; he has entered into partnership with the managers of both houses, and they have set up a kind of circulating library, for the vending of dialogue novels'.

Isaac Bickerstaff, after his good beginning with *Thomas and Sally*, gained and held supremacy as a concocter of musical entertainments, the success and quality of which are not to be judged from their brevity. *Love in A Village* (CG 1762) was popular for more than a century[1] and one of its songs, 'The Jolly Miller', is still sung. *Daphne and Amintor* (DL 1765) is a pretty piece, based on Mrs Susanna Maria Cibber's *The Oracle* (CG 1752), but *The Maid of the Mill* (CG 1765), taken from Richardson's *Pamela*, is a much more substantial work, and one of the first stage pieces to put forward the idea that love levels all ranks, a notion which did not receive a mortal blow as stage philosophy until *H.M.S. Pinafore* (1878), and was an unconscionable time a-dying after that. *Love in the City*, which also appeared in an abridgement called *The Romp* (CG 1767), and *The Padlock* (DL 1768), though they were successful, need not detain us. But *Lionel and Clarissa* (CG 1768), with music by Charles Dibdin, showed how firmly Bickerstaff had convinced himself and his audiences that love conquers all, and it held the stage for over a century. The comic serenata *The Ephesian Matron* (Hay 2 1769) need only be mentioned because its plot is the same as that of *A Phoenix Too Frequent* (Mercury 1946).[2] Though his most characteristic work is in his librettos for musical pieces, Bickerstaff wrote comedy as well, and *The Hypocrite* (DL 1768) provides a good portrait of an ignorant zealot in Maw-worm.

There remains in this decade a group of plays which, for one reason or another, call for special mention. The first is the happy collaboration of Colman and Garrick in *The Clandestine Marriage* (DL 1766), a comedy that has held the stage until the present day. It cannot be picked apart, assigning some portions to one author and the remainder to the other; the construction shows a neat economy which may be Garrick's, though there is more suspense and surprise than he employs in his unaided work; there is sentiment, but not at Colman's previous self-indulgent length; the language has a lustre that puts it with the best dramatic composition of the half century that includes Goldsmith and Sheridan.

In its treatment of the merchant class this play is satirical but not derisive; Sterling has a just opinion of his own merits, and knows how to realize his ambitions; he knows that intelligence is what wins the day, and he has that, though he lacks polish. The lovers are not inordinate in their affection, and we believe in them the more readily for it. Lord Ogleby is something new in the stage's long procession of men of fashion: he is a mass of affectation, but he

---

[1] It was performed at the Everyman, December 1923, and at the Lyric, Hammersmith, April 1928. *Lionel and Clarissa* was played at the Lyric, Hammersmith, October 1925.

[2] This plot also served Chapman for *The Widow's Tears*, *c.* 1612. The tale of the Ephesian Matron is to be found in the *Satyricon* of Petronius: for its subsequent use in literature, see Peter Ure, 'The Widow of Ephesus: some reflections on an international comic theme', *Durham University Journal*, New Series XVIII (December 1956), pp. 1–9.

is also shrewd; he is a wit, but he has a kindly heart and a sense of obligation becoming to his rank; he fights his years, but he has learned much from them. He is, indeed, an uncommonly well-rounded comic character.

Both Garrick and Colman rose well above their usual level in this collaboration; Garrick's polish but not his shallowness are present, and Colman's humanity sweetens the play without swamping it in a profusion of sentiment.

Garrick's unassisted hand may be judged in *A Peep Behind The Curtain* (DL 1767), which is one of those 'rehearsal' plays that both actors and audiences love. A somewhat perfunctory romance between Wilson and Miss Fuz frames a rehearsal of the first act of *Orpheus*, for which Barthélémon provided music. This is of the school of *The Rehearsal* (DL 1671) and is a predecessor of *The Critic* (DL 1779); like them it is of the 'insider' and 'studio joke' class of performance, with lots of amusing demonstration of theatre machinery and a group of dancing cows. The actor King, as Glib the author, is called upon to mock the stage deportment of the actor King; Saunders the stage carpenter is almost the first character of the kind to be allowed to protest that his vital contribution to the play is undervalued.[1] It is no wonder that audiences were delighted with it, and that it ran to 108 performances in its first year. What Garrick thought of it is a puzzle; he allowed the public to suppose that King was the real author, which may have been managerial cunning, or indifference.

The following year brought forward two comedies worthy of note. Hugh Kelly's *False Delicacy* (DL 1768) was successful; Oliver Goldsmith's *The Good Natured Man* (CG 1768) was not, but time has reversed the decision of the first season. Kelly's piece prospered because of its profusion of fine sentiments, but undoubtedly they clog the movement of the play, which contrives to be at once complex and weak. Duty to parents was refreshingly stressed, as a contrast to the undutiful runaway lovers so common in contemporary comedy. The theme of renunciation is strongly introduced, but is not allowed its resolution. Without the worldly characters of Cecil and Mrs Harley we should soon tire of the complexity of needless scruple which is all of the plot; clearly Kelly meant this to be amusing, but he has not had the comic art or the courage to make it so.

Goldsmith's play, on the other hand, is an unmistakable product of genius, and its waywardness is the result of great powers over which the author has insufficient control. It acts well, but leaves the audience confused, for the principal theme of Honeywood's self-destructive good nature is lost in the

---

[1] There is a hint of this in Shirley's masque *The Triumph of Peace* (1634) but not at Saunders's length.

splendid comic complexities created by Croaker and Lofty. These two characters have run away with the play, and the author has not chosen, or has been unable, to curb them. The scene in which the bailiffs occupy Honeywood's house and good-humouredly undertake to pass themselves off as his friends is one of the best things in eighteenth-century comedy; it is rooted in the barbarous hilarity of life itself, and not in any convention of stage wit.[1] That it was condemned as 'low' is evidence of nothing but how stiff-rumped (to use a term much in vogue in the theatre of the time) the convention-bound critics of the day could be.

Genius does not always go hand in hand with careful workmanship, and undoubtedly this is a flawed play. The management of the machinery of exit and entrance is not as skilled as Garrick or Colman would have made it. It is the vivid drawing of character that marks it as the work of a master hand, and the characters live through the freshness and pithiness of their language, which runs off the tongue with the smoothness and inevitability of phrasing that makes Goldsmith the darling of actors of Old Comedy.

The stage saw no tragedy of consequence at the end of this decade. There were a few reworkings of Greek themes. Murphy wrote a dull *Zenobia* (DL 1768); John Hoole, son of the machinist at Covent Garden, and a protégé of Samuel Johnson, saw productions of *Cyrus* (CG 1768) and *Timanthes* (CG 1770), two of his translations of Metastasio. Home's *Fatal Discovery* (DL 1769) was a worthy but undistinguished piece; he never entered the enchanted landscape of *Douglas* again.

One unacted play, however, was of substantial influence, and is still of interest. It is Horace Walpole's *The Mysterious Mother*, printed at his Strawberry Hill Press (1768) and subsequently republished in commercial editions. With all the amateurish fussiness which we shall meet again among literary men at the turn of the century, he explained his play and hedged it with conditions. So long as he circulated manuscript copies Garrick was not to see it; neither was Samuel Johnson. The reader must take note that the story is a true one, but quite unfit for the stage; one of the speeches had distinguished antecedents, being imitated from Lucan; Addison, on his deathbed, had said something very similar to what one of the characters in the play says; a picture by Salvator Rosa suggested another graceful touch. He fidgets as if he had built his play as a magpie builds its nest, out of bright scraps from everywhere. Above all the author of *The Castle of Otranto* wanted it known that his play was 'horrid'.

[1] It showed its quality in the Old Vic's production of the play at Buxton and in a provincial tour necessitated by the war in the autumn of 1939.

Indeed it is horrid. He penetrates deeper and more daringly than Home into the world of phantasmagoria and dream grotto where romance is to be found, and where the humbler creatures are the characters of melodrama. In his tale of a countess who lies with her own son, and bears a daughter whom that son later marries, Walpole goes far into the enclosed and darkling world of the psyche. And because a distinguished mind is at work we are able to ignore occasional lapses into bathos, and – worse – into pertness, because upon the whole the language is impressive, and the dramatic action swift. It is important as a harbinger of what is to come, though unfortunately its worthiest descendants are not among works for the theatre.

1770–1780

The ten years following 1770 offer some of the finest work of the half century, but also the inescapable procession of successful, workmanlike pieces that keep theatres open at all periods of history. Bickerstaff continued in his chosen line with *The Recruiting Sergeant* (DL 1770) and *He Would If He Could* (DL 1771): the former contains an elaborate interlude of dancing, a reminder of the size and versatility expected of an eighteenth-century company; the latter is a reworking from Pergolesi's *La Serva Padrona* (1733).

It is surprising to find Foote a champion of virtue in *The Maid of Bath* (Hay 2 1771): one Walter Long, a Bath citizen, had behaved with indecency towards a young lady, and Foote pilloried him in his play. It is hard to say whether Foote is more distasteful in his usual grossness or in his fit of virtue, for he introduced his own name into this play, and strutted unbecomingly in knightly guise. He was by this time fifty-two, and the loss of his leg was beginning to tell on him; this may account for a growing mannerism in his writing, which is to give the character he was himself to play a late entrance, carefully prepared by the rest of the cast: in *The Maid of Bath* and in *The Nabob* (Hay 2 1772) he does not make his entrance until Act II, which is late for the leading man in a three-act comedy. Garrick added to the merriment of this season with *The Irish Widow* (DL 1772), which provided Mrs Barry with a rattling 'breeches' and dialect part in a thin, brisk play that owes much to Molière's *Le Mariage Forcé*.

Richard Cumberland's *The West Indian* (DL 1771) is a well-managed play in the taste of its time, which was now leaning strongly towards sentimentality. With this writer sentimentality is made to take the place of any real observation of character. Belcour is a diminished Tom Jones, a rake with a good heart, and the other characters harp safely on a single string apiece; everything is subdued to the pointing of a moral. The great moment comes when Stockwell, the Unknown Father, or Fate With The Moneybags, reveals his identity and acknowledges his son:

> How happily has this evening concluded, and yet how threatening was its approach! Let us repair to the supper room, where I will unfold to you every circumstance of my mysterious story. Yes, Belcour, I have watched you with a patient but enquiring eye; and I have discovered through the veil of some irregularities, a heart beaming with benevolence, an animated nature, fallible indeed, but not incorrigible; and your election of this excellent young lady makes me glory in acknowledging you to be my son.

Try reading that aloud, seriously and with proper attention to phrasing and making the meaning clear to a hearer, and the quality of this play will manifest itself. It is stately and self-honouring, moral and sadly wanting in fresh air. The world of these sentimental comedies is a very small world. The didacticism of late medieval drama is here, unsupported by religious fervour or a real moral vigour.

The popularity of such plays can only be explained by the flattering echoes they gave back to the tone of society as theatre audiences represented it. *The Grecian Daughter* by Arthur Murphy (DL 1772) held the stage for fifty years. It is not strictly a tragedy (for in it the heroine, Euphrasia, preserves her father, her husband and her son, and maintains the Sicilian dynasty against a tyrant), but it was lachrymose, gloomy and much to the sentimental taste, and is called a tragedy in collections of drama, in *Biographia Dramatica*[1] and Genest.[2] It is, rather, a female dream of glory. Euphrasia saves the life of her father Evander by making her way to the

---

[1] *Biographia Dramatica; or, A Companion to the Playhouse* appeared first in 1764, was brought up to date in 1782 and was continued to 1811 in the 1812 edition, which is therefore the most useful. See II, 272.
[2] *Some Account of the English Stage from the Restoration in 1660 to 1830*, by the Reverend John Genest, 10 volumes (Bath, 1832), V, 323–4.

prison where he lies weak with starvation, and suckling him. Though this interesting scene takes place offstage, it is described with moral gloating by two agents of the tyrant, one of whom urges tyrants in general to

> . . . learn, that while your cruelty prepares
> Unheard-of tortures, virtue can keep pace
> With your worst efforts, and can try new modes
> To bid men grow enamour'd of her charms.

It is not easy for Euphrasia to surpass this purely feminine exploit, but she does so by employing 'a daughter's arm' to stab the tyrant, and after her father has cried

> My child! my daughter! sav'd again by thee!

she proceeds, nobly forgetful of herself, to apportion dignities to others.

Absurd though this play appears, a little reflection can partner its excesses in modern drama, and especially in the cinema. Only the language is strange; the promptings of the sentimental heart are familiar enough. The verse is smooth, though Murphy delights in the inversions of which Dr Johnson thought so poorly,[1] and it avoids the vice of echoing Shakespeare. The diction is fashionable; references to 'the social, generous tear' date it for the reader with a sense of language. But it is important to remember that it was popular; it suited the taste of its time.

That taste appeared to be remarkably sure of itself. It could, on the occasion of Weston's benefit at Drury Lane in 1774, weep at *The Grecian Daughter* and enjoy comic interludes between the acts, one of which was a humorous address delivered by Weston from the back of a pantomime rhinoceros. It could still shout down a play that failed to please it. It regarded hacked, rewritten and reshaped versions of Shakespeare as improvements on the original, and it welcomed George Colman's pleasing and melodious but utterly un-Miltonic version of *Comus* (CG 1772). Its sense of obligation to the past did not include English writers even of the first rank, and the

---

[1] 'He observed that a gentleman of eminence in literature had got into a bad style of poetry of late. "He puts (said he) a very common thing into a strange dress, till he does not know it himself and thinks other people do not know it. . . . For example, he'd write thus:

> Hermit hoar, in solemn cell,
> Wearing out life's evening gray.

Gray evening is common enough; but *evening gray* he'd think fine . . ." ' (Boswell's *Life of Johnson*, ed. George Birkbeck Hill and revised by L. F. Powell, III [Oxford 1934], p. 159, Thursday, 18 September 1777). This unnamed gentleman had innumerable companions among contemporary writers of tragedy.

Augustan veneration for Greece and Rome was giving place to an idea of tragedy that admitted of new and romantic settings without quite being able to abandon the Augustan gloom and rigidity.

William Mason was one of those who clung to Augustan principles. His *Elfrida*, produced first of all without his consent (CG 1772) and later with it and in a somewhat altered form (CG 1779), had an 'Old English' theme, but also a chorus in the Greek manner. When his *Caractacus* was performed (CG 1776), Mason was persuaded to permit some of his choruses to be declaimed by the Chief Bard, but he would not sacrifice them all. Mason was a better scholar than playwright, and perhaps this should be the judgement on all of those who sought to wed Greek form to non-Greek matter; it would be presumptuous to say that it cannot be done, but it is a matter of history that it has not been done.

Picturesqueness of milieu could not save the tragedy of this decade. Home's Spanish scene in *Alonzo* (DL 1773) was of no avail, nor did the charms of Peru do much for Murphy's *Alzuma* (CG 1773). Dr Paul Hiffernan's[1] *Heroine of the Cave* (DL 1774) was none the better for an Italian setting, nor did Dr Franklin's *Matilda* (DL 1775) gain from being laid in the time of William the Conqueror; Jephson's *Braganza* (DL 1775) lay of course in Portugal and Hoole's *Cleonice* (CG 1775) in Bithynia. *Edward and Eleonora* (CG 1775) had been prepared by its author, James Thomson of *Sophonisba* fame, for production in 1739, but was refused a licence for some supposed sedition; we may wonder if the appearance in 1775 of a play of such slight merit owed anything to its setting in Palestine; however, although the play has shallow roots in Euripides's *Alcestis*, it is very much in the taste of this decade, for it is on the theme of female nobility, and in it Eleanora sucks the poison from Edward's wound at risk of her life. *Eldred* (Hay 1775) was by the actor John Jackson, and its scene is 'Cambria'. Cumberland's *Battle of Hastings* (DL 1778) has a British theme, but its author cannot resist making Matilda speak of 'Pallas springing from the brain of Jove'; more than once the yearning for classical ornature led to kindred grotesquenès. Hannah More wrote *Percy* (CG 1777), Home made his last grasp at success with

[1] Of the unfortunate Paul Hiffernan (1719–77) *Biographia Dramatica* says:

> ... with no principles and slender abilities, he was perpetually disgracing literature, which he was doomed to follow for bread, by such conduct as was even unworthy of the lowest and most contemptible of the vulgar. His conversation was highly offensive to decency and good manners, and his whole behaviour discovered a mind over which the opinions of mankind had no influence.

Let those who believe that a consciously assumed bohemianism releases talent read any of Hiffernan's seven plays and reflect.

Alfred (CG 1777), and *Buthred* (CG 1778), the author of which cannot be unmistakably determined, is laid in the time of the Danish invasions; only the More work claims much attention now; Home presents Alfred the Great in the guise of a lover, and *Buthred* was short-lived; but all three are attempts to make British themes the stuff of tragedy.

The other tragedies of the close of the decade are of slight dramatic interest, but it is noteworthy that only an adaptation of Voltaire's *Semiramis* (DL 1776) by G. E. Ayscough was in the classical tradition. Jephson's *Law of Lombardy* (DL 1779), Mrs Cowley's *Albina, Countess Raimond* and Hannah More's *Fatal Falsehood* (CG 1779) all have what may be called romantic settings; the last of these was not a success, but the Epilogue by Sheridan is of interest, as it expresses in terms of elegant, amused condescension the attitude of the time towards female writers.

Charles Dibdin, whose chief fame is as a composer, was at times his own librettist; it was he who supplied the music for Bickerstaff's *Lionel and Clarissa* and *The Padlock*, and his own piece *The Deserter* (DL 1773) now achieved some success, though the prose speeches and verses are undistinguished. Foote's *The Bankrupt* (Hay 2 1773) is more than ordinarily disappointing and arbitrary in development, but its satire of the corrupt practices associated with bankruptcy is keen, and in Robin and Kitty it exhibits an amusing pair of servant lovers.

It is Oliver Goldsmith's *She Stoops to Conquer* (CG 1773) that illuminates the comedy of this decade. We do not enjoy it now as a mocker of sentimental fashions, but that was an important part of its interest for its first audiences. Garrick's Prologue (spoken by Woodward, dressed in mourning for the dying Comic Muse) gives pointed criticism of the theatre of the time:

> . . . But why can't I be moral? – Let me try –
> My heart thus pressing – fix'd my face and eye –
> With a sententious look, that nothing means
> (Faces are blocks, in sentimental scenes),
> Thus I begin – *All is not gold that glitters,*
> *Pleasure seems sweet, but proves a glass of bitters.*
> *When ignorance enters, folly is at hand;*
> *Learning is better far than house and land.*
> *Let not your virtue trip, who trips may stumble,*
> *And virtue is not virtue, if she tumble.*
>   I give it up – morals won't do for me;
> To make you laugh I must play tragedy.

The only hope for the languishing Comic Muse is the treatment of Dr Goldsmith.

The first encounter of Kate Hardcastle and Young Marlow is a mockery of the sentimental style: satire is too stern a word for this gentle rallying. Nor can we fail to note Miss Neville's extremely unsentimental concern about her fortune in the underplot.

It has been said [1] that the mainspring of the plot, in which two young men mistake a private house for an inn, is improbable; Goldsmith's reply was that it was based on a true story. [2] The point is of small relevance, for we accept the plot for the duration of the play. It is much better constructed than *The Good Natur'd Man*, and its deftness carries it lightly over the improbability.

Goldsmith had not lost his fondness for 'low' scenes: Tony Lumpkin's meeting with his friends at The Three Jolly Pigeons is 'low' by the standards of the time, and so also is Mr Hardcastle's scene in which he tries to make a motley group of servants behave like smart footmen – the kind of footmen satirized in *High Life Below Stairs*. Tony Lumpkin himself tends towards lowness, and has delighted audiences ever since because of it. And indeed the assumption of the character of a maidservant by Kate Hardcastle cannot have been acceptable to those who expected heroines to keep a high tone; she does it with humour, and this quality also gives freshness and life to her relations with her father.

All these elements are supported and illumined by the beauty of Goldsmith's language, natural and fresh to a degree only possible to genius, and glowing with humour, rather than with the flashing wit that Garrick possessed and Sheridan was to carry to its highest pitch in this period. When Synge wrote, 'In a good play every speech should be as fully flavoured as a nut or an apple', [3] he might have been describing the stage prose of Goldsmith. He is great in a realm where only the Irish playwrights of a later age have approached him.

The following year brings us nothing that has endured, but as the purpose of this survey is to consider what gave pleasure in its time, mention should be made of Dibdin's *The Waterman* (Hay 2 1774), in which the character of Tom Tug gave a name to the Thames watermen for many years to come, and from which the songs 'The Jolly Young Waterman' and 'Then farewell, my

[1] By William Woodfall, writing in the *Monthly Review* for April 1773 (XLVIII, 309–14).
[2] As reported by his sister, Mrs Hodson, *Collected Letters*, ed. K. C. Balderson (Cambridge, 1928), pp. 166–8; the incident of Mrs Hardcastle's drive is compared with a tale of a lady's terror on a coach journey in the *Rambler*, No. 34, in Boswell's *Life*, I (Oxford, 1934), p. 213, n. 5.
[3] Preface to *The Playboy of the Western World*, 1907.

trim-built wherry' are still occasionally heard. Popular also was the first piece by the soldier playwright who figures as a character in Shaw's *The Devil's Disciple*, John Burgoyne. *The Maid of the Oaks* (DL 1774) is conventional; Oldworthy prepares a *fête-champêtre* to celebrate the marriage of Maria to Sir Harry Groveby; she is a paragon, and proves to be Oldworthy's daughter and a great heiress; Oldworthy has concealed these facts lest pride and flattery corrupt her. In the underplot Lady Bab Lardoon humbles the lady-killer Dupeley by pretending to be a shepherdess. The piece is enlivened with much music and song, it offers fine chances for stage display, and as a fashionable touch a Druid makes an appearance at the end.

Foote's current piece was *The Cozeners* (Hay 2 1774); the writing is in his best vein and the characters of Mrs Fleece'em and Mrs Simmy are unusually good; this was Foote's last play but one, and in it vivacity for once gets the better of brutality. His own character, Mr Aircastle, does not appear till II. ii; he is an amusing creation, talking in rambling non sequiturs.

Bickerstaff's play *The Sultan* (DL 1775) has claim to be classed as a Women's Rights protest of a primitive order. Roxalana, an Englishwoman captured for the Sultan's seraglio, displaces the favourite Elmira, enchants the Sultan and secures the freedom of all his wives by her cheerful impudence and English superiority. This is not an operetta, though it contains a few songs. Dibdin also brought forward a non-musical piece in this season. *The Quaker* (DL 1775) is a renunciation play: Steady, the Quaker, wants to marry Gillian, but gives her up to Lubin, whom she loves; although his Quaker mannerism is mocked, he is shown as a man of magnanimity. This is one of those plays, dear to the simple heart, in which it is presumed that idealism is incompatible with sexual passion.

Garrick's pen was busy at this time with its last productions for the stage. His version of Ben Jonson, *The Alchymist* (DL 1774), was followed by *Bon Ton, or High Life Above Stairs* (DL 1775), which satirizes the adulteries of fashionable life and the follies of high-living servants in the four-handed amours of Lord and Lady Minikin, Colonel Tivy and Miss Titup; they are exposed by the country cousin, Sir John Trotley. It is a perfunctory play, and somewhat sour in tone for Garrick; it must have relied on deft and charming performance to pull it through. It may be noted that II. i, in which Miss Titup is concealed behind a chair by Minikin, and later discovered by Sir John, precedes the screen scene in *The School for Scandal* by just fourteen months.

Garrick's *May Day, or The Little Gypsy* (DL 1775) would not detain us if it did not display the author's last use of a theme that seems to have been a favourite with him. We have seen a son and his father as rivals in *Miss in Her Teens*, an uncle and nephew as rivals in *The Irish Widow*, and here we find the pattern again, for Furrow the farmer and his son William both want the Little Gypsy, and seek the May Day bequest of Squire Goodwill, which would bring them £100 with the girl; Furrow's daughter Dolly, disguised as an old gypsy, helps her brother to get the girl and the money. Garrick's farewell to the public as a playwright was with *The Theatrical Candidates* (DL 1775), in which Mercury announces an election contest between Comedy and Tragedy; when they have made their election addresses, they are surprised by Harlequin, who also wants to 'stand'. Mercury announces Apollo's decree, which is that all three must abide by the will of the public. It is a graceful trifle, with charming music by Arne, and it may be said to embody Garrick's managerial policy to perfection.

Richard Brinsley Sheridan's parents were both playwrights, and his father was an actor. Perhaps if he had not had the theatre so strongly in his blood he might have taken it more seriously. As it was, he took it lightly, both as a playwright and a manager, and who is to say that the results are not rhe better for it? His first play *The Rivals* (CG 1775) was somewhat carelessly plotted, and was withdrawn for repairs after two performances; ten days later it returned to the stage decidedly improved, but still with signs of hasty workmanship. In it Sheridan attempts nothing new: the character of Mrs Malaprop had already appeared as a type in Garrick's *Lethe* and in Murphy's *The Upholsterer*; Acres is the booby squire of a score of comedies, and affected heroines and irascible fathers had been two a penny for decades. But Sheridan made these dry bones live by a combination of high-bred merriment and a command of language which only Goldsmith, in a vein of his own, could rival. There is no grossness in Sheridan, as there is in even the best of Foote, and he has a comic vigour that far outdistances Garrick. Certainly he is not without originality when he can be bothered to summon it up. It is a happy inspiration to pair the level-headed Jack Absolute and the sensible Julia with Lydia Languish and the sentimentally self-tormented Faulkland, and we are persuaded, for once in eighteenth-century comedy, that their marriages are truly a reconciliation of opposites, and not simply a device to bring the curtain down.

Would that it were possible to say that this was a new dawn in comedy, but it was not. Foote's last work *The Capuchin* (Hay 2 1776) is a wretched production, an alteration of a play called *A Trip to Calais* which the Duchess of Kingston succeeded in suppressing before it appeared, as she knew that it contained a libellous satire upon her; *The Capuchin* contains a portrait of her chaplain (who had spread rumours that Foote was a sodomite) under the name of Dr Viper. And so poor Foote, a sad, dangerous, sardonic, coarse man, limps from the stage and the world.

The School for Scandal (DL 1777) establishes Sheridan as the greatest comic writer of his day. Its stagecraft is brilliant, and its satire of sentiment is keen, though its own ending is sentimental enough, and the character of Charles is in the tradition of the good-hearted rake. But Sheridan's sentiment is persuasive; the history of his own romance shows him to be a man of strongly chivalrous feeling, and it is precisely in chivalry that so much of the sentimental writing of the time was wanting. Joseph Surface rises above mere satire of a sentimental attitude; he is a philosophical villain, well aware of what he is and what he is doing, and calmly pleased with himself. He is far above the revengeful Lady Sneerwell, and her creature Mr Snake; he manipulates them. He is, indeed, Sheridan's finest creation, and one of the notable figures of English comedy.[1]

It is sometimes said that the 'scandal' scenes are in the Restoration vein, and certainly they are worthy to stand beside the great work of the end of the previous century. But this is not a belated Restoration play: we have only to compare the circle of the Teazles with that of Olivia in *The Plain Dealer*. The good breeding of *The School for Scandal* is characteristic of its own time, and of no other, and Sheridan's humanity is his own, owing nothing to fashionable sentimental attitudes. In this play, more than in *The Rivals*, his command of language is an unfailing source of delight, and even when it is complex there is a discipline within the profusion that makes it fall with apparent inevitability from the tongue of the player who has found its tune.

We may conclude a review of this decade with what is itself a perceptive comment on it. Sheridan's *The Critic* (DL 1779) is the best thing of its kind since Buckingham's *The Rehearsal*; it strikes deeper than Garrick's *A Peep Behind The Curtain*, not because Garrick lacked wit or art, but simply because the *vis comica* in Sheridan's nature is greater. The portrait of the household of Mr Dangle, the 'mock Maecenas to second-hand authors', gives us the tone of the critical society of the age as it was seen by its foremost wit; the tragedy written by Mr Puff is the tragedy we have been examining surveyed with genial irreverence through a quizzing-glass. This is one of the handful of great burlesques in our literature.

---

[1] See Charles Lamb's essay 'On the artificial comedy of the last century' for his description of John Palmer, the original Joseph, in this part. 'Plausible Jack' was a fat actor, a consideration to be remembered, as the finest Joseph of recent years, Sir John Gielgud, is a thin one.

1780–1790

A comedy that appeared at the beginning of this decade and held the stage successfully for more than a century – its last important recorded production being at the Court Theatre in 1913 – is *The Belle's Stratagem* (CG 1780) by Hannah Cowley. Neither Genest nor *Biographia Dramatica* speaks warmly of it,[1] but it provided good acting parts of the sort in which audiences like to see leading players; both Doricourt and Letitia Hardy have opportunities to show their paces, she by feigning a foolish simplicity and he by pretending to be mad; the disguise device has always been popular in drama, and here it is as the taste of the late eighteenth century enjoyed it. The writing is lively, if not witty, and there are several strong appeals to patriotism, exalting modest English womanhood above the ambiguous enchantresses of the Continent.

Thomas Holcroft's *Duplicity* (CG 1781) had bad luck at its first appearance and was more successful when it was tried again in 1796, reduced to three acts and renamed *The Mask'd Friend*. It deserves mention here because it was the first play from the hand of this prolific author which can be read: *The Crisis* (DL 1778) was not printed and does not seem to have been successful. *Duplicity* deals in terms of comedy with the mania for gambling that possesses Sir Harry Portland, and from which his friend Osborne delivers

[1] Genest, VI, 147–8; *BD*, II, 56.

him by fleecing him of his own and his sister's fortunes, which Osborne then restores with a vivid reminder of 'the distracted wife and widow's curse, the orphan's tears, the sting of desperation, and the red and impious hand of suicide' which follow the gamester. This is comedy principally because of the somewhat heavy-handed underplot. Holcroft was a man of remarkable spirit and courage, whose own life was a drama better than any he wrote;[1] comedy was not the true element of his mind, and he always moved in it as a traveller rather than a native.

Burgoyne's operetta *The Lord of the Manor* (DL 1781) detains us not by its intrinsic merit but because it is a kind of entertainment which was growing in favour at this period, a mingling of comedy and drama in which true love is exalted above wealth and rank, the spiritual benefits of rural life are warmly asserted and the call of blood overcomes the pride of elderly, wealthy relatives. This is the kind of piece satirized by Gilbert and Sullivan in *Ruddigore* (1887) and which achieved great popularity during the first three-quarters of the nineteenth century. The music for Burgoyne's operetta was by the accomplished William Jackson of Exeter, and when it was revived and revised by C. I. M. Dibdin in 1812, the additional music he wrote for it included 'The Dashing White Sergeant', still a popular dance tune. It is also worthy of note that the comic role of Moll Flagon was played by Richard Suett: 'breeches' parts for actresses and female roles for comedians are idiosyncrasies of the drama at this time that should not be forgotten.

A comedy of greater substance than these, that lasted out a century, was Charles Macklin's *The Man of the World* (CG 1781).[2] Its strength lies almost entirely in the principal character, Sir Pertinax Macsycophant, drawn, one may judge, under the influence of a detestation of the Scots that would have warmed the heart of Samuel Johnson. Sir Pertinax has raised his son to be a gentleman, and has thereby given the young man ideals of conduct beyond the understanding of his father, who has made a success in the world and a fortune, by acuteness and 'booing' – which is his pronunciation of 'bowing'. Playgoers have always been ready to believe that disagreeable and vulgar parents may have charming and high-minded children,[3] but the odd flavour of this play arises from the fact that Macsycophant has been drawn with so much strong feeling that he lives, whereas his gentleman son, Egerton, is a stick. Similarly the chaplain, Sidney, is represented as a man of fine feeling, but he listens to intolerable stuff from Sir Pertinax without protest; this

[1] See *Dictionary of National Biography*.
[2] It had been played in Dublin in 1764, but was not licensed in London until 1781.
[3] Witness Shaw's *Candida*.

may perhaps have been because Macklin the author did not choose that anyone should have lines that would seriously discommode Macklin the actor. Sidney, though a clergyman, never says a word about religion in a household that sadly needs spiritual counsel; he is, however, the exemplar of the fashionable theme of renunciation, for though he would like to have the heroine for himself he resigns her to Egerton.

Shallow psychology is common in the comedy of this period, but psychology so much awry as this is singular. The play draws all its strength from the character it most condemns; two philosophies of life are opposed, and the good one is factitious while the bad one is vital. The effect is to make us respect and almost like Sir Pertinax, as we grow impatient with the prigs who surround him.

The tragedy of this decade is interesting chiefly because of the rapidity with which the life leaks out of the Augustan tragic concept and reasserts itself in a kind of play that produces something like tragic effect but is nearer to melodrama. Walpole's *The Mysterious Mother* is an obvious influence on Richard Cumberland's *The Mysterious Husband* (CG 1783). This play gains by being written in prose, and considering the involved nature of the plot – the exclamation 'Complicated misery!' uttered by Dormer at the denouement must surely have raised a laugh at some time – the atmosphere of mounting horror is very well sustained.

It is a tale of incest, but, unlike Walpole's drama, it is incest of the spirit only; as Genest observes, 'the catastrophe is dreadful, but not disgusting.'[1] Lord Davenant, a widower with one son, has remarried; his second wife is a woman of great fidelity and beauty of character, who nevertheless cherishes a love for another man. But Davenant had previously married a young woman on the Continent, and left her after three months, giving her cause to think him dead. It is this young woman, Marianne, whom his son loves and marries; she is, as well, the sister of Dormer, the man Lady Davenant loves. Young Davenant discovers that he has married his father's legal wife before his marriage is consummated, so that physical incest is avoided, though the fact is blighting to his happiness and Marianne's. Davenant, tortured by remorse, kills himself.

Unlike *Douglas* or *The Mysterious Mother*, this drama does not take place in the closed world of romance. The Davenants live in fashionable London; they have friends who are not involved in their misery; no great length of time elapses during which they brood and lick their wounds; their unhappiness, though unlikely, is not inconceivably far-fetched. The consequence is

[1] Genest, VI, 270.

that this play has remarkable power, but does not grip the imagination as do the tragedies of romance.

The Augustan tragedy, though it had lost its impetus, lingered for another fifty years. Dr John Delap, a clergyman, brought forward his reconsideration of Euripides's *Heracleidae*, called *The Royal Suppliants* (DL 1781), which appears to have sunk like a stone. Mrs Brooke, the novelist and widow of a clergyman, wrote *The Siege of Sinope* (CG 1781) but seems to have been so careless that the classical names in her piece could only be made to scan by mispronouncing them. Samuel Jackson Pratt's *The Fair Circassian* (DL 1781) is a dull play of fraternal rivalry which a Persian setting does nothing to redeem. Jephson's *The Count of Narbonne* (CG 1781) is based on Walpole's *Castle of Otranto* and transfers some of the novel's romantic trappings to the stage, but misses the novel's atmosphere. Thomas Hull's *The Fatal Interview* (DL 1782) has not survived in print, and Richard Bentley's *Philodamus* (CG 1782) survived in print but achieved only a single performance.

These records of failure are significant because the managers of the patent houses obviously saw merit in these plays, supported them with money, undertook rehearsal, costumes and performance, and saw their hopes dashed. Tragedy languished not because the stage was not open to it, but because it repeatedly failed to strike the tragic note as the age desired it.

What was that note? The age was in the common predicament of not knowing clearly what it wanted, but knowing pretty clearly what it would not permit on the stage. Consider Hannah More's *Sacred Dramas* which appeared in 1782: the four plays are *Moses in the Bulrushes, David and Goliath, Belshazzar* and *Daniel*. They are brief, and are divided into parts rather than acts, and were not intended for performance. Here we have a clue to the failure of much tragedy of this era: too much that was nearest to the hearts of writers and audience was thought unsuitable to the stage. Miss More says of these pieces, 'It would not be easy, I believe, to introduce Sacred Tragedies on the English Stage. The scrupulous would think it profane, while the profane would think it dull' – although she reflects that Racine wrote *Athalie* 'in a dissipated country, and a voluptuous court'. Of her attitude towards these compositions, she says in her prefatory Advertisement, 'I reflected, with awe, that the place whereon I stood was holy ground' – and therefore unsuited to the stage. When playwrights believe that what is noblest and nearest their hearts is not suited to the stage they are unlikely to write tragedy of any consequence, and sanctimonious fusses about near-incest and silly points of scruple are made to serve their turn. The disease is a common one: the authors want to be vulgarly respectable more than they want to be artists; the audiences want to be thrilled but cannot bear to be disturbed.

Relevant to this is Cumberland's *The Carmelite* (DL 1784), which was a modestly successful tragedy by a recognized man of letters. What does it offer? First, a complex story. Matilda has appealed to King Henry I for redress against Hildebrand, who killed her husband St Valori many years earlier when he was returning from the Holy Wars. Hildebrand's ship is wrecked on the shores of the Isle of Wight, and Matilda's people rescue him and his companion and spiritual comforter, a Carmelite monk. Hildebrand has confessed his murder to the monk, and the monk has revealed to Matilda's old retainer, Gyfford, that he is none other than – St Valori! Matilda's champion in the coming trial by battle is her page Montgomeri, to whom she reveals at this juncture that he is the son of herself and the supposedly dead St Valori. But St Valori and Gyfford have seen her caressing this young man, and suppose her to be wanton. Hildebrand refuses to accept succour from Matilda, whom he has so deeply wronged, but he dies happily because the Carmelite reveals that St Valori lives. When at last all is explained, Matilda, St Valori and their son Montgomeri are united in happiness.

This play depends heavily on the fact that its characters confide their secrets to people other than those most directly concerned: they fear that too sudden joy might blast a wife, a guilt-ridden man, a son. One does not ask that common sense should dominate a tragedy; tragedy is rooted in emotions that set common sense at defiance. But tragic inevitability and solemn fatuity can be told apart by the intensity of the emotion aroused, and we know too well that the secrecy of the people in *The Carmelite* is dictated principally by the necessity to keep Act I at a decent distance from Act V. This is tragedy as conceived by Mr Puff and admired by Dickens's Theatrical Young Gentleman.[1]

The blank verse is journeyman stuff into which all the most effective tricks of rhetoric are lugged, to heighten matter that is obstinately flat; not soaring thought, but simulation of it, prompts this kind of writing. Similarly in the construction every device is used to excite the nerves without deeply involving the feelings. However sympathetically we may read it, we feel at the end that the author has been manipulating us to produce effects of tragedy from matter which has no tragic content.

Reading is not, of course, the proper method of judging a play. Genest tells us that Cumberland 'professes to have contrived the fable, and addressed every feature of the principal character, to Mrs Siddons' – and this explains

[1] 'Sketches of Young Gentlemen', in *Sketches by Boz* (1836).

much. *The Carmelite* is a vehicle for a particular star, and even the family resemblance of the Kembles is exploited by providing Sarah Siddons's brother with the role of her son, Montgomeri, in which he 'exhibited one of the finest forms ever seen on the stage'.[1] Mrs Siddons is enabled as Matilda to show most of the passions – all those she did best. But the tailoring of a role to the talents of a player rarely produces drama of any lasting worth. All through the period covered in this study we get too much of it, and when the playwright provides roles for himself, as with Foote, a kind of dramatic anarchy results.

Unhappily a great deal of pumped-up drama was made to serve the theatres of this decade. Again, Cumberland's *The Natural Son* (DL 1784) offers an example in the realm of comedy. It is in five acts, with barely enough provision to hold out for three, and although the author has provided a great deal of incident, it cannot really be called action, and the reader wonders why it might not proceed on the same lines for ten acts. The tale is that of Blushenly, an orphan without money, who does not think it right to marry Lady Paragon in that situation; when he discovers his parentage, and gets his inheritance, there is no barrier to the match. The dialogue is pleasant without being particularly witty or pithy, but there is far too much of it. In 1794 Cumberland trimmed it to four acts, which is still an act too many.

A consideration of the tragedy accepted for performance during the latter part of this decade tells us nothing new. The clutching at the picturesque continues in Cumberland's *The Arab* (CG 1785), a drama with whiffs of the Bible and Josephus about it. Dr Delap continued to lay Euripides under tribute in *The Captives* (DL 1786). Of greater interest, because more related to the thought of the time, is Frederick Reynolds's *Werter* (Bath 1785), but it was not a skilful adaptation of Goethe's novel. Jephson's *Julia, or the Italian Lover* (DL 1787) and Andrew McDonald's *Vimonda* (Hay 2 1787) are both tragedies of contrivance rather than of inevitability, and Mrs Cowley's *The Fate of Sparta* (DL 1788) was no more successful than her earlier *Albina, Countess Raimond* (Hay 2 1779). *The Regent* (DL 1788) was the work of Bertie Greatheed, and although it was moderately successful in the terms of the time, he did not try again. He belongs to the group of well-connected writers who tried their hands at poetry and tragedy without exerting themselves unduly. Of the same stamp was William Hayley, whose *Lord Russell* (Hay 2 1784), *Marcella* (DL 1789) and *Eudora* (CG 1790) were all written a few years before their appearance on the stage; he sought to persuade

[1] Genest, VI, 334.

theatregoers towards a high standard of morality, but seems to have gained little ground.

Further evidence of the growing success of women as dramatic writers is offered by the production of *The Widow of Malabar* (CG 1790) by Mariana Starke, a lady of some social pretension, and *Earl Goodwin* (Bath 1789) from the pen of Ann Yearsley, an untutored genius called 'the milkwoman of Clifton'. Neither piece held the stage long.

A woman writer greatly superior to these, who never attempted tragedy except as a translator, but wrote several excellent farces and comedies, was the witty Elizabeth Inchbald. She was no theorist, but had won her knowledge of the stage in the hard school of the strolling player; because of her personal beauty she also discovered a few things about love that were not to be found out by reading poetry, and she was successful in communicating her worldly wisdom to her audiences in a way they found palatable and recognizable. Her first full-length piece is *I'll Tell You What* (Hay 2 1785): it is not as skilled in workmanship as some of her later compositions, but it is in pleasant stage prose. Mrs Inchbald understood the art of writing lines that speak easily, even when the meaning is complex and the style profuse in the accepted 'elegant' manner of the time.

A good comedy to be recorded here is Burgoyne's *The Heiress* (DL 1786). He was not an inventive playwright, and his plot leans heavily on Diderot's *Père de Famille* (1758) and Charlotte Lennox's *The Sister* (CG 1769); this latter piece had but one performance, because for some reason, now forgotten, it was damned by the audience; certainly it lacks vitality. But vitality is precisely what Burgoyne's play possesses, and it arises chiefly from its spare, witty, fresh writing. It wavers into sentiment at times, for Burgoyne was not sufficiently original to rise above popular taste; it may also be said that the resolution of the plot is somewhat clumsy and prolonged. But it lives, and gave pleasure for several years.

Mention should also be made of Burgoyne's *Richard Coeur de Lion* (DL 1786), a musical piece though not quite an opera, even by the vague definition of the time. It is a good example of the type of play that is best called costume drama. Its plot is innocent of any intention to deceive by simulating nature: Richard is rescued from captivity by his love Matilda, who has disguised herself as a blind minstrel; it is she who leads the assault on the castle. This is simply an excuse for a love story, a quantity of agreeable singing, a display of scenery, some fighting, and a pretty girl in tights. But this combination has inexhaustible charm, and the addition of a dash of pseudo-history only makes it more acceptable.

Pseudo-psychology was equally popular in operas of this musically modest kind. In George Colman the Younger's *Inkle and Yarico* (Hay 2 1787) the young English adventurer Inkle is torn between an obligation to marry an English heiress, whose money he loves and towards whose person he is indifferent, or the savage maiden Yarico, whom he loves and who has, moreover, saved his life. Of course love triumphs, though avarice gives it a sharp tussle, and unquestionably Inkle talks better about the less attractive passion. This piece was popular for at least fifty years.

Holcroft's *Seduction* (DL 1787) has a somewhat serious plot in which the author's distaste for the world of fashion is apparent, but he has too much skill to let this spoil his play. The tone of the writing is light, and the care with which the minor characters are drawn gives it as much vitality as the artificial nature of the denouement – in which the seducer's go-between, disguised as the Sly Simpleton, proves to be the brother of his victim – will permit.

We may wonder, as we read these plays, what the servants of this era were really like. Except in Goldsmith, they are presented as modish imitators of their masters and mistresses, showing their wit, their affectations and their vices in little. This stereotype is varied occasionally by a faithful old steward, but otherwise it is rigid. Even Holcroft, whose sympathies were not wholly with the ruling class, shows us Lapelle the valet and Mrs Pinup the lady's maid just as they might have been in any other comedy of his time. Perhaps the truth is simple: this is how servants behaved – or at least as they liked to see themselves on the stage, looking down from the footmen's gallery.

The last comedy to engage us in this decade is *The Dramatist* (CG 1789) by Frederick Reynolds. Though it has not held the stage so firmly as some of its contemporaries, it has been seen from time to time, its last successful revival being at the Haymarket in 1927. The underlying tone is sentimental, but the construction moves the play along so swiftly, and the dialogue is so charming, that it never cloys. The character of the dramatist, Vapid, was somewhat resented, according to *Biographia Dramatica*, as 'one of the first of that numerous family, by which genteel and sprightly comedians have been converted into speaking harlequins'.[1] Tastes have changed, for we may now count Vapid's flights of fancy as one of the chief attractions of the play.

[1] *Biographia Dramatica*, II, 176.

1790–1800

During the second half of the eighteenth century roughly a hundred new tragedies were presented in the London theatres; of these nearly thirty made their appearance during the last decade, but there is little about them to call for individual comment; more and more, tragedy comes to mean 'productive of solemnly elevated feeling' and drifts towards romance. Music in tragedy grows from a song or two, often dragged into the action, to concerted pieces in which two or three characters and perhaps a chorus sing – a kind of useful musical shorthand for establishing the atmosphere of the merry greenwood or the robber's den. Comic scenes are more often found in tragedy, and Genest repeatedly complains of 'a jumble of T. C. and O.' in his notes on a play. Audiences have become less stringent in their ideas of what tragedy should be, and we must assume that absurdities in the printed text were obscured by bustling action and the attractions of well-graced players. Some new names appear among the writers of this sort of play. George Colman the Younger, son of the collaborator in *The Clandestine Marriage*, and himself a prolific playwright, brought forward *The Surrender of Calais* (Hay 2 1791), one of Genest's 'jumbles' but with some tragic intent. Murphy's last tragedy, *The Rival Sisters*, published in 1786, was produced (Hay 2 1793) without success; it is a 'regular' work, on the theme of Ariadne at Naxos, and without comic relief. Edward Jerningham, a poet of some accomplishment, proved that he was not a playwright with *The Siege of Berwick* (CG 1793); Henry James Pye attempted a tragedy on a moderate scale, in three acts, called *The Siege of Meaux* (CG 1794), which was more attentive to historical fact that many. James Boaden, a novelist, critic and biographer of Kemble, Mrs Siddons, Mrs Jordan and Mrs Inchbald (all very good reading, once one has become accustomed to the idiom), wrote five pieces of a serious nature during this decade, of which *The Italian Monk* (Hay 2 1797) was adapted from the romance, called simply *The Italian*, by Mrs Radcliffe, and *The Cambro-Britons* (Hay 2 1798) is of interest as evidence that the desire to draw dramatic themes from British history was still strong. Of this class also is *De Monfort* (DL 1800), which Kemble adapted from one of Joanna Baillie's 'Series of Plays: in which it is attempted to delineate the stronger passions of the mind'.

It need not be supposed from this uninspiring record that the theatre was dull at this time. The standard of acting was very high, and the tried-and-true repertoire provided it with meritorious plays. Some of the new comedies were excellent. Holcroft's *The Road to Ruin* (CG 1792) is his best work. If we accept the convention that young men who gamble away their fathers' fortunes are no more than generously wayward and may prove fine fellows in the end, we can admire Harry Dornton; certainly he is more attractively drawn than most such characters. We need feel no reservation about Gold-finch, a brilliant portrait of a witless young man of fashion; Old Dornton, the Widow Warren and Silky the usurer are full of life. Sophia, the heroine, is an attractive featherbrain. Even Sulky, the incorruptible family friend, is a real character, and not a walking compendium of moral precept. Not that the play lacks a strong moral bias: it was essential to Holcroft's nature. But he was sufficiently a man of the world and an artist to show it in the grain of his play, and not to apply it from without. This is a first-rate picture of society just below the aristocratic level, as it existed in the nineties. Holcroft's well-constructed, lively comedy has had a long life on the stage, and was last successfully produced in 1937, at the Ambassadors Theatre.

Mrs Inchbald's *Every One Has His Fault* (CG 1793) almost deviates from the surface comedy of the time into a play of deeper psychological insight. We sense from it that the writer knew human nature better than she dared to show on the stage; the desire – perhaps the commercial necessity – for regularity of plot and a balanced intrigue, with acceptable sentiments, hold it below what it might have been. But its dialogue is up to this writer's best level, which was colloquial without being trivial, and the differentiation of character is unusually subtle. If only she had felt free to give her unfortunates, Irwin and his wife, real faults instead of merely attractive weaknesses, she might have written a comedy of lasting merit. Even as it is her play held the stage for almost a century.

George Colman the Younger's most successful comedy, which held the stage till 1906, and might yet be seen, is *The Heir at Law* (Hay 2 1797); it was played all over England, and was a great favourite in America. It is the simple tale of the rightful heir who is thought dead, but returns to claim his fortune – not this time from a villainous uncle, but from Daniel Dowlas, a chandler who is astonished to find himself transformed into Lord Duberly. There is a dash of genius in Colman, a vigour of style that is accompanied by some slovenly workmanship. His plot here is trivial, and many of the scenes do nothing to advance the action; nevertheless these are the best scenes in the play. He has the real playwright's knack of bringing people together and making them talk absorbingly. Dr Pangloss, the best character, is not really necessary to the action; Zekiel Homespun, the Simple Countryman with the Heart of Gold, talks far too much for any good he does. But Pangloss is very funny, and Homespun provides the humbler part of the audience with a chance to enter into a strong league of sympathy with somebody on the stage. The lovers are tiresome; Caroline is no more than another part of Moreland's fortune, which he recovers, and because Moreland is a stick she is a female stick. But the comic characters are all first-rate, and we recall what they said long after we have forgotten what they did.

We need pause over John Philip Kemble's *Lodoiska* (DL 1794) only because it is a good example of the musical romance which is establishing itself as a favourite theatrical form at this time. It is a costume piece, written with all the licence afforded by fancy dress and a setting in a far-off land – Poland – which had romantic overtones for English audiences. Opera librettos are useful gauges of the amount of surface improbability audiences will swallow in return for a strong subjective experience: *Lodoiska* is a succession of highly charged incidents, supported by songs that establish the emotional tone. As Genest says, it is 'much better calculated for representation than perusal',[1] but the music by Storace contains the essence of its charm for several generations of playgoers who might have been surprised at being called opera-goers.

The taste of the time for sensation and marvels is reflected in the scandal that surrounded the production of William Henry Ireland's *Vortigern*

---

[1] Genest, VII, 333.

(DL 1796). This piece was announced as a newly discovered play by Shakespeare; it was the work of a youth who had, from his seventeenth year, imposed upon his father, an engraver and antiquary, with manuscripts purporting to be from the hands of several contemporaries of Shakespeare, for whom the father had a deep veneration; success led him to produce a version of *Lear* and some passages from *Hamlet*, supposedly in Shakespeare's hand; from this he was tempted to attribute to Shakespeare this play of his own composition, *Vortigern*, which understandably caused a sensation and secured the support and admiration of a number of eminent persons, not all of whom are to be blamed for being taken in. Boaden and Malone threw doubt on the authenticity of *Vortigern*, but by 1795 Sheridan had accepted it for production.

Whether Sheridan ever fully believed in the piece cannot now be determined, but it is pretty certain that by the time production was under way he knew it was a fake; certainly John Philip Kemble, who was to prepare it for the stage, and act the name part, knew it was not Shakespeare, and resented being party to such a folly. Ireland declared that it was Kemble's delivery of the line in Act V

And when this solemn mockery is o'er —

that finally turned the audience against it. But the audience would have had to be deaf not to know that Shakespeare had no hand in so jejune a tragedy. Thus Ireland, a writer of promise, was ruined at nineteen. Simple-minded as is his characterization, and tiresome his reliance on soliloquy, the play moves with a true Shakespearian rapidity. The verse is flat and derivative, and, as might be expected from a writer capable of so humourless a fraud, his Fool is a disaster. But the psychological interest of the piece does not attach wholly to Ireland: what sort of age was it in which so many influential men could be so deceived, and in which such a play could reach the stage?[1]

Costume drama was now firmly established; the type may be defined as that group of plays in which the action is laid in a bygone time not from historical or mythological necessity, but in order to exploit the picturesqueness of the costume and language of another era. Colman the Younger's *The Iron Chest* (DL 1796) was a fine early example of this long-lived genre. Sir

---

[1] *Vortigern* was published in 1799 (London) and again in 1832 with an additional explanatory Preface. See also *Miscellaneous Papers and Legal Instruments under the Hand and Seal of William Shakespeare including the Tragedy of King Lear* (London, 1796), and *The Confessions of William Henry Ireland* (London, 1805). Malone's *Inquiry into the Authenticity* . . . appeared in March 1796. A complete review of the affair is *The Fourth Forger* by John Mair (London, 1939).

Edward Mortimer, the principal character, is tortured by remorse because he has murdered a man who humiliated him; essentially noble, but burdened by a guilty secret, Mortimer is a Byronic hero before Byron. There are improbabilities in the plot, but they seem not to have disturbed audiences who kept it on the stage till 1879. The music by Storace adds a dimension to the piece, particularly by the rapidity with which it enables the band of robbers to establish an atmosphere of menace.[1]

If Colman was careless in construction and inclined to leave much of the hard work to his actors, he was a very Ibsen compared with Matthew Gregory Lewis, best known as author of *The Monk* (1796), whose *The Castle Spectre* (DL 1797) nevertheless had sixty performances in its first season and held the stage for a century to come. This is costume drama to which Lewis had added a jaunty romanticism of his own. His Prologue is of interest; romance is a 'fair enchantress' who haunts

> . . . graves new-opened, or midst dungeons damp,
> Drear forests, ruin'd aisles and haunted towers,
> Forlorn she roves, and raves away the hours!

In his words 'To The Reader' he brushes aside the objection that he has given his villain negro attendants on the shore of Wales. 'I by no means repent the introduction of my Africans,' he says; 'I thought it would give a pleasing variety to the characters and dresses . . . could I have produced the same effect by making my heroine blue, blue I should have made her.' This surely explains all his apparatus – sliding panels, spectres, animated suits of armour, and a misanthropic slave. They were for effect, and effect justified anything.

Doubtless it explains also the comic character of Father Philip. English audiences during this era were as ambivalent about Roman Catholics as some later ones have been about Marxists: priests and friars appear usually as villains (there are two such in *The Mysterious Mother*) or clowns. In *The Carmelite* it is assumed that a man could disguise himself as a White Friar, deceive everyone for twenty years, offer good counsel and ghostly support to anybody who needed it, and then fling off his habit to reveal a full suit of armour. 'Where a Friar was concerned, Lewis's mind was strangely warped', says Genest, himself a clergyman and certainly better informed.

Lewis appears to have been genially cynical about the stage. Certainly his

---

[1] Stephen Storace, 1763–96, wrote much music for the stage and a reading of the entry on him in Grove's *Dictionary of Music and Musicians*, Volume VIII, is a helpful reminder of the dependence of drama on music at this time. It was while supervising the rehearsals of the music for *The Iron Chest* that the composer fell ill and died.

comedy *The East Indian* (DL 1799), with its contrived and improbable plot and its use of effective odds and ends from *The School for Scandal* and Kotzebue's *Corsicans* (the first English version of which appeared the same year), suggests such an attitude. It may be said that this comedy was written when Lewis was sixteen; the reply must be that he had four years in which to revise it before offering it for production. He might surely have revised Mrs Slip-Slop (a name surely taken from *Joseph Andrews*), as Mrs Malaprop had shown all there was to be shown in that sort of fun nine years earlier. But Lewis was always wilful. Of interest is the curious Epilogue, in which the actor Bannister appears dressed as Queen Elizabeth; this must have been the point of the speech, for the words, though jocose, are barely coherent.

A great influence on the era to follow was Benjamin Thompson's version of August Friedrich von Kotzebue's *Menschenhass und Reue* (1789), called *The Stranger* (DL 1798). The German writer's power is undeniable; he has a depth of earnestness and a psychological insight far beyond any English writers' of the time. They feared to trespass too far upon real feeling, and relied on sensation and fretted nerves; Kotzebue's single aim was to touch and stir the heart. This play, apparently very severe on the guilty wife, gives her a defence: 'They do not truly honour virtue who can insult the erring heart that would return to her sanctuary.' In short, all the English plays in which wives or husbands were wrongfully suspected of infidelity had been playing with the subject: it is possible to sin and be redeemed by repentance. This play wrings every situation of its tear; the reconciliation of the estranged couple at the end by the need of their children may be sentimental, but it reaches its mark. This is a new note in drama.

It was another of Kotzebue's plays that gave the end of the eighteenth century one of its most admired successes, and a drama of which audiences did not tire for sixty years. This was *Pizarro* (DL 1799), translated by Sheridan, and also cut, adapted and fitted out with new songs. Indeed, the most admired single passage in the English version, in which Rolla addresses his soldiers on liberty, was entirely Sheridan's, and never failed to draw applause from audiences aware of the threat posed against them by Bonaparte's army. The part of Rolla was a favourite with three generations of leading actors, and his thrilling escape over the bridge, carrying the child, was only one of the excitements the play provided.

Mockery of *Pizarro* is easy. The popularity of the play assures us that this age had ears and minds and hearts responsive to a style of rhetoric of which Kotzebue was one master and Sheridan – the great parliamentary orator – was another. If we truly seek to know what *Pizarro* meant to its first audiences we may neither marvel nor despise, but must set ourselves to the delicate task of finding the path into the heart of it.

To dismiss any play that has won large acceptance over a number of years, simply because it seems artificial to our taste, is to be deceived by an irrelevance. All art is artificial, and to attempt to sift from it only what is timeless is a hopeless task. It is the artifice that determines its form and marks its content – however lofty and full of meaning for the first audiences – with the stamp of its time, and to belittle this element is to miss much of the quality of the whole. No work of art, however carefully it may be contrived to do so, escapes the spirit of its age and the conventions that govern the art of its age. No revival of a play from the past shows us the play its contemporaries saw. But if we, in our time, hope to elicit from the plays of the past the utmost they have to give us, we must bring a reasoned sympathy to the mode in which they are written and the cultural climate in which they grew.

The rhetoric of *Pizarro* is not luxuriant in comparison with the rhetoric of some of the successful plays we shall encounter in the eighty years that follow. Nevertheless it makes us wonder what sort of audiences were able to follow its complexities and be excited by them to outbursts of applause that stopped the show. The people in those audiences must have been keener of ear than we and trained to listen to speech with an attentiveness we reserve for music. They delighted in rhetoric as an art; they abandoned themselves to its persuasiveness; they valued the player whose vocal technique was equal to the demands of speech in this high-strained style – demands as exacting in their way as the elaborately ornamented arias of contemporary opera.

They encountered this and similar plays in a theatre where, at last, the picture-frame stage was triumphant, and where Garrick's efforts to keep spectators off the stage had been successful since 1763. They went to the theatre expecting a display of art in which the illusion of reality was a minor factor. The principal attraction of the evening, whether comedy or tragedy, was bracketed between a prologue and an epilogue, both of which treated it as a display, an entertainment, a show. A musical after-piece or a farce emphasized the supremacy of art, and made it plain that nature would be imitated according to well-understood conventions.[1]

The arbitrary nature of comedy plots – the sudden reform of disagreeable characters, the forgiveness of cruel or coarse impostures, the agreement that young and handsome people must necessarily be happy if they marry, all the nonsense of the little world in which the action is carried through – suggest that few people cared primarily about plot except as an ingenious fable that

[1] On this important change in the character of the theatre, see also Part I (2), pp. 29–31.

permitted display of character. And how was character displayed? Not so much in action as in speech. We may search these comedies for a long time before we find behaviour on the part of any character that really surprises us. But in the search we shall be arrested again and again by speech of remarkable pith, savour and wit, even among characters – such as heroines – who might not be expected to have this distinction.

The great masters of such dialogue are of course Sheridan and Goldsmith, and their individual vein is so clearly defined that we may fail to notice that they are working the same mine. But the lesser names of the half century achieve most of their distinction because of their facility in language. Garrick has many brilliant scenes, and redeems his most perfunctory productions by a sprinkling of fine lines. Foote, gross as he often is in thought, strikes out his dialogue to a fine edge. Colman is as adroit as Garrick, and Cumberland in comedy shows a deftness and lightness of tread that could not be deduced from his tragedy. Holcroft's serious undertones are heard through lines of great sprightliness and even the sentimental Bickerstaff is graceful and seemly and occasionally witty in his verse. The writers seem to have shared, not equally but all sufficiently, in a common command of languge that made it possible for them to say anything they wanted to say with style and address, reserving cant or slang for occasional use in depicting characters from low life or the sporting world. The charm, clarity and grace of this stage speech constitute the principal possession of the comedy writers of the age; like the eighteenth-century orchestra, it did not permit a wide range of colour, or overwhelming effects, but in the hands of masters it was masterly; employed by lesser artists it was still well bred and limpid.

The comedies of this period of fifty years are, taken as a whole, the products of minds observant but not reflective, worldly-wise rather than wise, finding expression in a style that is often elegant but rarely poetical. They as yet care little for fantasy or the charms of inconsequence. Their theatre is wholly a kingdom of this world, without any suspicion of the limitations of reason, and innocent of any intimations of a larger life. All is clear; it is a world without shadows. Their plays are diversions for men and women of the world, written by authors who understood men and women of the world. Perhaps it is ungrateful to suggest that men and women of the world make up a rather small part of society as a whole; obviously they, and those who sought to be like them, dictated the taste of the time.

It is the lack of any true depth of feeling that marks this comedy, as indeed it marks most comedy at any time. But the refusal to admit deep feeling in the theatre in the second half of the eighteenth century was far more serious in its effects on tragedy. The religious life of England was comatose in many areas, and where it was alert it was no friend to the theatre. Where religion, using the word broadly to suggest concern about the great mysteries of life and death, sleeps, there will not be much writing on the tragic level. The people in most of the tragedies we have considered believe in abstractions – honour, filial duty, the splendour of motherhood and the like – but behind these abstractions we sense only a feeble moral impulse; there is no God, or no gods, who will not be mocked and will strike the mocker down in his strength.

The writers of tragedy cannot be considered as in the same rank o importance as the writers of comedy. They are men with no tragic vision, except for Moore and – in one lucky play – Home. They are too often men in country vicarages, driven by a desire to astonish the world. Tragedy could be written within the Augustan confines, but not by men armed only with ambition and a narrow classical scholarship; they bow to the Augustan rules, but they have not the strength of impulse or the passion to make the rules look like laws. The flat, externalized world produced some fine comedy but it was the worst possible soil for tragedy.

No wonder, then, that by the end of the eighteenth century tragedy was moribund, and the passion and exuberance of serious feeling that might have nourished it was finding an outlet in a new sort of drama – serious but not tragic, passionate and unchaste – directed at another area of sensibility.

1800–1880

The most superficial glance at the period between 1800 and 1880 shows extraordinary achievement in every kind of writing except drama. Its poets, novelists and writers of *belles lettres* are familiar to every student of literature, but although it was a time of exuberant theatrical activity, the names of its playwrights are known only to specialists.

The reasons for this seemingly paradoxical state of affairs are complex and interacting; not all of them belong properly in this part of the book. In general terms it may be said that though many of the best writers would have been pleased to distinguish themselves in drama, they were unwilling to submit to the discipline of the theatre, which at this time was particularly vexatious to proud and original minds. It was also a factor that the rewards of the dramatist were trivial in comparison with those of the successful novelist or even the admired poet; more than ever the theatre was dominated by meanly commercial interests.[1] What drew the crowd was a display of brilliant acting; in theatre, as in music, it was the era of the virtuoso. Great actors chose to maintain their reputations in Shakespearian and other classic plays that had been cut to show their powers to advantage; they would also undertake contemporary plays which were sometimes no more than scaffolds

[1] On the dramatist's financial position, see also Part I (2), pp. 46-57.

upon which they mounted extraordinary creations of their own invention. But the tie between the theatre and literature, which we have seen wearing thinner during the fifty years already considered, dwindled to a thread as the influence of romanticism grew.

The first eighty years of the nineteenth century was a time of rapid increase in population, which concentrated in great cities, especially London. Here were new playgoers, many of them barely literate, who went to the new theatres[1] to be told tales and experience simple thrills. The chasm between their taste and that of fastidious men of letters could not be bridged; indeed, it would have been contrary to the social spirit of the time to try to bridge it. What had a Byron, a Shelley, even a Scott, to say to an audience of which an important part might be made up of coal-heavers, sweated milliners and sempstresses, costermongers, rat-catchers, dolls' eye-makers, dog stealers, pure-finders, rag-and-bone men, hawkers and all the rest of the *dramatis personae* of *London Labour and the London Poor*,[2] as well as decent but illiterate labourers and their wives, who wanted their money's worth on their night out? *Othello* they relished as a tale of jealousy, but upon Byron's Venetian play of a jealous husband, *Marino Faliero* (DL 1821), their judgement was Genest's – 'too much is said and too little is done.'[3]

Few writers of great gifts were fixed in their determination to write closet drama. Most were willing, and perhaps more than merely willing, to have their plays shown on the stage if the theatrical folk would respect their texts. Sir Walter Scott yielded to the suggestion of his actor friend, Daniel Terry, that he should write a play, and produced *The Doom of Devorgoil*.[4] He called it 'A Melo-Drama', and certainly it is as high in colour and as romantic in incident as many of the best plays that bore that description. Its principal plot concerns the pride of an old but poverty-stricken Scots house, the fortunes of which are restored when a ghost reveals a hoard of treasure concealed long before. The secondary plot is about a pair of peasant lovers, Blackthorn and Katleen, who disguise themselves as Owlspiegle and Cockledemoy, a demon barber and his apprentice, in order to torment a stupid parson, Gull-crammer.

[1] *Historical and Descriptive Accounts of the Theatres of London*, by Edward Wedlake Brayley, 1827, lists fourteen theatres; by 1880 *The Era* lists fifty-two.
[2] A sociological study of historic importance by Henry Mayhew, published in its final form in 1864 (London).
[3] Genest, IX, 91. On the new audience, see also Part I, pp. 7-8.
[4] The date of this play cannot be accurately determined, but a letter from Scott to Terry of 8 February 1818 (J. G. Lockhart, *Memoirs* [Edinburgh, 1837], IV, 125) alludes to it as recent and urges Terry to pass it as his own work. It was published in 1830.

These elements are not well joined, and the lively underplot tends to thrust aside the gloomy principal action. There are some excellent songs, of which 'The Bonnets of Bonny Dundee' has become famous, but Sir Walter was self-indulgent here: 'Dundee' runs on for eleven verses, with a rousing chorus after each. The dialogue is good throughout the play, but there is far too much of it. Many supernatural effects are required, and the author has appended footnotes suggesting how they might be achieved; all that can be said is that he had no notion of stage illusion, and would have been wiser to leave such things to those who had.

Unsatisfactory though the play is, we may wonder why Terry did not carve and cobble it into something for the stage. It is no worse than some of Terry's own adaptations of Scott's novels, which were successfully presented. Certainly it is better than Scott's later play *Auchindrane; or the Ayrshire Tragedy* (1830), a tale of feuding and revenge. Encouraged, Scott might have written drama as good as his novels. But he did not want to be known as a writer for the stage, and in a letter to Southey (April 1819) we may discover why:

> To write for low, ill-informed and conceited actors, whom you must please, for your success is necessarily at their mercy, I cannot away with. . . . Besides, if this objection were out of the way, I do not think the character of the audience in London is such that one could have the least pleasure in pleasing them. One half come to prosecute their debaucheries, so openly that it would degrade a bagnio. Another set snooze off their beef-steaks and port wine; a third are critics of the fourth column of the newspaper; fashion, wit and literature there is not; and on the whole I would far rather write verses for mine honest friend Punch and his audience.[1]

Scott was offered the best circumstances if he would seriously consider writing for the theatre:

> I remember declining [Byron's invitation] to write for the stage [DL] and alleging in excuse, not only the probability that I might not succeed, but the unpleasant yet necessary and inevitable subjection in which I must, as a dramatic writer, be necessarily kept by 'the good folks in the green-room.' *Caeteraque*, as I added, *ingenio non subeunda meo* [and other

[1] *The Private Letter-Books of Sir Walter Scott*, ed. Wilfred Partington (London, 1930; New York, 1930).

things not to be endured by my spirit]. Byron sprang up and crossed the room with great vivacity, saying, 'No, by G—, nor by mine either.'[1]

And yet this was the fate Byron suffered posthumously. Only *Marino Faliero* was performed in his lifetime (DL 1821) but Macready played *Werner* (DL 1830) and kept it in his repertoire, and also produced *Sardanapalus* (DL 1834). *Manfred* (CG 1834) and *The Two Foscari* (CG 1838) also reached the stage. Even *Cain*, which seems as little accommodated to the stage as anything of Byron's, has been given life by new techniques of presentation, and has been produced at Frankfurt in 1958 and Lucerne in 1960. But all these productions have involved cutting, rearranging and even rewriting to a degree that would have vexed Byron's proud spirit.

The most popular of his plays was *Werner*, and Macready achieved a substantial success in it, despite its atmosphere of gloom. But as a preliminary he cut the 3,171 lines of Byron's text to 1,631, and wrote an additional 143 lines of verse to bridge gaps caused by cutting, and to clarify and emphasize what Byron had left too vague for effective stage presentation.[2]

It was in Act V, scene i, that Macready introduced what was perhaps his most famous 'point' in *Werner*. He told a young actor how it came about:

> Carried away by the passion of the scene, he rushed down to Charles Kemble Mason, who played Gabor, and demanded, 'Are you a father?' Then he whispered, 'Say "No";' whereupon Gabor shouted 'No!' and Macready, in a burst of paternal emotion, rejoined:
>
> 'Ah, then you cannot feel for misery like mine!' and the pit rose at him.

This invention appears in the prompt copy, with the stage direction, 'Gets to chair and throws himself on it; after a pause, "Mark me, when you etc." ' The recorder of this interpolation refers to it as 'a sublime gag'.[3] No wonder Scott and Byron thought actors a low lot. But the actors knew what would make the pit rise, and the gentleman authors scorned to acquire such skill.

Some, of course, had a better initial idea of what would make a play than others. Coleridge had a native dramatic gift, and his *Remorse* achieved an honourable, if not glorious, run of twenty performances when it first

---

[1] Scott's marginal note to a letter to C. R. Maturin, 15 June 1815. The Latin, Lockhart says, should be rendered 'to say nothing of money matters'.

[2] From Gustavus Vaughan Brooke's copy of Macready's version, prepared for him in 1854 by Joseph Bedworth, prompter of the Theatre Royal, Birmingham, and now in the writer's possession.

[3] John Coleman, *Players and Playwrights I Have Known* (London, 1888), I, 47.

appeared (DL 1813) and was revived for a single night in 1817.[1] The atmosphere of tension between Moors and Spaniards is firmly established without being laboured; the melodramatic plot is sufficiently powerful to sustain suspense to the end, and the use of some of the supernatural elements in it shows a true sense of theatrical values. The scene in which a murder is foreshadowed by means of a picture is theatrically faulty, simply because pictures on the stage are rarely big enough or well enough painted to carry so much dramatic weight. The characters, though not strikingly differentiated in manner of speech, are well established as individuals, and certainly Dona Teresa and Alharda have more character, and more to do, than is usual among female roles in the drama of the time.

What raised the play well above competence is the quality of the verse. It is the work of a poet in a theatre where poets were rarely heard, and fustian was made to serve for verse. It is self-indulgent, as first plays often are: too many speeches are too long, which gives a sense of leisure when we need compression and an impulse forward. But *Remorse* suggests that if Coleridge had chosen to persist he might have been a dramatist of distinguished achievement.

Shelley thought so. *Remorse* was the only contemporary play he thought superior to *The Cenci* (1819), which he asked his friend T. L. Peacock to offer to Covent Garden. Although he was no playgoer he had firm ideas of what he wanted. The role of Beatrice was 'precisely fitted' for Miss O'Neill, and he would 'be very reluctant that any one but Kean' should play the Count.[2] Like Scott and Byron he had a poor opinion of audiences, but thought the play contained 'nothing beyond what the multitude are contented to believe they can understand'.

Because his theme was incest, Shelley's play had to wait until 10 March 1886 for a private performance, arranged by the Shelley Society at the Grant Theatre, Islington. Although the cast was a strong one and its attitude reverential, the faults of the play were apparent. It is slow to get under way, and the powerful single scenes in the third and fifth acts cannot redeem it. After the death of the Count the play loses the impulse given by its most vivid character, and even those who consider the last scene beautiful can hardly deny that it is theatrically lame. The Shakespearian echoes – especially those from *Macbeth* – are distracting and weakening. No quantity of good poetry can make up for so much clumsy construction, and it must also be said that

[1] 14 April, for the benefit of the actor Rae, who played Don Ordonio. (Genest.)
[2] Shelley's views are clearly set forth in his wife's Note to the published version of the play. It first appeared in the 1839 edition of the *Poetical Works*.

Shelley is nervous about his theme, perhaps from instincts of delicacy excessive in a playwright. If we are to be shaken by a horror, the horror must not be kept quite so much behind the arras.

Browning, whose exuberance might be thought to favour him, failed as a playwright. *Strafford* (DL 1837) survived for only five nights; *A Blot in the 'Scutcheon* (DL 1843) lasted three nights; *Colombe's Birthday* (Hay 1853) was his last work written to be acted and its reception was cool. Browning's fondness for psychological rather than physical action, and the difficulties of speaking his knotted verse, set Macready and the other actors against the plays, which underwent revisions that might better be described as maulings. The poet was high-mettled and lost patience with the actors who were not, apart from Macready and Helen Faucit, of the first rank. Yet we may feel, as we read his plays, that a sympathetic modern approach might yet reveal fine qualities. If Byron's *Cain* can succeed, is there not hope for Browning?[1]

Before we leave the poets for a time, brief mention must be made of Wordsworth, who wrote *The Borderers* in 1796 and made attempts to secure a production at Covent Garden the year following. He was not hostile to alteration, but it was not in the power of any amount of revision to make a play of this attempt to unravel 'the apparently motiveless actions of bad men'. He accepted the judgement of the theatre and did not publish the work until 1842. But if *The Borderers* will not do as a play we must recognize its virtues as a poem; the arguments in favour of what appears to be crime in the interest of a high conception of justice are engrossing, but they are useless in the theatre, being bodied forth in lumbering action and a kind of verse in which all the characters speak alike. Wordsworth could not make his metaphysics into good drama.

Thomas Love Peacock, who was charged with the task of presenting *The*

---

[1] In the autobiography of the American actor Otis Skinner, *Footlights and Spotlights* (New York, 1923), pp. 258–61, he describes a series of performances of *In a Balcony*, undertaken in the US in 1900 by Sarah Cowell LeMoyne as

> one of the genuinely artistic achievements of the American theatre . . . . I do not think we three actors of the short cast, Mrs. LeMoyne, Miss Robson and myself, ever approached a task with greater deference, or worked harder to make clear the difficult verse of Robert Browning . . . . Browning was never kind to the theatre in the matter of ease of delivery. For over an hour this little tragedy moves on argumentatively – intensely, even volcanically. At the finish I found myself exhausted from the mere physical work of 'putting over' Norbert. The result was well worth the effort. *In a Balcony* never failed to hold our audiences in breathless attention.

This, as opposed to the minatory spirit of Macready, seems to be what Browning needs from actors.

Cenci to Covent Garden without revealing the name of the writer, had theatrical connections, wrote criticism for the *Globe* and the *Examiner*, and tried his hand at playwriting himself. Three pieces from his hand survive: *The Dilettanti* is a farce, *The Circle of Loda* is a drama with a Norse theme, and *The Three Doctors* is described as a musical farce. All three are distinguished by the superior quality of their dialogue, which suggests the novels that were to come later. We need not agree with J. B. Priestley that they are 'crude affairs in which the author shows no sense of the theatre'.[1] On the contrary, he shows too much sense of the contemporary theatre for his own good; these plays are constricted and pinched to make them like other farces of the day; Peacock did not dare to be fully himself. This was indeed the fault of many a good writer who took a stab at playwriting and, because he wrote below his own level, was rebuffed.

Charles Lamb never dared to be himself in his theatre ventures. *John Woodvil* was published in 1802; it is interesting as the work of a literary antiquary, and is neither good enough to serve the stage, nor so bad as to be deplored. His attempt in the contemporary manner, *Mr. H.* (DL 1805), was deservedly damned: its theme is the sensitivity of the chief character about his name, which is Hogsflesh; this is feeble even for Lamb at his feeblest, and he cast it in the jocose, vulgar farce prose of the period. He never dared to exploit his vein of fantasy, or the brilliance of his native wit, in a play.

Doubtless he knew the temper of his time. Dickens, who suffered from no want of assurance, appears to have been daunted by the demand for slapdash, touch-and-go dialogue and plots of flat obviousness, and his pieces for the stage are hardly to be recognized as his work. *The Strange Gentleman* (St James 1836) does not seem to be from the hand which was at that time producing *Pickwick*; *The Village Coquettes* (St James 1836) was regarded as a vehicle for Hullah's music, and without the music it is little. *Is She His Wife ? or, Something Singular* (St James 1837) is of even less significance, and *The Lamplighter* (1838) is so spiritless a work that Dickens's friend Macready declined to produce it.

Collaboration seemed to work better. *Mr. Nightingale's Diary*, written in 1851 with Mark Lemon and first produced in the picture gallery at Devonshire House, provided Dickens the actor with an opportunity to assume six strongly contrasted disguises, showing his versatility as a comedian at its best. It is what theatre people call a 'vehicle' for his particular gifts, but is no

[1] J. B. Priestley, *Thomas Love Peacock*, in the English Men of Letters series (London, 1927).

better than a dozen other pieces – *A Day in Paris* (Victoria 1833), in which Mrs Selby played five parts, one as an army officer, for example – designed for quick-change artists. It is good of its kind, but it is not what we might hope for from Dickens. Neither is *No Thoroughfare*, the five-act drama in which he collaborated with Wilkie Collins. They had written it first as a Christmas story, then dramatized it for production (Lyceum 1867) with the popular melodrama actor Charles Fechter as the love-tortured villain, Jules Obenreizer. It was produced also in Paris (Vaudeville) as *L'Abîme*, with success. But even this is not in Dickens's best vein, nor in Collins's; the plot is absurd and the dialogue seems blunted.

Both Dickens and Collins wrote splendid melodramatic novels, fleshed out with descriptive passages that reveal the psychological truth that lies behind the vivid and apparently arbitrary action; the spirit moving their art often seems more theatrical than novel-like. The dialogue in their novels is alive, but it can rarely stand alone, as a score of adaptations for the stage, in which the dialogue has been isolated and compressed into a play, plainly attest. The dialogue and the descriptive and reflective matter form a unity. Dickens read aloud, as he himself amply proved, is admirably effective; Dickens as film, in which so much more of its totality can be captured, has been successful in our time; Dickens rendered down into a play has seldom been Dickensian.[1] And it appears that Dickens as a playwright, unable to be his own scene-painter and stage manager, and unable to play all the parts himself, was Dickens at his least characteristic, for he was trying to fit into an existing mould instead of forming a new one.

In a lesser degree this is also true of Collins, whose plays, though successful, brought nothing new or personal to the contemporary theatre. The great master of sensation needed the spaciousness of a novel in which to build up his characteristic effects. *The Frozen Deep* was privately produced at Dickens's domestic theatre in January 1857[2] and in the summer of the same year was revived by the excellent amateur cast of literary men and artists for several benefit performances, to aid the family of Douglas Jerrold.[3] Its first professional presentation was in October 1866 (Olympic), and Charles Reade noted

---

[1] Mention should be made of the very successful melodrama *The Only Way*, in which Sir John Martin-Harvey appeared over 1,000 times from 1899 until his retirement. But it reworks, rather than adapts, *A Tale of Two Cities*.

[2] Called the Tavistock House Theatre; the cast included Mark Lemon, Collins and several members of Dickens's family; scenery was by Telbin and music by Francesco Berger.

[3] Edgar Johnson, *Charles Dickens, His Tragedy and Triumph* (New York, 1952), II, 863–78.

in his diary: 'It is a pretty play . . . too much narrative; but after all, original and interesting, and the closing scene great and pathetic.'[1] Collins also produced stage versions of his novels: *Armadale* he dramatized twice, once by that name in collaboration with Régnier of the *Comédie Française*; he set this version aside as unsuccessful and the second dramatization, called *Miss Gwilt* (Globe 1876), was well received, though it was criticized for its 'unwholesomeness', which doubtless created interest among playgoers. *No Name*, dramatized with Wybert Reeve, was never performed in England, its life being confined to some performances in Melbourne, Australia.[2] *The Woman in White* (Olympic 1871), *Black and White* (Adelphi 1869) and *The New Magdalen* (Olympic 1873) – which was conceived as a play, but written first as a novel – complete the record of Collins's plays, of which the last was the most successful with the public.

Anthony Trollope did not take so long as Dickens and Collins to learn that the stage was not for him. *The Noble Jilt*, which he wrote in 1850, was sent to the comedian George Bartley for an opinion, and Bartley, in a letter of excellent practical criticism, condemned it as 'a five-act play without a hero!' Novels without heroes were growing in fashion, but a play without a hero was out of the question. Thrifty Trollope did not wholly lose his labour, however: in *The Eustace Diamonds*, written twenty-three years later, it is to this play that Mrs Carbuncle takes Lizzie Eustace, in chapter 52, and it is Bartley's criticism of it that she makes.[3]

Only literary piety could make us linger over Leigh Hunt's single tragedy, or the handful of plays by G. H. Lewes. Nor can there be any point in lingering over the plays by writers of undoubted reputation that were never intended for the stage. Their worth must be judged in other terms. Among this group – Matthew Arnold, George Eliot, W. S. Landor, Fitzgerald, Swinburne – only the name of Thomas Lovell Beddoes stands out as a writer whose failure to make any attempt to accommodate himself to the stage is a matter for serious regret. More successfully than Lamb, Beddoes sought to write in the manner of a former age; it is not quite just to say that he modelled himself on Tourneur and Marston – he recaptured their spirit and wrote original

---

[1] Quoted by Kenneth Robinson in *Wilkie Collins, A Biography* (London, 1951). Reade's diary is unpublished.

[2] Ibid.

[3] See *The Noble Jilt*, edited and with a preface by Michael Sadleir (London, 1923). Trollope also used the plot of his rejected play as the foundation for *Can You Forgive Her?* (1863). His only other play, *Did He Steal it?*, based on *The Last Chronicle of Barset*, was written in 1869 but not produced. It has been published, edited by R. H. Taylor (Princeton, 1952).

works from within it. But the length, the want of dramatic tension, and the self-indulgent poeticizing of *Death's Jest-Book* and *The Bride's Tragedy* suggest that he never meant them for any theatre save that 'mental theatre' of which lovers of the closet drama speak with enthusiasm. Those who do not respond to its charms feel that mental theatre, like mental lovemaking, demands a refinement of spirit given to few.

The last name to which we must refer is that of Tennyson, although little of his drama falls within the period discussed here. He was willing to have his plays shown on the stage, if the text were respected, by which he certainly did not mean that his text should be presented unchanged. He was fortunate in having Henry Irving as a friend, and it was Irving's acting version of *Queen Mary* (Lyceum 1876) which was given a respectable twenty-three nights' production. *The Falcon* (St James 1879) ran for sixty-seven nights. These plays were respectfully but not enthusiastically received, for in both of them the poetry was more vital than the drama, but not sufficiently vital to conceal the fact. In 1881 Irving gave an elaborate production to *The Cup*, Tennyson's short Roman tragedy, and kept it on the stage for over 100 performances. Tennyson's greatest stage success, *Becket* (Lyceum 1893), also belongs to the next volume, but it was part of the repertoire of Irving's later years, in the much altered version he had prepared in collaboration with the poet, and he acted it the night he died (13 October 1905). This version[1] is of the greatest interest, embodying as it does the elements that an actor-manager of distinguished abilities, but with also a firm hold on public taste, thought necessary to make a success of a poem not in itself strongly dramatic.

If the theatre during the first eighty years of the nineteenth century had merely been wanting in ideas and direction, it might have yielded to the talents of the original and greatly gifted writers whose works for the stage we have been considering. But that was not the case; it had ideas and a sense of purpose which, if not intellectually distinguished, were vigorous and practical. Plays of all kinds were wanted which would, in the most literal sense, 'fill the bill'; the demand for theatre entertainment was unremitting, and it is well for us to remember that the intellectual and emotional range which is now distributed among theatre, film and television was then the province of theatre alone.

Why, then, were these plays so rarely above the commonplace level as literature; why did a Bulwer succeed where a Scott failed? The answer was not primarily one of money; playwrights gradually asserted their right to a

[1] *Becket/a Tragedy/in a Prologue and Four Acts/by Alfred/Lord Tennyson/as arranged for the stage/by Henry Irving* (London, 1893).

share in the proceeds of success. Was it because actors and managers were hostile to literature? Certainly that was not the light in which they saw themselves, and by no means all of them were self-deceivers. It appears, rather, that the theatre at this time demanded qualities which did not need literary excellence either as justification or handmaid, and was able to provide a drama without it that kept the theatre prosperous. What these qualities were we shall now attempt to find out, using the chronological method that has already been applied to the last half of the eighteenth century.

1800–1810

By the beginning of the new century Augustan principles can no longer be said to be resisting those romantic ideas which, in the theatre, took the form of melodrama; the conquest of the theatre was assured, and although the mopping-up operations would go on for another forty years, the real fight was over.

Consider Thomas Morton's excellent comedy *Speed the Plough* (CG 1800) as an example of the way the struggle was going. Its generous five acts and its scenes of rural comedy suggest the eighteenth century; the characters of Farmer Ashfield and his Dame (whose concern for the opinion of the unseen Mrs Grundy on matters large and small is the best comic device in the piece, and has given a term to popular speech) owe much to the preceding twenty-five years. But the machinery of the plot hangs upon a lost heir, and mysterious parentage. Sir Abel Handy and his son Bob, with their enthusiasm for knowing best about everyone else's business, are observed with eighteenth-century eyes, and their dialogue is written in the supple, clean English which marked the best of the comedy we have already considered. But Farmer Ashfield's soliloquy in III. iii is an early example of the melodramatic comic man's dilemma when torn between right and wrong, and in it only the language is that of humble life; the sentiments are those of Nature's

Noblemen, with which class the succeeding eighty years will make us thoroughly familiar.

In the drama of the nineteenth century language is very often expected to be congruous with the sentiments expressed, rather than with the station and education of the speaker. Sir Philip Blandford, speaking of 'the canker that hath withered up my trunk', is already using the language of melodrama. Asked if he has a heart, he replies 'Yes; of marble. Cold and obdurate to the world – ponderous and painful to myself.' These expressions might rise to the lips of a baronet with a taste for florid speech, but when Susan, Farmer Ashfield's daughter, cries 'Oh man! ungrateful man! it is from our bosoms alone you derive your power; how cruel then to use it, in fixing in those bosoms endless sorrow and despair . . .', we wonder how the child of parents who express themselves in deep Mummerset came to speak so. Gradually we shall cease to ask such questions, which are irrelevant in melodrama, and learn also to accept breasts and bosoms as psychological centres quite as important as heads, and sometimes more so. When, as in *Speed the Plough*, we find that the denouement of the play is the rescue of the heroine from a burning house by the hero, and that the final scene of the action might be called Penitence, Pardon and Peace, we may be sure that the eighteenth century has lost its hold on the theatre.

Playwrights and probably the more acute members of the audience knew what had happened. George Colman the Younger's comedy *The Review, or the Wags of Windsor* (Hay 1800) seems superficially to break no new ground, but Colman was too astute not to have sensed the increased popularity of low comedy, and the play is in effect a vehicle for a comic trio – Looney MacTwolter the Irishman, John Lump the Northcountryman and Caleb Quotem the village factotum. It has the barest sketch of a plot, being concerned with Captain Beaugard's winning of the Quaker heiress Grace Gaylove, in spite of her guardian Mr Deputy Bull. When Beaugard's fortune is being told by Lucy – Grace's maid in disguise – she says 'I must give it to you in high-sounding language, for the fates are pompous.' Indeed the fates were pompous in the drama of the coming century, and for an excellent reason, which we shall hope to demonstrate when a sufficient number of fateful utterances have been examined.

John Fawcett's *Obi, or Three-Fingered Jack* (Hay 2 1800) is of interest as an early example of the pattern of full-stage sensation scenes interspersed with 'front' scenes of broad comedy and song which became characteristic of melodrama. The theme of West Indian magic is scarcely developed, and although Jack's grievances are set forth, they are not redressed; the whole force of the plot is devoted to bringing the white hero and heroine together

The black comics Tuckey, Quashee and Sam are shown as wholly devoted to their masters; they are humble helpers and servers. Nevertheless there are hints at possibilities of stronger drama, which are quickly negated. Quashee, a part for an actress dressed as a male liveried servant, says at one point: 'Ah, we poor blacks have a weary time of it, and are as much railed at as if the darkness of our skins were a sample of the colour of our hearts.' But she at once removes any possible offence from such a statement by singing 'Possum up a gum tree', to show that she need not be taken seriously. Jack's misfortunes are reminiscent of those of Oroonoko;[1] his beloved Olinda has been torn lifeless from his arms and in revenge Jack speaks of 'bursting like a whirlwind' on Ormond, the plantation owner. At the conclusion of the play Ormond frees his slaves. A sense of the wrongs of the slaves, and some uneasiness about acknowledging this feeling, is apparent in this play, crude though its workmanship is.

Clumsy construction is characteristic of the earliest melodrama; refinement in the use of its technique is slow in coming. The comedies that hold to eighteenth-century techniques therefore give an impression of superior literacy. Frederick Reynolds's *Folly As It Flies* (CG 1801) offers a good example; its dialogue is high-coloured but rational, in spite of traces of melodrama and sentimentality in its plot. Virtue is somewhat extravagantly rewarded, and folly is treated with drollery, rather than satiric rebuke. Similar comment serves for *Love Laughs at Locksmiths* (Hay 2 1802) by George Colman the Younger. The plot is as old as Plautus: Vigil, a painter of historical subjects, tries to keep at bay the suitors to Lydia, his beautiful ward; he is circumvented by Captain Beldare and his servant Risk, who disguise themselves as artist's models. It is a farce with songs[2] written to popular tunes; melodrama also included a good deal of singing, and one sometimes receives the impression that the playhouses of this era were very close to being musical comedy houses. The melodramatic element in Colman's play asserts itself in Beldare's boast of British freedom in his final speech. A farce more in tune with eighteenth-century models is James Kenney's *Raising the Wind* (CG 1803); its plot is a romantic intrigue dependent on the character of Jeremy Diddler, a short-sighted sharper, and it is arbitrarily resolved by a legacy. The dialogue is admirable.[3]

[1] *Oroonoko* was still frequently played and was seen at Covent Garden in 1792, 1795 and 1806.

[2] One of these is 'Unfortunate Miss Bailey', still popular.

[3] We learn from Lytton's *Money* that by 1840 Jeremy Diddler had become a byword, and in 1879 that notably short-sighted actor Henry Irving still counted the part one of his comedy successes. See Lawrence Irving, *Henry Irving* (London, 1951).

Melodrama was already using music for purposes more subtle than occasional songs. Cues for music and extended stage directions began to be a characteristic of the promptbooks. Thomas Holcroft's *A Tale of Mystery* (CG 1802) requires at Montano's entrance '*Music loud and discordant at the moment the eye of Montano catches the figure of Romaldi; at which Montano starts with terror and indignation. He then assumes the eye and attitude of menace, which Romaldi returns. The music ceases.*' Music is required '*to express discontent and alarm*', '*to express chattering contention*', '*to express pain and disorder*'. There are directions for '*Music of doubt and terror*', '*Threatening music*', '*Soft music but expressing first pain and alarm, then the successive feelings of the scene*'. Music is called for to accompany '*painful remorse*', followed by '*dejection*'. The stage directions are equally demanding. A storm with lightning, thunder, hail and rain is called for, and it must have taxed the stage manager to realize the direction '*Enter Romaldi . . . pursued as it were by heaven and earth*'. The dialogue between the wicked Count Romaldi and his servant Malvoglio is in a vein long worked by melodramatic authors:

ROMALDI: We are in his power.
MALVOGLIO: He is in ours.
ROMALDI: What are your thoughts?
MALVOGLIO: What are yours, my lord?
ROMALDI: Guess them.
MALVOGLIO: Executioners!
ROMALDI: Infamy!
MALVOGLIO: Racks!
ROMALDI: Maledictions!
MALVOGLIO: From all of which a blow may yet deliver us.
   (*Music : terror, confusion, menace, command.*)

This was something new in the theatre and when new it must have produced the expected thrill. A servant, Fiametta, not being bound by the high solemnity of the chief players, is allowed to express the impatience and indignation that supposedly were felt by the audience. This melodrama contains some of the elements that came to be stereotypes of such plays, and were mocked by Gilbert eighty years later; for instance, the villain is betrayed by a scar on the back of his hand, and there is a fight on a bridge. We should take special note of the character of Francisco, who is noble, long-suffering and dumb, whose story it has not occurred to anybody to ask about in eight years. If these things were original with Holcroft we should admire him as an innovator; his play, however, is a version of Pixérécourt's *Coelina, ou l'enfant du mystère* (1800).

Other melodramatic turns of plot, later to become commonplaces, are to be found in *Tekeli, or the Siege of Montgatz* (DL 1806), which Theodore Hook wrote when he was eighteen and sensitive to what was in the air; the sacredness of hospitality, mocked by Shaw in *Arms and the Man* (1894), and the moment of revelation when Tekeli and Wolf '*throw off their peasants' dresses and discover superb military habits*' are but two of these. The melodramatic extravagance of speech, meant to convey intensity of feeling rather than police court evidence, is exemplified by Alexina's declaration that she has a letter from Tekeli that she has 'bathed with tears for five long months'. The ending is of the kind satirized by the struggle between pirates and police in *The Pirates of Penzance* (1880).

The theme of picturesque affliction, exemplified in Francisco in *A Tale of Mystery*, is given fuller treatment in *The Blind Boy* (CG 1807) by James Kenney; the sweetness and passive suffering of Edmond, the boy of the title, was emphasized by having an actress of special charm, Miss de Camp, play the role. It is a plot of mysterious parentage: Edmond is of noble birth, heir to the throne of Sarmatia, but he wants to suppress this fact because he loves the humble Elvina, in whose peasant home he has been sheltered when hiding from the usurper Rodolph.[1] Even when he is restored to noble estate and takes Elvina with him Edmond remains a sufferer, because of his blindness and the physical delicacy which emphasizes it. We shall meet many examples of picturesque affliction in melodrama.

It would hardly be necessary to refer to M. G. Lewis's *Raymond and Agnes*, which had been presented at Covent Garden in 1797, if the author had not thought fit to bring it forward again in 1809, tricked out with even greater melodramatic extravagance; Lewis serves as an excellent barometer, marking the extreme of public taste rather than its median. Though the names of the characters are vaguely Spanish, the scene is the realm of Gothic romance. Agnes, the daughter of the Bleeding Nun, disguises herself as that apparition to escape from Lindenberg Castle; but the true Bleeding Nun misleads her lover, Raymond, and then, when Raymond rescues Agnes from bandits, appears to give them a spectre's blessing. There is play with drugged wine, much inexplicable vengeance and Lewis's customary lavish but ignorant use

[1] Prince Rodolph may well be the first character in melodrama of whom it is said, 'His father, the late Palatine, on his death-bed revealed to him the dreadful secret of his birth.'

of the apparatus of Catholicism for theatrical effect. It is a measure of what the public would swallow.

It was not only in the theatre that public taste had taken a strongly romantic turn. The process had been at work for twenty years past, and in 1802 John Boydell published his edition of Shakespeare, illustrated with 162 pictures painted by the leading artists of Britain. An hour's examination of these pictures is worth a volume of exposition of what the romantic taste of the time was, and how it might be expected to manifest itself on the stage.[1]

[1] A key to the popular attitude to Shakespeare is Charles A. Somerset's strange play, *Shakespeare's Early Days* (CG 1829), in which the handsome Charles Kemble played a sentimental, twaddling Bard, greatly troubled by apparitions. The reader is also referred to relevant portions and plates in *Shakespeare and the Artist*, by W. Moelwyn Merchant (London, 1959).

1810–1820

There is little to distinguish this period from that which went before, and
nothing arresting in talent or craftsmanship. W. Barnes Rhodes's *Bombastes
Furioso* (Hay 2 1810) is described as 'a burlesque tragic opera'. It is not a
burlesque in the sense of ridiculing any play, or group of plays, in particular;
it is intended to amuse solely by its absurdity, and one presumes the actors
brought great comic skill to it. The only reason for mentioning it here is its
success, and because it is an early example of the musical extravaganza which
is to become so popular, and which is, as Genest often says, 'better suited to
performance than perusal'. But in the next seven decades some of the
wittiest writing for the theatre took this form, and it counted among its chief
supporters literary men, journalists and Bohemians in general – successors,
in their fashion, to the 'wits' of an earlier day.

The era was apparently warmly disposed towards adaptations; what could
be read with pleasure might fitly appear on the stage. Thomas Dibdin's version of Scott's *The Lady of the Lake* (Surrey 1810) is simply contrived, for
Scott's couplets – with the smallest possible amount of additional matter –
have been allotted to the characters; the effect is inevitably to make the
dialogue seem short-winded. Nevertheless the piece is well managed, picturesque and full of chances for spectacle; the great combat between Fitzjames

and Roderick Dhu (played by Elliston and T. P. Cooke) is one of these, and the growing fondness for scenes of ritual is satisfied by the preparation of the fiery cross of war (II. ii) and the business of Fitzjames dipping a lock of Blanche's hair in Roderick's blood (II. iii).

Ritual is essential to M. G. Lewis's *One O'Clock, or the Knight and the Wood Demon* (Lyceum 1811), which is another tale of a lost child of high birth, recognized at last by a birthmark on the hand. It is called 'a grand operatic Romance', and contains songs and choruses; the music was by Michael Kelly and Matthew Peter King. The verses, however, are perfunctory and bad, for Lewis seems to have had little sense of language; he can make Una say of some new robes, 'They'll be the very thing', and then speak in empurpled fustian, without any intention of incongruity. But the ritual is effectively contrived: the usurping baron Hardyknute maintains his power by sacrificing a child every year, on 6 August, to Sangrida, the Wood Demon; Leolyn, the rightful baron, but a child and a mute (one of the army of the picturesquely afflicted), is endangered; the heroine Una saves the child, and Hardy-knute, having inexplicably forgotten that it is 6 August, himself falls a victim to Sangrida, whose ceremonies of sacrifice are the best things in the play.

Lewis also brought forward a reworking of his *The East Indian* (1799), called *Rich and Poor* (Lyceum 1812); the five acts have been reduced to three and the number of characters has also been decreased. It is of interest principally as a demonstration of what an instinctive playwright Lewis was; he has little conscious art, and his revision of the earlier play is clumsy.

Sturdier craftsmanship is that of Isaac Pocock, whose *The Miller and His Men* (CG 1813) kept its popularity at least until 1870. Although not primarily a musical piece, its score by Henry Rowley Bishop, which included four songs, some choruses of banditti, and one concerted number, or 'glee', contributed much to its success. The scene is Bohemia, and the miller, Grindoff, is clandestinely the chief of a gang of brigands; although for seven years he has had the high-mettled Ravina as his mistress, he seeks the hand of Claudine; her honest suitor Lothair joins the gang in disguise, draws Count Friberg to attack the mill with troops, and himself explodes the powder magazine concealed beneath the mill, for a spectacular finale.

Pocock's skill is demonstrated also in *The Maid and the Magpie, or the Fallacy of Circumstantial Evidence* (CG 1815). The charming Annette is accused of stealing a silver spoon; she has in fact sold a spoon of her own to a pedlar in order to get money to assist her father, a soldier accused of striking his superior; her mistress's spoon was stolen by a magpie. Although he borrowed the pretty story,[1] Pocock has used it well.

Borrowings from the French stage were constant and remorseless. A great success for many years was William Barrymore's *The Dog of Montargis* (CG 1814), adapted from Pixérécourt's *Le Chien de Montargis, ou la Forêt de Bondy* (1814).[2] Briefly, it shows how a faithful dog, aided by a dumb youth (again the picturesquely afflicted), brings his master's murderers to justice. It had also the assistance of music by H. R. Bishop.

It is now prudent to look once again at the lighter entertainment of the day, for it is from this source that one of the significant movements in the drama of the next 100 years will come. *Harlequin Hoax, or a Pantomime Proposed* (Lyceum 1814), by Thomas Dibdin, is a characteristic 'extravaganza' of the time. In it Patch, an author, proposes a pantomime which is violently wrenched in whatever direction the talents of the principal players (who were Liston and Miss Kelly), the resources of the manager's scenery, and the costumier's stock, choose to take it. It is very rough stuff, full of topical songs and parodies, and tailored to the charm and brisk delivery of popular players. It gives us a notion of what the taste of the day would accept and applaud. But something much better was to come in this line, and the man who was to mould the extravaganza into a modest work of art was James Robinson Planché, whose first work for the stage was *Amoroso, King of Little Britain* (DL 1818). The author was twenty-two, and he leans obviously on *Bombastes Furioso*; his piece – it was in fact a collaboration with some unnamed friends – achieved a gratifying seventeen performances. Planché's career continued until 1872, and encompasses 176 works of one sort and another[3] as well as a

---

[1] The extremely popular French original, by Jean Marie Theodore Baudoin d'Aubigny and Louis Charles Caigniez, was called *La Pie voleuse* (1815). Rossini used it as *La Gazza Ladra* (Milan, 1817), and H. R. Bishop borrowed from Rossini for *Ninetta, or the Maid of Palaiseau* (CG 1830).

[2] It was the insistence of Frau von Heygendorf, mistress of Karl August, Duke of Weimar, that this play be presented in the court theatre at Weimar, that led to Goethe's resignation as director on 12 April 1817. It was a regulation of the theatre that no dogs should be brought on to the stage. It may also have been the trickery of the performance (for when the noble animal sprang at the throat of the murderer, who expired shrieking, 'Call off the dog!', it was in fact leaping at a lump of sausage meat concealed beneath his collar) that offended the fastidious playwright. (*A History of Theatrical Art*, Karl Mantzius, trans. C. Archer [New York, 1937], VI, 271.)

[3] Of his dramatic works he writes:

> . . . I believe I may fairly claim 72 as original, 10 being written in conjunction with Charles Dance, and 62 by me exclusively. The remaining 104 consist of translations and adaptations from the French, Spanish, Italian, and German,

leading part in the revolution of stage costume in the direction of historical accuracy, and an appointment in the College of Heralds, in which he rose to be Somerset Herald. It will not be possible to consider any great number of his works in the pages that follow, but it must be remembered that there was no year between 1818 and 1865 in which the stage was not enlivened by something, and usually several things, from his swift and witty pen.

Let us conclude our survey of this decade with W. T. Moncrieff's first substantial work, *Rochester, or Charles the Second's Merry Days* (Olympic 1818). This is costume comedy, a classification of drama to be very popular at least until 1914. In it Rochester and Buckingham, forbidden the court by the King, take an inn at Newport and alternate in the roles of innkeeper and tapster. The Countess of Lovelaugh and Lady Gay come to the inn, and get the better of the noblemen by disguising themselves as servant girls. There is much talk of seduction and the free life of the court, but anything irrevocable is kept at arm's length, and there is a wholesome underplot of true love concerning Silvia Golden, ward of the miser Starvemouse, and Dunstable, a player. The King comes to the inn, and after he has been made the butt of a trick by his courtiers, he pardons them.

What is interesting about this play is its determination to use the historical setting as an escape from the sexual morality of its own day, without actually wounding the susceptibilities of playgoers who were already moving towards that body of moral opinion which is too narrowly labelled Victorian. A good deal of this sort of thing will appear on the stage before 1880. Characteristic of this class of play also is a harmless intellectual snobbery; there is mock Restoration language and fun about Puritans for those who know some history and have read a few Restoration plays; there are also Shakespearian echoes for those whose ears are sharp enough to catch them. This is an appeal to the educated part of the audience, which will not always be the fashionable part, but will grow as the century grows.

---

    alterations of early English comedies, or of dramas by modern authors which were
    confided to me for revision.

(*Extravaganzas*, 5 volumes [London, 1879], V, 330–1.) It is such an author as Planché who figures as Overton, the narrator of Samuel Butler's *The Way of All Flesh* (1903).

1820–1830

Having introduced Planché as a wit, it may be well to establish his reputation as an all-round man of the theatre by taking notice of one of his early and substantial successes, *The Vampire, or the Bride of the Isles* (Lyceum 1820). The story is Gothic: Ronald, Baron of the Isles, betrothes his daughter Lady Margaret to the noble Ruthven, Earl of Marsden, without being aware that Ruthven is a vampire; through the intervention of the gallant Robert she is saved from a dreadful doom. The piece takes full advantage of the fashionable belief that Scotland and its people were uncommonly romantic, and of the nine songs eight are written to Scottish airs. The rhetoric is in the high melodramatic vein. Ruthven soliloquizes thus (I. ii):

> (*Walking about, agitated.*) Demon as I am, that walk the earth to slaughter and devour, the little of heart that remains within this wizard frame, sustained alone by human blood, shrinks from the appalling act of planting misery in the bosom of this veteran chieftain. Still must the fearful sacrifice be made, and suddenly, for the approaching night will find my wretched frame exhausted, and darkness, worse than death, annihilation is my lot! Margaret, unhappy maid, thou art my destined prey! Thy blood must feed a vampire's life, and prove the food of his disgusting banquet.

Dying, Ruthven loses his command of language only with life itself. He pleads: 'Place me on yonder mound, so that my fleeting spirit may be soothed by the soft and tranquil light of yon chaste luminary.'

We cannot read this without a smile but, as has already been stated, one of the purposes of the present study is to attempt to consider these plays sympathetically; we cannot recreate them as their first audiences saw them, but we must recognize that they accorded with the taste of some sophisticated playgoers, and that Planché was a man of wide culture and learning, who was not writing tongue in cheek.[1]

This play introduced the vampire trap, still in use, which permitted T. P. Cooke, as the Vampire, to pass through solid pieces of scenery.

The first twenty years of the century saw few attempts at full-scale tragedy, as distinguished from grave melodrama. We now encounter Sheridan Knowles, who enjoyed substantial success as a writer of plays which produced a tragic effect upon contemporary audiences. His dramatic career continued until 1844, when he became a Baptist lay preacher and a strong anti-Catholic. The first of his works to achieve a London production was *Virginius* (CG 1820). Its plot is sufficiently Roman and it would be absurd to complain that it is seen in nineteenth-century terms, but it may be said that it is the mean of the nineteenth century, rather than its finest feeling, that informs the play. The wicked Decemvir, Appius, desires Virginia, daughter of the centurion Virginius; Claudius, a creature of Appius, declares that Virginia is not her father's child but was begotten by one of his slaves and is therefore his own; rather than see his daughter dishonoured, Virginius stabs her, and kills Claudius.

The weakness of the plot is the readiness with which Claudius's trumped-up story is believed. But we might ignore that flaw if the play were cast in poetry, and not in measured rhetoric and Shakespearian echoes, with long and windy speeches that seem to delay rather than support the action. Modern taste, also, is not attuned to the insistent, repeated assertions of the moral splendours and emotional delights of fatherhood. Nineteenth-century drama is popularly supposed to be much concerned with the dignity of motherhood; those who read widely in it will find that fatherhood is given at least equal

---

[1] During the seasons 1961–5 the London theatre saw productions of *The Devils*, *The Connection*, *Altona*, *Oh, Dad, Poor Dad*, *Under Plain Cover*, *Infanticide in the House of Fred Ginger*, *The Physicists*, *A Severed Head*, *Exit the King*, *Endgame*, *Marat-Sade*, and *Waiting for Godot*, as well as a programme by the Theatre of Cruelty. All of these plays make demands on their audiences which are not, giving due allowance to changes in psychological fashion, unlike those made by melodrama in its Gothic and other forms.

time, and may even have a modest advantage. Macready, the first Virginius, had a particular taste for roles sodden in paternal nobility.

Another notable father-drama is W. T. Moncrieff's *The Lear of Private Life* (Coburg 1820); it is melodrama rather than tragedy and takes advantage of every melodramatic privilege. Agnes, daughter of the good Fitzarden, elopes with Alvanley and has an illegitimate child; Fitzarden goes mad, and his unreason is partnered by the extravagance of his rhetoric until Agnes returns, is married by her seducer, and comparative sanity is restored to him. His excesses are musically accompanied by Handel's 'Tears such as tender fathers shed'; his reason returns when, in III. v, Agnes is shown to him, framed as if she were her own portrait. Again let it be noted that this play is rooted in what might be considered typically Victorian morality, though Victoria was not born until 1819, and did not come to the throne for seventeen years after this play appeared.

Such morality was at war with the disposition of the Regency, which was the background to such comic high jinks as those in Moncrieff's own *Tom and Jerry* (Adelphi 1821), adapted from Pierce Egan's *Life in London* (1821–2). There were in all seven Tom and Jerry plays within three years, which made use of Jerry Hawthorn, Corinthian Tom and Bob Logic, sometimes with little reference to Egan's originals. No wonder that authors who were unprotected against such raiding considered themselves ill-used. Moncrieff's play was on the stage before the last instalment of Egan's novel had appeared.

Egan's *The Life of an Actor*, which he did not complete until 1825, was also pillaged by Richard Brinsley Peake for his play of the same name (Adelphi 1824). The novel, which is of interest now for the insights it gives into the conditions of the theatre of its time, has little to do with the play, but the hero of both is called Peregrine Proteus. Peake's play, though entertaining, contains some rather disagreeable jeering by London actors at their less talented provincial brethren.

Fathers in comedy and farce continued to be deluded figures of fun, but the father of a seduced, or even slightly blown-upon, daughter in melodrama was like a lion in his righteous roarings. John Howard Payne's *Clari, or the Maid of Milan* (CG 1823) contains such a father. Clari is tempted from a virtuous peasant home by the Duke Vivaldi, who promises her marriage but does not mean to keep his word; her conscience is stricken by a play offered for her entertainment which shows her own predicament; she returns home a virgin, to the extravagant delight of her father, and the Duke, overcome with remorse, offers honourable marriage. It is curious that the city of Milan does not figure in the play, which, however, had one overmastering effect, in the song 'Home, Sweet Home', popular for decades and still occasionally heard.[1]

Sheridan Knowles wrote *Caius Gracchus* in 1815 and saw it presented with success in Belfast; it did not reach London for nine years (DL 1824). It is a dull tragedy, if indeed it is tragic when a bore dies. The plot is from Plutarch (himself so sprightly a writer, laid under tribute by so many men of dowdy mind) and the verse is dull, ungraceful and unvaried; everybody in the piece seems to speak with the same voice. Its reception owed something to the success of *Virginius*, and Knowles was a writer who improved; he did not again slip back to the *Caius Gracchus* level. His next play, *William Tell* (DL 1825), is better plotted, and the dialogue has a quality of nerve and a sense of movement that is truly dramatic. The story is the familiar one pieced out with the incident of Albert, Tell's son, guiding the tyrant Gessler to safety when he is lost and frightened in the mountains. There is also a subplot about Michael, a merry youth whose father, Waldman, is Tell's comrade in his struggle against the Austrians; Waldman thinks Michael is of no consequence, for he makes a mistake common to the solemn of supposing that jolly people lack pith; but Michael is second only to Tell in the task of freeing the Tyrol.

It may be noted that this is yet another father-play, and Tell's anguish at being compelled to endanger his son is developed as far as it can go without tumbling into bathos.

A play that was competent enough to be popular, but which secured a success far beyond anything that mere competence can explain, is John Poole's *Paul Pry* (Hay 2 1825); it achieved the remarkable total of 114 performances in its first season, and had its last London revival in 1874. It has a double plot: the principal action concerns the attempts of Grasp and Mrs Subtle, who are steward and housekeeper to Witherton, to fleece him and, in the housekeeper's case, to marry him; the subplot shows the determination of Colonel Hardy to choose a husband for his daughter Eliza, and the curious chance by which he hits upon Stanley, whom she has long loved. These two

---

[1] The music was by the ubiquitous and industrious Henry Rowley Bishop (1786–1855). In addition to his compositions for the theatre he was Professor of Music first at Oxford and then at Cambridge, and was the first musician to be knighted by an English sovereign (1842). Some of his music for Shakespeare plays – 'Bid me discourse' and 'Should he upbraid' – and the glee 'Chough and Crow' are still occasionally heard. Comment in Grove's *Dictionary of Music and Musicians* (5th ed.) points out that 'Home, Sweet Home' marks a very early use of the leitmotiv in opera, for it is sung by several voices, and a chorus, in a number of rhythms, to emphasize a dominating idea. The song's enduring popularity in Japan has been demonstrated in Kon Ichikawa's film *The Burmese Harp*.

conventional actions are tied together by the character of the inquisitive, interfering blunderer, Paul Pry, whose oft-repeated 'I hope I don't intrude?' is the catchphrase of the play. Pry is a good invention, and many actors have played the part tellingly, the first being Liston. For decades Paul Pry was as celebrated a fictional character as Mrs Grundy or Jeremy Diddler.

J. B. Buckstone's *Luke the Labourer* (Adelphi 1828) is one of the many plays we encounter in the nineteenth century which seem to be on the point of saying something about the hard lot of an oppressed class of society, but never actually do so; instead they deal with an individual case. The mainspring of the clumsy plot is revenge: Luke thinks that Farmer Wakefield helped to bring about the death of his wife Maria, and of this there seems no doubt; nevertheless, Luke's own dissolute habits were in part responsible, and as the play progresses Luke grows darker as Wakefield grows lighter. Luke plots with a gypsy to abduct the farmer's child Philip, and many years later assists a wicked squire in his design to seduce Wakefield's daughter. But Philip, now a grown man, returns from sea and puts all to rights; Luke dies of a pistol shot he intended for Wakefield. This is a melodrama of some power, and it held the stage for forty years as a provincial repertory piece. It has the faults of its kind: the scenes in which the returned son Philip remains unknown to his parents are unnaturally prolonged for stage effect, and the plot is resolved in a rapid scramble that is characteristic of melodrama of the less adroit sort. Its language, too, is of the kind that can have moved only a naïve audience, as when the child Philip appeals to his abductors in the words, 'Remember the vilest insect that crawls on earth moans for its young' (II. iv).

Melodramas directed at the naïve grow numerous in this decade. Edward Fitzball's *The Red Rover* (Adelphi 1828) was a popular example. The Rover, a Byronic free spirit who appears in contemporary illustrations in the picturesque kilted dress of a pirate (still to be seen in *The Pirates of Penzance* in 1880), is given to 'hysterical laughter' and to apostrophizing himself in the third person; he dies declaring 'His ship shall be the Rover's funeral pile.' But the play appears to be the result of hasty workmanship, for the Rover has lost his grip on events almost completely well before the fall of the curtain. The action is really concerned with Lieutenant Wilder, who disguises himself and ships aboard the Rover's pirate craft in order to protect Madame de Lacy and her ward, Gertrude, who have been deceived into thinking it an innocent passenger vessel. Even the Lieutenant is less important than his humble comrades Fid (played by T. P. Cooke) and Guinea, who are British tars of unquenchable courage, resource and high spirits. It may be that some of the

Rover's hysterical laughter is caused by the discovery that Lieutenant Wilder is in fact Madame de Lacy's long-lost infant.

Drama exalting sailors, however, could hardly fail if T. P. Cooke were in the cast, ready to perform his celebrated double hornpipe; Cooke had actually been a sailor, but this does not appear to have inhibited him in his many impersonations of stage seamen.[1]

The greatest of all his triumphs was in Douglas Jerrold's *Black-Eyed Susan, or 'All in the Downs'* (Surrey 1829).[2] William, a great-hearted fore-mast hand, whose wife is a 'craft', his handshake a 'grapple' and who advises villains to 'strike their false colours', is accused of striking his superior officer, Captain Crosstree, who had made an immodest proposal to William's craft Susan. But at the time of the blow William's discharge from the service was complete, and Crosstree was not therefore his officer. This information is withheld through the malignance of Susan's uncle, Doggrass, but is uncovered just in time to spare William from hanging.

The play is a skilful compound of melodramatic elements, and Jerrold's clever hand with dialogue sustains a congruity even in such vividly coloured speech. The most telling passage in the play is William's farewell to his wife in III. iv, which, sweet though its flavour may be, is poetry of a kind and irresistible in this situation; it was written to draw tears, and it did not fail. So effective, indeed, was this appeal to the heart that it was used by W. G. Wills in 1873 as a model for the king's farewell speech in *Charles the First*.[3]

As there was a school of nautical drama, so also was there a school of total abstinence drama to which Jerrold contributed. His *Fifteen Years of a Drunkard's Life* (Coburg 1829) was an early and notable example of the type; the best that may be said of it is that it is better than most of an undistinguished collection. Temperance dramatists never seem to be conscious of any need to argue their case, and this makes for bad art. In Jerrold's play his hero, Vernon, is a drunkard when the play begins, so the decline we follow is social and financial rather than moral. It is of interest, however, to observe that this

[1] The character of the stage seaman is admirably described in *The Quizziology of the British Drama*, by Gilbert Abbot à Beckett (London, 1847), along with many other stock characters of melodrama. The reader will find this an excellent satiric comment on much of the drama considered here. It should be remembered, of course, that nobody bothers to satirize anything which a large body of other people do not take seriously.

[2] The title is from John Gay's song, set to music by Richard Leveridge, called 'Sweet William and Black-eyed Susan', which Granville Bantock dates 'not later than 1723' (*One Hundred Songs of England* [Boston, 1914]). It was popular for 150 years.

[3] The story is told in *Henry Irving*, by Lawrence Irving (London, 1951), pp. 215–16. It was the veteran showman, Colonel Hezekiah Linthicum Bateman, who had this happy inspiration, apparently in his sleep.

play was liberally borrowed from by William W. Pratt, author of the great American success *Ten Nights in a Bar Room* (New York 1858). Compare this, from Jerrold, I. i:

VERNON: Now there was last night, Glanville, honest Tom Glanville, Brightly, Samford, and myself – how much do you think we murdered? how much, now? come, guess – You can't – you haven't imagination enough. – A cool two dozen, – we four gentlemen sat down to two dozen.

FRANKLIN: And pray, as you sat down as gentlemen under what characters did you rise?

and this, from Pratt, II. ii:

WILLIE: I say, Green, my boy, I'm deuced dry. How much wine do you suppose myself and three jolly fellows murdered last night? You can't guess? Well, we sat down to a cool two dozen.

GREEN: The deuce you did. Well, as you sat down as gentlemen, under what character did you arise? Ha, ha, ha!

Pratt has borrowed so carelessly that he has not even given Willie the cue word 'gentlemen'. Similarly, when Franklin rebukes Vernon for drinking after he has forsworn wine, the drunkard says: 'Yes, that is wine as wine – but this, this I take as medicine.' And when Green makes a similar comment to Willie, he replies: 'So I did. That is, wine *as* wine; but this I (*drinks*) take as medicine.' These quotations are so exact, and the two plays so similar in other small points, that we may suppose that Pratt was not a simple plagiarist, but a man who had seen or perhaps acted in the earlier play, and could not forget it. And, of course, the morality that applies to drink may not carry with it an objection to appropriating somebody else's lines.

Let us conclude the consideration of this decade by some comment on Planché's very successful melodrama *The Brigand* (DL 1829). It is noteworthy for its skilful use of a device popular in this era, which was contriving the stage setting and groupings of actors so that they were at some time *tableaux vivants*, realizing a popular picture; this might happen at the beginning, the climax or the ending of a scene. In *The Brigand* the pictures chosen are the popular series of 'banditti' pictures painted by Sir Charles Lock Eastlake, exhibited first in 1823, and famous by 1829. Thus the play begins with 'An Italian Brigand Chief Reposing' and continues with 'The Wife of a Brigand Chief Watching the Result of a Battle' after a few minutes; the final tableau is, appropriately, 'The Dying Brigand'. The device has the virtue of associating the play with something known and presumably admired in another art, and the effect may well have been handsome. In an era before the revolution in marshalling and arranging stage figures brought about by the visit to England of the Saxe-Meiningen company (1881), or the careful crowd management of Charles Kean, this was a move towards a more plastic use of the stage.

The Brigand was also well supplied with music, and the brigand's song, 'Love's Ritornella', achieved wide popularity. The story is of one Massaroni, a brigand who is the son of Prince Bianchi, governor of Rome, and a peasant girl whom he deserted, but of whose memory he subsequently makes a cult. Massaroni terrorizes a principal road to Rome, and robs in the Robin Hood style. He visits Bianchi's palace, to collect the ransom of a couple of French travellers, and after some pleasant Scarlet Pimpernel ironies he is discovered and shot, just as Bianchi finds out that the hated brigand is – his lost son! It is worthy of note that Massaroni has spared the life of one of the Frenchmen because he learns that his victim is, like himself, a foundling. Gilbert, who learned so much from Planché, uses this device for comic effect in *The Pirates of Penzance* (1880), in which the way to the pirates' hearts is to protest one's orphaned state.

Planché knows how to manage drama of this sort so as to get the most out of every situation without pushing it to the point of absurdity. Construction is one of his skills; the other is a dialogue sparer and wittier than most of his contemporaries could provide.

1830–1840

Douglas Jerrold's *The Mutiny at the Nore* (Coburg 1830) is a superior example of the large group of plays that hint at, but do not state, problems of social injustice. In part this coyness may be attributed to fear of the Lord Chamberlain's displeasure; his office, through its Reader of Plays, had to approve of every drama before it could be presented, and discussion of potentially inflammatory issues was not encouraged.[1] Therefore even a play about a mutiny that took place in 1797 had to be discreet in its references to injustice and brutality. But there was another reason for the fact that virtually all plays about injustice to sailors, soldiers, farm labourers and other oppressed groups deal with the problems as they bear upon a single character and his family, rather than as they affect a class: this was of the essence of melodrama, which appeals personally and emotionally, and works upon the individual's sense of injustice, rather than upon a political or social issue. The playgoer went to melodrama at the Coburg or the Adelphi to see *himself* on the stage, to thrill to a personal and inward rather than a generalized appeal.

In this play the leader of the mutiny, Richard Parker, seeks redress not only for the wrongs of navy men but for his own unjust usage; Captain Arlington has sought the favours of Parker's wife, and has menaced Parker's

[1] See also Part I, p. 39-40.

child; when Parker shoots him, and is hanged for it, he has vindicated his own honour.

The evidence of a large number of melodramas suggests that they appealed to audiences made up of individuals burdened with a strong but ill-focused sense of personal grievance, readily understandable in men and women caught in a rapidly changing society. Ignorance and limited opportunities kept them down, and prevented any understanding of their situation beyond a strong sense that somebody was against them, and their accusations were against individuals rather than the social system. The people who figure in *London Labour and the London Poor* were not thinkers but feelers; when Parker cries 'the spirit of man is aroused, walks abroad, and cries for vengeance', their minds turned to oppressors they knew, not to political generalities. Their wives and daughters, who knew how difficult, and perhaps unpractical, it was to preserve their virtue much beyond the age of fifteen, when conditions of daily work and domestic service were so strongly against it, nevertheless liked to see heroines who would accept death before dishonour. Personal honour was a luxury, but it was a luxury they would have liked to enjoy; melodrama offered them a vicarious enjoyment of it, in terms that went straight to the heart. It is callous to condemn melodrama for its excesses without attempting to understand the satisfaction it once gave to people who have since found other ways of meeting social injustice – without having yet appreciated how much of destiny has its root in character.

Much melodrama was no more than crude storytelling, like W. B. Bernard's *The Wept of Wish-Ton-Wish* (Adelphi 1831), which is Fenimore Cooper's romance (1829) arranged in scenes of weighty drama, usually taking place on the full stage, between which are sandwiched the buffooneries of Satisfaction Skunk and his family, performed as front-scenes. But even in its lesser manifestations melodrama might give substance to an ideal. H. M. Milner's *Mazeppa* (Royal Amphitheatre 1831) is Byronic in spirit if crude in dramaturgy. The sense of its being a 'grand equestrian spectacle', in which Mazeppa's ride bound on the back of the 'fiery, untamed steed' in front of a moving panorama is the great sensation, should not blind us to the fact that this was Byron for the people, and that some of the undoubted Byronic spirit gleams through it.[1] As a play about a long-lost son it was in a common melodramatic mould, and here again the audience's underlying sense of having been wronged might be expected to respond. The fantasy of being the child of parents more powerful and glorious than those actually known is one on

[1] It preceded all other works or reworkings of Byron on the stage except *Marino Faliero* (DL 1821).

which many psychiatrists since Freud have commented as frequent even among people in superior stations of life. Certainly the common figure, in the theatre of the nineteenth century, of the lost child who is at last restored to his rightful position in the world suggests that such a situation offered a satisfaction and a compensation to a considerable part of any audience.

Consider, as another example, Richard Brinsley Peake's *The Climbing Boy* (Olympic 1832); the little sweep is in fact the grandson to Sir Gilbert Thorncliffe, and his discovery and his restoration to his proper station is the point of the play. The plight of sweeps' boys is discussed, certainly, but the little Climbing Boy's friend Jack Ragg is released from the chimneys only to become the servant of his former companion. The deep, carking sense of being a wronged man is not easily separated from that of being a wronged child, and the mainspring of this plot and of so many others is poetic justice, with social justice coming a very bad second. Melodrama was the poetry of the poor, not a hortatory, socially oriented theatre.[1]

Sheridan Knowles was busily at work in this decade, consolidating and improving his position as one of the leading dramatists of the age. It was not easy work, for Knowles suffered from the serious nineteenth-century disability of being 'not quite a gentleman', with the additional handicaps of being an Irishman and an actor. An anonymous critic, writing in the *Athenaeum* of February 1847, said of him:

> . . . counting Burns at the head of the Uneducated Poets (an epithet, as we have often said, to which the freest meaning must be allowed), we think that Mr. Sheridan Knowles will keep his place in the annals of the British Theatre as the King of Uneducated Dramatists. He takes pride, if we mistake not, in nature as superior to art; at least, he never fails to assert such as his creed. He will, therefore, we imagine and hope, not feel aggrieved at the position which we assign to him among the poets of his country.

His publishers quote this judgement in the Advertisement to his *Dramatic Works* (1856), apparently regarding it as both complimentary and just.

The Uneducated Dramatist's *Alfred the Great* (DL 1831) is a ponderous

---

[1] Mayhew gives an account of a boy of four years 'having beautiful black eyes and eyelashes, a high nose, and delicate soft skin' who was discovered to be the stolen child of wealthy parents while he was sweeping chimneys in the home of Sir George Strickland (*London Labour and the London Poor*, II, 347–8). What appear to be extremes and absurdities in melodrama often prove to have roots in reality.

work, but *The Hunchback* (CG 1832) marks an advance as great as that of *William Tell* beyond *Virginius*. It is another play of paternal feeling, and it also makes use of the well-worn melodramatic device of picturesque affliction, but it does so with a depth and certainty of touch that marks Knowles as a man of uncommon gifts. Master Walter, the hunchback and disguised Earl of Rochdale, is a true transforming agent in the lives of Clifford, Wilford and Julia; he moulds their fates and he deals out correction and retribution with an authority not quite human, but nevertheless convincing. Master Walter is like one of those creatures of fairytale who chastens those he loves, and seems to have knowledge far beyond the common. He is indeed that popular figure of romance, the magician, and, as Knowles draws him, a dramatically compelling one. The language of the play is not distinguished, and it is not easy for us to accept the fact that Modus was once a coveted high comedy role. Knowles was not skilled in drawing women, and both Julia and Helen seem as heavy-handed in their wit as in their love.

As Knowles's fame grew, so did that of Jerrold. In this decade *The Rent Day* (DL 1832), *Nell Gwynne, or the Prologue* (CG 1833), *The Wedding Gown* (DL 1834) and *The Painter of Ghent* (Strand 1836) are all of interest but we can spare comment only for the first. The abuse of the absentee landlord was a real one at the time, but once again poetic justice is preferred to protest. Martin Hayward cannot pay his rent owing to unprovoked misfortune, and his goods are seized by the cruel and corrupt steward Crumbs; in the distraint Hayward's grandfather's chair is broken, and gushes forth a stream of coins; the landlord, no absentee profligate but that familiar figure of drama, Divine Correction, swoops upon Crumbs and disgraces him.

The self-pitying psychology of the play would offend us if it were not for Jerrold's gift of language; he has little poetry, but his prose is neat and witty and, by melodramatic standards, compressed. It is through his dialogue that he creates tension and reveals character, and we may guess that his plays acted even more pungently than they read, for the savour and relieving tartness of his lines render them eminently speakable.

Not so the trundling prose of W. T. Moncrieff, whose *Eugene Aram* (Surrey 1832) was nevertheless a provincial repertory piece for many years. Moncrieff was a hack and his dramaturgy is inept. The subplot of Rowland Lester and his father in this play is so prominent that it almost swamps the character of Aram; it may well have been substantially cut in production by the 'heavies' who liked Aram's scenes of lachrymose remorse. The handling of antecedent knowledge is also unimaginative. But the popular theme of the doomed man kept the play on the stage till Henry Irving persuaded W. G.

Wills to write him a better version of Bulwer's novel (Lyceum 1873) with a more sophisticated contrast of innocence and guilt. Moncrieff's play is mentioned here only to give a sense of what the mean of the drama of the decade was.

When melodrama rose above the mean it could produce a rousing success like John Thomas Haines's *My Poll and My Partner Joe* (Surrey 1835). Part of its power lies in its handling of the ambiguous theme of strong masculine friendship – that sense of the 'pal' or the 'mate', which in the upper-class world might become the comrade-in-arms; it is a quality which, if clumsily handled, degenerates into what Max Beerbohm called 'manlydom', but which has been at the root of much remarkable literature and some plays that have possessed strong appeal.[1] In this vivid nautical melodrama Harry Hallyard and his betrothed Mary sacrifice their fortune of £32 to save an old sailor from prison; the pressgang takes Harry and he leaves Mary in the hands of his comrade Joe; when Harry's mother reads an account of his death, she urges Joe to marry Mary, and when Harry returns from his four years aboard the *Polyphemus* – during which he has been important in capturing a pirate ship and a pirate gang – he is thunderstruck, and thinks he has been deceived by the two he loves most; the situation is resolved when Joe is killed by the breaking of a crane, uniting Mary and Harry with his last breath.

The tone of this play is strong and despite its high colouring it is congruous throughout. The problem of melodrama was its constant tendency to slither sideways into bathos; what is called 'real life' suffers, alas, from the same pull towards the ridiculous. G. F. Taylor could not control his material in *The Factory Strike* (Victoria 1836): when his unfortunate hero falls at the feet of a wealthy youth, crying: 'The son of my benefactor here! – let me kneel and worship you!' – the playwright has lost his grip. The title of this piece suggests some foreshadowing of the drama of social significance, but it is just another tale of a mill operative whose enemies are within, and not without. A strike impends because of the introduction of machines in a weaving mill; Harris, a villain, is leading the men to strike and Warner seeks to dissuade them; the factory is burned and Ashfield, the good master, is murdered. It is here that the piece goes astray, for in the subsequent three years the mill hands become a robber band, not unlike that in *The Miller and His Men*. But Warner will

---

[1] It needs no Freud to discern it in *A Tale of Two Cities* (1859) and the dramatic version of it, *The Only Way* (Lyceum 1899), in which Martin-Harvey played over 1,000 times, though here it is for a man of superior character, loved by the heroine, that Sidney Carton sacrifices himself.

not join them, and is threatened with the workhouse; he is relieved by Ashfield's son who returns from the Peninsular War and gives him one of those purses so common in melodrama, and which must surely contain huge bank drafts rather than any ordinary coin. Harris and his gang kill Young Ashfield, and Warner is accused, but is later vindicated. It is, in fact, a dismal drama of the Good Man Falsely Accused, rich only in self-pity, who is in the end arbitrarily relieved of miseries which appear to be inherent in his character. Warner, in fact, is a born loser, a numerous class of society to which this kind of melodrama brought some gleam of hope and reassurance.

Nevertheless, even such twaddle as this has a degree of dramatic power that derives from its evocation of genuine emotion – and self-pity is both genuine and widespread. There is no genuine emotion of any kind in Thomas Noon Talfourd's *Ion* (CG 1836), though it was gloated over in its day as a restoration of dignity and tragic grandeur to the stage. Macready thought well of it, and so did Talfourd's large circle of literary friends. It was seen from time to time till 1850. But in the hot-blooded, unintellectual and downright ignorant and vulgar theatre of its time it was a sport.

Its plot is classical indeed: a curse upon Argos is attributed to the ruling house by Apollo, and Ion seeks the king, Adrastus, to kill him and remove the blight; but Ion is strangely drawn to Adrastus, and we are not surprised when the priest Medon reveals that Ion is the tyrant's son; therefore it is Ctesiphon who kills Adrastus; Ion is crowned, and kills himself as a sacrifice for his city, whereupon the pestilence abates. The respectable, unmemorable verse evokes no sense of doom and only the palest, most vitiated sense of anything Greek. The action is slow without being stately. Talfourd seems to have escaped the atmosphere of his time less successfully than his friends supposed, for in recollection *Ion* emerges as one of Macready's plays about fatherhood.[1]

It was Talfourd's one success. *The Athenian Captive* (CG 1838) was slower and duller. *Glencoe* (CG 1840) may be mentioned here to complete an account of his career as a playwright; it tells the familiar tale of the massacre and is rather livelier than his preceding two plays. The author has made an attempt to supply the taste of his age for romance, but his play is marred rather than assisted by some attempts to create a supernatural atmosphere. Macready admired its craftsmanship, but craftsmanship could not preserve it for long.

---

[1] The part of Ion, which was originally played by Macready, became a favourite with Ellen Tree, the wife of Charles Kean; portraits of her in the role show us a very girlish youth. She had great success in it in the US, playing it at the Park Theatre in 1845.

33a Garrick as King Lear

33b John Philip Kemble and Sarah Siddons as Lear and Cordelia, 1801

35 Mrs Siddons as Isabella in Shakespeare's *Measure for Measure*

36a Sheridan's *Pizarro*: on the Covent Garden stage, 1804

36b Sheridan's *Pizarro*: with John Philip Kemble as Rolla

36c Sheridan's *Pizarro*: Edmund Kean a comparable pose

M.ʳ KEAN AS ROLLA

37 Edmund Kean as Sir Giles Overreach in Massinger's *A New Way to Pay Old Debts*

38a Phelps as Cardinal Wolsey

38b The Kembles in *Henry VIII*, showing Siddons as Queen Katharine, John Philip Kemble as Wolsey, Charles Kemble as Cromwell, Stephen Kemble as Henry VIII

39 Fanny Kemble in *Henry VIII* at Smirke's Covent Garden, 1831

40a Madame Vestris and her husband Charles Mathews Junior
in Bernard's *The Conquering Game*

40b John Liston with Vestris in Poole's *Paul Pry*

41a Macready's production of *The Winter's Tale*, 1837

41b Charles Kean's staging of the same play, 1856

42 Macready with Helen Faucit in Byron's *Werner*

43a Boucicault's *The Colleen Bawn* at the Adelphi Theatre (1860)

43b Boucicault's *The Corsican Brothers* at the Princess's Theatre (1852), with Charles Kean as the dying Louis dei Franchi

44 Sheridan

45 Goldsmith

46 Boucicault

47 Gilbert

48 Photograph of Henry Irving as Mathias in Lewis's *The Bells*, 1871

It is a waxwork ideal of the classical world that stands behind Talfourd's plays. The nineteenth century, during the years under consideration here, turned for its mythical inspiration and energy to a realm of the imagination which more often produces folk tale. Planché's instinct for this world asserts itself again and again. In *Riquet With the Tuft* (Olympic 1836) and *Puss in Boots* (Olympic 1837) he wrote leading roles for Charles Mathews which were admirably suited to that actor's vigorous and authoritative comedy style; Puss and Riquet are not lovable creatures of the nursery, but dashing grotesques with a strong whiff of brimstone about them; they give a constant impression of power, and we are never perfectly certain that the power will be benevolently used, for it rises from a source that recognizes but does not bow to nineteenth-century ideals. We feel that Riquet or Puss would have dealt with Adrastus very smartly, father or no. In consequence these pieces, slight as they are, engage and stimulate us as *Ion* cannot.

Not all of the characters who seem to come from the chthonian world have this touch of the diabolical. B. F. Rayner's *The Dumb Man of Manchester* (Astley's 1837) was popular for fifty years and even had a production in this century (Everyman 1928) because it opposed simple goodness to unprincipled intellect, the former being exemplified by the Dumb Man, a creature of instinct. Even more strongly is virtue associated with lack of ratiocinative power in *The Idiot of Heidelberg Castle* (Astley's 1838). Both Dumb Tom and the Idiot were played by Ducrow, a great pantomimist; it is of interest that a stage direction in the latter play reads '*Music piano throughout each scene when the Idiot is on*'; music was relied upon to suggest the uncanny, the instinctive, the world of feeling. Such characters seem to have appealed powerfully to audiences containing many people who, without being either mute or idiotic, nevertheless had difficulty in holding their own in the voluble world in which they lived.

Knowles's contribution to the latter part of this decade is one of his best plays, *The Love Chase* (Hay 2 1837). The plot is admirably constructed, even though the author has set himself the task of resolving three very different love affairs without giving any one of them extraordinary prominence. But he manages to pair off Sir William Findlove and the Widow Green, Waller and his Lydia and Wildrake and his wilful Constance with just the right amount of misunderstanding, and without too much meddling by the benevolent Trueworth. His weak point is his verse, though he brings to it everything that study can achieve. He has conned the Jacobeans and copied them, but he remains wordy, heavy-handed in metaphor and too fond of inversions. We feel that Knowles's lines must have been hard for actors to commit to memory. Bartlett's *Familiar Quotations* (centennial edition) does not regard anything of Knowles's as familiar except two lines from *Virginius*; the *Oxford Dictionary of Quotations* does not mention him. For a dramatist, being quotable has a special importance.

Happier, therefore, was Edward George Earle Lytton Bulwer-Lytton, first Baron Lytton of Knebworth, who had the power of providing words, as well as situations, that linger in the mind. His first play, *The Duchess de la Vallière* (CG 1837), was a failure, perhaps because it relies so heavily on the title role, and Lytton was not fortunate with women in art or in life. He has restrained the vigour of his men, and though Louis and Bragelone are well drawn, they are subdued to the lead. Macready observed with sound professional judgement that the play is too long for what is in it, though he must have been pleased by Bragelone's words of the Duchess:

> Now let her flee away and be at rest.
> The peace that man has broken – Thou restore
> Whose holiest name is FATHER! (*soft music*) (IV. ii)

In *The Lady of Lyons* (CG 1838) Lytton shows a better command of his craft, and we are pleased with the spectacle of a literate, sophisticated, powerfully dramatic intelligence working within the framework of melodrama. The plot is a strong one, and the theme of a proud and wilful woman being reduced to humility cannot have been uncongenial to the matrimonially battered author. But he wisely balanced it against the rise to full self-respect of Claude Melnotte, his hero, who rejects pretensions to distinction and achieves the real thing. The dialogue, which he varies by using both prose and verse, his talent for writing fluent and occasionally memorable lines, and his discreet use of long speeches – he includes a few effective and obvious 'arias' as Bernard Shaw was later to do – give the play a sense of movement that Knowles was never able to achieve by these means. The success of the play was great, and it was played by a succession of eminent actors and actresses in first-rank productions until 1919.

Successful as it was, however, Lytton was even more adroit in *Richelieu; or the Conspiracy* (CG 1839). It is fast-moving, ably plotted and varied in mood and dialogue; further, it exhibits a sophisticated humour extremely rare in melodrama. Its superiority to its predecessor lies in the central character, who is not markedly like the Richelieu of history, but who is unmistakably that archetypal figure called, by C. G. Jung, the Wise Old Man. Capricious, powerful, all-knowing, ambivalent and decidedly tricky, this character has been what actors used to call a 'sure card' ever since Shake-speare embodied it in Prospero. Provided with such lines as:

> Beneath the rule of men entirely great
> The pen is mightier than the sword. Behold
> The arch-enchanter's wand! – Itself a nothing! –
> But taking sorcery from the master-hand
> To paralyse the Caesars – and to strike
> The loud earth breathless! – Take away the sword! –
> States can be saved without it! (II. ii)

So in the same act, to a young man charged with a special mission:

> Fail – fail?
> In the lexicon of youth, which Fate reserves
> For a bright manhood, there is no such word
> As – *fail!* . . .
> Farewell, boy! Never say 'Fail' again.

And once again, in the climactic moment when he defies, in a ringing speech, the agents of the King, who would seize Julie de Mortemar, his ward:

> BARADAS: The country is the King!
> RICHELIEU: Ay, is it so: –
> Then wakes the power which in the age of iron
> Burst forth to curb the great, and raise the low.
> Mark, where she stands! – around her form I draw
> The awful circle of our solemn church!
> Set but a foot within that holy ground
> And on thy head – yea, though it wore a crown –
> I launch the curse of Rome! (IV. i)

Given such speeches as these, a melodramatic actor of great powers had room to move, and it is not surprising that *Richelieu* was acted by every notable player who could command it. Irving revived it four times, and Walter Hampden last played it in New York in 1930.

To conclude consideration of this significant decade it is necessary only to mention Dion Boucicault's *A Legend of the Devil's Dyke* (TR Brighton 1838), not because it is important in itself but because it is the first of roughly 150 plays from the pen of one of the great contrivers of melodrama. It was written when he was sixteen, and is an astonishing production for so young a man. It begins in the high comedy form of the eighteenth century, but grows extravagantly melodramatic at the end, when the villain dies of poison concealed in a ring. The underplot, in which the servant Teddy Rodent attends a Brighton ball disguised as a rich widow, might have pleased Garrick. But when the villain murmurs, 'Say, shall this hand be pressed by Hubert Stanley's kisses, or moulder in the worm's embrace', and expires at last, crying, 'My curse, my withering curse be on ye both!' we know that melodrama has marked the writer for its own.

1840–1850

This decade offers little to detain us, and an account of it is chiefly a record of plays successful in their own time that are interesting now only as evidence of the vagaries of theatrical taste. It was in 1843 that the monopoly of the patent theatres on legitimate drama was finally broken,[1] but this did not release any surge of repressed talent among playwrights; economic considerations, and the taste of the public, kept them very much as they had been before – that is to say, hacks condemned to hasty work, providing laughter or sensation in the mode that would sell. Only a genius could break such a mould, and although Boucicault was a genius of a kind in the melodramatic vein, he had not yet found his full strength. If we look for freshness here, we shall find it in Planché.

He explains in the preface to *The Sleeping Beauty in the Wood* (CG 1840) how he came to use the word which describes his most important contribution to the stage. He says:[2]

> I selected the subject of 'La Belle au Bois Dormante', and as the absurd regulations I have already described as fettering the minor theatres did not affect the patent houses, the vague title of 'Burletta'

[1] See also Part I (2), p. 43.   [2] *Extravaganzas*, II, 66.

was no longer necessary to designate the particular style of drama I had originated in England. 'The Sleeping Beauty' was therefore announced as an extravaganza, distinguishing the whimsical treatment of a poetical subject from the broad caricature of a tragedy or serious opera, which was correctly termed a 'Burlesque'.[1]

Planché was a writer of considerable delicacy of taste; the excessive and strained punning which makes tedious the productions of some of his imitators was not characteristic of his work, nor was he gross in his portraits of characters from mythology or fairy tale. He was inventive, and later in the century W. S. Gilbert was to help himself substantially to Planché's inventions, though, as he usually extended or bettered them, this cannot be called plagiarism. Surely Gilbert found inspiration for Pooh-Bah in the character of the Lord Factotum in *The Sleeping Beauty*:

> As Lord High Chamberlain, I slumber never,
> As Lord High Steward, in a stew I'm ever,
> As Lord High Constable, I watch all day,
> As Lord High Treasurer I've the deuce to pay.
> As Great Grand Cup Bearer, I'm handled queerly,
> As Great Grand Carver, I'm cut up severely.
> In other states the honours are divided,
> But here they're one and all to me confided.
> They've buckled Fortune on my back – until
> I really feel particularly ill!
> Young man, avoid the cares from state that spring,
> And don't you be a Great Grand anything. (I. ii)

This is what Gilbert makes of it in *The Mikado* (1885):

POOH-BAH: . . . When all the great officers of state resigned in a body because they were too proud to serve under an ex-tailor, did I not unhesitatingly accept all their posts at once?
PISH-TUSH: And the salaries attached to them? You did.
POOH-BAH: It is consequently my degrading duty to serve this upstart as First Lord of the Treasury, Lord Chief Justice, Commander-in-Chief, Lord High Admiral, Master of the Buckhounds, Groom of the Back Stairs, Archbishop of Titipu, and Lord Mayor, both acting and elect,

[1] On the term 'burletta', see also Part I (2), p. 42.

all rolled into one. And at a salary! A Pooh-Bah paid for his services! I a salaried minion! But I do it! It revolts me, but I do it.

NANKI-POOH: And it does you credit.

POOH-BAH: But I don't stop at that. I go and dine with middle-class people on reasonable terms. I dance at cheap suburban parties for a moderate fee. I accept refreshments at any hands, however lowly. I also retail State secrets at a very low figure. (Act I)

Gilbert's sharper satire would not have served Planché's purpose; he had no Sullivan to write music that supported and sometimes added another shade of meaning to his verses; he wrote to airs that already existed and although he was a deft rhymer even he sometimes strains the tunes unduly. We may feel that in the context of what was possible in his theatre Planché handled his ideas and his material with skill that commands strong admiration.

Bulwer-Lytton followed the success of *Richelieu* with *Money* (Hay 1840), a comedy in a modern setting. It has many virtues: the plot is ingenious and its development never flags; the characterization is firm and the dialogue good, and witty when required to be so; the play gives a strong sense of happening in the world of London society and not in a dream world of melodrama. We are not surprised that it held the stage as viable drama and not simply as a revival of a work from another age, receiving twenty-two important productions in London alone, the last being an 'all-star' revival at Drury Lane in 1911. But it has an idiosyncrasy which is clearer to our eyes than to those of the nineteenth century: it unites two attitudes toward its characters, and although this is successfully accomplished it weakens the play as a work of art.

Clara, the heroine, is presented to us very much as a girl of 1840; her sense of delicacy, her reticences, her 'womanliness' – to use the word as it would have been used by those who first saw the play – are of her time. Georgina, however, is from eighteenth-century comedy; a quality of hard-headedness, of calculation, united with charm, does not trouble us in Julia in *The Rivals* (1775) or Miss Neville in *She Stoops to Conquer* (1773) because it is contrasted with a heroine whose opposed qualities are of the same period, but it seems false to modern taste when Georgina opposes these things to Clara. Bulwer-Lytton clearly draws the inspiration for *Money* from the Old Comedy of the eighteenth century and he is brilliantly successful except with his hero and heroine, who belong to his own time. That is to say, Evelyn the hero is a man of 1840 in matters of the heart; in his dealings with the characters from Old Comedy he not only speaks their language but feels as a misanthropic hero of an earlier age might feel.

Money thus provides us with an excellent example of the problem that is even clearer in some of the costume drama of the nineteenth century: clothes, language and manners of an earlier age may be copied, but feelings and social attitudes always betray the time of a play's composition, just as a piece of 'reproduction' furniture declares itself to the informed eye. Bulwer-Lytton has been subtle; he has put his eighteenth-century comedy into the dress of 1840, but when he wishes to draw his audiences into concern for a romance, he has to write it in the mode of his day. Now, when we are psychologically further from 1840 than we are, perhaps, from 1775, the incongruity is clear to see.

The era had not found a high comedy style of its own, and reliance on that of the previous fifty years is easily understood; it was the mode in which the best modern comedy known to the writers of 1840 was still cast. It was to this mode that Dion Boucicault (or as he spelled it at that time, Bourcicault) turned when he wrote *London Assurance* (CG 1841) in thirty days. It was a great opportunity for a writer still under twenty to be asked to produce a modern comedy for Charles Mathews and Madame Vestris; he took the best models he knew and produced a high-coloured piece with clearly drawn characters that continues to play well. The play held the London stage until 1913, and when it was done at the Malvern Festival in 1932 it was not a museum piece, offered as an act of theatrical piety, but a live comedy. It was revived by the Royal Shakespeare Company in 1970. A spectator meeting it for the first time would have some trouble in dating it, until the final speech, in which Sir Harcourt Courtly speaks of 'the title of a gentleman' and says that it is 'out of any monarch's gift, yet within the reach of every peasant'. That is the voice of the nineteenth century, and it could not have been expected to appeal to audiences much before 1840.

London Assurance is evidence of a striving for literary as well as theatrical success, and Douglas Jerrold strove for this kind of distinction, nowhere more intently than in *Bubbles of the Day* (CG 1842). Like Boucicault, he seems to think that it was to be found in reliance on the manner of Old Comedy. His son quotes an unnamed contemporary critic[1] as calling it 'the most electric and witty play in the English language, a play without story, scenery or character, but which by mere power of dialogue, by flash, swirl and coruscation of fancy, charmed one of the most intellectual audiences ever gathered'. Jerrold was disappointed by its reception, saying that it was 'brought

[1] Blanchard Jerrold, in *Douglas Jerrold, Dramatist and Wit* (London, 1914), p. 327.

out as a forlorn hope at the fag-end of a season',[1] but looking at it now we see faults that contradict the enthusiast of 1842. The plot is too slim, and furthermore Jerrold's ideas about political life seem to have been too thin to convince for five acts; he does not know politics as, for instance, Trollope does. And it should be said here that Jerrold's wit, admired in its own day, now seems to have a bitter taste, a smack of grievance understandable in the light of his personal life but which does not make for good art. With Jerrold, nobody who was a success could really be fully honest or admirable, and this attitude gives his plays a savour not of satire, but of gall.

Certainly it must have been bitter to him to see the success of such mawkish stuff as *Jane, the Licensed Victualler's Daughter* (Pavilion 1840), which may stand for a whole school of drama, touted by its publisher as 'highly-instructive and moral'. Its dramaturgy is crude and its dialogue vulgar; its only interest lies in the fact that the downfall of the villain, Ralph, is attributed to want of education. Or what would Jerrold make of such crude exploitation of a great legend as H. P. Grattan's *Faust* (Sadler's Wells 1842), in which scenes of rough comedy are sandwiched between exhibitions of stage trickery, with Mephistopheles as a magician not readily to be distinguished from the contemporary John Henry Anderson, conjuror and actor, 'The Wizard of the North'? What is of interest in this piece is that enough of the legend lingers to give the play a certain authority, and that apparently it was a kind of authority an audience wanted. It is just this authority that saves *Sweeney Todd* (Britannia 1842), in which George Dibdin Pitt exploited crime, ghosts, horror, remorse and retribution in the coarsest terms; but there is a raw-head-and-bloody-bones impact about this shocker that gives it a life impossible to drama that lingers in the realm of Old Comedy, when Old Comedy has ceased to say anything strikingly contemporary. Nor can Jerrold have taken much comfort in the proliferation of nautical melodrama, a type of play to which his *Black-Eyed Susan* had given so much impetus. An example from this period is *Ruth, or The Lass that Loves a Sailor* (Victoria 1843), which was a rousing success in itself and suggested the secondary title of *H.M.S. Pinafore* (1878).

These plays are saved from literary squalor by their vitality, and it must have been this quality that made them successful on the stage. There is boundless vitality in W. T. Moncrieff's *Caesar, the Watch Dog of the Castle* (Victoria 1844). Victor, the rightful heir of Montfaucon, has been reduced by fate to a half imbecile condition in which he takes on the duties and

[1] Blanchard Jerrold, in *Douglas Jerrold, Dramatist and Wit* (London, 1914), p. 336, in a letter to Benjamin Webster.

something of the character of Caesar, formerly the watch dog. The audience is repeatedly made to feel dread for the human Caesar, because he has a dog's trusting simplicity, and does not at once detect Dervilliers, who pretends to be the rightful heir, as his enemy. But it is Victor who knows the whereabouts of the secret spring that reveals his father's sword, and with the restoration of his inheritance he recovers all his humanity and his wits. The lesson of the play is that it is not cleverness, but goodness, that triumphs; this, and the strong chthonic element in the play – what Englishman can doubt the moral grandeur of a dog? – and the appearance of the charming Miss Mary Ann Vincent, at this time a plump twenty-six, in a revealing dogskin, made the play a sure card.

It was not obligatory for a melodramatic hero to be stupid, or merely dog-like. *Don Cesar de Bazan* (Princess's 1844), by G. A. à Beckett and Mark Lemon, takes its principal character from Hugo's *Ruy Blas* (1838) and builds a play around him. Don Jose hopes to procure the beautiful gypsy, Maritana, for the King by marrying her to Don Cesar, who is under sentence of death; but Don Cesar escapes, claims Maritana, kills Jose and is made Governor of Granada.[1] The dialogue is jejune, and the character of Maritana is poorly fleshed out; only Don Cesar has a chance to shine in this play. But the character of the penniless aristocrat, swordsman, adventurer, chivalrous lover and wit was exploited in many melodramas of the 'costume' order until 1914.

Don Cesar is a pleasant contrast to the lachrymose, self-pitying heroes of the total abstinence plays, which seem to have drawn large audiences, not all of whom can have been abstainers. A very successful example was *The Bottle* by T. P. Taylor (City of London 1847). Some of its effectiveness must have lain in the obligation it placed on the actors to portray the eight Cruikshank plates, ranging from *One: the Happy Home* to *Eight: the Madhouse*; we may presume that the plates inspired the drama.[2] The play is decidedly not of the same order of artistic achievement as the pictures; the wearisomely didactic wife of the drunkard, his spiritless children, the snuffling, lacklustre quality of his downfall, and his subaqueous death – 'What mist is that which

---

[1] This play had a long life as the story of William Vincent Wallace's *Maritana* (1845), which, with Balfe's *The Bohemian Girl* (1843) and Sir Julius Benedict's *The Lily of Killarney* (1862), which took its libretto from Boucicault's *The Colleen Bawn*, constituted what Sir Thomas Beecham called 'The English Ring'. All three should be known to students of James Joyce, as much of the musical culture of Leopold and Molly Bloom is rooted in them.

[2] Anyone wishing more information about Cruikshank's extraordinary series may consult Laman Blanchard, *The Life of George Cruikshank*, 2 volumes (London, 1882).

is falling? What bubbling is this next my heart?' – have not the Cruikshank incisiveness and stimulating grotesquerie. But the evidence is that the play gave much satisfaction.

Two other melodramas of this decade ask for comment. The first is *The Black Doctor* (City of London 1846) from *Le Docteur Noir* by Anicet-Bourgeois and Dumanoir (Théâtre Porte-Martin 1846); it was played in Paris by Lemaître, and in England by the negro tragedian Ira Aldridge.[1] The story is of Fabian, a negro physician, who loves Pauline, a noble French girl; believing that she loves St Luce, he leads her to a spot where the rising tide will destroy them, and reveals his passion, to learn that she returns it. They escape, live in Paris, and when their marriage is discovered Fabian is sent to the Bastille; the Fall of the Bastille frees him, but he is killed by a random shot. What is interesting about this play is that Fabian is a physician, and thus a white man's equal, and an aristocratic white girl loves him for himself. We shall not encounter English or American drama with a plot like this for some time.

The other play of interest is T. P. Taylor's *Vanderdecken, or the Flying Dutchman* (City of London 1846). It is significant as an early example of the play with a 'dual role': the same actor plays the parts of Vanderdecken the noble sea captain and his alter ego Schriften, who describes himself in the last act as 'a wild and fearful being; in my bosom is hatred, in my heart not an impulse of humanity . . .'. Later he identifies himself plainly: 'My resemblance to your husband may appear strange to you. Let me avow that I am his evil genius.' This device was to become popular not only because it gave a leading actor a chance for a display of skill, but because its idea of the duality of man's nature is deeply rooted and responds to powerful appeals. Such a play as this looks forward to Stevenson's *The Strange Case of Dr. Jekyll and Mr. Hyde* (1886) but it looks backward many centuries to Ormuzd and Ahriman.[2]

At this point some reference must be made to John Westland Marston, whose career as a dramatist extended over forty-three years, during which he offered twenty plays; as with Talfourd, a literary coterie admired him and tried to bring him into prominence, but only his first play *The Patrician's Daughter* (DL 1842) gained anything approaching the degree of success they thought owing to his abilities. It is in blank verse, and its setting is

---

[1] Published as No. 460 in Dick's Standard Plays, the date is given incorrectly as 1841, and Aldridge is named as author; the English translation was in fact by Thomas Archer.

[2] This play was not Irving's *Vanderdecken* (1878), which was of Wagnerian inspiration and was the work of Percy Fitzgerald and William Gorman Wills.

contemporary; the self-made statesman, Mordaunt, aspires to the hand of Lady Mabel Lynterne and she loves him, but the Earl her father cannot countenance a misalliance, and Lady Lydia, her aunt, breaks off the affair by fraud. Later, when Mordaunt has proved himself by becoming a baronet, the Earl consents to a marriage, but Mordaunt publicly refuses it, and is reconciled to the broken-hearted Mabel just before her death, when the deception has been revealed. What was considered Mordaunt's cruel and ungentlemanly conduct aroused controversy when *The Patrician's Daughter* first appeared.

The play has powerful scenes, but the language moves sluggishly, and Marston has been no luckier than a thousand others in putting the necessary trivialities of daily life into blank verse. Dickens wrote a Prologue praising the play as a drama of modern life, crying 'Awake the Present!' But alas, is not the present, nor indeed any sort of life known at any time. Marston's aristocrats, like those of so many nineteenth-century playwrights, are the creations of a man who has seen aristocrats only on public occasions; his radical, Mordaunt, is no more convincing, for Marston has not given him any political opinions – only gaseous generalities. Marston belongs to that unhappy class of writers who strain their talent too far; he lacks emotional conviction and his attempts to feign it cannot deceive. Failure on a respectable level is a peculiarly melancholy study.

The comedy of the decade produced at least two durable pieces and a few others which are of interest. Charles Selby's *The Boots at the Swan* (New Strand 1842) was a farce favourite for many years. As far as language goes it might have been written any time after 1800, but its burlesque of melodrama marks it as belonging to the middle of the century. It is a rattling farce in one act and two scenes: to assist Higgins to win Emily (whose sister objects to the vulgarity of his name), Captain Friskly and Earwig, the boots of the title, disguise themselves as an escaped convict and a policeman. Friskly is one of the many characters who seem to owe their origin to Dickens's invention of Alfred Jingle; he is also not unlike Jeremy Diddler. Earwig is one of those parts into which a skilled low comedian may inject a great deal that is personal; descriptions of the way in which a variety of players have shaped it reveal how adaptable it is; except that Earwig is deaf, they have little to restrain them.

Having won the confidence of Charles Mathews with *London Assurance*, Dion Boucicault collaborated with the famous comedian in an adaptation, *Used Up* (Hay 1844), from a French original; it is a 'dual role' play but not in the serious sense of *Vanderdecken*; it tells of Sir Charles Coldstream's boredom; he is utterly 'used up' and seeks sensation in the pursuit of a widow, Mrs Clutterbuck; when her husband appears they fight and each thinks he has killed the other; Farmer Wurzel conceals the husband, and his niece Mary conceals Coldstream, disguising him as Joe the Ploughboy; in the resolution Mrs Clutterbuck is abandoned and Coldstream marries Mary.[1]

Planché's *The Drama At Home, or An Evening With Puff* (Hay 1844) is interesting for the information it purports to give about the languishing of the patent theatres and the rise of the 'minors' consequent upon the changes in the Licensing Act, but it now looks as if Planché saw more than was really before his eyes. A greater freedom and prosperity undoubtedly accrued to the 'minors', but the taste of their audiences did not change. People who had become accustomed to plays which contained songs, in order to comply with the Lord Chamberlain's regulations, expected songs still, and audiences at the Adelphi and the Victoria, which had delighted in melodrama for many years, had no mind to change their tastes.

The other part of Queen Victoria's 4 January 1849 entertainment, John Maddison Morton's *Box and Cox* (Lyceum 1847), is of interest not only because it is a durable farce that delighted several generations of playgoers, but because it is a good example of the mockery of melodramatic dramaturgy that is becoming apparent in the middle of the century. It is a play for the popular comedian John Baldwin Buckstone, who played Box the printer; he and Cox the hatter have been rented the same room by Mrs Bouncer, Cox occupying it by day and Box by night, as this agrees with their hours of work; they discover the imposture, but also that they are engaged to the same Penelope Ann, and finally that they are long-lost brothers. Their scene of recognition is in the finest melodramatic vein: 'Have you such a thing as a strawberry mark on your left arm?' 'No.' 'Then it is he!' The dialogue is in the vein of polysyllabic humour so dear to the Victorians. An examination of any large body of memoir or anecdote of the period suggests that a large number of people in all walks of society actually talked and wrote in this way, considering it the proper thing to do.[2]

---

[1] Queen Victoria, whose fondness for the drama, and especially for comedy, was strong, commanded a performance of this piece at Windsor on 4 January 1849, to be followed by *Box and Cox*. Among the guests of the queen and the prince consort, and four of their children, were Their Serene Highnesses the Princesses Amelie and Elise of Hohenlohe Schillingsfurst, the Chevalier Bunsen and Baron Stockmar. One wonders what Stockmar, not notably a merry man, made of it all.

[2] Consider, as an example, *The Memories of Dean Hole* (London, 1892; New York, 1893). Samuel Reynolds Hole (1819–1904), the learned Dean of Rochester after 1887, was

Let us conclude this consideration of the decade with the Brough Brothers' *Camaralzaman and Badoura* (Hay 1848) which gives us an example of the popular lighter entertainment other than that of Planché. It is in the punning style of the time, and its songs are written to familiar airs; its humour relies on the device of making supernatural and immortal beings slangy and fashionable according to the London fads of the day.

What impresses is the extraordinary vigour of this script and others like it. They abound in a restless and exuberant comic invention, which is the other side of the coin from the zest and gusto of the melodramas. These forms of drama are, in fact, two aspects of the same taste, and can only have been comprehensible to people of alert and agile mind. The people who followed such barrages of puns have progressed far in this respect beyond the audiences of the eighteenth century, who – without necessarily being dull of wit or unsophisticated – nevertheless relished a slower, more deliberative kind of fun.

---

much admired for his epistolary and anecdotal style; no one could call him a foolish or imperfectly literate man, and his manner of writing may be taken as representative of a large group of upper-class Victorians, and of less fortunate people who imitated them.

1850–1860

Adaptations from novels have not been considered hitherto in this outline of nineteenth-century drama, except in the case of two works by Pierce Egan where particular circumstances made it appropriate. The serial productions of Dickens and Bulwer were coarsely adapted for the stage, in some instances even before the original had been completed in monthly parts. Where melodramatic incident was strong it was exaggerated; eccentric characters, where they existed, were made occasions for shows of professional skill, especially in matters of dress and make-up. But Tom Taylor's *The Vicar of Wakefield* (Strand 1850) is of greater interest than these because it shows clearly the tendency noticeable in all ages to reinterpret the art of an earlier day in contemporary terms. It is literate and dramatically adroit, but it is strangely unlike Goldsmith: the unworldly Dr Primrose has become a 'heavy father', Thornhill is a thorough villain rather than a self-indulgent and thoughtless rascal, and Olivia herself has been made congruous with them.[1]

The Vicar is costume drama, and the type is very popular from this date until 1914. Another example was *Belphegor* (Sadler's Wells 1856), adapted

[1] The change in emphasis is not unlike that which took place when *Tom Jones* was made into a successful film in 1963, and those elements in it which would most appeal to a mass audience in the latter part of the twentieth century were selected and stressed without much concern for the nature of the book or the society it depicted.

by Charles Webb from the French original (Gaîté 1850) by Dennery and Fournier. In all, there were three versions of this piece, not including a burlesque. The period was that of Louis XVIII, so it had the appeal of a costume piece, but in feeling it is mid-century. The complex plot tells of the mountebank Belphegor who has a wife of noble blood, whose marriage to him might therefore bring about his death – for impertinence, one presumes; he suffers much and at last unmasks a villain, regains his wife and is pardoned. There is a well-managed scene of pathos when he discovers that his wife has left him, for excellent motives clear to the audience but not to himself. The familiar theme of a father's sufferings is exploited, and the great-hearted simplicity of the faithful comic man effectively used. The subject is that of virtue misprized and set at naught by rank and wealth; this is one of the most familiar and popular themes of melodrama and some reasons for its success have already been suggested; it will be further explored at the end of this study.

Although the heroines of the plays of this part of the nineteenth century are vital to the dramatic action, their roles are not always interesting psychologically; as people, they do not so much act as permit themselves to be acted upon; they rarely initiate anything vital to the plays in which they appear, and seem to be the feminine side of the hero's nature rather than autonomous creatures. For this reason *Ingomar* (DL 1851) is of special interest: it is a version by Maria Anne Lovell of *Der Sohn der Wildnis* (1843) by Baron Eligius von Münch-Bellinghausen. In it the heroine Parthenia goes fearlessly among the savage Allemani to beg release for her captured father Myron; when he goes free, she remains as a hostage, and by her beauty of person and character subdues the chieftain Ingomar; for her sake he accompanies her back to civilization, determines to become a Greek and devote himself to the arts of peace; his nobility of nature proves to be a rebuke to Greek craftiness.

Love has conquered all, but not, we may think, without some destruction. Ingomar, who first appears as a likeable and wildly noble savage, suffers a considerable come-down when he is brought among the Greek tradesmen from whom Parthenia springs. Ostensibly the play is about the redeeming power of love, and the couplet:

Two minds with but a single thought,
Two hearts that beat as one,

is reiterated as an expression of a splendid ideal. But the play is unpleasantly middle-class in its values, and its sentimentality disgusts. Its popularity –

and it was played as a London piece into the eighties and as a provincial piece until 1900 – seems to have arisen from the spectacle of a girl getting a man thoroughly under her thumb, by exhibiting a soft and winning external character, under which she exerts a whim of iron.

Two melodramas famous for their 'dual roles' make their appearance at this time, both based more or less distantly on French originals. The first is *The Courier of Lyons*, the Adelphi version (1851) by Benjamin Webster and the Princess's version (1854) by Charles Reade.[1] It is based on a true story of the Directory period, when an honest citizen, Joseph Lesurques, was in great danger because of his extraordinary resemblance to a murderer and robber, one Dubosc. In the play Lesurques is accused of robbing the Lyons coach and killing the postilion; even his father doubts his innocence, for he has seen one whom he takes to be his son standing over the body of the murdered man. The denouement of the play takes place in an attic overlooking the place of execution, where Dubosc exults as the man who so much resembles him mounts the steps of the guillotine. The Jekyll and Hyde role gives great opportunities to an actor of resource and compelling personality.

The other equally famous piece is *The Corsican Brothers* (Princess's 1852), of which the English version was by Boucicault. It is a play in which the 'call of blood' is the mainspring of the plot, for the Corsican twins, Louis and Fabien dei Franchi, are united by a strong sympathy that warns the other whenever one of them is in danger. When Louis is slain in a duel in Paris, Fabien sees his ghost in Corsica, and goes at once to avenge his brother. This is a 'dual role' in which the two principal characters are subtly differentiated, instead of being plainly hero and villain. It was also a play in which great scenic display was possible;[2] Boucicault's version was last seen in the English provinces, acted by Martin-Harvey, in 1924; he played it in Canada later still; a revision, by John Bowen, was presented at Greenwich in March 1970.

The best work of this period is in the melodramatic vein, and the two plays just described are literate and, on the whole, moderate in dialogue. Comedy continued to mean farce, such as Charles Mathews's immensely popular *Little Toddlekins* (Lyceum 1852); its general character is indicated

[1] The title was more correctly translated in Reade's 1877 version as *The Lyons Mail*; in this form it held the stage until 1930. Sir John Martin-Harvey's promptbook of Irving's version, which is in the writer's possession, shows interesting trimming and rephrasing of some of the more extravagant rhetorical passages, to accommodate them to twentieth-century taste.

[2] On the 'Corsican trap' devised for this play, see Part II (1), pp. 89-90.

by the names of the principal characters – Jones Robinson Brownsmith, Barnaby Babicombe of Babicombe Bay, and Captain Littlepop. Brownsmith has a stepdaughter of fifty, though he is himself a young man; she is an impediment to his marriage with Annie Babicombe, and he tries to palm her off on Littlepop, who will not have her; so Brownsmith marries his stepdaughter to Babicombe, marries Annie himself, and then tries to untangle their relationships. It is a characteristic Mathews piece, interesting for the skill with which the plot is managed, and the very long soliloquies which allowed Mathews to amuse the audience with his own special sort of comedy.

An example of the piratical attitude of the time towards literary property is J. Sterling Coyne's *Box and Cox Married and Settled!* (Hay 1852), which, however, lacks the neatness of Morton's original.

Certainly one of the best costume dramas of the era is *Masks and Faces* (Hay 1852) by Tom Taylor and Charles Reade; it was described by a contemporary critic as 'a very manly and right-minded little comedy'.[1] It has a 'literary' appeal for those who knew of the existence of such people as Peg Woffington, Cibber, Quin and Kitty Clive, but it treats of the theatre of 1750 seen through the eyes of 1850: Peg's goodness of heart is brought forward to excuse the irregularities of her life; whether her insistence on the possibility of virtue in an actress is intended for the eighteenth-century characters around her, or for the nineteenth-century characters in the stalls, we cannot quite determine. At any rate, she says:

> ... when hereafter in your home of peace you hear harsh sentence passed on us, whose lot is admiration, but rarely love, triumph but never tranquillity – think sometimes of poor Peg Woffington, and say, stage masks may cover honest faces, and hearts beat true beneath a tinselled robe.

Certainly the play is very well managed, and the scenes in which Peg relieves the distresses of the failed playwright Triplet and his hungry family are excellent comedy and valid drama by any standard.

These costume dramas, though high in colour, possess characters who are more than pawns in a narrative, and their situations arise from psychology as well as incident. Tom Taylor and John Lang collaborated in *Plot and Passion* (Olympic 1853); its period is 1810 and it tells of a Madame de Fontanges whose passion for gambling has compelled her to act as a spy for Joseph Fouché; he requires her to entrap a legitimist writer who is also the man she loves, but he is thwarted. If it now seems contrived in con-

[1] Henry Morley in his *Journal of a London Playgoer* (London, 1866), p. 58.

struction, it is not more so than the libretto of the popular opera *Tosca*, which it somewhat resembles. Such lines as 'Poison never seethed in the honey of these lips', and 'His kisses scald like molten lead', do no violence to the high key in which the action is pitched.

Not every dramatist was so successful in this demanding realm of composition. Charles Reade's *Gold!* (DL 1853) exploits the excitement of the Australian gold rushes, but succeeds only in producing a rather vulgar effect. His heroine vacillates unpleasantly, apparently with her eye on money rather than on true love; all the good people are stupid, inept and gullible and cannot keep their hands on gold even when they find it. The play would not be worth mentioning if it were not a demonstration that melodrama was not a class of theatre piece that anybody – even so able a novelist as Reade – could write if he abandoned his mind to it; it requires its own sort of discretion and logic, and a mingling of melodramatic elements will not produce a superior example of the type.

Indeed, sincerity of purpose lies at the heart of the best melodrama, even when the workmanship is as crude as it is in George L. Aiken's *Uncle Tom's Cabin*. This piece, which first appeared at the National Theatre, New York, in 1853, inspired several English versions; Nicoll records no less than nine, but as they all derive from Mrs Stowe's novel it is lost labour to try to disentangle them. All are crude enough in workmanship, but are alike in their dependence on strong situations, rapid action and the sandwich-like alternation of scenes of drama and of comedy. The theme of slavery was of course a powerful contemporary one, but cannot have accounted for the success of the play over at least sixty years.[1] But if we suppose that in many, or even all, the spectators of the play there was, so deeply buried as to be only half acknowledged, a suffering servant, an angel child and a Simon Legree, and that it was a truly dramatic experience to see these personal elements bodied forth on the stage, we begin to understand something of the appeal and success of melodrama.

It appealed not only to the nobler but to the more commonplace and even

---

[1] The writer first saw the play in rural Canada in 1922; although the company was from the US, George Harris had been given a telling line: 'And when at last I stand in Canada, beneath the British flag, I need never call any man "Massa" again!' It was played in nineteenth-century style: Little Eva ascended to heaven before our eyes, very affectingly; Liza crossed the ice on the Ohio River, while thwarted mastiffs (as being more dramatically impressive than bloodhounds) roared on the shore; in a final apotheosis Eva welcomed Uncle Tom into a gorgeous Eternity, while the Negro chorus offstage sang 'Nearer, My God, to Thee'. At the age of nine the writer was finely purged with pity and terror as indeed were all the seniors in his vicinity.

inglorious emotions, and to these self-pity and the pangs of misprized love belong. Charles Selby's *The Marble Heart* (Adelphi 1854) tells of a sculptor whose hard fate it is always to love unworthy women with marble hearts, and to neglect his mother and a humble, true-hearted girl in so doing. The first act, labelled 'The Dream!', takes place in the studio of Phidias at Athens, where the sculptor loves the unfeeling Aspasia, and neglects the adoring slave Thea: the subsequent four acts occur in the Paris of 1854, where the young sculptor Raphael Duchatlet is the passion-torn creature of the beautiful but heartless Mademoiselle Marco, who listens without shame – nay, with amused assent – to a song having the refrain, 'Yes! – 'tis the chink of gold you love!'; the sculptor neglects the poor orphan Marie, and recognizes her priceless devotion only when he is dying. His friend Volage – described as 'the Editor of a Fashionable Newspaper' – moralizes over Duchatlet's body: 'False ones of the past, false ones of the future! – woe to the man who loves you; – ye have ever been, and ever will be, ministers of ruin, misery, and death!'

The spectacle of a man snuffling over his ill-usage by a woman is as little pleasing as it is common; this play performs one of the functions of melodrama by giving consequence to such a situation, and the success the play enjoyed shows only how shrewdly the writer had penetrated into one of the back cupboards of the human spirit.[1]

Pratt's *Ten Nights In A Bar Room* made its appearance in New York in 1858 and soon became popular in England as well. Its debt to Jerrold's *Fifteen Years of a Drunkard's Life* has already been noted, and the crude didacticism of the play requires little comment. But it is interesting because of the character of Sample Switchel, the Yankee Comic Man: by means of him the author extracts all the comedy he can discover in drunkenness and exploits it with a skill he does not show elsewhere. In the end Switchel reforms, but by then the author has both eaten and had his cake, for he has had full use of a funny drunk all through his play. Turning the Vice into a figure of fun is a good old dramatic practice.

It is apparent that at this time, and until the end of the century, writers of burlesques and extravaganzas were able to count on an acquaintance with popular plays, a large body of legend and some aspects of the classics that certainly could not be assumed in any audience now. Halford's *Faust and Marguerite* (Strand 1854) is of small dramatic consequence; Halford himself

---

[1] The 'Note for the Managers of Provincial Theatres' after Act I of this play gives explicit instructions for simulating classical statuary by means of living models and is of great interest.

played Mephistopheles, and both Faust and Valentine were played by girls. What is interesting is the acquaintance the writer shows with Goethe's play, and the acquaintance he assumes in at least part of his audience. So also with R. B. Brough's *Masaniello* (Olympic 1857), which burlesques Auber's opera (1828) in punning dialogue and new words to popular tunes; it introduced an operatic mad scene, in which Frederick Robson was able to recall some of his successes, but an audience wholly unacquainted with the original might find it puzzling. So too with H. J. Byron's burlesque, *The Lady of Lyons* (Strand 1859); to see it before the original would be baffling, for it is a close parody, assuming a full knowledge of the play without which many of the innumerable puns would be flat. The opening speech of the Porter is of interest:

> Oh this won't do. I'll leave the situation,
> This porter's in continual fermentation;
> I am, from suffering these perpetual shocks
> By day and darksome night an 'ater-o'-knocks!

In a modern audience, one wonders how many would sense the pun on 'darksome night' and 'atra nox'? The Victorian ear was keen and ingenious.[1]

Consideration of this decade may end with two plays by Dion Boucicault, both belonging to the period of his residence in the US, although he exploited

---

[1] Harley Granville-Barker ('Exit Planché – enter Gilbert', *London Mercury*, XXV [1932], pp. 562–3) makes succinct comment on the punning craze in Victorian burlesque. He quotes from *The Field of the Cloth of Gold* (Strand 1868) by William Brough, in which the lost King Francis soliloquizes thus as he wanders in the forest:

> These fine old trees my view on all sides border;
> They're Foresters of the Most Ancient Order.
> Still, for their king thus trapping there's no reason;
> And so, *high trees*, I charge you with *high treason*.
> My royalty at least there's no mistaking:
> I've walked, till every bone tells me *I'm a king*.
> I'll lie down 'neath these boughs, for I protest,
> Walking, this *forest long*, I *long for rest*.
> Francis, full length extended 'neath these branches,
> Will be what's called *Extension of the Franchis*.

Says Barker:

> There is much art in the cumulative effect of this. 'Ancient Order of Foresters' is, of course, not a pun at all. *High trees – high treason* is a straightforward one, the pun direct; *till every bone tells me I'm a king* is the 'pun implied' for variety; *forest long – long for rest* is the 'pun reversed'. But it is all a preparation for the sheer impudence of *Extension of the Franchis* which should strike us 'twixt wind and water, and the skilled actor will see that his audience does not laugh till then.

them in London as soon as their runs in New York were completed. The first, *Jessie Brown; or the Relief of Lucknow* (Wallack's 1858), exploits emotions of loyalty expertly, and also gets the utmost out of the ballads, tartans, bagpipes and other national accoutrements of the Scots. It is not Boucicault at his best, but it introduces in the character of the Reverend David Blount, an army chaplain, a figure who seems to be new to the stage, and whose popularity in melodramatic drama, film and television is not yet exhausted; he is the manly parson, who finds the restraints of his profession troublesome when he would like to take a crack at the enemy; his struggle between faith and patriotism is an interesting development of the classic dramatic struggle between love and honour. The play ends with one of Boucicault's *coups de théâtre* as General Havelock appears with his Scots troops and the relief is accomplished.

The other play, one of Boucicault's best, is *The Octoroon; or, Life in Louisiana* (Winter Gdn 1859); love is a mainspring of the plot, and the theme resembles *Uncle Tom's Cabin*, but the treatment is sophisticated. The lines are drawn in melodramatic style; Zoe the Octoroon is beautiful and good; the Southerners are aristocratic and the Yankees white trash. There are mitigations of this general characterization, and the people in the play have an engaging humanity. It is a fine example of sensation drama, exploiting a slave auction, several fights, savage vengeance, the explosion of a steamboat, and – a novel stroke – the detection of a crime by means of photography for the first time on the stage. But it is sensation drama to which a substantial measure of art has been brought, and it was such plays as this that banished the cruder works to the provinces. The extraordinary vitality of some of these unsophisticated plays, however, kept them alive there for another sixty years.

1860–1870

By this time Boucicault was the unchallenged king of melodrama, and in *The Colleen Bawn* (Adelphi 1860) he produced one of his greatest successes. The London production followed the opening in New York by six months, and the London reception was even more enthusiastic than that in the US. 'The applause each evening is perfectly uproarious', reports *The Players*, in its issue of 15 September, and again on 29 September, 'it continues to attract not only crowded houses but *impossible* houses.' The play, like so much of Boucicault's work, is not wholly original, being adapted from Gerald Griffin's popular novel *The Collegians* (1829). What the playwright brought to it was his own strong sense of theatre, and this is exemplified not only in the contrivance of effective situations but in his management of character. In *The Colleen Bawn* he has made much of the character of Danny Mann, who has been crippled early in life by the folly of Hardress Cregan yet who lives to do Cregan's will, serving him with a fidelity that is uncanny. The relationship is developed to the point where we feel that Danny is really an externalized form of the evil in Cregan, and that when he is killed by Myles-na-Coppaleen, Cregan has been regenerated. The mythic or fairytale psychology which has been observable in several of the best plays of the melodramatic sort is accessible to Boucicault; it would be false to say that he commands it, for that would imply an awareness of it as an element to be exploited, but it is certainly a strong factor in his sense of theatre.

So also is his evocation of that spirit of renunciation that gives a bitter-sweet flavour to much of the best melodrama. Eily O'Connor, the Colleen Bawn, is wedded at last to Hardress Cregan, but we are aware that Myles loves her, and that he is better suited to her in several important ways than is Hardress; it is Myles and Eily we remember as a pair, and Danny we remember as the agent of another man's evil; Hardress is an ambiguous character, not quite lover or villain. It is this ambiguity that gives the play much of its undoubted fascination.

The novelty that most impressed the crowded London audiences, how-ever, was the freshness with which the playwright reworked the familiar material of the stage Irishman. Never before had romance and peasant poetry been so cunningly wrung from a figure long common on the stage. Absurd Irishmen and gallant Irishmen there had been in plenty, but Myles-na-Coppaleen, a rogue and a poet with a splendid vein of chivalry in his behavi-our towards women, and in addition to these gifts a funny fellow, was a seemingly magical creation. If his splendour is tarnished for us now, it is because Boucicault created a new idea of Irish character that even the Irish realism of more recent literature has not been able to destroy and it was imitated until its freshness was gone. It comes close to greatness, but never attains it; there is in Boucicault's melodrama a factitiousness that accounts for its immense popularity when new, and its failure to sustain the rubbing of time. But to come as close to greatness as he did is in itself no trivial accom-plishment.

Dependence on character, as well as on thrilling incident, is what makes Tom Taylor's *The Ticket-of-Leave Man* (Olympic 1863) a melodrama of superior quality. Its construction is adroit and its theme of social justice is treated with a degree of honesty not common in an era when the Lord Chamberlain's reader of plays was likely to take exception to anything that suggested criticism of things as they were. But it is the characters from humble life and the criminal part of society that make the play vivid. They are neither impossibly virtuous nor monsters of wickedness: Bob Brierly is not a stainless hero, but a young man who gets into bad company because he is wilful and somewhat stupid; May is a very nice girl, but she has not the preternatural moral splendour of the heroine of the melodrama of the forties; Hawkshaw is a credible detective, neither all-seeing nor impervious to harm, for he can be tricked and he can be hurt; Dalton and Melter Moss are small-time crooks. They all live, and move through scenes that convince, and give a sense of London life while moving the action briskly forward. This is melodrama, unquestionably, but it is also sophisticated realism superior to that of, for instance, *Caste*. We are not surprised that it ran for a remarkable 407 performances, and had five successful revivals during the following twenty-five years.[1]

Boucicault was not slow to exploit his successful Irish vein. *Arrah-na-Pogue* (Princess's 1865) was first given a Dublin production in 1864, and won the approval of the land which was, in time, to grow weary of Boucicault's concept of an Irishman. The roles of Shaun the Post and Arrah Meelish were skilfully tailored to suit Boucicault and his charming wife, Agnes Robertson; the theme of thwarted romance was given rather more emphasis than in *The Colleen Bawn*, but the strong card in *Arrah-na-Pogue* was the appeal to Irish patriotism: though the play was laid in 1798, the old revolutionary tune, 'The Wearin' o' the Green', with revised verses by the author, had a Fenian ring; it is evidence of the caprice of the Lord Chamberlain's licenser that it was allowed to remain in the text. But the strength of the play is Boucicault's creation of Shaun, the Irish rogue. Rogues were one of his specialities; it was in 1865 that he revised *Rip van Winkle* for Joseph Jefferson, touching up and strengthening the old play and giving the Dutch–American hero all the qualities that made his Irishmen irresistible. The rogue-hero is archetypal and readily adaptable to all nations.

The stagecraft of *Arrah-na-Pogue* received the signal compliment of imitation by Bernard Shaw, in his melodrama *The Devil's Disciple* (1897); the trial of Dick Dudgeon, in particular, shows Boucicault's influence.[2]

Not all melodrama at this time was cast in Boucicault's sophisticated mould. One of the most popular of all was *East Lynne* (Surrey 1866), which John Oxenford adapted from Mrs Henry Wood's novel (1861). But where she is subtle and persuasive, he is high-coloured and coarse, and only the long

---

[1] It appears that Taylor was not unwilling to have this play accepted as his unassisted invention, though it was an adaptation from a French original, *Léonard* by Brisbarre and Nus. Henry Morley comments: 'We know what would be said of a writer in any other department of literature, except only the stage, who, having translated into English with a few small changes and touches and a transformation of title, the book of any foreign author, should present it to the public as his own.' (*Journal of a London Playgoer* [1866], p. 312.) We are concerned here, however, with its fitness for the English stage, rather than with matters of literary morality, which in such affairs as this was in a confused state.

[2] Martin Meisel in *Shaw and the Nineteenth Century Theatre* (Princeton, 1963), pp. 195–8, discusses this matter in detail; the whole of this book is an interesting exposition of Shaw's debt to the theatre discussed here, and his lifelong dependence on its lessons in matters of theatrical effect.

success of his version on the stage persuades us that he knew what he was doing. In his hands the theme is virtually that of Rowe's *Jane Shore* (1713), in which 'that fatal fair, that cursed she' is brought to ruin and repentance not through her own weakness but through another's strength. Lady Isobel, though demonstrably not an honourable character, is an immensely sympathetic one, and she pays for her follies with death. The only explanation for the grip this play had when well presented was that there were many people in every audience whose guilt – real or in the world of fantasy – was stirred by that of Lady Isobel, and whose pity for her was in a strong measure also pity for themselves.

The drama of the last five years of this decade was dominated by the success of T. W. Robertson. His apprenticeship had been long: his first play, *A Night's Adventures* (Olympic 1851), was written when he was twenty-two, and was followed by thirteen years of indifferent success as a writer and actor until his first undoubted triumph with *David Garrick* (Hay 1864). Even this success was not immediate: the play had been very poorly received in Birmingham before the London production. The plot is an unhistorical absurdity: Garrick, while playing Romeo, has fallen in love with a girl in one of the boxes; the girl, Ada Ingot, has also fallen in love with him, to the dismay of her father, a rich London merchant; Ingot persuades Garrick to disgust Ada by his drunken behaviour at a dinner party, but the deception is discovered and Ada and Garrick are betrothed. The melodramatic elements are many and bluntly introduced; Garrick grieves for his mother, whose heart broke when he became an actor; old Ingot asserts a father's claims in a fashion that recalls Macready's fondness for father-drama; the glamour and pathos of the player's lot are exploited in terms that seem to owe much to *Masks and Faces*; the bittersweet of renunciation is strongly invoked.

Nevertheless this seemingly unremarkable play was a favourite with many leading actors, held the London stage till 1902 and could be seen in the repertoire of Sir John Martin-Harvey until 1928.[1] It gives an opportunity for virtuosity that could not fail in graceful hands, for in Act II Garrick pretends to be uproariously drunk, to the outrage of Ingot's guests; but – and this seems to be the secret – his drunkenness, though extreme, finds him a gentleman and a charmer still, and the London citizens about him are

[1] The text of *David Garrick*, like that of many another popular nineteenth-century play, was subjected to occasional revision and bringing up to date. Sir John Martin-Harvey's promptbook shows Robertson's text reworked by James Albery for Sir Charles Wyndham, with an additional scene of five typewritten pages for Martin-Harvey's use, written by the Reverend Canon Langbridge.

boors. This provides the audience with a rare feast of snobbery of a sort they continued to enjoy at least until 1914; the great success of Anstey's *The Man from Blankley's* (1901), which is a reworking of this situation, is another example. Indeed, the delight of seeing clever and accomplished people score off vulgar and ill-graced people is by no means exhausted in the theatre, and the only possible comment seems to be W. S. Gilbert's:

> It's human natur', p'raps – if so,
> Oh, isn't human natur' low![1]

Robertson's next play, and a decided success, was *Society* (Prince of Wales's 1865). Here one of this writer's principal defects exhibits itself: he wrote of conventional, upper-class life, but he does not seem to have been well acquainted with its underlying structure, and he is sometimes shaky in matters of detail that could easily have been checked. Three generations of theatre life, and what appears to have been a congenital underdog cast of mind, make him a poor commentator on the lives of people in privileged or easy circumstances. In *Society* his idea of the life of the people he depicts is jejune; his titled people have a sense of honour that is wholly concerned with money, yet their scorn of Chodd, the plebeian, is complete. Lady Ptarmigant appears to have been conceived simply as a character to produce laughs – the older woman who serves as an impediment to true love and whose point of view changes for no reason except the needs of the plot. Because its values are ill understood by the writer, the play now appears mechanical and muddled.

Ours (Prince of Wales's 1866) is an improvement on *Society*, for it is more carefully plotted and moves with ease. The characters, also, are fuller and more credible, with the exception of Lady Shendryn; Robertson seems to have been unable to deny himself the depiction of these older women of high position, though he has an absurd notion of what they were like – a notion that the reading of a few novels of Trollope would have corrected. This author's frequently praised device of contrapuntal dialogue, in which four characters carry on two conversations, seemingly at the same time, that show two opinions on the same subject, is displayed in Act II. But in the same act Robertson cannot resist the satisfaction of putting Blanche and Angus into a tableau which recalls to the audience Millais's picture of 'The Black Brunswicker'. Indeed, as we read Robertson we are aware that his dramatic imagination lacks vigour and courage and his psychology is stagy; he has some new ideas, but they are not powerful enough to overbear his

[1] 'Babette's Love', *Bab Ballads* (London, 1869).

commonplace sense of theatrical effect. In the social realm this is certainly so: nobody in this play of heroism steps outside the fashionable contemporary idea of chivalry – the silent sacrifice by the male to the supposed delicacy of women's feelings.

Caste (Prince of Wales's 1867) is generally acknowledged to be Robertson's finest play, and certainly it exhibits his strengths in matters of construction, natural dialogue and a well-controlled realism. It also shows his weaknesses – commonplace expression, an absurd notion of aristocratic feeling, and a mind not sufficiently powerful to be comic or tragic or romantic with any fullness of conviction, but with the stage cunning always to be fashionable.

The play has considerable subtlety on a small scale. The central problem of social position is fairly posed and the contrast between Old Eccles and the Marquise is telling. True, the Marquise shrinks from the idea that her son would debauch an innocent girl of a lower class, whereas this seems the logical solution of the problem to the parvenu Hawtrey and is assumed by Sam Gerridge; but such clever facets of the discussion are set at naught by the plain fact that Esther, the heroine, does not seem to be either the daughter of her father or the blood relative of her sister, being in fact nothing but the humourless, emotion-burdened heroine of conventional drama. Indeed it is Robertson's unfortunate habit to negate many of his real strokes of observation and truth to life by melodramatic situations that lack melodramatic strength, such as the confrontations that provide much of the development of his second act.

He is much happier when working within a framework of fantasy. *School* (Prince of Wales's 1869) is an idyll of the Cinderella order, and he fills it with characters of gentle comedy whose charm is undeniable. Robertson, the realist, is here pleasantly relieved of the need to be realistic. And before we blame Robertson too much, we must recall that the age did not encourage vivid characterization of women, especially young women. Wilkie Collins created girls with more grit and determination than these – in *No Name* (1862), for instance – but it was not the stage fashion of the time, and Robertson, having once found himself in the fashionable vein, was understandably in no hurry to desert it. The young ladies of *School* have undoubted charm, and that is what their author and the audiences required of them.

Robertson's realism, so often praised, seems upon consideration to have been more a matter of settings, ornamentation and the minor matters of deportment; he was a revolutionary stage manager, and an early example of the stage director; it would be wrong to underestimate his advances in such matters, but equally wrong to equate them with unusual ability as a dramatist – the kind of ability that rises above current fashion and establishes its own. In *Home* (Hay 1869) he is careful to specify the details of ornament and furnishing in his drawing-room setting which suffices for three acts; this in itself would lend support to the admirable scenes of comedy, and give them a sense of really happening in a recognizable upper-class house. But Robertson is too eager to assert his warm regard for womanhood in a type of comedy in which, when handled by such a master as Feydeau, womanhood must take its chance. And he is prepared to bring his curtain down on a sentimental and melodramatic denouement that robs the piece of any character that has been earlier established. Robertson was ahead of his time in several significant aspects, but he had not the artistic or intellectual stature to break the melodramatic mould or even to reshape it significantly, as did Boucicault.

Nevertheless, Robertson rises well above the achievement of such a playwright as H. J. Byron, one of whose great successes, *Uncle Dick's Darling* (Gaiety 1869), belongs to this era. As a play it is a cheat, for all the anguish that Uncle Dick endures is undergone in a dream, in which he sees his darling Mary as cruel and false; he wakes to find her all that he believed her to be. Apparently the play was given value by the fine quality of the acting of Toole as Uncle Dick and Irving as the stuffy Mr Chevenix, but it remains a piece in which the emotions of the audience are aroused in a way that is negated by the discovery that it has all been a dream. This does well in fantasy, but when serious and sentimental ideas are trifled with it is simply an imposture, and the dishonesty is unpleasant. Robertson never stooped to such trumpery; within his limitations he was honest.

No consideration of this decade would be complete without some reference to the many burlesques that enlivened it, all of which are signs of a changing taste. H. J. Byron's *The Rosebud of Stinging Nettle Farm* (Adelphi 1863) is a burlesque of a type of melodrama already becoming old-fashioned; it is of interest because it gives us, as a good burlesque should, much of the essence of what it mocks. This piece also pillories the arbitrary nature of melodramatic plot – an arbitrariness that Byron was ready to exploit in *Uncle Dick's Darling*. It suggests, too, that melodrama without sensation – wrecks, explosions, fires and the like – was running its course, and that the older works could only be preserved if the demonic genius of an Irving expanded their emotional scope.

The burlesques often show an ingenuity and wit superior to that of many of the original plays that supplied the ordinary fare of the stage. Byron's *Esmeralda* (Strand 1861) and *Little Don Giovanni* (Prince of Wales's 1865) and F. C. Burnand's *Faust and Marguerite* (St James's 1864) and *Black-Eyed Susan* (New Royalty 1866) are all good and representative examples of their kind. Their humour rests on a comic reversal of the original plot, presented with elaborate scenery, plenty of songs in which new words were set to popular airs, dialogue that was a network of elaborate puns, and the 'travesty' element in which girls played the heroes and comedians the heroines; they were exuberant, fast and witty in the mode of the time, and they were for audiences that no longer responded to the farce form of the first forty years of the century – a form that had grown fragile and wooden with the passing of time.

1870–1880

If farce was dwindling, light comedy was flourishing, for it was a favourite form of entertainment with the better-educated and superficially sophisticated audience which had begun to make its appearance in the theatre after the middle of the century.[1] But a fashionable, or partly fashionable and predominantly middle-class, audience makes for a narrowing of vision in the theatre – an insistence on what such an audience admires, and will accept as a representation of the life it knows. The larger-than-life figures of melodrama, and the emotionally expansive heroes and heroines of such a comedy as *Money* give place to the pleasing but spiritually unassuming men and women of Robertson's comedies and such successful pieces as James Albery's *Two Roses* (Vaudeville 1870). Its plot is well managed, its dialogue is witty but not brilliant and its characters are well realized without probing beneath the commonplaces of accepted notions of what men and women should be. Digby Grant is a good 'eccentric comedy' lead, and Caleb Deecie, who is blind, has the special authority that used to attach to picturesque affliction, but he uses it very mildly; the two roses, Lotty and Ida, are nice girls, just sufficiently witty and charming to impress the nice girls in the audience as flattering likenesses of themselves. There is nothing in this popular play to

[1] See also Part I (1), p. 14.

disturb anyone, and its reward was a satisfactory 294 performances and five revivals in twenty years.

Whether this polite conventionality impeded the growth of W. S. Gilbert as a playwright, or whether the philistinism that is to be found in all his work was truly characteristic of his mind, is a puzzle that will not quickly be solved; the likelihood seems to be that Gilbert was conventional and rebellious at once, and that the earthbound spirit of some of his fantasy and the sourness that underlies much of his comedy are the result of this conflict. He had made a beginning with *Dulcamara, or the Little Duck and the Great Quack* (St James's 1866), which is an extravaganza on *L'Elisir d'Amore* (1832); he had done a good deal of apprentice work before the success of *The Princess* (Olympic 1870), based on Tennyson's poem and itself the basis for the operetta *Princess Ida, or Castle Adamant* (Savoy 1884) for which Arthur Sullivan wrote the music; *The Princess* contained songs written for existing music. We see here much that is characteristic of Gilbert's work throughout his career: his wit has a sour but not displeasing aftertaste; he is a splendidly accomplished versifier without the emotional range of a poet; his moral outlook is conventional without being at ease in its conventionality, with the consequence that an exacerbated mockery often breaks through and suggests an underlying savagery of spirit. Gilbert, like many a humorist, seems to have been an angry man and a disappointed idealist; but never, in his work, does he give rein to the ferocity that so often characterized his wit in private life.[1]

His success was great, and his industry unflagging; of his more than seventy plays only a few can be mentioned, but as he was thrifty of his comic devices an acquaintance with the best of the thirteen operettas he wrote with Sullivan will reveal them all. The partnership with Sullivan supplied what Gilbert sorely needed – an ameliorating and truly poetic element; Sullivan's sweetness of spirit and his genuine if circumscribed musical genius create the atmosphere in which these brilliant works live; nor was Sullivan's music deficient in wit, as an examination of his scores will reveal to anyone who knows the operatic repertoire of his day and the music of Schumann, which was one of his special delights. Sullivan might have made something better

---

[1] Gilbert's wit was the terror of his acquaintance. The actor Seymour Hicks (*Between Ourselves* [London, 1930], pp. 49–53) says, 'he seemed incapable of geniality'; when someone said to him 'Mrs. So-and-so was very pretty once', his reply was 'Yes, but not twice'; so also he replied to the secretary of an amateur dramatic society, who had asked what Gilbert thought of his club, 'Oh, not so much a club as a bundle of sticks.' He did not confine his barbs to small fry: it was he who described Beerbohm Tree's performance of Hamlet as 'funny without being vulgar'. See also Hesketh Pearson, *Beerbohm Tree* (London, 1956).

of *The Palace of Truth* (Hay 1870); certainly the 'changed souls' theme of *The Gentleman in Black* (Charing Cross 1870) is very much better when it becomes the 'changed babies' of *H.M.S. Pinafore* (Opera Comique 1878). Gilbert called this sort of thing 'topsy-turveydom' and it is the realm in which his best work is done, as such a modest piece as *Creatures of Impulse* (Court 1871) shows.

The greatest deficiency of Gilbert's comedies, as distinguished from his fantastic productions, is his failure to create pleasing or interesting women. Too often, if they are not mindless heroines of seventeen, they are scheming middle-aged viragoes, mocked for their ugliness, foolishly concerned to conceal their years and pitifully avid for men. *Randall's Thumb* (Court 1871) is a characteristic example of Gilbert's light comedy: Buckthorpe believes himself to have committed a murder, though in self-defence, and thus comes 'under the thumb' of Randall, himself a criminal known to the police as 'the Rum Customer'. Its technique is impeccable; much of the dialogue is very funny; but the dominating spirit is tainted with the author's ambiguous attitude towards women.

Pygmalion and Galatea (Hay 1871) was regarded by contemporary critics as Gilbert's best play; it was an undoubted success, enjoying ten important London revivals, the last in 1919, but modern readers may feel that the classical plot has been stuffily Victorianized. Galatea comes to life, and it appears that she may come between Pygmalion and his wife Cynisca; any interference with the marriage vow is unthinkable, so Galatea returns to stone, after a scene of renunciation. The atmosphere is oppressively middle class, in spite of Pygmalion's insistence on his station as an artist; Cynisca is conceived as a small-souled shrew, who regards blindness as a proper punishment for an erring husband; there is a prurience about the attitude towards sex in the play that shows Gilbert at his least likeable. The success of the play is a comment on its age. As we survey his career we may be glad that in *Thespis, or the Gods Grown Old* (Gaiety 1871) he made his first redemptive contact with Sullivan.

The littleness of spirit that troubles us in Gilbert's plays, and which was at least in part a reflection of the taste of his fashionable audience, did not dominate the whole of the theatre. *The Bells* (Lyceum 1871), by Leopold Lewis, was an adaptation from *Le Juif Polonais* by Erckmann and Chatrian, but as a stage success it was the creation of Henry Irving. As literature it need not detain us, but as Irving played it the piece became an evocation of a world where people were larger than life, where emotions reached beyond common experience, and above all a world of poetic justice; in fact, the world of the best of melodrama. If *Two Roses* was the realism of the day, we need not wonder that audiences responded eagerly to the greater psychological satisfactions of *The Bells*.[1]

Not all Irving's melodramas are capable of suggesting to us that they were once vehicles for great acting. W. G. Wills's *Charles the First* (Lyceum 1872) is a determinedly poetic piece, loaded with metaphor, simile and self-conscious archaism to a degree that makes absurd the author's claim in his preface that he 'had looked to the monuments of the grand Elizabethan age' for example. It is a falsification of history, for though it is possible to think that Cromwell was a rogue, it is absurd to present him as a fool, which is what Wills does. The play is too blatantly weighted to provoke pity for the king, and it serves now only to corroborate the remark of the elder Dumas that one should never ravish history unless one is capable of getting a child by her.

The hold of melodrama, which now usually meant also costume drama, was strong. Wandering Jew plays recur in the history of drama[2] and there were three of them in 1873, of which the best was *The Wandering Jew* (Britannia 1873) by George Landor Whiting, adapted from Eugene Sue's romance (1845). It is a rapidly paced play, filled with stirring incident, but there can be no doubt that the Jew himself makes it so, even though he appears only occasionally as a *deus ex machina*. It is the largeness of scope, the room they give for imaginative extension, that explains the popularity of these works that are so easily mocked. *The Two Orphans* (Olympic 1874), adapted by John Oxenford from the French of Dennery and Cormen, is a strongly sentimental piece, set in 1785; it wrings the heart with the spectacle of two orphans separated on their arrival in Paris from the country, and the menaces to the virtue of Henriette, endured while her blind companion, Louise, supposed to be her sister, is made to beg in the street by the vicious beldame La Frochard; of course they both are saved and discover that Louise, the blind girl, is of high estate before the play ends. It is significant that this play was French, and had a European reputation; melodrama was not an English phenomenon. It is also significant that so sentimental a play held the stage for at least twenty years and was filmed in 1911, 1915 and 1922; obviously it has elements in it that millions of people want, and that drama of manifestly greater literary merit sometimes fails to give them.

[1] For an eye-witness description of Irving's performance in the role of the haunted Mathias, see *Henry Irving*, by Gordon Craig (London, 1930; New York, 1930), pp. 47–59. It should be noted that *The Bells* was never called a melodrama during Irving's lifetime, an indication that the term had already acquired a pejorative connotation.

[2] E. Temple Thurston's play on this theme (not from Sue) was played at the New Theatre in 1920, and had five revivals, the last in 1953.

Not all these desired elements are lachrymose: high-hearted romance and chivalry are among them, and *Lady Clancarty* (Olympic 1874) by Tom Taylor provided these so successfully that it held the stage until 1907. In it Lord and Lady Clancarty, who were married at the ages of fifteen and twelve, and who have been parted for ten years, meet again but are unknown to one another; he has been serving James II in exile, and her father and brother are adherents of William of Orange. Clancarty, though a Jacobite, is a gentleman first, and he warns King William of an assassination plot; at last he is pardoned by the king and is united with his wife, with whom he has fallen in love. It is an agreeably sophisticated and literate play, and interesting in that, like *David Garrick*, it permits the audience a generous portion of vicarious snobbery.

Snobbery is a strong element also in *The Shaughran* (DL 1875), which is the last exhibition of what Gilbert, in *Patience* (1881), was to call 'the pathos of Paddy, as rendered by Boucicault'; the audience is invited to take sides with the impoverished but noble-minded Irish aristocracy and their devil-may-care peasantry against an unprincipled squireen who dares to aspire to a lady's hand. It is obviously commendable to be either upper class or lower class, but not to be on the steep and thorny road from low to high; the convolutions of feeling that make such plays as this successful with a predominantly middle-class audience are the concern of the psychologist or the sociologist. A modern reader may be puzzled to know what it is that makes Corry Kinchela so objectionable to all the other characters; it is simply because he is described in the dramatis personae as 'a Squireen', with the implication that he is a social climber and has the characteristic mean-ness of spirit which was associated with this type of person in the nineteenth century. The puzzle is in no way rendered easier of solution by the fact that by far the ablest man in the play is Conn the Shaughran, a fiddler and mani-festly of strong artistic temperament. Making money seems to be the only talent unworthy of applause.

In this era we meet with plays whose popularity is far less easily explicable in modern terms than are those of Jerrold or Sheridan Knowles, and this is because they are for audiences either in themselves fashionable or desirous of seeing what is in fashion. Such a play is H. J. Byron's *Our Boys* (Vaudeville 1875), which, for all its trashy dialogue and thin psychology, ran for 1,362 performances on its first production (a record for the time), and was revived at intervals until 1914. The 'boys' of the title are Talbot Champneys and Charles Middlewick, respectively the son of a county magnate and a wealthy retired butterman; both are 'trumps' and too proud to knuckle under to their domineering fathers; of course fathers and sons are reconciled at last. The prurience already commented upon in some of the work of Gilbert is marked in the productions of the less gifted Byron, and the 'tease' scene in Act III, when the heroines think the boys have a woman concealed in their lodgings, is a masterpiece of squirming Victorian nastiness. It is an error to think that sex was not presented on the nineteenth-century stage with erotic intention; at its best it is as subtly erotic as the paintings of Tissot and at its worst it drops to the level of the seaside postcard.

No useful purpose is served by pursuing Gilbert's career through all the plays he wrote during this decade. Sometimes he offers a charming piece of sentiment, as in *Sweethearts* (Prince of Wales's 1874), which does not aim very high, but gains stature by the completeness of its achievement. Sometimes he strives to be topical, as in *Charity* (Hay 1874), in which he essays the problem of the woman who has 'fallen'; he begins with the assumption that this is the offence for which no forgiveness is possible, and then loads the dice so heavily in favour of his heroine that she seems less to have fallen than soared, so noble and sinned-against is she; thus his play is safe from criticism, and may have deceived some audiences into the notion that they were thinking deeply about a moral problem.

If Gilbert is uncomfortable and commonplace when he touches realities, he has a featherlike touch with farce. *Tom Cobb, or Fortune's Toy* (St James's 1875) is all invention and fun, sustained for three acts by delightful comic dialogue. We can hardly believe that he is the same man who contrived the leaden *Dan'l Druce, Blacksmith* (Hay 1876), a costume drama that draws heavily on *Silas Marner*, and is sodden with the 'thees' and 'thous' of 'period' dialogue. It is in such plays as *Engaged* (Hay 1877) that we find his best inventions – the seemingly dewy but financially astute maiden, the unwilling suicide looking for someone to dissuade him, the man who confesses that he is irresistible to women. Deliver Gilbert from the shackles of what he assumed to be serious, and he takes wing splendidly.

This is the secret of the operettas he wrote with Sullivan: he need not be serious or reassuringly moral. These musical pieces which have been so lovingly preserved into the present day by the family of the original impresario, Richard D'Oyly Carte,[1] are an invaluable aid to the student of nineteenth-century drama, for countless traditions of posture, delivery and

---

[1] The writer, as a schoolboy, took part in productions of four of these works that were directed by a stage manager who had been trained under Gilbert's stage manager at the Savoy; he insisted on strictly traditional performance, and his warmest commendation was, 'Children, Mr Gilbert would have liked that!'

emphasis are preserved in them, from the melodrama Gilbert remembered well and mocked with affection. Such theatrical fossils are especially apparent in *H.M.S. Pinafore* (Opera Comique 1878), *The Pirates of Penzance* (Opera Comique 1880), and *Ruddigore, or The Witch's Curse* (Savoy 1887), and to have seen them performed by the D'Oyly Carte Company is to have seen the nautical, pirate and 'domestic' melodrama of the 1820–50 period through a glass of champagne. Indeed, all the Savoy operas, as they came to be called, relate to an earlier stage, and often it is the stage of which R. L. Stevenson wrote in 'Penny Plain and Twopence Coloured' (1887).

It was a stage by no means dead at the end of the period here under consideration. *The Wreckers* (Britannia 1878) by Fred Marchant and Cecil Pitt, a stage manager's copy of which is in the writer's possession, shows that in this thrilling realm of dark secrets, foundling heroes and true-hearted funnymen, nothing had really changed since 1820. Nor had the manner of hasty composition been markedly influenced by the careful techniques of more sophisticated drama, for the excisions, additions and overwritings speak of a theatre in which the authors worked against time, racing along well-understood paths.

Conclusion

The chronological plan of this consideration of the drama between 1750 and 1880 was adopted in order to show, so far as the scope of such a study allows, what actually happened in the theatre during a period of 130 years. Though talent was abundant, no playwright of dominating influence arose, and the theatre gave no leadership in the revolution of taste that dismissed Augustan ideals in favour of those of the Romantic movement. Indeed, Augustan taste lingered rather longer in the theatre than elsewhere: it was congenial to an audience in which the weight of judgement was on the side of men of classical education, and it appealed to reason. The romantic taste which superseded it appealed, on the contrary, to feeling; thus it won the favour of the women, though women were not, for several decades, a strong element in the theatre audience; but the new taste appealed to the new audience of people whose education was neither classical nor extensive, but who were not for this reason intellectually inert, and who had a strong sense of what they expected a play to be.

What they wanted was vitality, which was a quality the waning Augustan taste notably lacked. Its tragedy was gloomy and insipid; its comedy was better, but by 1800 it was too plainly a comedy of stereotypes, enlivened by a skilled use of language – very much a 'literary' comedy. What the new taste demanded was a kind of play that was very like a dream, in that it set the dreamer directly in the heart of the action, bodying forth deep though ill-defined feelings and offering compensation for some of the insufficiencies of waking life. All vital drama has something of this character; the romantic spirit of the new age demanded it in generous measure. Few plays during the first fifty years of our period met this requirement; *Douglas* and *The Gamester* were notable exceptions. The Gothic drama and its successor, melodrama, strove consciously to follow the new path. The purpose of the new drama was to explore that inner world of the psyche where the un-finished business of life is to be found – the wounds that have not been healed, the sorrows that have not been assuaged, the loves that have not been requited, the sense of having been used less than justly by life – and to offer the solace of chivalry, constancy and renunciation; it asserted the existence of a Providence that would give the good man, after heavy trials, his due. For the tragic concept of a Fate indifferent to merely human and personal concerns it substituted poetic justice.

As the mainspring of drama it exchanged a desiccated classicism for a vital, if often coarse, humanism. Nothing in melodrama is without meaning or attributable only to chance; its often excessive reliance on coincidence reflects a nineteenth-century desire to understand and explain fortune – a desire not far from the wish to command fortune. It exchanged the reasoned and polished language of the eighteenth century – a language quite as useful for disguising lack of content as for explicating it – for the hot and sometimes absurd language of passion. 'I must give it to you in high-sounding language, for the Fates are pompous', says Lucy to Beaugard, when she tells his fortune in *The Review* (1800). Why are the Fates pompous? We find a clue in *Memories, Dreams, Reflections* by C. G. Jung. Describing the complex technique by which he explored those fundamental patterns he calls 'archetypes', he writes:

> I wrote down the fantasies as well as I could, and made an earnest effort to analyze the psychic conditions under which they had arisen. But I was able to do this only in clumsy language. First I formulated the things as I had observed them, usually in 'high-flown language', for that corresponds to the style of the archetypes. Archetypes speak the language of high rhetoric, even of bombast. It is a style I find embarrassing; it grates on my nerves, as when someone draws his nails down a plaster wall, or scrapes his knife against a plate. I had no choice but to write everything down in the style selected by the unconscious itself.

. . . Below the threshold of consciousness everything was seething with life![1]

It is from the source thus explored by Jung that much of the literature of romance comes, but the melodramatic playwrights, many of them men of humble gifts and limited sensibility, seem often to have transferred the bombast of their inspiration directly to the page without any of the alchemy observable, for instance, in the dramatic verse of Byron or Coleridge. But even at its worst, melodrama continued to draw on that realm where 'everything was seething with life', and to transfer as much as possible of that extraordinary psychic vitality to the stage. The plays, so neglectful of the externals of reality, were psychologically convincing because they spoke from these depths to corresponding depths in their audiences.

Melodrama had another source of eloquence in the music that suggested its name. A thorough study of the music that accompanied melodrama cannot be attempted here, but it should not be forgotten; unlike the acting of Kean, Macready and Irving, it is recoverable through a study of existing scores written for particular plays. Reference has been made to the many directions for music in Holcroft's *A Tale of Mystery* (1802); the score for Kenney's *The Blind Boy* (1807) is an early example of melodrama music that achieved sufficient popularity to warrant publication. But most of this music remains in manuscript, and the humbler theatres had simple themes of 'hurry music', 'combat music' and 'love music' applicable to many plays, and comparable to 'stock' scenery.

A superior melodrama would as a matter of course have a score of its own. A characteristic example is M. E. Singla's music for *The Bells*.[2] It begins

---

[1] *Memories, Dreams, Reflections (Erinnerungen, Traüme, Gedanken)*, trans. Richard and Clara Winston (New York, 1963), pp. 177–8.

[2] Unpublished; the description offered here is from Irving's full score, in the writer's possession. It is of interest to compare Singla's score, so carefully fitted to the dramatic necessities of *The Bells*, with what served as incidental music at the beginning of the century. In Michael Kelly's music for *Pizarro* the 'Grand March in the Temple of the Sun' is the work of Kelly himself, but he has borrowed the 'March of Priests and Priestesses' from Gluck; some of the songs are Kelly's, but there is one each by Sacchini and Cherubini. The published music for *The Castle Spectre* consists of a song in an idiom that Kelly may have thought to be Celtic, a scrap of a 'Spectre Song', twenty bars of music for horns, a clarinet and a piano, to be heard 'from the Oratory when the Ghost appears', and a 'Jubilate on the Ghost's retiring'; obviously more music than this must have been used in production, and one presumes it was chosen from the popular repertory, much as in the days of silent film, when 'thematic cue sheets' were provided for the pianist, so that he could select suitable music from perhaps 1,000 pieces known to him. Sometimes, as in *The Red Cross Knights* (2 May 1799), a composer of eminence, in this case Thomas Attwood, provided settings for the necessary songs, drawing upon Mozart

with a substantial overture. After an attention-claiming flourish of ten bars it goes at once into a theme of sleighbells, jingling in trotting rhythm above an accompaniment of bassoon and strings. Irving did not trust to any chance orchestral effect, but used special bells chosen to produce the particular mood of mystery he wanted. After twenty-three bars of this a succession of four themes illustrative of various elements in the play are developed, ending with a formal 'finale' succession of fateful chords to take the curtain up. The music is scored for an orchestra of fourteen instruments, with percussion in addition. There are twenty-seven music cues in all; some are of substantial length, to introduce the second and third acts and to support ensemble scenes; others are of a few bars only, to emphasize climaxes in the action. The music, without being distinguished, is literate and sophisticated, using folk-song themes to suggest the rustic setting of the play, but now and then employing these with ironic intent – to suggest, for instance, the peace and innocence of the village while Mathias is struggling with his burden of guilt. Themes accompanying the vision of the Polish Jew, or Mathias's mounting dread, are simple and dramatically effective, but not trite. This score is obviously a valuable element in creating the total effect of the play; its relation to the drama and the quality of its workmanship are characteristic of many others.

If the language of melodrama was the rhetoric of the archetypes, the logo-daedaly of the extravaganza may perhaps be called their wit. One of the

---

when he chose, and securing an important trio from another well-known composer of the day, J. W. Callcott. We can only suppose that scores assembled in this way, though they certainly supported the drama and created atmosphere, gave an impression of opera rather than of music subservient to a dramatic unity; action must have stopped until the music had made its effect, which was to be pleasing rather than to explain character or suggest psychological action. But the stage directions for *A Tale of Mystery* (1802) show how music, even if not specially composed for the play, was being put to more effective use as a guide and spur to emotion. This was true 'melodrama', as it was understood, for instance, by Liszt, who experimented with spoken words and musical accompaniment as sensitively as any musician who has ever given his mind to the problem such a combination creates. But we must constantly remind ourselves that any theatrical convention, once it has been accepted, passes unnoticed by the greater part of every audience. Audiences at *Pizarro* doubtless found the music they heard suitable; critics rarely commented on Singla's music for *The Bells*; in our own time cinema scores of great sophistication and sometimes of distinction (Ralph Vaughan Williams's seven film scores between 1940 and 1949 come to mind) are not objects of special interest to audiences, for they are not so much heard as felt. It is as an assistance to feeling, rather than as an intellectual pleasure, that music enters the theatre, and the many ways in which it has performed its task offer a subject of the greatest interest, though it still awaits its careful historian.

principal charms of these entertainments was an ingenious anarchy of language, pun being heaped upon pun until the listener might well suppose that nothing he heard meant exactly what it said. The writer does not seek to push this psychological approach to the language of the nineteenth-century drama to an extreme, but Freud has argued that wit is a means of seeking relief from unconscious pressures and inhibitions, and certainly the nineteenth century had its full share of these.[1] Freud says that young children play with words as if they were objects, until the necessities of growth force them to accept logic and reality; but by recapturing the pleasure of word play, something of the freedom and happiness of childhood is also recaptured. By this means, like melodrama, the extravaganzas seek to slip past the gates of reason, and to appeal to their audiences on a deeper level; in a social setting where the reality and earnestness of life was so often and so powerfully asserted the agreeable madness of the language of extravaganza must have offered a delightful surcease.

If what is written here seems to stress the claims of melodrama at the expense of drama that sought to give a more measured and externally realistic representation of life, it is quite simply because melodrama was self-assured and vital whereas the other drama was tentative. However crude the effect might sometimes be, the melodrama authors did not wholly shrink from that battle with troll folk in the crypts of heart and head which Ibsen said was the essence of life;[2] so far as the conventions of the nineteenth century permitted, they attempted to deal with much that was personal, subjective and psychologically daring, and we must sometimes be astonished by the vividness with which, in the first fifty years of the nineteenth century, they made the essence of the Romantic movement available to sections of the public that would be unlikely to encounter it in any other form. Melodrama was the accepted mode of the theatre of the first eighty years of the nineteenth century; Shakespeare and other classics were offered to the public in the melodramatic style and with their melodramatic values emphasized. Melodrama was Dionysian on a generous scale; the playwrights like Robertson and Gilbert were but waveringly Apollonian, and when they sought to evoke strong emotion it was half-hearted melodrama that they wrote. The best writers of melodrama were by no means wanting in literary merit,

[1] Sigmund Freud, *Wit and Its Relation to the Unconscious*, trans. A. A. Brill (London, 1905). The section on puns, being translated from German, is not especially illuminating, but the argument of the book as a whole is strongly relevant to our theme.

[2] In a letter to Ludwig Passarge (16 June 1880), quoted in Michael Meyer, *Henrik Ibsen*, II (London, 1971).

though none emerges as an artist of the first rank; it is unjust to dismiss their work because a few of the melodramas that are now remembered for their absurdities of plot and language have given the term 'melodrama' a pejorative cast. If melodrama does not accord with a high ideal of literature, it suggests that the theatre can get along without obviously literary content for a surprisingly long time, but that it cannot endure without emotion and passionate appeal.

It has sometimes escaped the attention of scholars whose preoccupation is chiefly with literary matters that a substantial quantity of the best melodrama is still vital and popular in the repertoires of the opera houses and ballet theatres of the world, and that as opera and ballet they engage the deeply serious attention of some of the foremost theatre artists of our time, drawing large and by no means simple-minded audiences. It is only the emphasis that has changed: music has replaced language as the primary means of expression, and language supports music. A fine performance of *Rigoletto* or *Le Lac des Cygnes* is an experience through which we can discern, and by no means dimly, the quality of melodrama at its best. Nor is it irrelevant that opera and ballet are international in appeal, as was melodrama during the period when translation, adaptation and downright stealing quickly wafted a new play through Europe and America. If we look for a supreme genius of melodrama we shall find him in no playwright but in Giuseppe Verdi; nor should the operas of Tchaikovsky be neglected by anyone who seeks to recapture the bittersweet, haunting quality of the costume drama of the nineteenth century.

If the period 1750–1880 offers little to the scholar intent upon literature, it will long continue to provide a feast for the scholar of the theatre, for it was splendidly and variously theatrical.

Bibliography

I Social and literary context

Several standard works are indispensable for anyone doing serious research in the period 1750–1880. One of these, *The London Stage, 1660–1880; Part 4*, ed. George Winchester Stone Jr (Carbondale, Ill., 1962), is concerned with Covent Garden, Drury Lane and the Haymarket during Garrick's managerial tenure, 1747–76; *Part 5*, ed. Charles Beecher Hogan (Carbondale, Ill., 1968), extends this coverage to 1800 and also takes account of the rise of the new theatres. Both volumes contain not only a vast amount of accurate theatrical information and a day-by-day account of the repertory, but also comment on audiences, trends in taste and moral attitudes in the theatre. Essential also is Allardyce Nicoll, *A History of English Drama, 1660–1900* (Cambridge, 1966). The volumes for 1750–1900, III–V, contain valuable introductory chapters on the theatre, on the audience, and on actors, managers and authors. The only extensive bibliography for our period is James F. Arnott and J. W. Robinson, *English Theatrical Literature 1559–1900: a bibliography incorporating Lowe's Bibliographical Account* (London, 1971).

Descriptions of audience behaviour and contemporary attitudes to the stage can profitably be obtained from the English translation of Prince Hermann von Pückler-Muskau, *Tour of a German Prince*, 4 vols (London,

1832). Pückler-Muskau was a visitor to the London stage in the 1820s; an account of earlier tourist reaction to English theatres and audiences is given in John A. Kelly, *German Visitors to the English Theatres in the Eighteenth Century* (Princeton, NJ, 1936). There is interesting social comment, as well as reactions to particular plays and actors, in two minor records: *The London Theatre, 1811–1866*, ed. V. C. Clinton-Baddeley (London, 1966), a selection of theatrical items from the diary of Henry Crabb Robinson; and *The London Theatre in the Eighteen-Thirties*, ed. A. C. Sprague and Bertram Shuttleworth (London, 1950), a similar treatment of the journal of a theatre-loving clerk, Charles Rice. A great variety of information on the licensing of theatres, the role of the Lord Chamberlain, the attitudes of and the censorship exercised by the Examiner of Plays, the composition of audiences, the income of play-wrights and their relations with managers, the 'decline of the drama' and a host of other matters, can be found in two sets of parliamentary committee proceedings: the *Report from the Select Committee on Dramatic Literature* (London, 1832) and the *Report of the Select Committee on Theatrical Licences and Regulations* (London, 1866).

Several theatrical histories either contemporary with or close to many of the events they relate are relevant to the first two sections in this volume. Benjamin Victor, *A History of the Theatres of London and Dublin*, 3 vols (London, 1761–71), although too early for much of our period, is interesting on the Garrick years at Drury Lane. Alfred Bunn, *The Stage*, 3 vols (London, 1840), while a justification of Bunn's complicated managerial activities, has much that is valuable on the theatre of the 1830s. Percy Fitzgerald, *A New History of the English Stage*, 2 vols (London, 1882), ends its survey of patent theatre history in 1843; Henry Barton Baker, *History of the London Stage*, 2nd ed. (London, 1904), concludes in 1903 and is much more extensive, especially in treating nineteenth-century West End and East End playhouses, their character and their audience. Neither book is always accurate, but there is much information in Baker unavailable in more modern studies. Henry Morley, *Journal of a London Playgoer* (London, 1891), a personal record of theatregoing from 1851 to 1866, comments mostly on performances and plays, but also remarks on audiences and social attitudes. More general and historical in nature, as well as socially more interesting, is Edward Dutton Cook, *A Book of the Play*, 2 vols (London, 1876). Henry James, *The Scenic Art* (New York, 1957), has three essays on the London theatre in 1877, 1879, and 1880. William Bodham Donne, *Essays on the Drama* (London, 1858), is a collection of critical essays touching on general subjects, and Clement Scott, *The Drama of Yesterday and Today*, 2 vols (London, 1899), contains the theatrical memories, from the 1840s to the 1890s, of the leading critic of his day.

Scott's work tends to diffuseness and anecdote, and these qualities, combined with inaccuracy, confused chronology and tedious irrelevancies, are the major sins of the innumerable theatrical memoirs, biographies and autobiographies of the eighteenth and nineteenth centuries. However, collectively they represent a large mass of material, some of it extremely valuable, and the better written and more reliable ones are significant works in their own right. The following provide a variety of useful information concerning audiences, the prosperity of the theatre, the position and income of the playwright, the copyright laws, the Examiner of Plays, public taste, etc.: Thomas Davies, *Memoirs of the Life of David Garrick*, 2 vols (London, 1780; repr. New York, 1969); James Boaden, *Memoirs of the Life of John Philip Kemble, Esq.*, 2 vols (London, 1825; repr. New York, 1969) and *Memoirs of Mrs Siddons*, 2 vols (London, 1827; repr. New York, 1969); Frederick Reynolds, *The Life and Times of Frederick Reynolds*, 2 vols (London, 1826); Thomas Dibdin, *Reminiscences*, 2 vols (London, 1827); *The Memoirs of Charles Dibdin the Younger*, ed. George Speaight (London, 1956); R. B. Peake, *Memoirs of the Colman Family*, 2 vols (London, 1841); 'J. W. Cole' [J. W. Calcraft], *The Life and Theatrical Times of Charles Kean*, 2 vols (London, 1859); Edward Fitzball (originally Ball), *Thirty-five years of a Dramatic Author's Life*, 2 vols (London, 1859); Squire and Marie Bancroft, *Mr and Mrs Bancroft on and off the Stage*, 2 vols (London, 1888); J. R. Planché, *Recollections and Reflections*, rev. ed. (London, 1901).

Of these memoirs, only those by the Dibdins and Fitzball offer much comment on the audiences of minor theatres and their tastes; the remainder concentrate on the patent theatres and the main West End houses. Henry Mayhew, *London Labour and the London Poor*, 4 vols (London, 1861–2; partially published in numbers, London, 1851), has something on the theatrical taste of costermongers and audience behaviour in the Victorian Theatre. Thomas W. Erle, *Letters from a Theatrical Scene Painter* (London, privately printed, 1880), is a series of hostile but vivid impressions of East End audiences that is also valuable for its account of acting and staging outside the West End. Several pieces by Dickens are relevant here: 'The Theatrical Young Gentleman' in *Sketches by Boz* (London, 1837) describes the theatrical taste of this representative of the working class; 'The Amusements of the People', *Household Words*, 30 March and 15 April 1850, deals with the behaviour, composition and attitudes of audiences in working-class melodrama houses; 'Two Views of a Cheap Theatre', in *The Uncommercial Traveller* (London, 1860), treats of the same topics with specific regard to the Britannia Theatre. Two modern studies, Albert E. Wilson, *East End Entertainment* (London, 1954), and Frances Fleetwood, *Conquest: the Story of a Theatre Family* (London, 1953), contain non-West-End material of interest.

The standard work dealing with the complex history of the Licensing Act and the attack upon patent privileges, down to 1843, is Watson Nicholson, *The Struggle for a Free Stage in London* (London and Cambridge, Mass., 1906). A helpful general background to the question of the income of playwrights is A. S. Collins, *The Profession of Letters* (London, 1928). Thomas J. Thackeray, *On Theatrical Emancipation and the Rights of Dramatic Authors* (London, 1832), is informative on the comparative earning power of French playwrights as well as on the legal position of dramatists and their relations with managers prior to the passage of the Dramatic Copyright Act. John Coryton, *Stageright* (London, 1873), is a summary of laws then in force relating to dramatic copyright; a later work of the same kind is Bernard Weller, *Stage Copyright at Home and Abroad* (London, 1912).

This section of the bibliography can conclude with several modern studies. Both J. J. Lynch, *Box, Pit, and Gallery* (Berkeley, Calif., 1953), and Harry W. Pedicord, *The Theatrical Public in the Time of Garrick* (New York, 1954), concern themselves with social analysis of playgoers, audience behaviour and audience attitudes in the London of Garrick and Dr Johnson, but Pedicord's is the more scholarly and authoritative work. George Rowell, *The Victorian Theatre* (Oxford, 1956; new ed. 1967), is a general introduction to the period 1792–1914, with some comment on the changing nature of audiences and their tastes. One of the best histories of the nineteenth-century theatre, including chapters on London life and the stage, the theatrical monopoly, the command of audiences and an appendix on the income of dramatists, is Ernest Bradlee Watson, *Sheridan to Robertson* (Cambridge, Mass., 1926).

II (I)   Theatres and stages

Anon., 'A New Stage Stride', *All The Year Round* (31 October 1863); *The Art Journal* (London, 1853); J. Boaden, *The Life of J. P. Kemble* (London, 1825); Colley Cibber, *An Apology for his Life* (London, 1740); Clément Contant, *Parallèle des principaux théâtres modernes de l'Europe* (Paris, 1859); Percy Fitzgerald, *The World behind the Scenes* (London, 1881); 'David Groove', letter in *The Great Gun* No. 7 (London, 1884); *The Industrial World* (October 1932); Frederick Lloyds, *Practical Guide to Scene Painting* (London, nd–?1875); Raymond Mander and Joe Mitchenson, *London's Lost Theatres*

(London, 1968); Edwin O. Sachs, *Modern Opera Houses and Theatres* (London, 1896-9); Richard Southern, *Changeable Scenery* (London, 1952), 'Concerning a Georgian proscenium ceiling', *Theatre Notebook*, III (1948), 'Interesting matter relating to the scenery, decorations etc. of the Theatre Royal, Tackett Street, Ipswich', *Architectural Review* (August 1946) and 'The picture-frame proscenium of 1880', *Theatre Notebook*, V (1951), *The Victorian Theatre, a pictorial survey* (London, 1970); William Telbin Jr, 'Scenery', *The Magazine of Art* (1889).

II (II)   Actors and their repertory

(i) GENERAL

Useful as initial general introductions to the performers and managers of the period 1758-1880 are such standard works as Allardyce Nicoll's *A History of English Drama 1660-1900*, III-V (Cambridge, 1966), G. C. D. Odell's *Shakespeare from Betterton to Irving*, 2 vols (London, 1920; repr. New York, 1963), E. B. Watson's *Sheridan to Robertson* (Cambridge, Mass., 1926), and the relevant volumes of *The London Stage: Part 4, 1747-1776*, ed. George Winchester Stone Jr, 3 vols (Carbondale, Ill., 1962) and *Part 5, 1776-1880*, ed. Charles Beecher Hogan, 3 vols (Carbondale, Ill., 1968). *Actors and Actresses of Great Britain and the United States*, 5 vols (New York, 1886), the title of which is self-explanatory, is a monumental survey by Brander Matthews and Laurence Hutton ranging from the Garrick period to the date of publication. Still extremely informative is the pioneering work by Karl Mantzius entitled *Skuespilkunstens Historie*, V-VI (Copenhagen, 1916-17), translated into English as *A History of Theatrical Art in Ancient and Modern Times*, 6 vols (London, 1903-21).

Arthur Colby Sprague's investigations of Shakespearian performance traditions – *Shakespeare and the Actors* (Cambridge, Mass., 1944; repr. New York, 1963) and *Shakespearian Players and Performances* (Cambridge, Mass., 1953; London, 1954) – shed valuable light on the prenaturalistic actor's approach to his role. Related in spirit is the three-volume study by William Winter entitled *Shakespeare on the Stage*: First Series (New York, 1911), Second Series (New York, 1915) and Third Series (New York, 1916).

Reliable scholarship devoted specifically to the development of acting styles in this – or any – period is rare. Of particular interest here are Lily B. Campbell's 'The rise of a theory of stage presentation in England during the eighteenth century', *PMLA*, XXXII (1917), and two classic articles by Alan S. Downer entitled 'Nature to advantage dressed: eighteenth-century acting',

PMLA, LVIII (1943; reprinted in *Restoration Drama*, ed. John Loftis [New York and Oxford, 1966]) and 'Players and painted stage: nineteenth-century acting', *PMLA*, LXI (1946). Carefully documented book-length studies covering this subject include Bertram Joseph's *The Tragic Actor* (New York, 1959) and Edwin Duerr's *The Length and Depth of Acting* (New York, 1962). *The Eighteenth Century Stage*, ed. Kenneth Richards and Peter Thomson (London, 1972), also contains several relevant essays on acting.

(ii) OLDER SURVEYS AND CONTEMPORARY SOURCES

A considerable number of stage histories and surveys of actors' careers appeared during the period. Among the more useful and familiar of them are: H. Barton Baker, *Our Old Actors*, 2 vols (London, 1878); John Genest, *Some Account of the English Stage*, 10 vols (Bath, 1832); Thomas Gilliland, *Dramatic Synopsis of the Theatre* (London, 1804) and *The Dramatic Mirror, Continuing the History of the Stage . . .*, 2 vols (London, 1808); John Westland Marston, *Our Recent Actors*, 2 vols (London, 1888); W. C. Oulton, *A History of the Theatres of London*, 2 vols (London, 1796) and *A History of the Theatres of London . . . from the Year 1795 to 1817 inclusive*, 3 vols (London, 1817), and *Oxberry's Dramatic Biography and Histrionic Anecdotes*, 2 vols (London, 1826).

Selected source documents for further study have been made available by A. M. Nagler in *Sources of Theatrical History* (New York, 1952) and by Toby Cole and H. K. Chinoy in *Actors on Acting*, new rev. ed. (New York, 1970). The latter volume also contains an exhaustive bibliography of works on the history of acting.

(iii) THE GARRICK ERA *1750–76*

The standard biographies of Garrick include Thomas Davies's *Memoirs of the Life of David Garrick, Esq.*, 2 vols (London, 1780; repr. New York, 1969) and Arthur Murphy's *The Life of Garrick*, 2 vols (London, 1801; repr. New York, 1969). To these may be added Percy Fitzgerald's somewhat later but valuable *Life of David Garrick: from Original Family Papers*, 2 vols, rev. ed. (London, 1899). Further source material may be found in *The Private Correspondence of David Garrick*, ed. James Boaden, 2 vols (London, 1831–2) and Garrick's *Letters*, ed. D. M. Little and G. M. Kahrl, 3 vols (London, 1964).

Among the many studies of various aspects of Garrick's career, the following titles offer particularly valuable information: William Angus, 'An appraisal of David Garrick: based mainly upon contemporary sources',

Quarterly Journal of Speech, XXV (1939); Kalman A. Burnim, *David Garrick, Director* (Pittsburgh, Penn., 1961); Frank A. Hedgcock, *David Garrick and his French Friends* (London, 1912; repr. New York, 1969); Joseph Knight, *David Garrick* (London, 1894; repr. New York, 1969); Mrs Clement Parsons, *Garrick and his Circle* (London, 1906; repr. New York, 1969); Harry W. Pedicord, *The Theatrical Public in the Time of Garrick* (Carbondale, Ill., and London, 1966); and Cecil Price, *Theatre in the Age of Garrick* (Oxford, 1973).

Contemporary titles shedding additional light on Garrick's acting style include Joseph Pittard's *Observations on Mr Garrick's Acting* (London, 1755), David Williams's *A Letter to David Garrick* (London, 1772), and Joshua Steele's unusual *Prosodia Rationalis: or An Essay Towards Establishing the Melody and Measure of Speech*, 2nd ed. (London, 1779), which uses a system of musical notation to record Garrick's delivery in *Hamlet*. Some of the best commentary on Garrick's art is to be found in descriptions of his acting by foreign observers. Especially relevant in this respect are the comments of Georg Christoph Lichtenberg in *Lichtenberg's Visits to England as described in his Letters and Diaries*, trans. M. L. Mare and W. H. Quarrell (Oxford, 1938; repr. New York, 1969), by Jean Georges Noverre in his *Letters on Dancing and Ballets* (London, 1951), and by Denis Diderot in *The Paradox of Acting* (New York, 1957).

An anonymous work entitled *An Estimate of the Theatrical Merits of the Two Tragedians of Crow Street* (Dublin, 1760) is a useful acount of the acting of Barry and Mossop. Treatments of Macklin's career include William Cooke's *Memoirs of Charles Macklin* (London, 1804; repr. New York, 1969), James T. Kirkman's *Memoirs of the Life of Charles Macklin, Esq.*, 2 vols (London, 1799), and E. A. Parry's *Charles Macklin* (London, 1891). A recent biography is W. W. Appleton's *Charles Macklin: An Actor's Life* (Cambridge, Mass., 1960).

Relevant biographies of other actors of this period include *The Life of Mr James Quin, Comedian* (London, 1766) and Thomas Davies's *A Genuine Narrative of the Life of Mr John Henderson*, 2 vols (London, 1778). Lively accounts of the ladies on Garrick's stage are numerous. Eminently readable are: *An Apology for the Life of George Anne Bellamy*, 6 vols (London, 1785), *An Account of the Life of That Celebrated Actress, Mrs Susanna Maria Cibber* (London, 1887), Percy Fitzgerald's *The Life of Mrs Catherine Clive* (London, 1888), Augustin Daly's *Woffington* (Troy, New York, 1891), and J. Fitzgerald Molloy's *The Life and Adventures of Peg Woffington* (New York, 1897). Lewis Melville's *Stage Favourites of the Eighteenth Century* (London, nd) offers a more general survey of the careers of these actresses.

A number of more widely ranging theoretical and critical works deserve the close attention of the student of the Garrick era. Important treatises on the theory of acting and its practical application include: James Boswell's *On the Profession of a Player* [1770] (London, 1929), Samuel Foote's *Treatise of the Passions* (nd), John Hill's *The Actor* (London, 1750; revised and enlarged, 1755), Roger Pickering's *Reflections upon Theatrical Expression in Tragedy* (London, 1760), and Thomas Sheridan's *A Course of Lectures on Elocution* (London, 1762). Related to these sources is Earl R. Wasserman's study, 'The sympathetic imagination in eighteenth-century theories of acting', *JEGP*, XLVI (1947). Relevant critical collections include Thomas Davies's *Dramatic Miscellanies*, 3 vols (Dublin, 1784: repr. New York, 1969), Samuel Derrick's *The Dramatic Censor* (London, 1752), and Francis Gentleman's *The Dramatic Censor, or, Critical Companion*, 2 vols (London, 1770). Richard Cumberland's *Memoirs* (London, 1806; repr. New York, 1969) and Tate Wilkinson's *Memoirs of his own Life*, 4 vols (York, 1790), both provide useful details about the theatre of the period. Finally, estimates of many of the performers of this era are to be found in Charles Churchill's *The Rosciad* (published in *The Poetical Works of Charles Churchill*, I [London, 1844]) and in Thomas Wilks's *A General View of the Stage* (London, 1759).

(iv) 'THE KEMBLE RELIGION' *1776–1812*

Of primary importance for a study of John Philip Kemble and Sarah Siddons are James Boaden's *Memoirs of the Life of John Philip Kemble, Esq.*, 2 vols (London, 1825; repr. New York, 1969), and his *Memoirs of Mrs Siddons*, 2, vols (London, 1827; repr. New York, 1969), Percy Fitzgerald's *The Kembles*, 2 vols (London, [1871]; repr. New York, 1969), and Thomas Campbell's *Life of Mrs Siddons*, 2 vols (London, 1834; repr. New York, 1969). More recent studies include Mrs Clement Parson's *The Incomparable Siddons* (London, 1909; repr. New York, 1969) and Herschel Baker's *John Philip Kemble, The Actor in his Theatre* (Cambridge, Mass., 1942).

Supplementary information may be gleaned from such sources as: *An Authentic Narrative of Mr Kemble's Retirement from the Stage* (London, 1817), *The Covent Garden Journal*, ed. J. J. Stockdale, 2 vols (London, 1810), Frances Ann (Fanny) Kemble's *Records of a Girlhood* (New York, 1879), *The Life of John Philip Kemble, Esq.* (London, [1809]), Sir Walter Scott's 'Review of Boaden's *Memoirs of the Life of John Philip Kemble*', *Quarterly Review*, XXXIV (1826), and John Ambrose Williams's *Memoirs of John Philip Kemble, Esq.* (London, 1817).

Some related pieces on specific roles and productions include H. C.

Fleming Jenkin's 'Mrs Siddons as Lady Macbeth and as Queen Katharine' in *Papers on Acting*, ed. Brander Matthews (New York, 1958), John Philip Kemble's *Macbeth and King Richard the Third* (London, 1817), Theodore Martin's 'An eye-witness of John Kemble', *The Nineteenth Century* (February 1880), *A Review of Mrs Crawford and Mrs Siddons in the Character of Belvidera* (London, 1782), and *A Short Criticism on the Performance of Hamlet by Mr Kemble* (London, 1789). Later related studies include Harold H. Child's 'Shakespearian productions of John Philip Kemble', *Shakespeare Association Papers*, XIX (Oxford, 1935), a useful treatment of Kemble's approach to his acting texts, F. J. Marker's 'From Covent Garden to the Bowery: Kemble and Hamblin promptbooks for *Henry VIII*', *Theatre Survey*, IX (November 1968), David Roston's 'John Philip Kemble's *Coriolanus* and *Julius Caesar*: an examination of the prompt copies', *Theatre Notebook*, XXIII (1968), and 'John Philip Kemble's *King Lear*', *The Eighteenth Century Stage*, ed. K. Richards and P. Thomson (London, 1972).

For a biography of Cooke, see William Dunlap's *Life and Memoirs of George Frederick Cooke*, 2 vols (London, 1815; repr. New York, 1969). Eliza O'Neill's career is described in C. I. Jones's *Memoirs of Miss O'Neill* (London, 1816). The endeavours of the Infant Roscius are the subject of J. Merritt's *Memoirs of the Life of William Henry West Betty, Known by the Name of the Young Roscius* (Liverpool, 1804) and Giles Playfair's *The Prodigy (Master Betty)* (London, 1967). Books about other figures in this period include B. Fothergill's *Mrs Jordan, Portrait of an Actress* (London, 1965) and Jane Williamson's *Charles Kemble, Man of the Theatre* (Lincoln, Nebraska, 1970).

Theoretical and critical works relating to the period in general are Gilbert Austin's *Chironomia; Or, a Treatise on Rhetorical Delivery* (London, 1806), Henry Siddons's *Practical Illustrations of Rhetorical Gesture and Action* (London, 1807), which is the English version of J. J. Engel's *Idéen zu einer Mimik* (Berlin, 1785–6), and Thomas Holcroft's *The Theatrical Recorder*, 2 vols (London, 1805; repr. New York, 1968).

The impressive body of English dramatic criticism which began to appear during the Kemble era constitutes both a rich mine of information about acting and an independent subject for study and delight. William Archer and R. W. Lowe's three volumes of *Dramatic Essays* (London, 1895) collect the most significant theatre criticism of Leigh Hunt, William Hazlitt and G. H. Lewes (together with John Forster). All three of these major critics have written about a variety of the performers under discussion, and their essays constitute the most important single source of commentary on acting in

England from Kemble to Salvini. The Hazlitt volume has been reissued as *Hazlitt on Theatre* (New York, nd), and it contains selections from the critic's *View of the English Stage* (1818) and *Criticisms and Dramatic Essays of the English Stage* (1851). Equally significant for a study of late eighteenth-century and early nineteenth-century acting are Leigh Hunt's *Critical Essays on the Performers of the London Theatres* (London, 1807) and his *Dramatic Criticism*, ed. L. H. and C. W. Houtchens (New York, 1849; London, 1950). *Victorian Dramatic Criticism*, selected and introduced by George Rowell (London, 1971), provides a handy sampling of the criticism of this period. The Archer and Lowe volume on G. H. Lewes should be supplemented with his supremely important *On Actors and the Art of Acting* (London, 1875; repr. New York, 1957 and 1968), which spans the entire period from Edmund Kean to Salvini.

Astute critical observations of a non-public nature are to be found in the selections from the diary of Henry Crabb Robinson entitled *The London Theatre 1811–1866*, ed. Eluned Brown (London, 1966). A fuller sampling may be had in Thomas Sadler's *Diary, Reminiscences and Correspondence of Henry Crabb Robinson*, 2 vols (Boston, 1869). Charles Lamb's commentaries may be read in *The Art of the Stage as set out in Lamb's Dramatic Essays*, ed. Percy Fitzgerald (London, 1885).

(v) FORCES OF CHANGE *1814–43*

Although William Hazlitt remains the foremost connoisseur of the art of Edmund Kean, the numerous biographies of this actor provide useful supplementary information. Nineteenth-century memoirs of Kean include F. W. Hawkins's *Life of Edmund Kean*, 2 vols (London, 1869; repr. New York, 1969), J. Fitzgerald Molloy's *The Life and Adventures of Edmund Kean, Tragedian: 1787–1833*, 2 vols (London, 1888), and Bryan W. Proctor's *The Life of Edmund Kean*, 2 vols (London, 1855; repr. New York, 1969). Biographies in this century include M. Willson Disher's *Mad Genius: A Biography of Edmund Kean* (London, 1950), H. N. Hillebrand's *Edmund Kean* (New York, 1933), and Giles Playfair's *Kean* (New York, 1939).

Principal sources of information about Macready are Sir Frederick Pollock's edition of *Macready's Reminiscences*, 2 vols (London, 1875) and William Toynbee's two-volume edition of *The Diaries of William Charles Macready 1833–1851* (New York and London, 1912; repr. New York, 1969). The *Journal of William Charles Macready 1832–1851* was abridged and edited by J. C. Trewin (London, 1967). Further light is shed on his career by Juliet Pollock's *Macready as I knew him* (London, 1884), William Archer's

William Charles Macready (London, 1870), J. C. Trewin's *Mr Macready* (London, 1955), and Alan S. Downer's *The Eminent Tragedian, William Charles Macready* (Cambridge, Mass., 1966).

Macready's managerial techniques are illuminated by Charles Shattuck's editions of promptbook facsimiles, *William Charles Macready's 'King John'* (Urbana, Ill., 1962) and *Mr Macready Produces 'As You Like It'* (Urbana Ill., 1962). These may be supplemented with George Scharf's contemporary iconographic record, *Recollections of the Scenic Effects at Covent Garden Theatre during the Season 1838–39* (London, 1839).

Regarding Helen Faucit, see Theodore Martin's *Helena Faucit* (London, 1900) and her own essay *On Some of Shakespeare's Female Characters* (London, 1899), Fanny Kemble's *Records of a Later Life*, 3 vols (New York, 1882), John Vandenhoff's *Dramatic Reminiscences* (London, 1860), *Leaves from an Actor's Note-Book* (New York, 1860) and *An Actor's Notebook, or The Green-Room and the Stage* (London, 1865), Lester Wallack's *Memories of Fifty Years* (New York, 1889; repr. New York, 1969), and *A Memoir of Charles Mayne Young*, 2 vols (London, 1871) by the actor's son Julian Charles Young all contain valuable information pertaining to the general period in which these performers flourished.

Accounts of the contributions of Madame Vestris may be read in Charles E. Pearce's *Madame Vestris and Her Times* (London, 1923), Leo Waitzkin's *The Witch of Wych Street: A Study of the Theatrical Reforms of Madame Vestris* (Cambridge, 1933), and William A. Armstrong's 'Madame Vestris: a centenary appreciation', *Theatre Notebook* II(1) (1956). Two recent biographies are William W. Appleton's *Madame Vestris and the London Stage* (New York, 1974) and Clifford J. Williams's *Madame Vestris: a Theatrical Biography* (London, 1973). The careers of the elder and the younger Mathews have been documented in a series of volumes which constitute a mine of information about this period: they include *The Life and Correspondence of Charles Mathews the Elder*, ed. E. H. Yates (London, 1860), Mrs Anne Mathews's *Memoirs of Charles Mathews, Comedian*, 4 vols (London, 1838), and *The Life of Charles James Mathews, Chiefly Autobiographical*, ed. Charles Dickens, 2 vols (London, 1879).

The life of R. W. Elliston, whose career as a manager brought him into contact with most of the major figures discussed here, is recounted by George Raymond in his *Life and Enterprises of Robert William Elliston, Comedian*, 2 vols (London, 1846; repr. New York, 1969).

(vi) NEW THEATRES FOR OLD *1843–80*

Several collections of theatre criticism are useful for a study of this portion of the period, including Henry Morley's *Journal of a London Playgoer from 1851 to 1866* (London, 1891), Morris Mowbray's *Essays in Theatrical Criticism* (London, 1882), Dutton Cook's *Nights at the Play* (London, 1883), and such Clement Scott items as *From 'The Bells' to 'King Arthur'* (London, 1897) and *The Drama of Yesterday and To-day*, 2 vols (London, 1899). A few of the essays in Henry James's *The Scenic Art* (New York, 1957) bear upon the closing years of this era. Such theoretical works as Gustave Garcia's *The Actor's Art* (London, 1888) and Percy Fitzgerald's *The Art of Acting* (London, 1892) afford interesting comparisons with earlier treatises of this kind.

Older standard biographies of Phelps are John and Edward Coleman's *Memoirs of Samuel Phelps* (London, 1886) and W. May Phelps and John Forbes-Robertson's *The Life and Life-Work of Samuel Phelps* (London, 1886). Shirley S. Allen's *Samuel Phelps and Sadler's Wells Theatre* (Middleton, Conn., 1971) is a more current study. A useful additional source is Sir Johnston Forbes-Robertson's *A Player under Three Reigns* (Boston, 1925).

The Life and Theatrical Times of Charles Kean F.S.A. by 'John William Cole' (pseudonym of the actor J. W. Calcraft), 2 vols (London, 1859), may be supplemented by William G. B. Carson's *Letters of Mr and Mrs Charles Kean Relating to their American Tours* (St Louis, 1945) and Muriel St Clare Byrne's reassessment of Kean as a producer, 'Charles Kean and the Meininger myth', *Theatre Research*, VI (1964). The only full-length account of Fechter's career, Kate Field's *Charles Albert Fechter* (London, 1882; repr. New York, 1969), devotes a chapter to his revolutionary Hamlet. Sullivan is described by Robert M. Sillard in *Barry Sullivan and his Contemporaries*, 2 vols (London, 1901), and deified by Bernard Shaw in *Shaw on Theatre*, ed. E. J. West (New York, 1957).

Information about Marie and Squire Bancroft may be found in their own *Mr and Mrs Bancroft on and off the Stage*, 2 vols (London, 1888), their *Recollections of Sixty Years* (London, 1909; repr. New York, 1969), and Squire Bancroft's *Empty Chairs* (London, 1925).

The vivid stories of Salvini told by Shaw, James, Fanny Kemble, Lewes and others may be measured against E. T. Mason's careful transcription of *The Othello of Tomasso Salvini* (New York, 1890) and *Leaves from the Autobiography of Tomasso Salvini* (New York, 1893).

The beginning of Henry Irving's management marks the close of this period, and the careers of Irving and Ellen Terry fall outside its scope. For this very reason, it would seem logical to offer a brief guide to the mass of published material describing these performers.

Irving's own *The Drama: Addresses* (London, 1893; repr. New York, 1969) deals, despite its title, mainly with the art of acting. From the multitude of full-length accounts of this actor and his career, a dozen useful titles might be selected: William Archer's *Henry Irving* (London, 1883), Auston Brereton's *Life of Henry Irving*, 2 vols (London, 1908; repr. New York, 1969) and his *The Lyceum and Henry Irving* (London, 1903), Edward Gordon Craig's *Henry Irving* (New York, 1930; repr. New York, 1969), Percy Fitzgerald's *Henry Irving: A Record of Twenty Years at the Lyceum* (London, 1893), Charles Hiatt's *Henry Irving: A Record and a Review* (London, 1899), Laurence Irving's *Henry Irving: The Actor and his World* (New York, 1952), Henry Arthur Jones's *The Shadow of Henry Irving* (London, 1931; repr. New York, 1969), Walter H. Pollock's *Impressions of Henry Irving* (London, 1908; repr. New York, 1969), H. A. Saintsbury and Cecil Palmer's edition *We Saw Him Act: A Symposium on the Art of Sir Henry Irving* (London, 1939; repr. New York, 1969), Bram Stoker's *Personal Reminiscences of Henry Irving*, 2 vols (New York, 1906), and William Winter's *Henry Irving* (New York, 1885).

Ellen Terry, Irving's illustrious leading lady, speaks for herself in her *Story of My Life* (London, 1908), which later appeared in an enlarged edition entitled *Ellen Terry's Memoirs*, with additional chapters by Christopher St John and Edith Craig (London, 1933; repr. New York, 1969). Clement Scott's *Ellen Terry* (New York, 1900) and Roger Manvell's later work of the same name (New York, 1968) are valuable supplementary sources. Charles Hiatt provides an account of the actress's roles in *Ellen Terry and her Impersonations* (London, 1898). *Ellen Terry and Bernard Shaw: A Correspondence*, ed. Christopher St John (London and New York, 1931), triggered Edward Gordon Craig's *Ellen Terry and Her Secret Self* (London, nd), with its free-wheeling attack on the 'poke-nosed old woman with an idle and vindictive tongue' which Craig always felt Shaw to be.

III Playwrights and plays

The reader who seeks to acquaint himself with the drama of the 1750–1880 period will be obliged to search in the catalogues of large libraries for many of the plays he wishes to read. The plays mentioned in the present essay, however, will be found with a few exceptions in a number of large compilations.

For the 1750–1820 period, three large works will be of the greatest useful-ness. They are: *Bell's British Theatre*, 20 vols (London, 1776–8), to which a four-volume supplement containing farces was added in 1784; Richard Cumberland's *The British Drama*, 14 vols (London, 1817), is useful not only for its texts but for biographies and criticisms; the largest compilation is the work of Elizabeth Inchbald, the first series of which, called *The British Theatre*, was published in 25 vols (London, 1808) and also contained bio-graphy and criticism; it was followed by *The Modern Theatre*, 10 vols (London, 1811), and was completed by *A Collection of Farces*, 7 vols (Lon-don, 1815). The modern plays and the farces are without biographical and critical material, but all plays in the series are asserted to be printed 'from the prompt books under the authority of the managers'. Another useful volume is *A Collection of the Most Esteemed Farces and Entertainments Performed on the British Stage* (Edinburgh, 1792; no editor is named, but the publishers were Silvester Doig and William Anderson of Stirling: 6 vols).

For plays of the nineteenth century, the reader must depend primarily on T. H. Lacy's *Acting Edition of Plays, Dramas, Extravaganzas, Farces etc.* which fills in all 101 vols, and includes 1,485 plays. Important also is John Dicks's *The British Drama* in 12 vols, each of which contains from fourteen to twenty plays. Of great importance are the publications of the house of Samuel French, which took over Lacy's enormous list in 1873. Because so many of Lacy's and Dicks's plays were published for sale at 1d. each, they are cheaply printed, and cannot always be found in good condition. The strain of reading five acts printed on double-column pages, each column running to eighty-six lines of the type called 'ruby', adds substantially to the fatigues of research in this realm.

For those who cannot find what they seek in these compilations, two articles by R. C. Rhodes, in *The Library*, XVI (1935), give a longer list of sources, and much the same material is in *The Cambridge Bibliography of English Literature* (Cambridge, 1940), III, p. 585 (rev. ed., Cambridge, 1969, III, pp. 1123–4).

Apart from collections and long runs of plays by Lacy, Dicks and French, the plays of some dramatists have been collected: see *The Dramatic Works of David Garrick*, 3 vols (London, 1798); *Comedies and Dramas* by Douglas Jerrold, 2 vols (London, 1853); *The Dramatic Works of James Sheridan Knowles*, 2 vols (London, 1856); The *Extravaganzas of J. R. Planché*, 5 vols (London, 1879); and *Original Plays by W. S. Gilbert*, 4 vols (London, 1902). The reader who seeks an example of modern editorial skill applied to the drama of this period will find it in the four volumes of *English Plays of the*

Nineteenth Century, edited by Michael R. Booth (Oxford, 1969–73), and in George Rowell's *Nineteenth Century Plays* (Oxford, World's Classics, 1953). For the American Drama of the period the reader is referred to the invaluable twenty-one volumes of *America's Lost Plays*, gen. ed. Barrett H. Clark (Princeton, NJ, 1940– ; repr. Bloomington, Indiana), and to *Representative Plays by American Dramatists*, edited by Montrose J. Moses (New York, 1918; repr. New York, 1964).

PLAYWRIGHTS

The most useful source of information on most of the playwrights mentioned in the text is the *Dictionary of National Biography*, but readers who wish to gain a surer sense of the theatre during the time under discussion may wish to augment its sober record with contemporary works which may not be so reliable in matters of fact, but which are touched by that illuminating mendacity which marks so much writing about the theatre.

The bibliographical guide to the section of this volume on 'Actors and their repertory' contains many of the titles which are relevant to this section also, and it is needless to repeat them. In addition to Genest's *Some Account of the English Stage from the Restoration to 1830*, 10 vols (Bath, 1832), the student will find useful *Biographica Dramatica or A Companion to the Playhouse* (London, 1812), in which the earlier work of David Erskine Baker and Isaac Reed is brought down to 1811 by Stephen Jones; it contains accounts of playwrights as well as plays and is a useful guide to contemporary opinion. For the nineteenth century it would be impossible to give here the names of all the biographies and personal memoirs which would fill out a knowledge of the playwrights and the circumstances in which they worked. A few of particular value are Thomas Holcroft's *Memoirs*, completed by W. Hazlitt, 3 vols (London, 1816; repr. ed. C. Colby, 2 vols, London, 1925); *The Life and Times of Frederick Reynolds*, 2 vols (London, 1826); Thomas Dibdin's *Reminiscences of the Theatre Royal, Covent Garden, Drury Lane &c*, 2 vols (London, 1827); *Random Records* by George Colman the Younger, 2 vols (London, 1830); James Boaden's *Memoirs of Mrs Inchbald*, 2 vols (London, 1833); *Memoirs of Charles Mathews, Comedian*, by Mrs Mathews, 4 vols (London and Philadelphia, 1838–9); John Coleman's *Players and Playwrights I Have Known*, 2 vols (London, 1888); *The Life and Reminiscences of E. L. Blanchard*, by Clement Scott and Cecil Howard, 2 vols (London, 1891); *The Diaries of William Charles Macready*, ed. William Toynbee, 2 vols (London, 1912); and *Douglas Jerrold, Dramatist and Wit* by Walter Jerrold, 2 vols (London, 1914).

MELODRAMA

For discussion of the nature of melodrama the reader may turn to *Crime and the Drama* by H. Chance Newton (London, 1927), *Blood and Thunder* (London, 1949) and *Melodrama* (London, 1954) by M. Willson Disher, and *English Melodrama* by Michael Booth (London, 1965). Newton had seen melodrama and loved it, Disher delighted in it, and Booth sifts it, sympathetically but with scholarly discretion. All three are useful in their different ways.

Much about the manner in which nineteenth-century plays were conceived and acted may be divined from such a satirical book as *The Quizziology of the British Drama* by Gilbert Abbott à Beckett (London, 1847) and a very serious work, *Theatricals and Tableaux Vivants for Amateurs* by Charles Harrison (London, 1882).

Index